A.C.W

with love

from   J.R.L.

July 8. 1949

WINNINGTON-INGRAM

ARTHUR FOLEY WINNINGTON-INGRAM

WINNINGTON-INGRAM

THE BIOGRAPHY OF ARTHUR FOLEY WINNINGTON-INGRAM
BISHOP OF LONDON 1901-1939

S. C. CARPENTER
DEAN OF EXETER

(1858 — 1946)

HODDER AND STOUGHTON
ST. PAUL'S HOUSE, LONDON, E.C.4

FIRST EDITION . . JUNE, 1949

MADE AND PRINTED IN GREAT BRITAIN FOR
HODDER AND STOUGHTON LTD., LONDON
BY EBENEZER BAYLIS AND SON, LTD., THE
TRINITY PRESS, WORCESTER, AND LONDON

CONTENTS

CONTENTS

PREFACE

THE invitation to be the compiler of this book came to me from Bishop Curzon, till recently of Exeter, and the Bishop of Leicester. They were then the Suffragan Bishops of Stepney and Willesden in the Diocese of London, and their Chief was still at Fulham. I learned at the same time that the suggestion was not unwelcome to the family. The Bishop of London himself knew about it, and he once said that he was glad that I was to be his biographer. When he retired in 1939, he sent me all his engagement-books for the years of his London episcopate. Apart from that, the only reference that he ever made, so far as I know, to the proposal was the wholly characteristic remark, "Of course, I might outlive dear old Carpenter!" That did not happen, and at his death I began to collect material. I waited till then because the commercial advantage of producing a biography while the subject of it is still very clearly remembered seemed to me to be outweighed by the indecency of canvassing for recollections of a man still living.

It has not been an easy book to write. As is well known, the Bishop's life was made up of innumerable personal contacts, things which are hard to recapture on paper. And even when they have been to some extent recaptured, the attempt to weave them into a continuous narrative sometimes results in broken threads. I have been helped past all expectation or desert by friends of the Bishop, who have contributed press-cuttings, letters and reminiscences in great numbers. Some of them I forbear to mention, for reasons connected with the nature of their reminiscences. Among those whose help I am at liberty to acknowledge with great gratitude are Miss Winnington-Ingram, the Bishop's sister, Mrs. Grice-Hutchinson, his niece, and the Reverend Edward Winnington-Ingram, his nephew. Others to whom I owe a large debt are Mrs. H. L. Paget, the Reverend Ernest Bramwell, the Reverend P. B. Clayton, the Dean of Hereford, several ex-Chaplains, notably the Bishop of Leicester, the Bishop of Jarrow, the Reverend T. L. Manson, S.S.J.E. and the Reverend H. G. Thomas; and those who lent or gave me

3

press-cuttings, Mrs. Grice-Hutchinson, Miss St. Hill Bourne, Miss
O. M. Bancutt, and some whom I have not been able to identify.

Contributors on a smaller scale, but not less welcome, were
the Master of Marlborough, Miss Pearce, Miss Catton, Canon
Alexander, Canon Spencer Leeson, Canon R. A. Edwards, Arch-
deacon Sharpe, Miss Major of the London Diocesan Office, the
Reverend Arthur Holmes, the Reverend Kenneth Ashcroft, the
Reverend A. M. Cazalet, Mr. H. T. A. Dashwood, the Vicar of
St. Peter, London Docks, Canon Tatlow, Prebendary Dunn,
Prebendary Merritt, Mr. Clifton Kelway, Mr. L. E. Jack, and the
very numerous senders of what may be called minor reminiscences,
a few of whom are named in the text. I am also indebted to the
Editor of the *Church Times* for leave to use cuttings from his paper,
and for other help. I have made grateful use of Mr. Charles Herbert,
Twenty-five years as Bishop of London, and Mr. Percy Colson, *Life of
the Bishop of London*.

As will be seen, I have made no attempt to construct anything
like a history of the Church of England during the years of the
Bishop's life. There are episcopal biographies in which such a
course is appropriate, and indeed essential, but this is not one of
them. I have followed a roughly chronological order, but chiefly
I have sought to paint a picture of the man. There are no doubt
some to whom the portrait will seem over-critical. To others it
will seem not critical enough. I am content to let such censures
cancel one another. If it is the first duty of a biographer not to "set
down aught in malice", a second is that he should "nothing
extenuate".

Long as the book is, I am conscious of gaps in it. I had indeed
written another chapter, called "Some Causes", dealing with the
London Public Morality Council, the National Mission of Repentance and Hope, the Bishop's work for the Church of England
Temperance Society, and some minor activities, but the book was
long enough without that.

The Archbishop of York suggested to me in a letter that what
were at that time the forthcoming biographies of William Temple,
Cosmo Gordon Lang and Arthur Foley Winnington-Ingram should
together do something to kindle a renewed faith in the Christian
cause and in the vocation of the Church of England. In the *Life of*

William Temple by my friend, Dr. Iremonger, the hope has already been abundantly fulfilled, and many are looking forward eagerly to Mr. Lockhart's pages. Within the limits of my own province, I have found for myself the encouragement of which Dr. Garbett speaks, and it is my hope that it will be shared by others.

The laborious duty, which to anybody else would have been irksome, of translating an unsightly and much corrected autograph into a legible typescript, has been shouldered by my wife, herself a scion of the Foley family.

Bishop Charles Curzon has kindly read the book in proof, and has enabled me to remove some inaccuracies, but he must not be held responsible for any of the statements or sentiments contained in it.

S. C. CARPENTER.

I

EARLY DAYS

Every Biography, said Mr. G. W. E. Russell, no mean authority, should begin with a pedigree. It may seem dull, but it often illuminates what follows.

Arthur Foley Winnington-Ingram was born on the 26th January, 1858 at Stanford-on-Teme Rectory in Worcestershire, his father being Rector of the Parish.

The family came originally from Cheshire, but they had lived in Worcestershire since the seventeenth century.

Sir Francis Winnington, Barrister-at-Law, Master of the Bench of the Middle Temple, Treasurer of the Inn in 1675, and for a short time Solicitor-General, had been born in the City of Worcester in 1634, and had Stanford Court as his country seat. He also leased from the Crown the Manor of Bewdley, from which in the twentieth century Earl Baldwin took his title. His grandson Thomas (1696-1746) sat in Parliament for Worcester from 1726 to 1746, and was one of Walpole's Whig supporters.

The Winningtons were one of the leading families in the County, and the reigning head generally sat in Parliament for one of the County divisions. In 1751 Edward Winnington was made a Baronet. He married Miss Ingram of Ribbesford House, one of twenty children, all of whom survived. One of his sons, Edward, married a Miss Foley, thus forging a link with the Foley family. He had a son who adopted the name of Winnington-Ingram. In course of time the Reverend Edward Winnington-Ingram, father of the Bishop, was appointed to the family living at Stanford, a parish of which the population to-day is said to be 285. These facts explain how "Foley" and "Winnington" and "Ingram" came to figure in the Bishop's name.

His mother was Marie Louise, third daughter of Henry Pepys, Bishop of Worcester, a younger brother of Christopher Pepys, first Earl of Cottenham. Her mother was Marie, *née* Sullivan, who died in 1885, aged 89. The Bishop of Worcester was descended from John Pepys of Cottenham, Cambridgeshire, great-uncle of the Diarist. The Pepys family had lived at Cottenham since the time of Elizabeth, and they are often mentioned in the Diary.

The Bishop's father was Rector of Stanford for forty-six years, and died in 1891. Mrs. Winnington-Ingram lived to be a very remarkable old lady, residing for many years at Bournemouth, devoted to her Bishop-son, as he to her, but always thinking of him as still a boy, in which, as will appear from these pages, she was perhaps not far wrong.

Worcestershire is a beautiful county, and it is generally agreed that Stanford is set in one of the most charming parts of it.

Mrs. Sherwood, author of *The History of the Fairchild Family*, had been born in the Rectory. Her father, Dr. George Butts, who was *inter alia* Vicar of Kidderminster, built the house and lived there. Mrs. Sherwood, who had spent some years in India, thus wrote of it:

> I have travelled far, but I have never seen any region of the earth to be compared with Stanford—the verdant and rich English scenery, where every feature of the landscape of a somewhat northern climate is so assembled as to compose the most extraordinary beauty.

The parents of the Bishop are described as "the last owners of the undivided Lordship of Ribbesford".

The Rector was a "Squarson", that is, Squire and Parson in one. When the Bishop went to Ribbesford in March 1926 to dedicate a window given by his brother Edward—who exactly fifty years before had been inducted as Rector of Ribbesford, and later became Rector of Ross and Archdeacon of Hereford—in memory of their father, he said:

> Those who smiled at that old type of clergy knew little that the best was shewn in Worcestershire. "My father knew as much about cattle and gardens and crops as a farmer, yet he never placed in the background his Ordination as a minister in the church". The village people round Stourport and the farmers of Ribbesford recognized his experience, and would like to pay this tribute. They were no ordinary people. My dear father was a fine old character. He was to us boys what a gentleman ought to be, one loved. My dear old mother you knew far less of in Ribbesford than they at Bournemouth. Partly for financial

and health reasons, she went away to live there, where she spent the last twenty-five years of her life, well known by many people in that locality. She lived to an advanced age until her death two years ago. She lived to see her ten children, thirty-seven grandchildren, and twenty-four great grandchildren, and she reigned in our hearts like a queen to the last. With my father at Stanford and mother at Bournemouth ended a long family connection. The memorial window was given in fulfilment of the vow made by my brother nearly fifty years ago.

Arthur was the fourth child of ten, and it may be confidently assumed that he learned many useful things in the rough and tumble life of so large a family. Life was quite simple. The father taught the boys to swim in the river. Arthur shot rabbits and became fond of fishing. A neighbouring clergyman, Mr. Moncrieff, helped the boys to construct some home-made golf-links. Arthur is described as "not mischievous, but full of fun", and thoughtful for others. When his old nurse died, he wrote from Marlborough what has been described as "a remarkable letter", which has not survived. He said once that he used to read as a boy Andrew Murray's *With Christ in the School of Prayer*. There are a few stories of this period. On October 7th his eldest brother wrote from Rugby:

> Walter Pownall looks very well and is going in for the Navy. I'm sure, if he passes, Arthur will, for he's fearfully dense for his age. Do get Arthur to go in for the same thing. He's made for it all over. He'd be always cheerful and jolly under any circumstances.

In January, 1868, Arthur was sent to a Preparatory School at Hartney Wintney in Hampshire. After he had been there for a few weeks his brother wrote:

February 23rd, 1868

> I have had a letter from each of the boys. Arthur said he was head of his class for the week. Arthur says that he likes hockey better than football, which is a heresy he must be got out of somehow.

And on May 30th, 1868:

> I am so glad to hear of Arthur's successes, but we must not make him conceited: do you think there is any chance of doing so?

He went to Marlborough in February, 1871, at the age of twelve with a Foundation Scholarship. He was in B2 House. F. W. Farrar had just become Master. Farrar was a famous preacher, and a volume of his School Sermons, "In the Days of thy Youth," has been very widely read.

Ingram's record at School was good, but not very distinguished. He played games, but did not excel. In Cross Country Running he was the School hare. He worked hard, and became a School Prefect in 1875. There is extant one of his old school-books, a copy of the Philoctetes of Sophocles, in T. K. Arnold's School Series. On the fly-leaf is written in a boyish but quite legible hand:

A. F. W. Ingram,
Upper Fifth,
September 28th, 1874.

There are some pencil notes in the text, mostly of those technical grammatical terms which were beloved by the classical master of those days, Synizesis, Synecfonesis [sic], zeugma, brachylogy, etc. Occasionally "Irony" is written, and, against several of the choruses, "Revise". There is no note after line 687, which suggests that the Form read rather less than half the Play. Two years later, when he was in the Sixth Form, he passed the Examination for the Oxford and Cambridge Higher Certificate in Latin (Livy and Virgil), Greek (Sophocles and Demosthenes), Mathematics (Elementary), Scripture and History. In 1877 he passed in Greek (Aeschylus and Thucydides), Mathematics (Elementary), Scripture (Greek Text) and History. In Latin (Cicero and Virgil), he obtained distinction.

In 1877 he went up to Keble College, Oxford, with a Scholarship and a School-leaving Exhibition. Keble was a new Foundation, dating only from 1870. Since 1850 the Church in Oxford had lost many of its old privileges. The younger generation of Churchmen, led by Gore and Scott Holland, were eager to grapple with the new situation, but some of the older Tractarians were inclined to despair of the outlook for religion. Liddon once went so far as to speak of Christian work in the University as "combing the hair of a corpse". Keble College, of which Pusey and Liddon were the chief promoters, to which both Mr. Gladstone and Lord Salisbury were generous benefactors, was intended to arrest the decay and also to keep alive for ever the memory of John Keble, Fellow of Oriel, Professor of Poetry, Village Priest and pattern for all time of steadfast faith. As Professor Sir Richard Jebb, M.P., said at Selwyn in 1895:

It is difficult to imagine a higher tribute to departed worth than that a man's name should be chosen by those who knew his life, as a designation of a College, and should thus become as it were a permanent symbol of those qualities which it is desired to reproduce in the rising generation.

Among Oxford Liberals, flushed with the victory that Newman's secession, a Royal Commission and the resultant Acts of Parliament had given them over the old clericalism, Keble College was not at first popular, partly because it returned to old tradition as a Church College and partly because it departed from a more recent tradition in that it deliberately aimed at plain living, combined with high culture of the mind. It was accused of being reactionary, monastic and all sorts of things. In fact, the Liberals, except those who were really liberal, behaved to it in a thoroughly illiberal way. But Talbot was the ideal first Head. He was intellectually able, an Examiner for Greats, a strong Churchman, eminently reasonable, and "well-connected". He and his staff, which included Lock, Mylne, Spurling, Aubrey Moore, Arthur Lyttelton (who went from Keble to be the first Master of the sister-foundation, Selwyn, at Cambridge) and H. O. Wakeman, together with the irresistible charm of Mrs. Talbot (née Lyttelton), made Keble, and it soon gathered both academic and athletic reputation. The architect of the College buildings was Butterfield, whose designs were good, but he was fond of rather garish bricks, and these in 1877 had not yet toned into the Oxford scene. Even to-day Keble Chapel is not admired by everyone.

Ingram's career at Keble was successful, but not glorious. Well-grounded in the Classics at School, he secured a First in Mods, and a Second in Greats, a record which proves that he was at that period a well-read and accomplished young man. He did not play cricket (it was almost the only game at which he never became proficient), but he is believed to have played football. Hockey had not at that time attained its present vogue. It is certain that he coxed the College Eight, and he once spoke of himself as having rowed Bow in the Torpids. At Keble, as at Marlborough, he was known as "Chuckles".

One thing at Keble which made, as he says, "more impression on me than all the Sermons I ever heard in Chapel" was a young don insisting, at the risk of his life, on ministering to an undergraduate dying of a most infectious disease.

It is probable that the greatest impression of all was made by Edward King, Professor of Pastoral Theology. There were his professorial Lectures, and there were little talks once a week in an outhouse attached to his Canonical House at Christchurch, which to many young men were as "good news from a far country". Ingram never lost his love and reverence for King. King was his spiritual father, and in later days, when both were in the House of Lords, his political disciple. He used to say to Ingram, "If I am in doubt, because of my increasing deafness, how to vote, I follow you." There is a touching little letter, written by Bishop King's Chaplain to Ingram, which he says that the old Bishop on his death-bed had instructed him to write:

> Thank him most sincerely (for his letter). Tell him that his life and faith has been one of the greatest comforts, and a confirmation of my faith. I hope he will long continue in his diocese to preach the Gospel that so much needs to be preached. I pray God to maintain his faith and his love and his courage and to refresh him with an increasing consciousness of God's presence and love. "God spake once, and twice I have also heard the same, that power belongeth unto God." "With God nothing is impossible."
>
> From your loving and grateful friend,
E. LINCOLN.

While he was at Keble, his brother had just become Rector of Ribbesford. Ingram stayed with him there, and helped him to coach a crew on the river and taught in the Sunday School. The recollection of an old lady still living at Bewdley is that "he was very popular with the young men, and seemed to have a good influence on them". He used to read the Lessons at Ribbesford Church and superintend at Wyre Hill Sunday School in the morning and teach there in the afternoon. At one time he was tutor to Mr. Robin Wilson, who lived at Severn House.

In his last years at School, and during his time at Keble he went through what he described afterwards as "mental misery". No one knew of it. He was outwardly as cheerful as ever, but he would walk round the School playing-fields and think about it. He became doubtful about the truth of the Christian religion. He had been brought up in the Faith, and had accepted it quite happily and unquestioningly. But now he began to wonder—Was the Resurrection of Christ true? Is the whole thing a dream? How can we reconcile earthquakes with the love of God? In the second half of his Oxford time he read for Greats, always an invigorating and disturbing process. Some are unsettled by it. Others are reassured. No one is unmoved. It is right that it should be so. The risk of unsettlement must be faced. As Carlyle said, "Man's first answer is yes; his second, no; and his third answer, yes." Less unhappily introspective than Arthur Hugh Clough, less negatively confident than W. K. Clifford, less blankly defeatist than a great number of his contemporaries, who never tackled their second-hand doubts with any first-hand resolution, he had a period of great distress. This was the only light that he had ever seen, or heard of, and now it was flickering and, it seemed, in danger of extinction. Happily, he went the right way to work. He consulted a wise elder brother, who told him in a long, re-assuring letter that he was not the wicked boy he thought he was, that there was no harm in asking questions, that they were the natural questions of one who was passing from boyhood to manhood, that our Lord was very kind to the honest doubter, Thomas, and that there was a Bible promise that "those who will to do the will of God should know of the doctrine, whether it be of God". He had heard that Charles Bradlaugh, when as a young man he had taken his doubts about the Old Testament to a clergyman, had been told that he was very wicked, and he was greatly relieved by his brother's sensible advice.

In the second place, he had enough good sense to remember that on the first Low Sunday, "when the disciples were assembled", Thomas was with them. Ingram remained in the Christian fellowship. He did not give up saying his prayers and he did not give up going to Communion. Some of those who are afflicted by intellectual uncertainties allow these practices to be the first things that are dropped. They ought to be the last.

He consulted the Warden of Keble, but Talbot was always so eager to be fair to both sides that it occasionally marred his usefulness as a counsellor. Creighton once said of him at Keble, "His only fault is that he carried fairness almost to a vice; no one can be so fair as he talks." And a Leeds Churchman once said of him, "He has no use for me. You see, I am not a Quaker, or any kind of Nonconformist, and I have no religious doubts." Talbot was a king among men, but he reigned, and ranged, over so large an area that an undergraduate, who only wanted to be directed to a house about two streets away, might well be puzzled by him.

At all events, Holy Orders, which had been in general the prospect, now receded. On leaving Oxford, he accepted a travelling tutorship for three years, and went on the Continent with his charge, an uncertain believer but a practising Churchman. There, as he said, he sorted out his ideas. While he was in Germany he encountered a German Baroness, who said to him contemptuously, "What, you are a University man, and still believe in the wonders?" She apparently meant the miracles of the Gospels. This rather put him on his mettle, and he began to read more carefully and constructively. He also found help from the parents of his pupil. The father, a well-known Judge, advised him to "soak himself in the Gospels".

One of the books that helped him was Flint's *Theism*, a book that has served many in its time, but is now out of date. Flint answered the questions that were asked in the nineteenth century, the sort of questions that are hinted at in Tennyson's *In Memoriam*, arising out of the apparent waste and cruelty of Nature, "red in tooth and claw". Flint's answers were the re-stated Argument from Design, the evidence of Conscience and the reasonableness and power of the Christian Creed.

Another book that helped him much was R. W. Dale on the Atonement, a book not actually much read to-day, but one which, partly because it is Dale, and partly by reason of its subject, is more durable than Flint's. Ingram summed up its teaching in later years by saying "that it had taught him that somebody had to keep the broken law of God, for nobody had kept it".

A third book which was of service to him was a famous classic, William Law's *Serious Call to a Devout and Holy Life*. It has helped many, including Samuel Johnson and John Wesley. Hurrell Froude once called it "a clever book". Keble, who heard this, said nothing at the moment, but later remarked—"Froude, you said just now that

The Serious Call was a clever book. To me that sounds much the same as if you had said that the Day of Judgment will be a pretty sight."

Speaking at Birmingham in 1905, soon after Bishop Gore became Bishop of that city, he said that, like many other young men, he had been steered through his difficulties and perplexities, and brought to a firm belief in the Christian Faith, now his most priceless possession, chiefly through Bishop Gore. *Lux Mundi* was published in 1889, and Gore had been a graduate resident at Oxford or at Cuddesdon since 1875. He also said in later life that he had owed much at this time to Liddon's Bampton Lectures.

In an unpublished autobiographical fragment, written at the end of his life, Ingram says:

> Looking back, I could see the mistake I made during those days. The Spiritual Eye consists of three parts, (i) The Imagination, (ii) The Conscience, (iii) The Spirit.

> (i) First, the Imagination, the formative power of the Brain, which conceives great ideas, as opposed to the critical power of the Brain, which we call The Reason. This Imagination finds it very hard to believe that "God can do great things". The Incarnation, in other words, seems too good to be true. There is no reason in the world why God should not come to earth in Human Form, but it simply seems too good to be true. Here Browning, as usual, sets us right. When David in Browning's famous Poem, "Saul," feels a great desire to help the stricken Saul, he says:

>> What I suffer for him whom I love,
>> So didst Thou, else here the parts change:
>> The Creature surpass the Creator.[1]

> In other words, if the Boys who died in "The Battle of Britain" were willing to give their lives for others, and God either can't or won't, they are all morally greater than God, which is absurd.

> (ii) Then the Conscience of course has to be clear. "Where were you, Sir, last night?" asked the Colonel of the young Subaltern who was airing his views about the mistakes of Moses. He knew that it was an uneasy Conscience which lay behind that talk. It is not by any means always a faulty conscience that leads to Unbelief, but it sometimes does.

[1]This is an inexact and composite quotation from the poem.

(iii) Then, thirdly, with regard to the Spirit. It must breathe the air of Heaven. It does not belong here at all.

> "Not in entire forgetfulness,
> And not in utter nakedness,
> But trailing clouds of glory do we come
> From God, who is our home."
>
> (Wordsworth)

And if the Spirit doesn't breathe its native air, it cannot live on earth, and therefore to give up Prayer is to give the Spirit no chance to live. Prayer is only Breathing, breathing the air of Heaven. But if the Imagination, The Conscience and The Spirit all work together, The Eye is single, and "If thine eye be single, thy whole body shall be full of light".

It was, then, by the Mercy of God and the Guidance of the Holy Spirit, that I at last saw the light and believed in the Gospel, which I have now preached up and down the world for sixty-two years.

All this explains why he was not ordained Deacon till he was twenty-six, three years beyond the minimum age. It is often a good thing to do this. In 1881 not all young men, as John Morley unsympathetically pointed out in *Compromise*, were ready to pledge themselves for life at twenty-three.

He did not go to a Theological College. He had been at Keble. Keble is not a Theological College but it is a Church College, and Keble men have more opportunities than those of some other foundations, of learning what an ordered Christian life is. And his conscientious and methodical habit of mind had taught him during those next three years many things. Still, a biographer who was allowed to spend some time at Cuddesdon may be pardoned for thinking that it is a pity that he did not go to Cuddesdon—or one of the other Theological Colleges. He would have learned there, easily and happily, what he had to teach himself laboriously in later years. That he did learn it the following pages will abundantly testify.

He was ordained Deacon by the Bishop of Lichfield on Sunday, March 19th, 1884, and Priest less than a year later. His curacy was at St. Mary's, Shrewsbury. He preached his first sermon in Stanford Church.

II

SHREWSBURY AND LICHFIELD

AT Shrewsbury he was very happy. St. Mary's is a fine old Church with a lofty tower and spire, dating in part from Norman days, with some beautiful old glass. It occupies a commanding position on high ground near the Castle.

The young curate had of course very much to learn, but he had a good Vicar in Archdeacon Lloyd, and he said afterwards that the Senior Curate and his wife took him in hand, as Aquila and Priscilla took Apollos, and "taught him the way of the Lord more perfectly". His own recollection of his experience there was that he discovered what it was to be needed and to be able to help people. In the unpublished manuscript mentioned in the first chapter, the Bishop says:

I found to my astonishment that an ordinary man like myself, as I then was and am to-day, could be looked upon as a kind of Earthly Providence by about 2,000 poor people of my District. At School and at the University one is more or less self-absorbed; but here, to my infinite delight, I found that I could really be of use to others. It was a revelation to me that the sick would listen for my footsteps to come and cheer them in their sickness, that people of all sorts should come to me in their troubles, that a congregation should seem to listen with pleasure to my youthful sermons. I learnt then the meaning of Our Lord's words that "we are to lose ourselves to find ourselves". I also for the first time saw the Gospel in action. I shall never forget one incident which occurred in my first year. I sat up all night with a little girl of 14 in the Infirmary, to which we Curates were Chaplains. It was bad enough there those long hours to hear her say "Oh dear, oh dear," over and over again. She died about 3 in the morning. It was far worse to meet her mother, who had been summoned too late, and take her down into the Mortuary. I shall never forget her piercing shriek, "My little lamb, my little lamb," and I realized, as I tried with stumbling words to comfort her, that nothing that I had read at Oxford of Plato and Aristotle was of any use to meet real human anguish, except faith in the Risen Christ, which I had so recently learnt to grasp. What I said I can't remember, but it seemed to help her, and I realized that, if you do have to throw away the light of the world, there is no other light to light up this darkness. What I was taught at that first death-bed I found true in a hundred cases.

Mr. M. J. Harding, sometime Manager of Lloyd's Bank, Shrewsbury, wrote in 1946, at the age of ninety-two, that he well remembered Ingram's first sermon at St. Mary's. It "touched us all and made us eager for more". It was on the text—"Be ye followers of God, as dear children." "His Vicar brought him for introduction to my family, and we were much struck by the loving kindness he shewed from the first day. He quickly became endeared to the whole parish, and, when he left, his loss was deeply deplored."

The Rev. F. C. Stamer writes:

It was my lot to follow him in the only curacy he ever held, viz., at St. Mary's, Shrewsbury, and I can testify to the irresistible charm of him as a young man, and the wonderful influence he exerted over all who came in contact with him, especially young people. He was a diligent visitor and his visits to the sick especially were much looked forward to and appreciated. In Church it was the same, and he filled the beautiful church with people drawn from every Parish in the town, and his preaching was most telling. Our Vicar, Archdeacon Lloyd, once asked me and my fellow-curate, Herbert Glennie, what was the secret of Ingram's success, and he said it was that he always forgot self in whatever he was doing.

His churchmanship at this date was rather inchoate. He said to a gathering of Evangelical clergy in London in 1911 that he had left Keble, not only without knowing the difference between High Churchmen and Low Churchmen, but without knowing the difference between a Churchman and a Dissenter. He was of course a Churchman by tradition. His faith in the central doctrines of Christianity had been shaken and then re-established, but nothing had occurred to make him doubt that, given Christian faith, his natural religious home was what it had been at Stanford, Marlborough and Keble, the old Church of England. During his years at Shrewsbury and Lichfield, he said that he had determined with an unbiased mind to find out the truth about the Church. In this he was greatly helped by Canon Scott Holland's famous book *Creed and Character*, which has consolidated the faith of many. There emerged in his mind the idea of the Divine Society, the Church, founded by the Son of God and inspired by the Holy Spirit. He came to a full and firm belief in the ministry of the Church, the Sacraments of the Church, the Creeds of the Church, and the prayers of the Church. Those were the four corner-stones upon which he took his stand, and upon which he stood that day. He expressed the opinion that Evangelicals as a body would make a great mistake if they were ashamed and afraid of the word Catholic, especially as every time they said the Creed they expressed their belief in the Holy Catholic Church.

He still knew nothing, or next to nothing, of Anglo-Catholicism. It was in fact a much rarer thing, and, to most church-people, a much more alarming thing than it has since become. But he was deepening his personal faith, and learning to exercise that wonderful pastoral power that remained with him all his life.

He was long remembered in the town. A Shrewsbury School Master wrote to him nearly twenty years later, when he became Bishop of London:

My dear Ingram,

I guessed that you would receive 3,000 letters, or more, and therefore I refrained from writing before, but I do not like to think that no one should send you a letter from a School where you are held in such affectionate remembrance. For all your friends in Kingsland I want just to say how happy and thankful we felt for London's sake when we heard the news of your appointment. I trust that they will shortly give you one or two more Suffragans and that you will have health and strength to stand the work. Your old Salopian friends in St. Mary's parish are in a great state of pride and jubilation and talk—some of them—as if they had helped you on the way to Fulham!

The Bishop of Lichfield had his eye on the young man, and after only eighteen months in his curacy carried him off to Lichfield to be his Domestic Chaplain. The duties were no doubt less onerous than they are to-day. The Bishop's engagements were not so numerous, and his correspondence not so heavy, as Ingram's were at a later date in London. But it was a very useful stage in his training. He learned there the importance of being methodical and tidy, and he had contacts with a great variety of people, clerical and lay. He acquired experience of the problems which arise in parishes and also of the sort of thing which both clergymen and laymen from time to time wish to have brought to the attention of the Bishop, without approaching him directly. This sort of inside knowledge was of great service to him afterwards. A Bishop's Chaplain learns to understand parochial clergymen as parochial clergymen learn to understand laymen, not by being one of them, but by constantly having to be with a great many of them. He says that Mrs. Maclagan "tried to spoil him". There was a little Church where he ministered, and he lectured at the Theological College, where he played games and made friends with the students. He began there his work of preaching Parochial Missions. One was at St. Faith's District in the Parish of St. Mary Wigford, Lincoln. A priest, who was then curate in the Parish, recalls that he was "quite wonderful".

It was all very happy and comfortable, and no doubt there were plenty of people who told him, or could have told him that, like Nehemiah, he was "doing a great work, and must not come down". But he had his scruples. He was a cog in the machine. He was carrying on. He was maintaining the good work, and it was a holy, spiritual work. But could he not initiate something? Some pioneer task? Something more difficult and more laborious than his present job?

Suddenly it seemed to come. Bishop Webber of Brisbane was seeking recruits for his vast diocese. Here is Ingram's own story of it:

The reason I remember the sermon is this. I was at Lichfield. I was very comfortable; I had the dearest little Church, in which I preached every Sunday evening. I was honorary lecturer at the College, and played games with all the young men—twenty to thirty young men—who were my great friends. I was treated much too kindly by the Bishop, whose private Chaplain I was. Everything was *couleur de rose*. At that time the Bishop of Brisbane, Bishop Webber, came over to try to find someone to take the place of my dear old friend who was called to his rest so suddenly the other day, Bernard Wilson, who was his chaplain at Brisbane. He talked to me, but the old Adam was against it, and I did not want to go. I felt, however, that the call could not be resisted, and in that service, for the Church Guilds of the diocese, I was waiting for the voice of Heaven to decide. An old man, Canon Twells, preached—I can see him now; I knew him afterwards as a personal friend; and this only shews how a sermon may speak home: I can still hear his short sentences ringing through the Cathedral, as he pointed out "to every man his work". That was the deciding message to me. In the evening I offered myself to go, never dreaming, of course, that I should not be sent.[1]

The message was no doubt reinforced by his recollection of what Edward King had said in his hearing at Oxford a few years before, words which he often quoted:

Now, gentlemen, remember, when you are ordained, you are ordained for the world.

The Bishop of Lichfield, after a week's consideration, declined to let him go, or at least exercised so much pressure on him that he felt obliged to withdraw his offer. It may be that the following letter from Mrs. Maclagan to the Bishop had something to do with this:

I saw plainly in the Cathedral at Evensong, I have nothing but selfish reasons against the sacrifice. The loss to the diocese, to ourselves, to the English Church in which I looked forward with almost a mother's pride to see him win a high place—will be all gain to the struggling Church in the Colonies, and his brilliant talents and bright cheerful spirit a perfect godsend to the lonely Bishop—But alas! I am very selfish, and the hot tears will rise in spite of myself, and it will be a very big piece of my heart and a very happy slice out of my life that will go to the Antipodes. I have been telling myself for some months that the present state of things was too good to last, but I only thought of his going to a parish of his own in the diocese; such an uprooting as this never came into my mind. I feel now as if I had put it into Bp Webber's head, for before he ever saw Mr. Ingram when he was detailing all his needs to me, I said "Take what you can get from here, only don't set your affection on our Chaplain, for we cannot spare him." I always felt so happy when he was with you with his bright, boyish ways, taking you out of your cares and lightening your loads, and now there will be the anxious work of beginning again with a stranger. Oh dear! I mustn't write about it any more, or I shall splash the paper and make blots. . . .

[1] *The Mysteries of God*, 238.

21

From this it appears that some at least already saw that Ingram was marked out for some high and responsible work in the Ministry of the Church. It may well be that the Bishop of Lichfield expected that some other more imperious call to work, for which he was obviously the man, would come before long. And, within six months, it came.

It appeared that a new Head was needed for Oxford House, Bethnal Green. Here indeed was an opportunity for someone who wanted to break some fresh ground. It would perhaps be over-romantic to call East London virgin soil, but at least it had largely become fallow, so far as the Gospel was concerned.

To H. B. Bromby, Vicar of St. John's, Bethnal Green, afterwards Vicar of All Saints', Clifton, son of old Bishop Bromby, who lived at Lichfield, belongs the credit of the first suggestion. He saw that Ingram was the man for Bethnal Green.

The circumstances at the time might have seemed fortuitous, a vacancy arising, the recommendation of a friend, the fact that Ingram was known to the Warden of Keble, who was Chairman of the Oxford House Committee, but we, who have the advantage of being wise after the event, shall not err in seeing the hand of God in it. The two events, the volunteering for Brisbane and the call to Bethnal Green, together provided the material for Scott Holland's little joke, "He started for the East, but never got further than the East End."

Bromby wrote to him on October 21st, 1888:

My dear Ingram,

Henson tells me that Oxford House is offered to you. I am so glad and I do earnestly hope that you will accept it. There is a glorious work to be done, and I do believe that you are the man to do it. At the University Club there are 1,000 men and it is a place that can so well by God's help be moulded. It may become a great Evangelistic centre and may leaven the whole neighbourhood. I don't speak now of all the other work both among the people and for University men who are drawn to the House.—At any rate I earnestly beg you not to decide against coming until you have been here to see the place and its possibilities. I verily believe this to be a real call. I feel with you so much in the anxiety this will cause you and I pray from my heart that you may be granted wisdom and guidance.

His mother wrote:

My dear Arthur,

I was very much excited by your letter this morning, which I received in my room quietly, and my first impressions were, what an honour it was for you to be chosen for such a work for God, and I felt so thankful. But Father, who is of a much more practical spirit, soon talked my enthusiasms out of me, and I can now only offer my sympathy and earnest prayer that you may be guided right. I think your own Bishop, too, will take a commonsense view of the case, and will not be led away. Whatever you decide, it will be a good thing to have the practical side of the question put as clearly as Father has put it. You have not private fortune enough to make you independent of salary, and want of funds would cripple you much. I do not quite know what your duties would be, but, I suppose, to organize the work of the younger men, and preach in Mission Halls &c. There would be much that you are well fitted for, if your health would stand the confinement and bad air, but you are not one of the very robust ones, I can see. Let us know your decision as soon as possible. Father has written you a long letter.

He was utterly without experience of such work. He does not even seem to have visited East London, as hundreds of under-graduates and young graduates did, on his invitation, during the next nine years. But it was evidently a man's job, and in the end he said "Yes". One thing that helped him to the decision was the advice of old Bishop Abraham, who had been Selwyn's right-hand man in New Zealand. He said:

I have learned through my long life that a man is called for the work he is fitted for. I think you are fitted to draw these young men from Oxford to Bethnal Green. Go and do it.

There was much sorrow in Lichfield at his departure. Here is a letter from the daughter of a friend and neighbour:

Dear Mr. Ingram,

I am so glad to hear about you—I think it's splendid and I hope you'll get on and be very happy there—We shall miss you very much when we go to Lichfield and I expect all the Lichfieldites will weep and tear their hair! I hope you won't bury yourself there though, and that we shall see you again soon.

With best wishes,

I remain,

Yours very sincerely,

The Bishop of Lichfield released him, and invited him to preach the Advent Ordination Sermon before he went. The text was Hosea XI. 4: "I drew them with the cords of a man, with bands of love." He was very fond of this passage, and constantly quoted it all through his life. It was the text of a much later sermon in Sherborne Abbey in 1939, and it was the method of his work, not only at Bethnal Green, but throughout his whole life.

III

OXFORD HOUSE

THERE was a time when the land to the East of the City of London was open country. In 1504 Sir Thomas More wrote to John Colet, then Vicar of Stepney, whose father Sir Henry Colet, had his country house, with its beautiful garden-walk, in the parish:

> Wheresoever you look, the earth yieldeth you a pleasant prospect: the temperature of the air fresheth you, and the very bounds of heaven do delight you. Here you find nothing but bounteous gifts of nature and saint-like tokens of innocency.

It is also interesting to remember that Pepys, when the great Fire of London was raging, stored his treasures at the country house of Sir William Rider at Bethnal Green.

Much water has flowed under London Bridge and down to the sea since those halcyon days. The bucolic solitudes of Colet's parish and of Pepys' "Reception Area" have been replaced by factories and whelk-stalls, by some broad and busy highways, and about five hundred miles of undistinguished and almost indistinguishable habitations, and the supposed saint-like innocence of sixteenth-century peasantry by the sharpness of the East London boy. Sir Walter Besant in his *East London*,[1] describes it as a city of many trades, but a city with no hotel and no bookshop.

At the beginning of the nineteenth century it had become isolated and neglected, and, in the main, if we except the more prosperous outer suburbs, a city of the poor. The Ecclesiastical Commission, founded as a Commission of Enquiry in 1831, and made permanent in 1836, a body of which Bishop Blomfield of London was the life and soul, did it good service. They laid hands on some of the large revenues of St. Paul's Cathedral, hitherto used to maintain a number of Prebendal benefices which were sinecures or very nearly that, and with the money so acquired they founded

[1] Published in 1901, the year in which Ingram passed from Stepney to London.

parishes in East London. Bethnal Green in 1830 had but two Churches, one mission and one school for its population of 73,000.

Blomfield was reproached, not least by Sydney Smith, for robbing the Cathedral, but he had a strong case. He said very justly: "They blame me for these measures, but they will hereafter confess that those very measures have been the saving of the Church."

And it did make for the saving (if that too human word may be allowed) of the Church. In fifteen years Blomfield had established in Bethnal Green alone ten Churches, ten schools, twenty-five clergymen and eleven parsonages, and much the same elsewhere. Mr. T. S. Eliot's *The Rock*[1] does justice to his energy in building and founding, and even if he sometimes thought that, if only a Church could be built, the parish would straightway be evangelized, he certainly made a great difference to East London. Ingram, speaking of this in 1940, said:

> What we do now is to send down a man first and give him a mission room which can afterwards be called the "Hall" of the parish. He then gathers the people round him and with help from the centre they build their church, and look upon it as theirs.[2]

Anyhow, as a result of Blomfield's work, the clergy of the district were still left with large populations, so large as to make parish work laborious, and, in the deepest pastoral sense, impossible, but the conditions were no longer so outrageous as they had been. There were parishes of a size, which, if it could not be called reasonable, was nevertheless not quite fantastic, and there were endowments which, with the taxation and cost of existence then prevailing, did produce something like a living wage. At one end of the ecclesiastical scale such parishes as St. George's in the East and St. Peter's, London Docks built up a strong Church life, and at the other end great work was done by such men as W. W. Champness at Whitechapel. And there was Samuel Barnett, who was *sui generis*, at St. Jude's, Whitechapel and Toynbee Hall.

In 1878 Walsham How became the first Bishop of East London. He had the curious title of Bishop of Bedford, a survival from the

---

[1] This play was acted in London at the Sadler's Wells Theatre in 1934, in aid of the Bishop's Forty-five Churches Fund.
[2] *Fifty Years*, 2.

days of Henry VIII, but East London was his district. He brought Eton to Hackney Wick in 1880, and Christchurch to Poplar in 1881. He was really the first prophet of the new spirit uniting East and West, though even before that Thring of Uppingham had seen the possibility of associating Public School boys with the work of the Church in desolate places.

These enterprises represent the beginning of the Settlement Movement, one of the best social phenomena of the last quarter of the century. Toynbee Hall was not actually the first, but the Barnetts were the father and mother of all Settlements, including those which sprang up in America. The Barnetts paid their first visit to Oxford in 1875:

> We used to ask each undergraduate as he developed interest to come and stay in Whitechapel, and see for himself. And they came, some to spend a few weeks, some for the Long Vacation, while others, as they left the University and began their life's work, took lodgings in East London, and felt all the fascination of its strong pulse of life, hearing, as those who listen always may, the hushed, unceasing moans underlying the cry which ever and anon makes itself heard by an unheeding public.[1]

Barnett believed that the cure was friendship:

> Inquiries into social conditions lead generally to one conclusion. They shew that little can be done *for*, which is not done *with* the people. It is the poverty of their own life, which makes the poor content to inhabit "uninhabitable" houses, and content also to allow improved dwellings to become almost equally uninhabitable. It is the same poverty of life which makes so many careless of cleanliness, listless about the unhealthy conditions of their workshops, and heedless of anything beyond the enjoyment of a moment's pleasure.
>
> Such poverty of life can best be removed by contact with those who possess the means of higher life. Friendship is the channel by which the knowledge—the joys—the faith—the hope which belong to one class may pass to all classes.[2]

Scott Holland said of him:

> He surprised us by his quiet common sense. He had nothing about

[1]*Life*, 303.
[2]*ib.* 307.

him which excited us. He sometimes spoke with awe and bated breath about things that seemed to us commonplace enough. Once for instance in Balliol Hall he had described to breathless undergraduates all that might be possible to them if they came to work for the poor in East London, and then he mentioned as a culmination to their dreams and aspirations that possibly at last they might become Poor-Law Guardians! There was rather a sudden fall in the excitement for the moment at this vision of the East End, but we saw gradually that this meant that you would have got to the very heart of things in a way that really touched the life and needs of the poor.[1]

Archbishop Lord Lang, himself one of the pioneer workers for the Settlement idea, said:

Our conscience felt the rebuke of the contrast between the wealth of inheritance and opportunity stored up in Oxford and the poverty of the life lived amid the mean streets and monotonous labour of East London. In a vague way we felt the claim of that poverty on our wealth. Could anything practical be done to meet it? The answer to that question was important. If it had not come, the movement might have drifted into mere vague sentiment or academic talk. It came that November evening. The Vicar of St. Jude's, Whitechapel, Mr. Barnett, then in the prime of his life, in his fortieth year (1883) read a paper in which he sketched the plan of a "University Settlement in East London". "Something," he said, "must be done to share with the poor the best gifts." Let University men become the neighbours of the working poor, sharing their life, thinking out their problems, learning from them the lessons of patience, fellowship, self-sacrifice, and offering in response the help of their own education and friendship. "This," he said, "will alleviate the sorrow and misery born of class division and indifference. It will bring classes into relation; it will lead them to know and learn of one another, and those to whom it is given will give."[2]

Among the names of those who first saw what Barnett meant, and worked for him at the University or lived with him in Whitechapel are those of Arnold Toynbee, Sidney Ball, Alfred Milner, Lewis Nettleship, A. L. Smith, W. H. Forbes, Arthur Sidgwick, H. Scott Holland, C. G. Lang, C. L. Marson, F. S. Marvin, J. A.

[1] *Life*, 309.
[2] *ib.* 310.

28

Spender, E. T. Cook, a notable list. And in the background were the seniors, Jowett and T. H. Green, encouraging the young men. Also behind the Movement, especially the Cambridge Settlements in South London, was the large, prophetic mind of Westcott. At a later date Mr. C. R. Attlee was among the residents of Toynbee Hall.

At that time the conscience of West London, of the Universities and Public Schools, and of the country houses, was stirred. Generous instincts made a number of healthy and well-educated young men, who themselves had great social advantages, feel that they could not be content with the extreme segregation that had come about in London. It was picturesquely said that "all those who eat jam live at one end, and all those who make jam at the other". This is not factually accurate, because at that time jam was cheaper than butter, and bread and jam was a staple diet. London children were often given a piece of it for their dinner, to be eaten in the street. In the early years of the century Walworth and Battersea children, at a school treat, would clamour for bread and butter, rather than bread and jam. If, however, you substitute the making and wearing of fur coats for the making and eating of jam, the comparison is accurate.

Public opinion had been greatly stimulated by the books of Henry George, by a series of newspaper articles by G. R. Sims, called "How the Poor Live", and by a tract written by Mr. Mearns on behalf of a Committee of Free Churchmen, called "The Bitter Cry of Outcast London". A little later Morrison's "Tales of Mean Streets" and Whiteing's "Number Five, John Street" were widely read.[1] Best of all was C. F. G. Masterman's "From the Abyss", which, with "The Condition of England", made Chesterton say that Masterman "was the only man who could make the map of England crawl with life".

Some of the fashionable "slumming" which ensued consisted in distributing half-crowns, a process not merely useless but pernicious. And some of the conscience-pricking only resulted in large Mansion

---

[1] I can remember a Cambridge Meeting about 1900, at which Mr. Whiteing spoke on behalf of Cambridge House, Camberwell. On the advertisement was printed an extract from his book, suggesting that the residents in a Settlement did not really get inside the people's lives. For that it was essential to live in John Street. At the Meeting he explained that he had not intended to disparage Settlements.

House Funds for the Unemployed, too much of which was absorbed by the ingenious cadgers. The modern Social Services were then unborn. The Salvation Army was already doing valuable redemptive and constructive work. Dr. Barnardo opened his first Home in Stepney Causeway in 1867, and began sending boys to Canada. The C.O.S. was fighting mendicancy and promoting thrift. The wiser among the clergy had their Relief Committees, and were trying to separate in the minds of their parishioners two totally different things, the practice of religion and the hope of gain. But even when Ingram went to Oxford House in 1888, there were parishes which were what St. Jude's, Whitechapel had been when Barnett became Vicar in 1873. The tiny congregation consisted of old women who were intent on establishing their claim to participation in parochial charities. Ingram himself said that in his Shrewsbury curacy his predecessor was described in some houses as a very generous man, who had distributed half-crowns. He was determined that he would not do this, but to his horror he discovered that it was said of him after he had left.[1] He also tells of one old lady who by extreme ingenuity had become possessed of no less than eleven blankets at Christmas time.

The Settlement was a serious and constructive business. It was an attempt to know and to befriend. It deprecated casual relief, given to obvious and importunate poverty. Oxford chose East London, and Cambridge went to that larger and even more desolate area that lies along the South Bank of the river. Men fresh from the studies and sports of the Universities went and lived among the poor, and made friends with them. They attended the Meetings of C.O.S. Committees and discovered what "case-papers" were, and how laborious it is to compile them, they visited homes, they collected savings, they boxed, they ran through the streets with the club athletes at night, they played cricket and football on Saturday afternoons. They became members of Care Committees, they sent children for a fortnight into the country.[2] And sometimes, as

---

[1] It was in fact true. All his life he distributed half-crowns, and larger sums, to those apparently in need. He could not help it.

[2] All this was as a rule very efficiently organized. But there was a Camberwell story that the correspondence of one amateur helper was allowed to get into some confusion, with the result that when the day came, he received streams of telegrams like this: "You promised us twenty girls. Boys are arriving by every train."

Barnett is said to have suggested, they reached the summit of a career by becoming Guardians of the Poor! Some men lived for years in the Settlement, and, like T. H. Urwick, Douglas Eyre, Percy Alden and, in South London, R. A. Bray and Charles Masterman, became experts in sociology.

Bishop Luke Paget said very wisely:

> It seemed to break down barriers of which they were vaguely ashamed, and to provide a chance for the contacts and the friendly gestures they wanted to make. It was almost inevitable that, in some cases, people forgot what had been done already, and gave an exaggerated sense of venture, enterprise, and even courage to what they meant to do. That could hardly be avoided, but, all the same, there was, I am sure, an immense force of kindness, of true love of God, at the heart of the movement to which School and College Missions were due.[1]

Oxford House, of which James Adderley was the first Head, was opened in 1883. Technically, it is older than Toynbee Hall (1884) but the idea of the Hall had long been in Barnett's mind, and its opening only meant that some young men who had been living in Whitechapel lodgings now lived together. Oxford House was founded as a definitely Church Settlement. There was an idea that Barnett "rather kept his Christianity in the background".[2] And it was felt that there was room for another foundation. It is curious that E. S. Talbot, who was one of the founders of Oxford House, was reproached by William Bright, that pillar of orthodoxy, for being over-inclusive.

The truth about Barnett is that in what would now be called his rather old-fashioned and Broad Church way, he was intensely Christian. Only he felt that in East London there were many "walls to be thrown down" before people could be expected or indeed were able to become Christians. Oxford House soon found exactly the same thing. Many hours of Ingram's time had to be spent in duties which could be called secular. But there was always a religious purpose behind it.

[1] *Life*, 86.
[2] This was said in my undergraduate days at Cambridge by a high-minded disciple of Westcott. He had no special knowledge of Toynbee Hall or of East London, but it was a common impression.

The Oxford House tradition was from the first that of Keble rather than of Balliol. Barnett was troubled because a Church Settlement in East London was thought necessary, but both he and Adderley were tactful, and, though the supporters of the two Settlements were sometimes a little controversial, they worked side by side. Talbot, for his part, always stood firmly with Westcott and Gore and Scott Holland in believing that Christian faith must have a direct bearing on industrial problems. In fact Oxford House stood for the principles of the Christian Social Union, or, as it is now called, the Industrial Christian Fellowship.

The first Head was the Rev. The Hon. J. G. Adderley, generally known as Father Jim. He went there as a layman, and was presently ordained Deacon with a title at St. Andrew's. He was a character in his day. Devoted, mercurial, better at the short-term than at the long-term policy, he had been as an undergraduate at Christ Church an amateur actor of some note. He was drawn by the inspiration of Luke Paget to East London. There he was a socialist priest, in a day when such were rather rare. He had a singular capacity for making friends with all sorts of people, peers and paupers, and putting them at their ease. He paid out of his own pocket for the training of not a few young men for the Ministry. His stories, *Stephen Remarx*, *The New Floreat*, *Behold the Days come*, were widely read. When he became too old for active work he went back to live in East London. He wrote very generously to Ingram:

> I thank God that you have been appointed to the work, chiefly because I know that you will keep in the forefront of it the Christian and spiritual character of it, and will do much to realize what was always my ideal when there (but God knows how imperfectly I did my part).

He was followed at Oxford House for a short time by Hensley Henson, a man of brilliant gifts,[1] but hardly those of the precise kind that Bethnal Green could understand. Buchanan, who lived at the House, wrote on November 6th, 1888:

> What we want in Bethnal Green is quiet, unobtrusive, steady work,

---

[1]The late Sir Richard Lodge once told me that he had examined Henson for Greats at Oxford, and that his papers were the best that he had ever read.

32

with wide sympathy, large-hearted charity, and inexhaustible patience
... H.H.H. has been a regular tornado.

Ingram succeeded him at the end of 1888. His first impression
was one of the extreme respectability of East London. He had read
of "Jack the Ripper", and had heard stories of wife-beating, but he
soon perceived and ever afterwards affirmed the fundamental
decency of the London poor. "See them as far as Temple Bar," he
would say to anxious mammas, "and they will be all right from
there." Almost at once the place hummed with life. He had no
experience of such work. He was a countryman, and life at Keble,
in the well-ordered parish at Shrewsbury, and in the Bishop's Palace
at Lichfield had not taught him much about great cities. He said
long afterwards:

I found a population so little outwardly Christian that only one
per cent. went to Church or Chapel, and yet, underlying that indifference and even hostility to the Church, there was deep capacity
for love, and, as we shall see, even worship, which had to be drawn
out by long and patient work. That great saint, Bishop King, had
given a motto to the Oxford House when it started out from Oxford,
"Rub lightly". He had packed up all his furniture to go to Lincoln
and only had a match-box left in his house. He caught sight of the
inscription on the box, and made it his text. He could not have taken
a better text, for even if I had collected thirty men from Oxford
instead of the three I found there, and built a new house for £150,000,
we still had to work for seven years before any definite religious
result was produced. We "rubbed lightly" ... and endeavoured by
love and kindness to evoke that spiritual power which we felt must
be somewhere down in that mass of humanity. We acted very much
as Field-Marshal Montgomery acted before the Battle of Alamein.
He worked and worked away to undermine the defences before the
tanks could go through, and it was not until after seven years that
"the tanks went through" with us.

In 1888 the success was all in the future, but Ingram knew that
men whom he had admired and trusted at Oxford were thinking
very deeply about East and West,[1] and about ways in which the
twain could be made to meet, and he had a burning desire to be of

[1] See p. 70.

C

service. His love of God, his love of men and his passion for the redemption of men's lives made him the ideal East London parson. He soon began to see what he describes in a talk to the Leeds clergy:

> There is a great joy to the faithful minister in *seeing the Church slowly grow before his eyes*. He knows that he has to build it as Christ built it originally by first getting a nucleus which he can trust, and building on that. When Christ had got together His faithful disciples, He said, "On this Rock I will build my Church"—and so does the faithful pastor say, "On this Rock will I build my Church."

East London at that time was far from being a spiritual wilderness, though there were parts of it which seemed untouchable. Here is Sir Walter Besant's description, written with friendliness, but not exactly from within, of its Church life:

> There is at the present moment no more active clergy in the world than our own; there is no organization more complete than that of a well-worked London parish. The young men who now take Holy Orders know, at the outset, that they must lead lives of perpetual activity.[1]

Many of them had been at their work too long and were dispirited. One elderly clergyman said to Ingram: "I walk about my parish and no one knows who I am." "How long have you been here, Sir?" "Twenty-five years," was the sad reply. Yet this was the parish of which J. E. Watts-Ditchfield was afterwards Vicar. It was filled to over-flowing, and the rents of houses near the Church were raised by sixpence a week.

There was clearly very much that wanted doing. There was still the isolation from the culture of London, the unemployment, the casual employment, the large class of those who had gradually become unemployable, the alien problem, the slum-houses, the constant shifting of population, the lack of public spirit, the indifference to spiritual things, almost the incapacity to entertain the idea that there are spiritual things, the common notion that, while religion may be true enough, it does not matter, and the practice of it, except perhaps at a Watch-Night Service, is probably hypocrisy.

[1] *East London*.327.

34

There were the toil-worn mothers, with almost no labour-saving devices in their homes, the girls who worked in the factories and had a good time in their own way until they married and sank into household drudges like their mothers. There were the men, mainly of two kinds, those who led decent, uncultured, and except for their family affection, uninteresting lives, and those who gambled or found drink "the shortest way out of Hoxton". There were the boys, who worked on the tail-boards of vans or at some other blind-alley occupation, and in the evenings ranged the streets in gangs of about nine, of whom one was by natural gifts the leader. And there were some criminals.

There was also some political prejudice to break down. It happened that among the early residents were some members of Lord Salisbury's family. The House was thought in some quarters to be a Conservative dodge. It was even supposed by some that Ingram was a candidate for Parliament. It soon appeared, however, that the House had no politics, and would back any effort for social betterment. This was found hard to believe, but it was eventually accepted. Ingram became a trusted leader, and one of his successors, Mr. Michael Seymour, was elected Mayor of Bethnal Green.

Here is, in Ingram's words, a Sunday picture:

> You must prepare your minds for this, that a vast majority of the men in your district will have spent their Sundays for the last twenty-five years, and their fathers before them, in the following way: they will have lain in bed until about eleven or twelve, having been up early all the week; they will then go round when the public-houses open, which they do at one; they will have what they call a "wet" till three, when the public-houses close; they will then have dinner, the great dinner of the week, which the missus has been preparing all the morning. Then comes a lie down on the bed in shirt sleeves until five, with a pot of beer and *Lloyd's Weekly*; then follows tea, and after tea a bit of a walk round to see a friend or relation; then fairly early to bed to make up for the very late Saturday night, and to be ready for work in the early hours of the morning.
>
> Let us face facts then: it is that Sunday you have got to turn into a day of spiritual rest and worship.[1]

When Ingram arrived on January 1st, 1889, the available equip-

[1] *Work in Great Cities*, 13.

35

ment at Bethnal Green did not amount to much. The original Oxford House was only the old Day Schools of St. Andrew's, Bethnal Green. There were three residents, and there was only room for four. The annual income was £700, and they were in debt. An appeal was issued for £14,000. Money was at once collected, Lord Brassey being a generous donor, and a freehold site was bought. Ingram used to say in after years that it was a vacant plot and the only things on it were a dead cat and the brick that had killed it.

The foundation-stone of a new House was laid in 1891 and in 1892 the House was opened by the Duke of Connaught, in the presence of two Archbishops, the Bishop of Lichfield having in the meantime become Archbishop of York, the Bishop of London and a large number of well-wishers. The House had thirty residents, and the annual income had risen to £2,000. Ingram was all his life a very successful money-raiser for Church objects. He used to say that, when he died, his epitaph would be "Last of all, the beggar died also". He collected money and enlisted support from all quarters. The Webbe Institute was founded by the Webbe family. The Repton Club was carried on by Old Reptonians. There was the Oxford House Club and the University Club, and Oxford House played a large part in the establishment of the Federations of Working Men's Clubs and Boys' Clubs, and in the work of the London Playing Fields Society.

Ingram never forgot that Oxford was his chief source for human material. Sir William Anson, Chairman of the Oxford Committee, was a tower of strength. Ingram paid constant visits to Oxford, and his charm and eagerness attracted men of all sorts to Bethnal Green. One, afterwards a Diocesan Bishop, came for three months and stayed for two years. Douglas Eyre, Barrister-at-law, the devoted and indispensable second in command, spent his life there. Among other duties, he was one of the band of essayists who, in a volume called *Church Reform*, edited by Charles Gore, prepared the way for most of the reforms that have since come to pass. One sentence of his essay lingers in the memory. Speaking of some policy which was alleged to be prudent, he said, "It appears to me that the Church is blasted with this kind of prudence."

There is no more wholesome and attractive human type anywhere than the best kind of English undergraduate. Ingram collected many of them. Some were ordinands already. Some, fired by his example and his shrewd discovery of a hitherto unrealized vocation, sought and received Holy Orders, and have done good work in the priesthood all over the world. What Archbishop Lord Lang said of his first introduction to Oxford House will appear later in this book.

The Reverend Ernest Bramwell, known at the House as "Brammy", was, as he says himself, a thoughtless undergraduate, who had no use for missionaries, but consented to meet Ingram at lunch. He was attracted, and when Ingram borrowed a pair of shorts and ran beside Bramwell's College Boat in the Torpids, it seemed that here was a sportsman, whose meeting might be worth attending. At the Meeting Ingram captivated them, and when he said, "If you have nothing particular to do in the Vac, come and stay with us and see what we are doing,"

I went. My first impressions were, what a nice house, what splendid clubs etc., for working men, and how fried fish smelt, and what crowds of people, who all looked very much the same, all very interesting but drab. In the House were Oxford and many Cambridge men, and they all had different jobs assigned to them; they were all full of the Head's enthusiasm, and there was a delightful spirit of friendship and welcome. Religion of course there was; there was the Chapel at the top of the House. It was thought as natural with the Head to have Service in the Chapel first thing as it was to have breakfast. Nobody was pressed to attend but everybody did. All this made a very great and deep impression on my mind.

After taking his degree Mr. Bramwell became a resident:

On Monday morning the Head presided at a Chapter Meeting, and each man was given a definite piece of work for the day. The evening was the time when each man went to his Club, either men or boys, and a wonderful organization it was. The Head always had the knack of getting the right man on the right job. One sometimes wondered how he got through all he did in the day, and the answer to that was Method. He was the most methodical man I have ever met, everything had its exact allotted time and it was never broken. For instance, so much time after getting up for prayers, so much time for letters and interviews—so much time for exercise, etc., etc. His rule got broken, however, when the doctor ordered him to sit down and be quiet, for at least half an hour, after lunch. This was a trial, and he would sit and read the *Spectator* for exactly thirty minutes, and off he went. Exercise was an important item, and there was at the House a Fives (Rugby) Court, and tremendous games used to be played there. I don't think I ever heard of anybody who defeated the Head at Fives. A four would play as hard as possible, and the Head was as wily and crafty as possible. But the game would only last a certain length of time, and he had to be bathed and changed for some engagement. The story is told that as usual the time was cut to the exact minute, and after the game he rushed upstairs, turned on the bath, got his clothes off and jumped into the bath. Unfortunately the bath had been painted that morning and when he got out his feet and back were thick in white paint. There was no time to clean it off so he pulled his clothes on over it. He had to go and preach, and he said they did not know what a whited sepulchre was addressing them! He always looked upon exercise as an important item in life.

Nobody would say that the Head was musical, but he loved a good song, especially a good chorus. Sunday nights, when everybody was in the Common Room at the House, there was generally a first-rate sing-song, and the House could boast of some excellent performers. Then too there was started at about that time the Bethnal Green Orchestra and Male Voice Choir. Under the conductor, Barry, a large orchestra was got together, with players from the West End, East End, Queen's Hall professionals, and once a week a Concert was given at one of the big Club Halls. But the point of the Concert was an address given by the Head half-way through the Programme. This must have been an extremely difficult thing to do. How to grip a large audience's attention in the middle of a concert, to grip it so tight that you could hear the proverbial pin drop, was wonderful except to those who knew the Head and that wonderful power of his of "putting it over". There was always that compelling and wonderful influence.

A young man came to Ingram once and said: "I have lost my faith. What can I do? Will you have me at Oxford House?"

"Certainly," I said, "if you will come and pray with us, and not talk about your doubts." I had thirty other young men in the House. "Yes, I will come," he said. And he came and for five years he worked among the poor, and he never talked about his faith at all. What was the result? Why, in working for others his faith came back to him:

he saw the Gospel in action. He saw that the only thing that did any good in the slums was faith. He saw faith in action. He has been for years a most respected clergyman in the Midlands.[1]

Some went on to business or the Law or other calling. But all had seen, not only a slice of vivid London life, but also what the East Londoners began to see—"Behold, now, I see that this is an holy man of God, which passeth by us continually." Ingram's example and his joyous faith appealed to the best that was in them, and called the best out of them. And the work, illuminated by the torch of his leadership, was fascinating. There is no exaggeration in the words used by Ingram in a sermon at St. Paul's:

> May I not appeal to the experience of this mass of human souls as to whether in their own measure they cannot certify that service for others, however imperfect, brings joy? I would ask the young University man who has gone down to live in the midst of the poor whether he has ever known in all his life such peculiar and subtle happiness as he has known during the months or years during which he has done it? Not one, but dozens of such men have looked up into my face and said, "We never knew, we had not the slightest idea until we served down here, what true happiness means."[2]

Among those whom he drew in were many who had gained athletic distinction at the University. Among the first was F. J. K. Cross, a famous runner. He even had at one time a "Blues Committee" at Oxford. Asked once if this was a considerable asset for work in East London, he replied that just at first it was. The boys in the Club were interested to meet a man who had rowed the gruelling course from Putney to Mortlake, or had played against Cambridge at Lord's, but this did not last long. Character was the thing that mattered. At the same time, as we all know, it happens that athletic capacity does very often carry with it capacities of a more spiritual kind.

Most of the men were turned into the Clubs. Here are Ingram's own words about Clubs. Speaking of Clubs for the average decent East London boy, he says:

[1] *Nine Christian Virtues*, 47.
[2] *Under the Dome*, 100.

39

Get a nucleus; ask half-a-dozen or a dozen to tea; broach your project; get leave from the Vicar to use the school-room or the mission-room; buy a few games and get the most good-natured female relation you have to buy a bagatelle board. Begin small and let it grow slowly; make all members pay an entrance fee of three-pence and a subscription of a penny a week to pay for the gas, etc. As soon as you can form a committee of the boys themselves, give them the authority to keep order. Nominate your first committee, but let the Club elect at least half afterwards. Do not give the power of admission or expulsion, or they may do to you what they did to a clergyman I knew on receiving this power, namely, passed a rule that no more should be admitted, and captured the fine new premises that had been built for the original twenty-five.

Have plenty going on; it's idle hands that break up furniture. Have, if possible, plenty of room; it's crowding that spoils discipline. Cater for body, mind and spirit; have plenty of games for the body; as you progress, get up a class or two for the mind. They will at any rate be ready to learn carving, possibly shorthand. A few will really like to go on with reading and writing, though they will be shy to say so; and if there is a Paris Exhibition going on, they will sometimes learn French. They never do go to the Exhibition, but they always think they might.

Then on Sunday, have a Bible-class connected with the Club; but, if you take my advice, you will not make attendance at it a test for coming to the Club. I know that in saying this I am going against the practice of many good workers, but it touches a question about which you will have to make up your mind for all clubs: Is it for Jacob or Esau?[1] . . .

For the very rough boys, who are lawless, and occasionally in trouble with the police, he says:

I can only summarize what you have to do with them. Let them box in your presence for three months: it is the only thing they can do or care to do. After three months, advance gradually to dumb-bells. Have a few papers in another room for the quietest, and after six months get a bagatelle-board, but don't be surprised, as Mr. Legge says, if they mark this advance in civilization by prodding holes in the ceiling with the bagatelle cues, which gives the ceiling the appearance of a cloth target after a Gatling-gun has been shooting at it.

[1]This, and the following extracts, are from *Work in Great Cities*.

40

In other words, it comes to this. I assume that you are going down into your districts to attack the real problem, and not some fancy problem, which you think ought to exist. If you are, then "take the human animal as you find him, and touch him at any point where he can be touched". Let your heart go out to these lads, so generous, so loyal, and so true when you know them; love them—that is the main thing, and then how to win them, "love will find out the way".

About men's clubs, speaking from experience of one club of eight hundred, another of three hundred, and from watching and sharing the work of the sixty clubs in the Federation, he says:

Here again you must at once make up your mind whether you are going to cater for Jacob or Esau; if for Jacob, then make any rules you like; there ought not to be the slightest difficulty in working a quiet club for your Church working-men. They have already got the very thing to which you hope some day to lead Esau. They have got "religion", the safeguard of righteousness and the bond of peace. The clubs I speak of are for Esau, and, as a first step to making him religious, have no religious test: let him be as free from being "button-holed" in your club to join anything against his will as a Bishop is free from being "button-holed" in the Athenæum to join the Land League. Have no political test either, of course: it is a *social* club you want; it is a union of men as men, to raise the life of man. Begin small and educate a nucleus, then have your committee, just as with the boys.

Your club must be an effective "cut out" of the public-houses which flame at every corner, there is no good in wasting your breath in abusing publicans; it is useless, besides being usually quite unfair. Devote your energies to cutting them out. Let me quote an incident which I narrated in my article. I was visiting in the London Hospital, and found myself sitting by the side of a broken-legged publican. When he heard who I was, he began asking about the welfare of several of our club-members. I asked him how he knew them. "Oh," he said, "they were regular customers of mine before they joined your club; I had a public-house close down your way."—"Are you still there?" I asked him. "No, sir, I've moved a little further off."

Then with regard to religion, by all means have a voluntary Club Bible-class, and once a quarter a club service in the Church, also voluntary, but to which you will find some will come who never come at any other times. But apart from anything directly religious which you will be able to introduce, you will have this inestimable blessing in your parish work, you will *know* the men of your parish; the barrier between you will be broken down; you will be able to visit them in their own homes on quite a different footing. The very working of the club, in which you are working shoulder to shoulder, will weave you into a brotherhood you can get in no other way; and as you patiently watch your chance year after year, it will go hard if some of them, at any rate, will not take from a friend the faith which they refused to take from a stranger.

Other men were set to work in Provident Collecting. In East London at that time the existence of the Post Office Savings Bank was not enough. Somebody must call every Monday morning and collect the shilling or the sixpence and take it to the Bank.

Birds of passage could be used in the season for the Children's Country Holiday Fund. More permanent workers, with the requisite capacity, could serve on the Sanitary Aid Committee, and armed with their knowledge of ball-traps, gullies and the provisions of the Housing Act, treat on behalf of some tenant with the Local Authority. A Barrister would attend once a week as Poor Man's Lawyer, and give free legal advice. One of the great pieces of social work done by Oxford House was the preservation of six-and-a-half acres of open space in Bethnal Green, which, in defiance of a 200-year-old Trust, was in danger of being built on. It had been improperly used as the site for an asylum, and when that went, houses were on the point of springing up. Ingram secured it for the public and became Chairman of the Trust which was to guard it for ever. In later life, when he was President of the Industrial Commission of the Church Assembly, there were some members of it who alleged that the Chairman could only wave his hands and say, "All my life I have been a worker for Social Reform." They perhaps did not know that in his young days he had worked untiringly and successfully at the task of bringing to bear the Christian Gospel on the actual facts of industrial life.

All the time the life and spring of the whole work of the House was Ingram. "Give a chap a chance," said Buchanan, one of the Settlers, at the meeting at which Ingram was introduced. They did, but he took it with both hands. This is the testimony of residents and observers, and it can also be inferred in another way. In 1895 he was invited to deliver the annual course of lectures on Pastoral Theology at Cambridge. Many famous men have given those lectures, and much good advice has been heard by successive generations of Cambridge ordinands, but it may be doubted whether any course has ever been more stimulating and more popular than that of 1895. Professor H. E. Ryle, afterwards Bishop of Exeter and Winchester, and Dean of Westminster, not a man to use words lightly, said in his introduction to the published book, *Work in Great Cities*, which has already been quoted in this chapter, that:

> Many of us, I am confident, were deeply moved by the perfect simplicity and admirable directness with which Mr. Ingram spoke, out of the fulness of his own experience, and if I may add, out of the riches of his sympathy with young men. We, in Cambridge, gained some insight into the secret of the influence which he wields as a leader of the band of Oxford men, who are now living in East London, "making their hardest task their best delight".

Professor Ryle wrote personally to him:

My dear Ingram,

It is very good of you to have thought of making such a suggestion. It would be a great privilege to be thus associated with a course of lectures which I enjoyed so keenly and found truly helpful, and I very readily consent to do what you propose. May I say it? The greatest joy has been to get to *know* another fellow-worker. It is a joy beyond all analysis, and to love the brotherhood is a commandment with promise, of which the fulfilment is often as sudden as it is sweet.

The men are very grateful to you: and several of them have expressed the hope that the lectures will appear in a book form.

> For your kindness,
> I too am,
> Yours gratefully,
> HERBERT E. RYLE.

In these lectures Ingram unconsciously gave picture after picture of his own ideals. He strove manfully against egotism. In the lecture on preaching he said:

> You will notice that I am afraid in this lecture of giving many illustrations, for fear of it being supposed that I consider myself capable

of carrying out the advice which I give to you; but one personal incident I might tell to illustrate this point.[1]

Nevertheless, he was there to put his experiences at the disposal of younger men. Ideals and principles and reminiscences come tumbling out together, and it is not difficult for other eyes to see self-revelation, innocent, edifying and even inspiring, in such passages as these:—

Speaking of the qualifications for Ministerial work in great cities, he said:

(i) First we must believe with all our hearts in our message. We must have thought it carefully out, and prayed over it, and spoken it to our own hearts, and quite made up our mind that Christianity, in its full meaning, as understood by the Holy Catholic Church, to which we belong, rightly understood and practically applied by all classes, is the cure for all our ills: that in the most literal sense, from all evils in the present life as well as in the future, there is no other name by which we can be saved except the name of JESUS CHRIST OUR LORD.

(ii) We must be able to say why we believe this; we must be able, not necessarily to argue, but to give clearly and forcibly the reasons for the hope that is in us. The time has long passed when any statement will be taken on the mere word of the clergyman. The very first visit to a hospital may lead to a question which will go to the roots of the faith. In the midst of that restless host we have to bear firmly and calmly on high the banner of the faith once delivered to the saints.

(iii) We must believe in our mission: This is essential in any age or in any place, but it is a special need when the forces loom so huge against us in the great cities. We want men with a strong sense of mission, who have heard the cry of the great deep calling unto deep; who have heard the voice of God cry, "Whom shall I send?" and the voice of humanity cry, "Who will come to us?" and who have answered, "Here am I: send me," and who know that God has sent them, through the hands of His servants.

(iv) We need men who are methodical. It is hopeless in any sphere of life to do much work unless the day is mapped out and every hour carefully accounted for; for it is perfectly childish to enter

[1] The incident was the story which he often told about "the chain of sin". See p. 128.

44

upon such a campaign as mission work in great cities involves, unless the campaign is conducted day by day with punctuality, precision, and self-discipline. I have only to refer you to the lectures of one of my predecessors in this lectureship—Canon Gibson on "Self-Discipline"—to give you the opportunity of learning in the best possible way how such self-discipline should be carried out; punctual time for rising, prayer and meditation: Mattins, either by yourself or in church, the teaching in the School, the morning's read, the hours for visiting, Evensong, the club or class—it has all to be methodized, and yet filled from end to end with loving zeal, which blends the whole day with its varied parts into one sacrifice well-pleasing to God, which is our reasonable service.

(v) We want bright men—men who, as they go into some of those dark little homes, will take a little sunshine with them; men who, when they enter a club, will set others at their ease, and who can pacify any small dispute in a good-humoured way. Especially is this required with open-air work, when almost everything depends on being able to keep the crowd in good humour and so carry the day.

(vi) We want sympathetic men, who will never weary of the tale of sorrow, but who yet are clear-headed enough not to let their hearts overbear their judgments.

(vii) We want, in view of the excessive drinking, men who, for the sake of others, will be teetotalers. There is no need of violent fanatics who will turn Teetotalism into the only Gospel, but undoubtedly there is a need of men who, in view of the "present distress" think it right to waive their rights; who, with Christ before them as their pattern, not from any Manichaean notions of the world, "please not themselves" in this for the sake of the weak brothers for whom Christ died.

As a matter of practical convenience you will find it a great help. I was haranguing 400 men the other day in the Beckton gas-works during dinner-hour, and was just in the middle of my dis-course, when a man shouted out, "Are you a tot?"—"Yes," I said. "Oh, all right—go on, then: if you wasn't, I wouldn't listen to you."

(viii) Lastly, we want patient men. There's an old saying, "It's dogged that does it", and undoubtedly it's dogged that does it in mission work in great cities.

In the lecture on "Unbelief, and how to meet it", he said:

And if moral integrity is the first—and, after all, what is it but the "breastplate of righteousness" we heard of long ago—we must put secondly the *shield of faith*. Yes, important as knowledge is, we must put faith before knowledge. It's believing in these things which carries conviction, not being able to argue about them; it's believing in a living God, "above our path, about our bed, and seeing all our ways." It's living in the sunshine of the faith that God's love is rising on us regularly as the morning sun; it is the steadfast morning prayer by which we rise into a new atmosphere, and come down with a new glory in our souls; it's believing in a Saviour who is with us "all the days", to console, to strengthen, and guide, and who yet, though with us all the days, has appointed fixed trysting-places where He will meet us in a special way; it's looking on the Church, not as some external organization which has to be kept up for its own sake, but as a "Divine Society", founded by Christ to be the most perfect brotherhood the world has ever seen, to be the arms and hands and feet by which he might gather in the world; it is looking on the Sacraments, not as something which gets between the soul and Christ, but as ropes which bind us to our Guide; it is believing in the Holy Spirit as an ever-present Worker in our own hearts, in our districts, through our preaching, in our visiting, and who yet comes at times, like Confirmation and Ordination, with special gifts and powers; in other words, it is faith in historic Christianity, without which no man may tread the dark valley, but with which upon his arm there is no weapon forged in the armour of hell which can move him by a hair's breadth from his mission of love.

It could hardly be bettered as a short description of the ideals of a town parson's life. And if the question be asked: "How did he know that?" the answer must be that he knew it in the only way in which a man can ever know things of that kind. He knew it by experience.

Lastly, in the Lecture about visiting, is this:

What then is the workmanlike way—I had almost called it the scientific way—of drawing souls to God? Surely, as a rule, *the gradual way*. "I drew them with the cords of a man, the bands of love," says the Almighty to Hosea; and it was by the bands of loving influence that Jesus Christ drew round Him, not only the weary and heavy laden, the children and the mourners, but the young men of the world, and Matthew the publican, and women like Martha, to whom the home was everything. Sometimes, of course, one must flash in some question, or raise the voice in loving warning, and even conceivably ask that very question of which we have spoken; but it will not be before we have thrown round them the meshes of loving influence, and made it possible for them to feel, whatever we say to them, "faithful are the wounds of a friend".

There is always "the next step" for them to take. That man never prays; that child is unbaptized; that boy is unconfirmed; that woman never comes to church: it is that next step, whatever it is, not as a mere form, but definitely as an outward and visible sign of turning over a new leaf, of conversion, trying to please God better, that you have to get them to take, and you visit them for that purpose. "I will lead them on gently," quotes Bishop Wilkinson from Genesis, in one of his beautiful works, "according as their strength will bear, lest, if I overdrive them one day, all the flock will die."

He himself found the work fascinating:

The most glorious and enthralling work in which a man can be engaged. I am going to tell you that it is going down into the mud of the streets after the lost coin, that it is sharing the Good Shepherd's search for His lost sheep—aye, and His joy in finding it too.

There were queer incidents:

I will tell you what may possibly happen when you knock for the first time at a door. After long hesitation it will be opened by a little girl about half a foot; you will hear a distant voice from the wash-tub in the rear, "Well, Sally, who is it?" Then Sally will answer at the top of her voice, "Please, mother, it's religion." You will require all your presence of mind to cope with that.

He gained his intimate knowledge of the people by constant visiting. Speaking to clergy at Leeds during this period, he said:

It is not too much to say that no one can preach well and effectively to an ordinary congregation, who either does not visit, or has not visited. The real secret of being able to preach easily and effectively is to know your people; in other words, it must be pastoral teaching. I suppose many of you will experience what many have experienced in the past—and that is, working away slowly and painfully at a subject

47

in the morning, and then finding after the afternoon's visiting, from sheer contact with real sorrow, real difficulties, and real problems, a sermon comes into the mind easily and naturally; in the morning it was up in the air, an abstract way of dealing with a subject; in the afternoon it came out of the fulness of the heart, to comfort actually sad people, to convert living sinners, and to explain real perplexities.[1]

Until he became Rector of St. Matthew's, with a cure of souls, it was *ad hoc* visiting, to look up Club absentees, or to visit sick members. From time to time there would be a sudden accident:

What awful work it is!—half-an-hour beside a gashed and mangled frame with life fast oozing out, and no sort of preparation for death; no prayers, no penitence, no power of amendment, often half-conscious, and with wife and children weeping round. Truly, if ever one needs, at one time more than another, to throw oneself wholly upon God, it is then!

Or here is an illuminating reminiscence:

Take the case next of the man who has fallen ill, or has had an accident, but *has some days, or even weeks to lie*, either to live or to die. Take the case of a young gymnast who fell in Oxford Hall. It was quite an easy trick he was doing, he had done it dozens of times before; but he was careless this time and fell, and in falling he cracked the top of his back-bone. He was just twenty-five, but he had never been baptized, had seldom or never said a prayer, and never been to church or chapel. I went at once, when I heard of the accident, to the hospital to see him. I scarcely knew him for he had not long joined the club, but the first thing he said was, "I have never been baptized." He was dead from the shoulders down, but the doctors thought he would live some days. I had to crowd the Gospel of a lifetime into these few days. I paid him constant short visits. He was very good and patient and attentive. I baptized him after a time, taught him some prayers and hymns, and at his own request tied on to the ropes above his bed, for he could move neither hand nor foot, that most beautiful hymn which he died repeating.

"O my Saviour, lifted
From the earth for me,
Draw me in Thy mercy
Nearer unto Thee."

[1]*Good Shepherds*, 15.

For such visits and such help the relatives were pathetically grateful. Sometimes they forgot all about it before long and went back to their old way of life, but it was said that the congregation at the Sunday evening service in Oxford Hall, popularly known as Ingram's 'All, had been almost entirely built up at the death-beds of relatives. It was a piece of real Good Shepherd work. A friend writes:

I am sure as a preacher he was at his best in the Old Mission Room at Bethnal Green.

All the time he was raising money for the work of the House. The days of his great begging at Bournemouth and Eastbourne and Torquay were not yet, but even at that time Mr. Bramwell writes that:

He was certainly an arch-beggar, but again it was all that wonderful infectious enthusiasm. He meant every word he said. One of his principal efforts was always to be raising money for the Oxford House and Bethnal Green, as later on he worked terribly hard for the East London Church Fund. Apart from often and often preaching in West End Churches, he was for ever addressing drawing-room meetings and telling the West End what was being done in the East End. It was certainly wonderful how his appeal went home and the financial help came rolling in. It was not the money only but the lively interest many took in what was going on in Bethnal Green. It is true to say that sometimes the enthusiasm would sweep him off the correct line and truth got a wee bit stretched. A wise friend described him "an unsullied soul, but incapable of the truth". Not altogether fair, the latter part, as it only amounted to a little enthusiastic exaggeration.

Not content with the West End he determined to see what he could do with his home county of Worcestershire. A tour of the county was arranged, and off we went, the Head and three of us Residents. It was a most delightful tour in the summer. We stayed in jolly big houses and had lots of tennis, etc. Then in the afternoon our hostess would arrange a garden-party and when all her friends and neighbours had come, we took seats on a little platform in the garden and told them about Bethnal Green and East London. We felt a little bit like the good young man who dies in the last chapter because the Head, who of course spoke first, would talk of us as young men who were giving up so much to look after their poower brothers in East

London. Not a bit of it; we were just loving life. The crab of the Head speaking first was, that before the meeting we used to pool our stories and anecdotes, and then portion them out. He would invariably bag all our stories.

Then there was the evidential work. On Sunday afternoon, in summer in Victoria Park at the Christian Evidence Society Stand, and in winter in a hall, he would give lectures and answer questions. The Park was a great place for the airing of opinions. Secularist orators had pitches there, as well as the adherents of curious forms of religious belief. Ingram was distressed to see young boys vigorously applauding the destructive and sometimes blasphemous statements of opponents of the Christian Faith. It is true that he said in 1939:

> I lectured for nine years in the open air in East London, and I never heard a word said against Jesus Christ Himself. I have heard plenty of criticisms of the Church, but always on the ground that the Church had ceased to represent Jesus Christ.[1]

but it may be that a charitable memory had a little softened the bitterness of the attack. He had said in 1904:

> I have myself had to stand Sunday after Sunday in the open air, practically the only one in that particular crowd who profess belief at all. On the secularist side was open unbelief, and scoffing at Christ and the Bible, while all round were men and boys joining in it, and what cut my heart most was to see the boys there. I stood alone amid a hostile crowd, not one of whom professed belief in a single word of the truths of the faith I preached.[2]

and in 1899:

> There is the secularist at the street corners and in the park, using these very dangers and this suffering to persuade the boys and girls, the women and the men gathered in knots around him, that the Bible is a pack of lies, that the clergy are impostors, that the Lord Jesus Himself was either deceived or deceiver, and sowing in their hearts the seeds of distrust and disbelief.[3]

[1] *Secrets of Happiness:*
[2] *Faith of Church and Nation*, 104.
[3] *Banners*, 204.

At all events, something had to be done:

> I determined therefore to carry the work into the enemy's country
> and procured a small platform and advanced into the crowd which
> assembled every Sunday in Victoria Park. We had with us at the
> Oxford House a man with a singularly raucous voice (he subse-
> quently became a Dean!). I got him to come and sing the Old Hun-
> dredth, and, as I expected, the extraordinary noise attracted a little
> crowd; and I then ascended my little pulpit and addressed them on
> why we were Christians and the good reasons we had in believing
> in the Christian Faith. I afterwards found it better to advance to the
> Secularist's platform and ask leave to answer what he had said, which I
> was always courteously allowed to do.
> Then by a stroke of good fortune the central platform in the Park
> became vacant, and by the popular vote of the Park I was hoisted up
> to be the chief Park lecturer. It was indeed a great opportunity, and I
> only wished I had been more worthy of the occasion.[1]

He soon discovered that it was essential to be familiar with the
case of the opponents. A well-qualified theologian might deliver
his carefully argued lecture on "The New Testament" or "Why I
believe in Christ", and then be rather taken aback by the suggestion
that the books of the New Testament were all drastically revised
in the fourth century, and are very different from what the authors
originally wrote.[2] Ingram worked hard at the secularist books,
and harder still at the building up of his own constructive case. He
put his points in a homely way and had no hesitation about raising
a laugh. But he was too chivalrous, and also too wise, to attempt to
score off his opponents in a personal way. His crowd was always
much the largest in the Park.

His own teaching is contained in the series of little books, *Old
Testament Difficulties*, *New Testament Difficulties*, *Church Difficulties*,
Popular Objections to Christianity, *Papers for Working Men*, *Reasons
for Faith* and so on, which were published by S.P.C.K., and had
large circulations. They seem now a little old-fashioned, and many

---

[1] *Fifty Years*, 8–9.
[2] I believe that this suggestion, which has actually been made, but is quite fantastic, arose
out of the perfectly accurate statement, made by Textual Critics of the New Testament,
that there was a "recension" in that century. This merely means that existing MSS were
compared with one another, and a revised text came into use. It differed from the ancient
text about as much as the text used in making the Authorized version differs from that which
lies behind the Revised Version.

of the books on which he depended are out of date. But he worked hard at it, and it was exactly the kind of thing that was wanted. The *Oxford House Papers*, to which scholars of the calibre of Sanday contributed, were on a larger scale.

Ingram tells a story of the early days. He asked a large audience of men what subject they should tackle on the following Sunday afternoon. It is probable that he had given them some kind of lead, but as he told the story, four hundred voices shouted like one, "Eternal Punishment." He added: "There was a nice topic for a young man to undertake at a week's notice."

Some of the questions were the stock objections, Cain's wife and the stipend of the Archbishop of Canterbury. It has never been discovered exactly what he did say about Cain's wife. The question is only difficult if it is supposed that Adam and Eve were two individuals, and that they and their sons were the only human beings then upon earth. If, however, it is supposed that "Adam" means Primitive Man, a being whose life covers centuries, perhaps millennia, who may have existed in more than one part of the globe, there is no difficulty. Ingram, when the subject came up in after years, used to say, "Oh, we buried her in Bethnal Green years ago." His attitude to Biblical problems was what would to-day be described as a very mild and cautious criticism. About the Archbishop he used to say that he was a trustee who was compelled to spend all his official stipend and perhaps more, if he had any, on inhabiting and maintaining Lambeth Palace.

Some of the questions went deeper. A very frequent difficulty was "Why do we suffer pain?" There is a summary of his answer in a lecture about Pain:

The substance, then, of what we understand about pain amounts to this: it is a danger-signal both to man and animals, without which death and loss of limbs would be far more frequent than they are. It is administered as mercifully as is consistent with this object. It does not necessarily demoralize, but only when the will rebels and turns what might ennoble into something that demoralizes. It is immensely illuminated by the life and words of Christ, who at once bore it, soothed it, and comforted it, and though still, like many other things, a mystery, it is a mystery of which we are justified in saying to ourselves:

52

"Take it on trust a little while,
Soon shall ye read the mystery right
In the full sunshine of His smile."[1]

Of course what he then said, or afterwards wrote, is not the last word on the subject. It is a popular, and, if judged by the highest philosophical and theological standards, superficial treatment of profound themes. All the same there was power and understanding in the concluding paragraph of an article called "Why did Christ die?" in *Papers for Working Men*.

Once united to Him—and the union needs a responsive effort on man's part—but once united to Him, and there is no legal fiction about being saved by Him. You cannot help being saved by Him. The Head cannot be the Saviour and the members unsaved; the Vine cannot be Redeemer, and the branches unredeemed; unless the branch "abide not in Him", it cannot be cast forth and wither. There is no more room for controversy about faith and works; the faith that joins and keeps joined must, even as it admits the grace of remission of sins, admit also the grace that flowers into good works. We are justified by faith, but it is a faith that *worketh by love*.

Why did Christ die?

Can we find, then, a better answer than the hymn the children sing as they play quietly by the shore of truth, the depth of which we try in vain to fathom?

"He died that we might be forgiven,
He died to make us good,
That we might go at last to heaven,
Saved by His precious blood."[2]

Or this to Boys:

What do I mean by saying that Jesus loves you? What does love mean? Think of some one whom you know loves you on earth: think of those laymen who move perpetually among you night after night here: you know three things about them:

(i) *They don't mind the least how much trouble they take* about you.

(ii) They *sympathize with you* in your troubles and difficulties.

(iii) They *do it all for nothing*; they get nothing by it.

[1] *Popular Objections to Christianity*, 34
[2] *Papers for Working Men*, 24.

Now, the Bible would call all that *love*; it would say, "They, beholding you, love you"—it is a labour of love.

Multiply that ten thousand-fold; picture that combination of *self-sacrifice*, *sympathy* and *disinterestedness*, and then increase it infinitely, and you have some idea of the love of Jesus for you,

(i) He has cared for you enough to die for you.

(ii) He feels the deepest sympathy in all your troubles and trials.

(iii) He has done it all for no reward except the crown of thorns and the Cross.

"*Jesus, beholding you, loves you.*" I said that to-day to a boy on his death-bed, and repeated it until he seemed to believe it; a changed look came into his face; he seemed to turn and meet Christ's loving gaze.[1]

Scholarly or not, it helped those who heard it. When he left the Park, he had a testimonial in the form of a beautiful cabinet made in Bethnal Green by a man who had been converted by the Sunday lectures, which was subscribed for by the rest of the audience. What pleased Ingram most was that his secularist opponents joined in the testimonial, as they said that he had always treated them in a gentlemanly way.

Part of his advice to young preachers was that, as they wrote or otherwise prepared their sermons, they must see their congregation in their mind's eye all the time. This he unquestionably did himself. He loved the East Londoners, and he elicited their love. In Victoria Park and in the streets he was a popular figure, but in the homes of those to whom he had ministered either there or in his own church, he was beloved. The writer is of the opinion that the title "Father" is best used for members of communities, though he allows that there are some priests from whom somehow the title cannot be withheld. It had not become the fashion in Ingram's day in East London, but, if it had, he would have borne it. An Evangelical member of a Parochial Church Council in Lancashire once capped something that the Evangelical Vicar had said by bursting out with, "Now I know exactly why Roman Catholics call their clergy 'Father'." Fifty years later Ingram would have been greeted by every ragged urchin in the street with, " ' 'Ullo, Farver," and he would have been "The Farver" to all the people in his parish.

[1] *Addresses to Working Lads*, 60.

54

He used a reminiscence of his Oxford House work in a sermon at St. Pancras Church in 1906:

> That God leads us, and does not drive, is the explanation of many of the difficulties that have been sent up to me. Why are there sin and evil in the world? What was the necessity of the Incarnation? Why the astounding miracle of the Atonement? What is the good of the Church? The answer to every one of these questions is that God leads and does not drive. I remember so well in the old East End days, when the young men of the boating club connected with the Oxford House came to ask about their rowing on Sunday morning, and I explained to them that I could not remain their president if their club races were held on Sunday morning; that it was impossible for me to commit myself to the principle that Sunday morning was the time for a boat-race, but that I had no right, as president or head of Oxford House, to dictate to them as individuals what they should do, for I lived down there to try and lead them to better ways of spending Sunday mornings; and the deputation, with that perfect frankness and trust which they always gave me, looked up and said: "We quite understand, Mr. Ingram: you have come down here to lead us, and not to drive us." They could not have hit off the work of a priest of God, if he works faithfully in the spirit of God, more perfectly straight than that.[1]

The intense sympathy which he felt for East Londoners is illustrated by a curious fact. As a young man he spoke in the way in which a parson's son, born in Worcestershire and educated at Marlborough and Oxford, usually speaks. In East London, and ever afterwards, he spoke in what must be called something of an East London voice. There was no coarseness or vulgarity in his tone, just a friendly vestige of the fact that he had "heard the East a-callin'".

In 1895 Bishop Temple pressed him to become Rector of St. Matthew's, Bethnal Green, the mother church of the district. It was a dignified old Wren Church, built for preaching, but the life of the parish was not vigorous. Ingram said later, "There were only seventeen people in the Church when I looked in." The dialogue at Fulham Palace was characteristic:

"They say I shall be overworked."

"But we don't think of that, do we?"

[1] *A Mission of the Spirit*, 73.

"Mr. Lawley" (Vicar of St. Andrew's, Bethnal Green, afterwards Lord Wenlock), "thinks it would be a mistake."

"You'll convert him in two years."

"Is it your Lordship's wish that I should do this?"

"Oh, yes, and, what is more, you'll be instituted *to-morrow*."

"But I am going for my holiday to-morrow."

"Then you must go the day after."

On the next day he attended at Mr. Lee's office and was instituted. As he rose from his knees, he records that a glint came into the Bishop's old eyes, and he said, "You'll be able to catch the six o'clock, if you're quick."

Actually, he put off his holiday for a little, and explained his new duties to the crowd in Victoria Park the next Sunday afternoon. Before long he became Rural Dean of Spitalfields, and the Bishop of Stepney (Forrest Browne) wrote:

My dear Rural Dean,

By how many more titles, all redolent of help and co-operation from you, am I in course of time to call you! I have only this moment seen it in the "East London Observer". People complain that the Bishop of London does not himself appoint the Rural Deans. In this case it did not matter who appointed, there was only one man in anyone's mind. May you rule your flock with the rod of a Rural Dean, of a *decanus rusticanus* as the old French Statutes of Cathedrals used to put it. In Spitalfields that should mean a sinecure. You won't make it one.

Yours sincerely,
G. F. STEPNEY.

He still lived at Oxford House, and drew his stipend of £150 a year, with board and lodging. The Rector's stipend was used entirely for parish purposes. The Rector had hitherto been paid by a half-penny poll-tax on the inhabitants of Bethnal Green, a terrible arrangement, which Ingram changed as soon as he could. The Ecclesiastical Commissioners bought out the poll-tax scheme, at the cost of some diminution of the income. Ingram put in two admirable curates, Marshall and Philpotts, who lived at the Rectory, and the large, shabby Rectory garden became a sort of playground for the people of the parish. It was hard work, but it was of course a great advantage to the Rector that he could call on the House men to visit and teach in his parish.

He gives an account of it in the *Secrets of Victory* (1946):

The result was marvellous. It was the lay people that did it, and that is the great point of the Report on the Conversion of England, that it is the Lay people who will have to do it again. The result of our seven years' long work was shewn. The gay crowd climbed up every rickety staircase, knocked at every door. "But we hate the Church," was the reply. "Oh, no," they said, "*We*, whom you have learnt to love all these years, *are* the Church; you didn't realize that we were the Church." The 17 in Church went up to 100, then 200, then 400, and you should have heard them singing at Evensong, just the ordinary Evensong of the Church of England, with tunes to the Psalms they could sing, and popular Hymns, and Lessons with short explanations to precede them, and you would then be convinced that the working people of England could be taught to love the Liturgy of the Church of England. "How I did hate those Psalms," said a young policeman to me; "but now I love them." There is no reason, if the Church can be in full strength, as it has never yet been, why it should not have the nation at the feet of God, and we shall have shewn no proper Thanksgiving to God for His Glorious Victory, until every parish church and every Cathedral of the British Empire *rings* with the praise of God.[1]

Preaching in his old Church in 1929 he said:

You will understand I am sure, that there is no pulpit in the world to me like this one in Bethnal Green. Since I was here I have preached in thousands of churches up and down the world, but the two years that I spent as Rector of the Parish Church here are written indelibly upon my memory. Very few of you here to-night will remember that time, now thirty-five years ago. When I was asked by Bishop Temple, when working at Oxford House, to undertake the work of this parish with its ten thousand people, I felt very doubtful whether I should be able to combine the two. But in those days we had five curates, ten lay workers, and ten lady workers who visited the people, knocking at every door, and inviting personally almost every man and woman to come to church. I always picture on a Sunday evening this church packed to overflowing, with not a single place vacant,

[1] *The Fruits of Victory*, 45.

even in the gallery, and the thought of those thrilling mission services which we used to have night after night has warmed my soul ever since. I honour these splendid men here who are to-day toiling on year after year, but some day I want to see those galleries crammed as they were in the old days, and to feel that old-time enthusiasm which existed then. It could be done again, if only there was an adequate staff to cope with the work, and if only men and women would respond adequately to God's demands.

Mr. Bramwell describes a Watch-Night Service:

The Head got up into the pulpit and just let himself go with a great outpouring of his spirit. Imagine the scene—the Church full of people who had poured in from the street and from the pubs with all the noise of hooters and bells outside. The Head had them, after speaking, on their knees in dead silence as the New Year came in, those people, silent and deeply touched. They gave themselves away perhaps as they started applauding at the end.

Meantime the House was going full swing, and for two years the Rector was Rural Dean of Spitalfields as well. It was almost more than flesh and blood could compass. In fact it was more, but by the mercy of God there was available the grace which makes men sufficient ministers of a new covenant. Wherefore he fainted not, for though the outward man was weary, yet the inward man was renewed day by day.

During his time at Oxford House Ingram was pressed several times to consider other work, always of the nature that is sometimes called "promotion". In April 1893 he was sounded by the Bishop of Christchurch, N.Z., about the bishopric of Wellington. It was not a firm offer by the appointing body, but it appears from such letters as have survived that there is reason to believe that it would have gone forward, if Ingram had agreed. In September 1894 the Bishop of Newcastle pressed him to become Vicar of Newcastle. "It wants a man," he wrote, "earnest, loving and sympathetic and strong, to make that great Cathedral the centre of a life which shall pulse through the city and radiate through the diocese. Will you come and be that man, God helping you?" In November of the same year came an invitation from the Bishop of St. Alban's to be Vicar of Chelmsford and Archdeacon. In April 1896 the Provost of Oriel wrote:

My dear Ingram,

You know that we are suffering a great loss in Lang's departure for Portsea. Amongst other results this College has to appoint a new Vicar of St. Mary's.

At our meeting to-day it was agreed *nem. con.* that you were the fittest man in the judgment of us all to take his place and gather up the many threads which he is dropping.

It was thought best that, as a preliminary step, I should write to you semi-privately and ask if there is any chance, let me say hope, of your being able to leave London and come here. If so, the College would proceed to formulate proposals more definitely. On this head I will not say more now than that we should all do our best to give you a position in connection with this College both useful and dignified.

I need not add how much I should welcome you personally.

I remain, my dear Ingram,

Yours always sincerely,

L. R. PHELPS.

In May 1896 the Bishop of Lichfield, who had no doubt heard of all or some of the refusals of the foregoing offers, wrote rather diffidently:

My dear Ingram,

I suppose there is not the slightest chance of my being able to tempt you to undertake the Archdeaconry of Salop and the charge of St. Chad's, Shrewsbury.

The position would not be lucrative but of wide influence.

Yours most sincerely,

AUGUSTUS LICHFIELD.

There is no record of his replies to any of these letters, or to an offer, which is known to have been made, to become Rector of Stoke-on-Trent, or of what he thought of them, but it may be conjectured that by this time he felt that he was wedded to East London "till death us do part", and that his later moves were acceptable because the sphere of both of them included Bethnal Green. It appears from some later correspondence that about 1900 he was a good deal talked of as a possible Bishop of Liverpool, but there is no reason to believe that he was invited by the Prime Minister to go there, or that he would have accepted, or indeed that a much better choice for that particular diocese was not made in

Dr. Chavasse. The only "might have been" of that kind which could ever be anything of a regret to his friends (and that not on all grounds) is that he did not leave London at the height of his powers to become an Archbishop in the Dominions. It is, however, on record that he did once offer to resign London and become Bishop of "any poor diocese in Canada", but the Archbishops felt that he must stay where he was.

IV

STEPNEY

No one was surprised when in 1895 Bishop Creighton invited Ingram to become Bishop of Stepney. Creighton, without actually making over to his Suffragans[1] the episcopal charge of a district, had returned to some extent to the devolution principle of the pre-Temple days. For most purposes the Bishop of Stepney was the Bishop of East and North East London. "I choose you," Creighton is reported to have said, "not because I think you will do it well, but because I cannot think of anyone who would do it better." He also said once, "Don't ask me what my suffragans do; they go where they like, do what they like, and say what they like, and I get the blame." And in 1898 he wrote to Arthur Lyttelton, on becoming Bishop of Southampton:

I think it much nicer to be a suffragan bishop than a diocesan bishop. You have all the sweets and escape the bitters of the episcopal office.... Therefore make the best of it while you may.

It was the diocesan bishop's point of view, not always shared by the suffragans.

East Londoners had mixed feelings. They were to lose "Mr. Ingram", though the old name clung at his reappearances among them, and they were to receive him back again in a larger, more distinguished, but also more diffused capacity. He would no longer be able to devote himself to Bethnal Green in the old way, but Bethnal Green would have the altruistic satisfaction of knowing that he was now in a position to do much more for Poplar and Hoxton and Whitechapel and Shoreditch than the occasional visits or the annual mission in one parish had allowed. To Poplar and Hoxton and Whitechapel and Shoreditch it was almost pure gain.

[1]The word is used throughout this book in its popular sense, of a bishop who assists a diocesan bishop in a diocese. The correct use of the term is different. The diocesan bishops of a province are the suffragans of the Metropolitan. Thus the Bishop of London is a suffragan of the Archbishop of Canterbury.

It was not that they now had for the first time someone who could care for them. Their Bishop had always done that. But they felt that they now had someone as their Bishop who knew them intimately.

To Ingram himself there came now a larger picture of East London as a whole. Bethnal Green had been a little pool of poverty, for the most part rather slummy. He now saw more clearly what Sir James Paget had seen when his son Luke Paget first went to the Church Mission:

> Before I ever saw it, my father walked all the way from Hanover Square to Poplar, and he summed up his opinion in words which I shall always remember: "My dear Luke, I don't pity you a *bit!*"
> He saw what I never got tired of seeing: the splendid width of the East India Dock Road, with dock-gates and shipmasts at the end of it; and Poplar Church, and the recreation ground, and the rows of nice houses, and—for he was a Yarmouth man—the tokens of foreign travel and seafaring life, the flying fish in bottles, the albatross wings, the Oriental curiosities which used to adorn some of our windows. He certainly liked the look of the place.

Ingram succeeded Bishop George Forrest Browne, who was translated to the See of Bristol. Browne was a learned man, of great power and with an immense capacity for affairs, who, as a Cambridge don, had held several University offices and discharged the duties of them all with vigour and success.[1] With all this, he was, or seemed, rather formidable. He visited and confirmed most faithfully, but he was more at home instructing the St. Paul's Lecture Society or in the pulpit of the Cathedral than in the neighbourhood of Wapping Old Stairs. When he died at the age of ninety-six in 1930 the Bishop of London spoke of "the extremely firm but kind way in which he ruled his district".

The Cathedral comes into the story because the bishopric was then held, and continued to be held till the translation of Cosmo Lang from Stepney to York, with a Canonry at St. Paul's. There

---

[1] It was of him that this story was told at Cambridge. A distinguished foreigner had been conducted from College to College and was much impressed, but not quite satisfied. "But where," he said, "is the University?" At that moment Professor Browne was seen walking rapidly, with papers under his arm, to some meeting of the Council of the Senate, or the General Board of Studies, or the Press Syndicate. "There," said the guide triumphantly, "there is the University."

are as a rule no funds available for the payment of suffragans. They
have to be maintained by making them either Cathedral Canons or
parochial incumbents. The Cathedrals or parishes do not always
like this arrangement and they are sometimes known to invoke St.
Peter as the saint who is most likely to understand their case, but
there seems no help for it.[1]

On becoming a Bishop he was admitted by his old University of
Oxford to the Degree of Doctor of Divinity *honoris causa*. It was
the custom at that time for both the ancient Universities to confer
this degree on *alumni* of their own who became Bishops or Deans.
This is not now done, and diocesan Bishops, if they do not already
happen to be Doctors, receive the Lambeth D.D. which is, by ancient
custom, that of the Archbishop of Canterbury's own University.[2]

He was consecrated at St. Paul's on St. Andrew's Day (November
30th), 1897. It was announced on the Service Paper that the Archbishop of Canterbury would be the principal Consecrator, but he
must have fallen ill, because the Cathedral Book shews that the
consecrating bishops were the Bishops of London, St. Alban's,
Lichfield, Bristol, Rochester, Marlborough, Southwark and
Colchester and Bishop Barry and Bishop Bromby. The Preacher
was Prebendary Shelford, Rector of Stoke Newington. The congregation included two hundred of the East London clergy and many
deputations of old friends. An eye-witness (Mr. Ernest Rowell)
writes:

> It was a sight that I shall never forget. Outside the Cathedral were
> horse and pony traps from the East End, feeding from their nose-bags,
> the owners of which were in that great congregation in the Cathedral.
> It was a moving, impressive sight during the singing of Bright's
> beautiful hymn, after the Celebration of the Holy Eucharist, "And
> now, O Father, mindful of the love".

The only other hymn was "Blessed City, Heavenly Salem". The
Service was Stanford in B Flat, and there were two short anthems
by Gounod and Benedict, composers popular at that time.

[1]As I have written this, I must be allowed to add that the episcopal Canon of Exeter, the
Right Reverend W. F. Surtees, as well as being a most efficient suffragan, discharges every
duty at the Cathedral with complete and overflowing faithfulness. It can be done, but at a
cost.

[2]Veracity wrings from me the admission that this has been, ever since the death of Archbishop Benson, the University of Oxford.

So Ingram became Bishop of Stepney and Canon of St. Paul's. It was a new life for him, but he was completely unspoiled by his elevation. A friend wrote to him and said: "I suppose I mustn't go on calling you 'old chappie'. He replied, 'If you don't go on calling me 'old chappie', I shall never write to you again. With the new housekeeper saying 'My Lord' every second minute, and the children in Bethnal Green saying 'Oh, my goodness, look at 'is trahsers,'[1] your saying 'Old chappie' is the only thing that keeps me well, except sitting as I am now in an old sweater and knicker-bockers and going off to play golf with a colonel who is called 'Old Foozle' on the links."

2 Amen Court, which had been in past years the home of Gregory (before he became Dean) and Browne, and has since been occupied by Cosmo Lang and Canon Alexander, lies, as is well known, in one of the quiet spots in the City of London. These houses have a curious origin. King Charles II borrowed a small sum of money from the Dean and Chapter of St. Paul's, and to their surprise paid it back again very soon. Puzzled by this, they took advice about it. They consulted courtiers, and, it may be, even the King's physicians, and decided that it must be the King's intention to borrow presently a larger sum and not repay it. They quickly retained the services of Sir Christopher Wren and sank their money in "bricks and mortar", the earliest use of that expression in the English language, and built the Canons' Houses. Sure enough, before long, the King asked for a larger sum. They were full of dutiful regrets, but they had no more capital to lend.

One of his first acts was to convert one of the upstairs rooms into a bathroom,[2] and there are stories of interviews with the clergy carried on through the bathroom door. "All right, old boy, I'll come and confirm on the twenty-fifth. Just let me finish drying and I'll make a note of it."

His work was twofold. He had to care for the spiritual welfare of East and North East London. There were at that time 208 parishes

[1] A newly-consecrated Bishop was once walking the streets of Plymouth, when he over-heard this conversation between two boys behind him. "I say, Bill, what's that?" "Oh, I know. It's a Highlander going to a funeral."

[2] The Wren houses had at first no bathrooms. There is a St. Paul's story that Canon Newbolt would have liked to instal one, but Dr. Liddon, his great master, and his predecessor in the house, had not had a bathroom, and so he held his hand. Canon Mozley, who succeeded Newbolt, felt that, Liddon or no Liddon, the time had come when there must be a bathroom.

in the Deaneries of Stepney (41), Spitalfields (23), Shoreditch (21), Hackney (27), Islington (23), with as many incumbents, 340 assistant-curates, and a population of nearly two million souls, more, as the Bishop used to say, than the population of Birmingham, Manchester and Liverpool put together. Many of them were living in terribly crowded conditions. It was said that in East London 400,000 people lived in single tenement rooms, 40,000 lived five in a room, 8,000 lived seven in a room, and some actually lived ten in a room. The Bishop said to Cambridge Undergraduates that he had never seen the legendary case in which there were five families in one room, one in each corner and one in the middle, and they got on all right until the family in the middle began to take in lodgers. But the official statistics were bad enough. The Bishop, preaching for the East London Church Fund in Westminster Abbey in 1898, described the conditions and added:

I only have to ask you to think over what that means. I don't say from a physical point of view; the death-rate shews that. In one crowded district the death-rate is constantly from 22 to 27 *per* 1,000, compared with 18 *per* 1,000 in the rest of London. The overcrowding is undoubtedly the cause. But think of the morals! Oh, fathers and mothers who come here this evening, think if you had to bring up your own dear boys and girls five or six in a room, the only room in which to eat, sit, and sleep; think what it would mean for the morals of the children. Think how hard it would be to bring them up in decency at all. You will understand from this what a tremendous problem this overcrowding means to the parish clergy working in the East End.[1]

In the same sermon he said:

Three children in one of our poorest districts were observed playing by the Board School Master. He asked them what they were playing at, and one of them replied that they were playing at "Home". One of them was father and the other was mother. Father was beating mother when the policeman—the third child—came and took him up. If you can imagine that being "home" in the minds of those children, you will realize what havoc in the homes of East London drink works.

[1]*Banners*, 201.

E

Moreover, the population was constantly shifting. As families prospered a little, and the boys appeared at the Club in collars instead of knotted handkerchiefs, they moved from Whitechapel to Walthamstow. Sometimes, not having prospered particularly, they moved into the next street. Sometimes, having been particularly unprosperous, they put their "sticks" on a barrow by night, flitted to a remote street, and were lost sight of. It was reckoned that in some parishes the communicant-roll would have almost completely changed in five years or three times in fifteen years. All this made parish work very difficult. The clergy worked magnificently, but the numbers, the conditions and the removals were rather daunting. Ingram made it his business to put fresh heart into them. "All his days," in Mr. Bramwell's words:

> Were spent getting in touch with his clergy in East London and there were some wonderful heroes among them, men who had spent their lives working away in some out of the way slum parish. He was a great inspiration to those men.

His work was not all personal. He had not forgotten his old Christian Social Union principles and the policy of what is now called Moral Welfare. He said in St. Paul's:

> What can I do? you ask.
> One thing at any rate you can do. If you are taking rent from property, see that it is sanitary, see that the tenants are treated like men and not like animals: do not leave it to an agent, and ask no questions if the rent is paid. You can do more. You can join a Sanitary Committee of the Mansion House Council, or start a committee where one is not started. The one in Bethnal Green is worked by a lawyer, and has on it doctors, surveyors, one or two gentlemen of leisure, and working-men. Or perhaps most useful of all, you could go and live in a poor district, and after a time get elected on to the local Vestry, and when you have got the confidence of your colleagues, get them to use the large power put in their hands by the law, to close houses and enforce sanitation.

Nevertheless, a good deal even of this work was intensely personal. He would constantly refer in St. Paul's to an experience of a day or two before:

If you could have come, my friends, yesterday with me as I went to give the Communion to a young man in the prime of life who was being choked with cancer, with only two more weeks to live, and if you could have faced death side by side with him, and seen him go up to his death as bravely as any young officer ever went up to the mouth of the cannon, you would appreciate more what the Cross is. If you were more with those who are falling, as it were, off earth, and as they fall into the abyss are caught by the Cross and lifted up to heaven, then it would come over you what comes over some of us at times with overwhelming force, that life would be impossible and hopeless without the Cross.[1]

Or this, on Sunday evening in Westminster Abbey:

Only this afternoon, after an afternoon sermon at Whitechapel at the institution of a new vicar, I was summoned by one of the curates of Whitechapel to go with him to a man who had sent a special messenger to ask me to go before he died. I went with the curate up a long staircase to the very top of the house, and there, two hours ago, was a man lying dying. He had round him every comfort, he had by his side, at his beck and call, his friend who had fetched me. He had searched him out in this upstairs room, and was acting as his constant friend. I knelt by him and prayed by him, and spoke to him, and sat some time by him. That is the sort of thing that is going on every day up and down the district. Ask who it is that places flowers by the bedside, who brought that jelly? It is the East London clergyman or his parish worker, who, by his constant visiting, is the friend of the district. I often think, as I see that silent army going forth to their work, of the beautiful lines of the American poet:
"The den they enter grows a shrine,
The gloomy sash an oriel burns,
Their cup of water warms like wine,
Their speech is filled from heavenly urns."[2]

These parishes were of all ecclesiastical complexions. Ingram always sought peace and ensued it, and, if sometimes he found more than was really there, it was a form of wishful thinking that did him great credit. Preaching in St. Paul's on the Sunday after the London Church Congress over which Creighton presided in 1899, he said:

[1] *Banners*, 110.
[2] *Ib.* 207.

My friends, if you would go night after night through a great district like East London, you would find the underlying unity. I go from parish to parish, and I find the High Churchmen, with his mission services and often his prayer meeting, preaching the Gospel in simple language to the people; I find constantly those who are called Evangelical eager about Confirmation, greatly alive to bringing their people to Holy Communion, and a substantial Church teaching and a substantial Church principle underlying them all. I have no sense of superintending a divided Church in East London.

He himself went everywhere, and became the friend of all the clergy, and of a surprisingly large number of the people in the parishes. He exemplified the new meaning wittily given at a later date by Paget to the ancient Catholic formula *Quod ubique, quod semper, quod ab omnibus*,[1] but he felt acutely the need for more workers. For them he appealed to the Universities and to West London:

There is a parish which sent me a letter yesterday to say, "We have no workers, we have no one to visit, what are we to do? Send us some ladies to visit the people, or some men to work."[2]

He wanted to bring to bear the intelligent sympathy of kind-hearted and—it is a real point—well-dressed people, for those who were sick, tired and broken, or what is sometimes lightly called irreclaimable. He told people at drawing-room meetings in West London what the East End was like. He knew—none better—that if a sick man is to be converted to God during the period of his sickness, or if a broken life is going to be built up into a Christian character, it means constant visits of, say, half an hour each for weeks together. This needs a large staff of helpers, regular or voluntary.

His appeal went home. One rich man came to him and said:

I am tired of writing cheques for charities, and merely subscribing to this and that. What I want myself is personally to serve. I want to go and tell somebody myself personally about Christ and His love. Can you give me half a dozen invalids in East London that I can go and visit personally?[3]

The Bishop of course could do that quite easily, and did it. And that

---

[1] Paget translated this, "Everywhere, always, and generally by omnibus."
[2] *Banners*, 210.
[3] *Twenty-five Years*, 75.

man satisfied his desire by making friends with East Londoners and giving them personal service in the evenings, after a day's work in the City.

He needed not only workers but money. The chief sources were the East London Church Fund, and the Bishop of London's Fund. The latter was for the whole diocese, but East London had a good share of it. For this he was an untiring beggar. The story of his great begging at such places as Bournemouth, Eastbourne and Torquay belongs chiefly to his "London" days, but he had begun it at Bethnal Green, and he carried it on vigorously as Bishop of Stepney. A friend says, "He worked terribly hard for it." He set himself in his last year the "target" of £20,000, and was delighted when on entering the Hall for the Bournemouth meeting in January 1899 to receive the following telegram from Mr. Walsh, the Secretary, who had never broken into verse before:

> Bishop, set your mind at ease,
> And tell the meeting, if you please,
> That £20,000, though late,
> Has come at last for '98.

There has survived an anonymous letter:

> Harrow, 28th November 1898.
> I heard your sermon in Chapel last night, and will you accept the enclosed for the East End Fund. I am a Harrow boy still, but I will come and help you some day. I had almost given up the idea till I heard your sermon last night.

Over and above this begging for the Fund, he would often appeal for special cases. He said one Sunday afternoon in St. Paul's:

> Take Love. We spoke last Sunday of love, and I would thank from my heart those three generous souls, one of whom sent fifty pounds for the poor ruined old Rector of Bow, another five pounds, and one who has spent the week in collecting thirty shillings in half crowns for the East-end hospitals.[1]

At another time in the Cathedral he shewed that an appeal of a different kind had gone home:

[1]*Banners*, 53.

It was a touching restitution that a young man of this congregation made, two Sundays ago, when, with a conscience touched with penitence at his breach of love, and for having murdered hope, he gave fifty pounds a year to the rescue work of the diocese.[1]

All the begging meant hard work and much travelling, and there was always a good deal of routine administration, but he never allowed himself to become the servant of machinery. He was always the friend of the clergy and the people of East London. He was fond of quoting Matthew Arnold's Sonnet:

'Twas August, and the fierce sun overhead
Smote on the squalid streets of Bethnal Green,
And the pale weaver, through his windows seen
In Spitalfields, look'd thrice dispirited.

I met a preacher there I knew, and said:
"Ill and o'erworked, how fare you in this scene?"—
"Bravely!" said he; "for I of late have been
Much cheer'd with thoughts of Christ, the *living bread*."

O human soul! as long as thou canst so
Set up a mark of everlasting light,
Above the howling senses' ebb and flow,

To cheer thee, and to right thee if thou roam—
Not with lost toil thou labourest through the night!
Thou mak'st the heaven thou hop'st indeed thy home.

Arnold, communicant as he was, did not share the whole of Ingram's, or of his own father's, faith, but he respected it, and to a considerable extent he understood it.

Ingram was fond of claiming that light would some day come from the seemingly dark East. He ended the Westminster Abbey Sermon already quoted by saying:

If in that way we work together, this Church of East London will have a new glory to shed upon the Catholic Church of CHRIST. It was said once by one of the Canons of this great Abbey that every new race, as it comes to the Church—Chinese, Egyptian, Indian— sheds a new glory of its own upon the Church. And East London,

[1] *Banners*, 58.

when it is once converted, will shed a new glory on the Church of CHRIST. If we act up to what we know, East and North London shall be flooded with light—"the light that never was on land or sea," the light which the world can neither give nor take away.[1]

It was this steady championship of East London, and belief in it, that won him the love of East Londoners. He said of our Lord that:

It was within Him like a spring working by law, a spring which had all the regularity, as well as the spontaneity, of some beautiful spring among the hills, and it was at the service of every sufferer that came to Him; but He never hurt people when he tried to comfort them, because He gave them the nerving and strengthening sympathy of love. And then, again, notice how constant it was with Him. He was never too tired to be kind. He might be disappointed forty-nine times, but the fiftieth time found Him perfectly ready still. Wake Him up from His sleep, and He is ready to do an act of mercy. Place Him, tired, by the well, and He is ready there to try and help a sinful soul.[2]

He might perhaps have said about himself that he tried to make that the law of his own life, but to observers it seemed that the kindness always came bubbling out spontaneously. One of countless examples is related by an old friend:

Dr. Ingram was walking along the Mile End Road to a Meeting on a very wet night when he saw an old woman sitting in the gutter selling chestnuts. She was ill-clad, and much exposed to the rain. The bishop took off his mackintosh and put it round the shoulders of the old woman, and then proceeded on his journey, arriving at the Meeting all wet.

It was not only "St. Martin" acts of that kind, it was not only the constant readiness to visit a sick-bed at a moment's notice, but it was something which East Londoners perceived to be behind all that, which won him their love.

One incident will illustrate this. He was re-opening a Church in Bethnal Green. There was a very slight disturbance of some kind at the West End of the Church. The Bishop did not even notice it.

[1] *Banners*, 210.
[2] *The Afterglow of a Great Reign*, 52.

71

But somehow the rumour got about and went through the district in five minutes that their Bishop had been insulted by "ignorant" people in that Church. When after a talk in the Vicarage about the work of the parish, the Bishop came out to go home, a huge mob had assembled. Many of them were not Church-goers, but they all cheered when they saw him and said, "We've come to see you safe home." He told them that he was in no danger, but nothing would satisfy them but to march behind him for a good half-mile, until he found a cab which took him back to Amen Court.

Mr. Bramwell writes:

> He was at this time closely in touch with all the leading men in Church and State and knew many very intimately, but it never made him any more important in his own eyes, and an old East End friend would be given as great a welcome as the Prime Minister. There must have always been with him a strong sense of the brotherhood of man.

The other half of his work at this period was at St. Paul's. The Canon-in-residence used at that time to preach on Sunday afternoons during his three months of residence every year. His colleagues were Newbolt, Scott Holland and Archdeacon Sinclair. He consulted Scott Holland about his method of preaching. Should he preach written sermons as Holland himself, with immense effect, always did? Or should he prepare as well as possible, and then preach without notes? Holland advised him to do as he had been accustomed to do. He took the advice. He once told Canon Alexander that the only sermons he wrote out in full (with the exception, it may be supposed, of those preached on great National Occasions, or before a University) were those of Easter Day evening in St. Paul's. The notes of the sermons were afterwards written up, with the aid, in some cases, of press reports in the *Family Churchman* and the *Church Family Newspaper*, and published in *Under the Dome*, *Banners of the Christian Faith*, and *The Afterglow of a Great Reign*.[1] It was perhaps a good thing that he went on in the old way, partly because it was his natural way, and also because parties of East Londoners came to St. Paul's on Sunday afternoons, and they would have been disappointed if they had found he had changed his style

---

[1] In the Preface to *Under the Dome*, the Bishop, then Bishop of London, acknowledges the help of his Chaplain, the Reverend H. P. Cronshaw, in turning "the reports of sermons delivered extempore into readable chapters".

too much. In no respect did he change it much. An eye-witness records that once in the pulpit something went wrong with his collar. He tore it off and went on.

Under the Dome includes five sermons delivered on special occasions, to the Guild of St. Luke, to H.M. Judges, on the Sunday after the London Church Congress, on the return of the City Imperial Volunteers from service in South Africa, and at the Annual Church Parade of the London Rifle Brigade, whose Chaplain he was.

Banners of the Christian Faith contains sermons on Faith, Hope, Love, Penitence, Prayer, Intercession, Charity, One God and Father, One Lord Jesus Christ, One Spirit, One Body, One Bread, all given in St. Paul's in 1898, and two others. "Two reasons," the Preface says:

> lead me to publish them—one that at the time that they were delivered they produced so many questions and letters from members of the congregation as to seem to shew that they were not wholly out of touch with what people were thinking, and hoping; and, secondly, that there seems a need of a book to put into the hands of the ordinary layman to explain in a popular way the main truths which a consistent Churchman holds.

In one point he was betrayed by his fondness for a telling illustration:

> There was a little lad in a London street, on one of our foggy days, seen to be holding in his hand a stick with string attached to it. Some one asked, "What is it that you are holding so tightly in your hand?" and the lad replied, "I am flying my kite; it is up there right in the midst of the cloud and fog. I saw it go there." "But how do you know that the kite is there at all? You can't see it." "No," said he, "but I can feel it pull." I use that trivial illustration for a purpose.

He did not realize that if there is a fog, there is no wind, and a kite will not fly. But eliminate the fog and replace it by a passing cloud, and the illustration stands.

Miss Pearce writes:

> My brother and I used to go round every Sunday afternoon after our Sunday School and steal in at the South Door of the Cathedral and pass through the barrier to stand near the pulpit. If Winnington-Ingram was preaching, we were sometimes faced with a large placard

—CHURCH FULL—which meant that there was no standing-room in that vast building.[1]

In his first sermon at St. Paul's he said:

It is always a solemn thing to any man in any place to begin a new ministry. In the old place everything has been so familiar. There have been the faces of men and women whom he has learnt to know and trust as friends. There gradually has grown up such spiritual sympathy between a man and his people that it became at last like standing up before five hundred or a thousand friends. He knew where the old faces were sure to be: he knew why they were there. But in a new ministry all is changed. New faces front the preacher. Those who come wonder to themselves whether they will find any help in him, whether there will grow up between him and them any of that subtle spiritual confidence without which preaching is in vain. If that is the case in any church, how much more is it in St. Paul's Cathedral! Here there fronts the pulpit a great sea of faces, most of whom are quite unknown, and will always remain unknown; a great sea of humanity with unknown troubles, unknown difficulties, unknown cares. And as one stands and faces them there is borne over one almost a sense of hopelessness. When one thinks how the Gospel has been preached from this pulpit by men ten times as able as oneself, in ten thousand ways, is it any good, one asks oneself, to stand up and try to find an entrance into hearts closed as yet to the old message, or find as good a way to the hearts of those who have accepted it?

And yet there is a passage in a poet which comforts one to-day:

"To the sentinel that hour is regal
When he mounts on guard."[2]

In the front row, under the Dome, would often be found Lord Salisbury. "That young man's sermons," he is reported to have said, "help me more than anyone else's."

Two of the things that dwelt most in his own recollections of those days were, first, the Tuesday Bible Class for the workmen of the Cathedral staff, where many a discussion was started which was carried on as they worked in the coal-house or on the roof of the Cathedral, and, second, his relations with the Choristers. He had not

[1] The Reverend E. H. Pearce, afterwards Bishop of Worcester, was at that time Vicar of Christ Church, Newgate Street and Chaplain to Christ's Hospital.
[2] *Banners*, 1-3.

the literary skill of Holland, who wrote a charming song about "Four and twenty white birds, baked in a pie," the pie being the Dome of St. Paul's, but he made friends with them:

> I used in those days to take my exercise on a bicycle in the early morning, and timed my ride so as to meet them on their early walk on the Thames Embankment. As I appeared coming from the Temple direction, there was a rush to meet me; the first prize was my right arm, the second my left, and the third was my bicycle, and I was always pleased that my two arms were considered higher prizes than to ride my bicycle![1]

On Saturday afternoons there were parties of East Londoners to be taken round the Cathedral and to hear stories of the building and of the lives of some of the warriors and others who lie buried there. After that there would be tea at 2 Amen Court.

One of the big sermons of this period was that preached before both Universities at different times. It is printed in *Banners* and there also lies before the writer an old copy of the *Cambridge Review* for December 7th, 1898, containing a full report. It was fifty years ago, and the Universities do not now inherit the Public School Chapel tradition to the old extent, but in the opening sentences he diagnosed acutely the situation as it was:

> If old University men were asked where and when they could get apart from the rush of life, and quietly look at the present in the light of the past, they would probably answer that it was when they were able to spend a quiet Sunday at their University itself. There is a permanence about a great place, which gives a sense of continuity to life and which brings up by a law of association the thoughts and feelings of the past, while at the same time it humbles by its very greatness the individual himself. And if, further, an old University man asked what, in the light of such quiet introspection, he had learned since his University days from the experience of life, which had been more or less completely hidden from him when he was up at the University, he would often have to confess that it was a living belief in the Power of the Holy Ghost. Think for a moment how easily the great language of religion glides off us in our University days— repentance, conviction of sin, miserable sinners, the love of God, the Sacrifice of the Cross—it has all come down to us through echoes of

[1] *Fifty Years*, 17-18.

the School Chapel from the days of the nursery; it is all right and proper, and the thing to believe, but is it not also often to us, during our undergraduate days.

"A tale of little meaning, though the words are strong?"

I for one never wonder at the sharp shock of doubt with which a boy in the sixth at school or a young man reading for Honours at Oxford or Cambridge, suddenly wakes up to find how double-edged are the tools he has been carelessly playing with in his hand, and to grasp the real import of the awful language he has been so casually taking on his lips.

He then goes on to speak of the three tests of the pervading influence of the Holy Ghost in a University. They are:

   (i) Unity in Diversity.
   (ii) A growing and increasing faith in Jesus Christ.
   (iii) The presence of a missionary spirit.

There is a plea for more clergy and more workers for India, Africa, East and South London, and for surrendering the personal life to the leading of the Spirit, and the end is:

Get back then to the old times of prayer again, if you have been led away to give them up; take out again the old Bible; come back to your School Communions; remove that bad habit which has grown upon you and has crushed but not, thank God, crushed out, the Divine fire; heap on the fuel of some bit of work, however humble, done for God and your fellowmen; and the fresh breeze from heaven will fan again to life the dying embers; the old love will come back again into your cold heart with new force; the power of the Holy Ghost will stir and quicken within you and foster every sign of life, and you will do your part to make the Universities—what they were meant to be—great signs in England of Christian Unity, Christian Faith, and Christian Love—pillars of cloud by day, and fire by night to guide the nation to the Promised Land.

The Canonry made him a familiar figure in the City. It was said by a resident that:

If it was known that he was passing down Cheapside, the shop-keepers would all come out on to the pavement to wave to him in the hope of getting a nod or a smile.

A young woman employed in Paternoster Row saw his cassocked figure disappearing into the Archdeacon's house, and remarked, "The finest purple passage I ever saw."

He had plenty of admirers. A friend writes:

That he had many and devoted women admirers goes without saying, and, though not wishing to be unkind, I think they went rather too far in their devotion. There were such a lot of them. I believe he was never known to comment on it.

One incident, a little later, was sensibly dealt with by a wise matron. There was a young woman who sent him letters and presents. She said she was in love with him. "She was obviously a psychological case. We did not know any psychology in those days. I shook her. It seemed to answer. Short cuts are often useful."

During his time at Amen Court he had a very disturbing personal experience. He rather suddenly became engaged to be married to the daughter of a peer, a lady "noted", as was said in a newspaper, "for her splendid carriage and beauty". The engagement was said by some to have been engineered by a matron who was very fond of him, and thought, as matrons often do, that a nice young man ought to have a nice wife. The engagement after a short time was broken off. Those who were near to him at the time knew that it was a great blow to him, but he said very little. It was sometimes said that parental pressure had been brought to bear, but it was generally believed that the lady came to feel that she was not suited for the life which she would have to lead as Ingram's wife. If that was so, it was a very wise decision, a discovery much better made before than after marriage. He was known to say afterwards about it that it had perhaps been a good thing after all, as his single life made it more possible or at least easier to do some of the things that he had done. A friend writes: "I think he was right, though I sometimes wished he had had a sensible wife to protect him at Fulham later."

There is a letter from Bishop Wilkinson written on the occasion of Ingram's appointment to London, but referring to this experience, which says:

God has revealed Himself to you in these dark months when everything seemed to have slipt beneath your feet, and you found that

He was a sure refuge, that under His shelter you could rest till the storm had spent its strength.

To a friend Ingram said at the time "God is helping me through." To another friend he wrote in August 1899: "I look upon it just as a trial sent from God for my good, and as a fresh consecration to my work. 'Stand upright on thy feet,' is my text for next Sunday, and I am trying to practise what I have preached for fifteen years, to take trouble 'standing up', and with steadfast faith in God's Love." One last quotation from Mr. Bramwell, about "days off":

According to his unfailing rule he must have his day off in the week for exercise, and golf was his game. I was asked to play one day with him and went into his room at 2 Amen Court to meet him and go together. He was changing for golf. I was surprised to see him bandaging his legs with a rubber bandage. He said he had had for years varicose veins or, as he said the East Ender called them, "various" or "bellicose" or "very close" veins, and never went without band- dages. No wonder his legs looked so thin in his Bishop's gaiters. Playing golf with him was always a bit strenuous, he was so keen. He had been known to drive off first from the tee and, not waiting for his opponent to drive, to gather up his clubs and start running to his ball. He was certainly wonderful on his days off, he was like a boy let out from school—with never a thought of East London, St. Paul's or anything. And he certainly did not look like a Bishop with a horrible old pair of knickers with the tags sticking out.

Truly it could have been said at this time, as it perhaps was said by some, that if the Prime Minister were willing to make an experi- ment in the next appointment to the Diocese of London, here was an interesting experiment ready to his hand. Ingram himself seems to have had no idea of it, and had written to Lord Salisbury to com- mend the name of Edward Talbot. The actual offer was made in the first instance to Bishop Davidson of Winchester, and he was pressed by Archbishop Temple to accept, but the medical verdict was decisive. The essential evening work would have been beyond his strength. The offer was then made to Ingram. One intimate friend advised strongly against acceptance, but the Archbishop and Bishop Davidson pressed him to undertake the work, partly at least on the ground that it was too heavy for anyone but a man of full strength.

In actual fact, he did not seem at this time to be a very strong man. One who had known him at Shrewsbury writes: "When he went to London, I gave him five years to hold it, as he was not strong-looking as a young man." In any case, the prospect was formidable, especially for one who knew both London and Bishop Creighton intimately, but, so far as evening work was concerned, it had no terrors. That had been part of his daily routine for many years. There is no record of his self-communings and prayers, but it may safely be conjectured that they were something like those of the prophet—"Then said I, Ah, Lord God! behold, I cannot speak; for I am a child. But the Lord said unto me, say not, I am a child: for Thou shalt go to all that I shall send thee, and whatsoever I command thee, thou shalt speak." (Jeremiah i. 6, 7.)

V

LONDON—THE EARLY YEARS

THERE were some who were surprised when the still young Bishop of Stepney became the still younger Bishop of London. There had been an attempt just before to persuade the authorities to make him Chaplain-General to the Army, but, much as he would have done in that office, there was even more that he could do as Bishop of London. His appointment was not really surprising. He had made an immense impression as a leader and as a preacher, and of all living ecclesiastics he was incomparably the most attractive, both to the man in the street and to those in authority.

To begin at the top, it is likely enough that, in spite of her general predilection either for the Dean Stanley type of clergyman or for those who spoke to her most confidently of recognition after death, Queen Victoria, if she had lived longer, would have agreed to his nomination. She liked what she had heard and seen of him. In 1899 he was preaching for the second time at Windsor, having passed in that year through what he describes as "a trying personal experience", of which he hardly supposed that the Queen would have heard. But she said to him, "I have been thinking a great deal about you this year, Bishop." To her memory the Bishop paid a very charming tribute in four sermons preached at St. Paul's, and published under the title of "The After-glow of a great Reign". The four sermons are entitled—Her Truthfulness, Her Moral Courage, The Rainbow round about the Throne, and the Law of Kindness. There is in them no word of personal reminiscence, only a simple desire to link the lessons of the Queen's devoted life with the supernatural inspiration of the Christian Gosepl. He did not forget to include in the fourth sermon a plea to remember the over-crowded slum-dweller, those whom "we miscall the Hooligans", and the child who had no Christian teaching.

Nevertheless, it was King Edward VII who appointed him. To King Edward the advice tendered by Lord Salisbury was almost

certainly most congenial. Ingram was the kind of man he liked.
And he was always a good friend. There is an amusing story of the
Bishop of London's first visit to Sandringham. It was the week-end
just before his enthronement. Lord Salisbury was present, and he,
with the Bishop and others, were sitting at dinner. The Prime
Minister, who was both rather absent-minded and very short-
sighted, said in a voice that could be heard across the table, "Who is
that good-looking young clergyman? I seem to know his face."
The King replied: "He is the man whom you have just recommended
for the see of London." It must have been embarrassing for Ingram,
but after dinner the King took him aside, and said: "Dear old
Salisbury is growing rather forgetful. But you mustn't mind. Only
this afternoon I found him gazing at a photograph of me. He shook
his head and muttered sadly, 'Poor old Buller!'" All the same,
Lord Salisbury knew what he was doing when he made the nomination. No Prime Minister, not even Mr. Gladstone, was ever more
zealous to appoint the right men to bishoprics. Within a year of
Ingram's appointment he nominated Charles Gore to be Bishop
of Worcester and Cosmo Gordon Lang to Stepney. Lord Salisbury
said himself of Ingram, "He will be the busiest man in England."

To the Bishop was assigned the duty of preaching at the Coronation. The sermon was written, and indeed printed. The title of it
was "The Heart of a King" and the text was "God looketh not as
man seeth, but God looketh at the heart", but it was never preached.
The King was taken ill, and an operation for appendicitis became
necessary. It was very urgent. Only the day before the Bishop was
in Westminster Abbey, actually in the pulpit, adjusting the stand
for the sermon the next day. Lord Esher came up to him there and
then and said with strong emotion, "Bishop, there will be no
Coronation to-morrow; the King is desperately ill, and is being
operated upon this morning. Will you give out to the Choir that
there will be no Coronation?"

As all the world knows, the operation was successful, and by
August the King was strong enough to bear a shortened service.
The sermon was cut out, and when the King asked: "Who was to
have preached the sermon?" and was told, "The Bishop of London,"
he replied, "That's all right, he is the last man to mind the sermon
being cut out." The King, who had his likes and dislikes, had a

81

F

warm regard for Ingram, and his usual greeting when they met was, "Well, Bishop, not working too hard, I hope." In 1901 the King granted to him a very rare privilege, which continued until the Bishop's death. It was freedom to drive through the Horse Guards. Anyone may walk there, but no one, save by the express permission of the King, may drive.

To return to the Diocese of London, the *Church Times* said of the appointment:

In addition to the fact that Bishop Winnington-Ingram is a *persona grata* to the general body of Churchmen, we view his approaching elevation with unbounded pleasure, because it argues a new departure in the right direction. His claim to promotion is not based upon his discovery of some new properties in the particle ἄν, nor upon his having birched dull youths up the steeps of Parnassus, nor upon the qualification of being a safe and colourless nobody, or a political partisan, or a popular preacher. On the contrary, he has served his apprenticeship as a parish clerk in the diocese he is about to rule. He has worked amongst the very poorest of the poor. He has had practical experience of the difficulties "the poor parson of a town" has to encounter. He has been, if anyone has, one of the working clergy of the diocese, and his tenure of the post of Bishop-Suffragan, brief though it has been, has proved, in a very special degree, the means of interesting the wealthier members of the Church in London in the wants and trials of the poorer.

The *Church Times* said a week later:

We have no desire to see the College of Bishops recruited from the ranks of the unlearned and the undignified, but we cannot help thinking that the Church has greatly suffered in the past from the selection of men whose learning and dignified bearing removed them from all sympathy and fellowship with humbler folk.

This may have been founded on fact in 1901, but it need not be so, and we have had some notable examples since that date, not least at Canterbury itself, shewing that learning and dignity do not separate their possessors from ordinary people.

A leader of the Evangelicals, the Archdeacon of London (W. M. Sinclair), said in his sermon at St. Paul's on the next Sunday afternoon that:

It was his privilege to give the first public welcome to the new Bishop. He had known him as curate, as head of Oxford House, as Canon of St. Paul's, and as Bishop-Suffragan. If ever there was a man who lived by the power of Christian sympathy, it was he. The whole diocese would rejoice to have as their leader and ruler one so whole-hearted. What had given him his rapidly-acquired influence over the educated people in the West of London? What obtained him his power over the East-end population? What had attracted the enormous crowds who had come to hear him preach at St. Paul's? It was the earnestness of his single-minded belief, the self-consecration to his work, the consistency of his life, the simplicity of his devotion, the absolute sincerity of his affectionate sympathy for every sort and condition of men with whom he had to do, from the highest to the lowest. With a guide of such primitive faith and zeal, such plainness of life, such happy unworldliness, such cheerful optimism, such unflagging energy, such frank and open and attractive friendliness, such unruffled good humour, they looked forward under God's blessing to prosperous and progressive days for the Kingdom of God in that mightiest and most perplexing of all the dioceses in the world.

The Lord Mayor of London sent a telegram:

> The citizens of London heartily congratulate the diocese and the metropolis on your lordship's appointment, and send hearty wishes for your happiness and success as their Bishop—

a message which pleased Ingram so much that he kept it, though he hardly kept anything of that kind, and the words have been copied into this book from the original. His colleague, Canon Newbolt, gave him a Service Book with the inscription *Ecce ego, quia vocasti me* (1 Samuel iii. 5). He used it till it fell to pieces.

Among other letters received was one from a young man, bearing a distinguished name, which began:

My dear Father-in-Christ,
    I must not let you become fully Bishop of London without telling you—as perhaps a disciple may—with what affection and happiness I watch you mount this great "Stool". Affection makes what happens to you a personal matter to many of us. We share in and delight in and are proud of your wonderful lot.

His own brother Alfred wrote:

83

My dear Arthur,

I open my paper this morning to see that you are Bishop of London! Ten thousand congratulations! And yet I know how you are feeling the responsibility. I shall pray often for you—but don't let the work kill you. You must think of yourself and how important it is now that you should keep well. I think my *chief* feeling was fear about the work though I feel the tremendous honour in your being Bishop of London. I know it came as a surprise to you, though all the same it was just the *very best* appointment that could be made. I felt that all along.

To Mr. Kensit, the leader of the ultra-Protestant party, the appointment seemed deplorable. The *Westminster Budget* for March 15th, 1901, records that he said:

> The Protestant Party will look upon him as a most dangerous man, as during the time he has been Suffragan Bishop of East London he has done all in his power to help on the Romanizing movement.

But Mr. Kensit always had his own peculiar and rather rigid point of view, and his own way of defining "Romanizing". Another Churchman, described by a secular newspaper which cannot now be identified as "a stern and unbending Protestant", said:

> The choice is a wise one. Dr. Ingram is a High Churchman, and to many of his views I am strongly opposed; but he is a man of splendid character. He is not great in scholarship, and on matters of opinion he often errs; but he is one of the most devoted workers and one of the most lovable men in the Church. He will make a great Bishop of London.

Prebendary Barker, Rector of St. Marylebone, one of the senior among the London clergy, and what was then called a Broad Churchman, said to a representative of the *Westminster Budget*, who asked him his opinion of the appointment:

> "I am greatly pleased with it. It is a pleasant surprise."
> "Do you think the older clergy will object to his age?"
> "Not in the least! The Bishop is a *persona grata* with clergy and laity alike—with the West End and with the East End. He is young, and though he did not take a Double First at the University, he is a man of intellectual attainments, as well as a striking personality."
> "You regard the appointment as good for the diocese at large?"
> "Undoubtedly!"

The same paper continues:

At Oxford House it goes without saying that there is great rejoicing. One of the Bishop's "boys" now at work in the world outside was met by a correspondent by the merest chance to-day on the top of an omnibus in the Bethnal Green Road. "Eh, have ye 'eard the grand news?" said the young man. "Our old 'Ead at Oxford House is the new Bishop of London, God blesss him. 'E be a mon. Us Lancashire folk—I comes from Bolton[1]—don't care much for Bishops, but 'e be a mon and a straight mon, and what 'e 'as done for me and many more lads none can tell. I seed 'em first in Victoria Park a-tackling them 'ere Hatheists, and my word, it wor a sight. Then I joined 'is club, and I and all my mates would do anything for 'e. I am just back from the front, and a-going to see my old mother when I reads this 'ere good news of me old 'Ead a-becoming Bishop of London. God bless 'im, 'e'll do summat, and workin' men will love 'im." Our correspondent pressed the young man to give his name, but he said, "The old 'Ead would not like it."

The total number of letters was about three thousand.[2] They came from people of every sort, omnibus-drivers and conductors, young artisans, former opponents in Victoria Park, friends in West London, schoolboys all over England. The Bishop said at the Annual Meeting of the East London Church Fund in March:

The undeserved affection which has breathed through them, and the promise of so many prayers, has inspired and helped me more than I can say. But yet, above and beyond all that, there is to-day upon me the awful sense of responsibility. Then, again, it is a most true sadness and difficulty to have to leave the dear old East-end. Some people may have imagined that some other way of spending one's evenings might be more enjoyable than travelling about on the tops of omnibuses and trams every night for three years, but I can assure you that I have enjoyed it thoroughly. I regret deeply that my nights will not

[1] I cannot help thinking that the speaker did less than justice to Bolton, of which I was Vicar for seven-and-a-half years. Boltonians have a great regard at least for their own Bishop of Manchester. Some of them took it ill that Blackburn was chosen as the see-city when the Diocese of Manchester was divided in 1927. "What's the matter wi' Bolton?" they said. It was unreasonable, because Blackburn was chosen on geographical grounds. Otherwise. . . !

[2] In the last week of his time at Fulham he read 2,000 letters, written to him in 1901, and then burned them all. Those that are here quoted are from a small collection of documents that came into the possession of Mr. H. T. A. Dashwood.

be spent in that way now. I am not going, I can assure all my numerous advisers, including the *Spectator* of this week, to attempt to be my own Suffragan. There are several things which I shall carry away with me from East London. First of all, I shall carry away with me a picture of the most absolute devotion on the part of the East-end clergy. Yes; I will say to you City men who are present, that you have not yet realised to the full all the debt which the citizens of London owe to the clergy of North and East London. I have seen them, night after night, toiling on, year after year, some for ten years, some for twenty years, and some even for thirty years, down in those slums, seeking no earthly reward. This is the work which the East London Church Fund is supporting; and I wish to bear witness, at this meeting, to what I have seen at close quarters. Then, again, I shall carry away with me a wonderful picture and memory of the whole-heartedness of the East-end people. I still hope to retain in my arm the muscle which I have developed by shaking hands at East-end Church "Socials". . . . I do believe that I shall try to work fairly with all parties in the Church. I think that the East London clergy will be ready to admit that I have at least tried to administer East London fairly, and I count it a great happiness that I have as many friends amongst one party as among the other. Therefore, do strengthen my hands, that I may carry on this vaster task in the same fair spirit. Then, again, receive and back up my successor. . . . Lastly, back up the East London Church Fund. There is a kind of magic about this Fund. It blesses him who gives as well as him who takes; it blesses him who works it as well as him who receives from it; and it seems to bind East and West in a kind of loving brotherhood. I say, stick to the Fund, work with it—it is the fairest-worked fund in England—put all your enthusiasm into it, your love, your sympathy, and your prayers, and never rest content until East London has become the Kingdom of the Lord and of His Christ.

There was of course no Consecration, inasmuch as Ingram was already in Episcopal Orders. The next thing was Homage to the King. This relates only to the emoluments of the see. The income of each see at one time arose from the estates of the see, which were far from uniform in value, and were granted afresh by the monarch to each new Bishop. They are now pooled and are in the hands of the Church Commissioners, by whom the Bishops are paid quarterly, but the Bishop does not draw any stipend until he has done Homage.

The final stage was enthronement, or, more correctly, Inthroniza-tion, in the Cathedral on Tuesday, April 30th. This in the Southern Province has for centuries always been performed by the Arch-deacon of Canterbury. Enthronement has no legal force, but it is a convenient way of publicly presenting the new Bishop to the diocese. Sydney Smith was very contemptuous in 1828 about Archbishop Howley being enthroned at Canterbury by proxy.

Ingram's Enthronement was a grand occasion. The Lord Mayor and the Sheriff attended in their robes of state. The Bishop, the Dean and Canons all wore their magnificent festival copes. The *Church Times* called it:

a stately and well-ordered ceremony, which we hope we may take as a happy augury of his rule. It is worthy of note that the Press comments on the ceremonial—which, it must be confessed, was elaborate enough to have been pronounced, a few years ago, extravagant and even dangerous—expressed more than approval, even admiration. The fact is that in spite of occasional fits of nervousness, the public mind has been educated to a surprising degree. It begins to understand that ceremonial, whether in Church or State, has a distinct value, provided it is seemly and expressive.

Enthronements are often in the afternoon, but this time it was in the morning. The Service was Holy Communion (Stainer in A), with, as always, a *Te Deum* (Martin in A). The Bishop was the celebrant, and only those communicated who were about to take the oath of canonical obedience. Among them was Cosmo Gordon Lang, Ingram's successor. The Bishop's own oath was as follows:

Ego Arturus Foley, Episcopus Londiniensis, promitto et juro ad haec Sancta Dei Evangelia per me hic inspecta, quod secundum ap-probatum hujus Ecclesiae morem in ea residebo; quod jura libertates et approbandos Ecclesiae consuetudines servabo et observari faciam; quod bona et possessiones Ecclesiae inventa servabo, et alienata pro viribus revocabo; sic me Deus adjuvet, et Haec Sancta Dei Evangelia.

On leaving the Cathedral after the Service, the Bishop was enthusiastically cheered by a great crowd which had assembled in St. Paul's Churchyard.

After the Enthronement the Bishop lost no time in getting to work. In the afternoon he presided over the executive of the Bishop of London's Fund; and he spoke at the Annual Meeting of the "Fresh Air" Mission, at which he said that he was glad that his first words in public after his enthronement should be for the children of London; at 5.30 he had an engagement at some place which cannot now be deciphered, and at 7.30 he dined with a large party of the London Clergy at Sion College. On the next day he helped to consecrate Lang.

Enthronement is a big word. It suggests pomp and stateliness. Ingram could be stately, on stately occasions, but he was never pompous. He could indeed pass from grave to gay very quickly. A young curate, not long from Oxford, who was ordained by Ingram at one of his first Ordinations in St. Paul's, said in conversation that he had been startled, and, possibly, a little offended, when the Bishop, after being very splendid and very solemn in cope and mitre at the service, said to the young men, "Now then, you chaps, come along and have a cup of coffee. I am sure you want it after all that."

This reminiscence may be reinforced from fiction, but the fiction of a master, Mr. George W. E. Russell. In his superb *Londoner's Log Book*, the Guild of Fishers in Deep Waters in the Parish of St. Ursula, Stucco Square, was distressed by the breezy manner and slangy vocabulary of "Blazer" Bumpstead, the new curate. During the holidays of the Vicar, he put some audacious verses in the Parish Magazine. The Guild ladies were indignant, and thought of complaining to the Bishop. "But," they said, "this new Bishop likes that sort of young man, and calls them 'old chap'. I suppose they remind him of the people with whom he worked in the East End."[1]

At all events he was enthroned and he had to face the prospect of living at Fulham Palace and in London House, St. James' Square. He had never been an enthusiast for Bishops' Palaces. He had been attacked many a time in Victoria Park about the seemingly large incomes of the Bishops. Then he had been accustomed to say that a Bishop's income was an unaudited Trust Fund for himself and the

---

[1]For further light on Bumpstead, the curious reader is referred to the same writer's *Afterthoughts*, where under the title of the *Parsons' Team*, he describes a great football match. "Bumpstead" is believed to be a composite portrait of two of the real men there mentioned.

diocese. Soon after he succeeded to London, he allowed a rumour to get out that he proposed to give up Fulham Palace. This, he confessed afterwards, was a *ballon d'essai*, and he soon discovered that the diocese was "dead against him". All his instincts rebelled against the idea of living alone, but for a chaplain and domestic staff, in a mansion with a park round it, and he was also in point of fact embarrassed for money. He had to pay the large fees which became due not only to legal officials but even to Government Departments on succeeding to a diocesan bishopric, and he had to borrow £5,000 to furnish the two houses. A book called the *Fatal Opulence of Bishops*, affirming that the spiritual efficacy of their work was seriously hindered by large incomes, had lately aroused some attention, and the Bishop, commenting on this at the Festival Dinner of the Corporation of the Sons of the Clergy[1] in May, 1901, said that, for his own part, he was now in front of one of the most appalling crises that he had ever faced in his life. Three years later he published a Balance Sheet, a copy of which is appended.

London.

(*From the London Diocesan Magazine*)

Having no home-life, I feel that it falls upon me to fight this battle for my brethren, who naturally might feel a greater delicacy than I do, in disclosing the actual expenditure of their homes, although I have no sort of doubt that their balance-sheet would tell the same story as mine.

The partial disclosure of anything leads to misunderstanding. The black headlines, "£5,000 lost in three years", in one of the leading evening papers suggest speculations on the Stock Exchange, or Bridge, if not "The Turf". I have, therefore transcribed as accurately as possible the balance-sheet from May 1, 1903, to May 1, 1904, the accounts dating in each year from May to May, as the first instalment of the income of the See was paid to me on May 1, 1901. The expenditure of one year is very like the expenditure of another, with one exception, and that is (as I have explained in a note) that the repairs on the two houses come every five years, and the large excess of the expenditure over income this year was due to the fact that the repairs on Fulham Palace had to be done during the year.

[1] The Corporation is so called because it was founded in the seventeenth century by some London Merchants, who were themselves sons of clergymen. Its object is to relieve clerical poverty. It has in the course of three hundred years collected and distributed a very large sum of money.

And that brings me to the use of these old "Church Homes". It is an open secret that I was in favour personally of getting rid of one or other of these large houses on entering on the See, and it is clear that a small flat in the centre of London, and possibly a cottage just outside, would meet my own personal requirements; but after nearly four years' experience now of what use can be made of these houses, I am not sure that it would equally meet the needs of the Diocese. I have just said good-bye to forty ordination candidates who have spent here the last two days. I ask myself, without Fulham where should I entertain them? It would be terrible to go back to the days when candidates had to put up in some dioceses at hotels and public-houses, and had no such quiet and devotional days as have preceded the ordination to-day, and which precedes all four ordinations in the year.

Then I fear that the clergy and their wives would miss the great garden parties numbering 3,000 in the summer; I should miss myself the 300 children of the clergy who, with their mothers, will assemble here on Innocents' Day, but my own disappointment would be no argument by itself; unless I am much mistaken, 300 children would be disappointed too, which matters very much.

The boys who use the field for football and cricket would have to go without. Then in the summer every Saturday brings its 100 factory girls or boys from the slums, or tired women, or men's club, to have tea in the garden: and perhaps, best use of all, here in the cool of the garden, the tired workers come and spend a week at a time, and the sick child whose home is some East-end vicarage without a garden gets back her colour in the old church home, which is hers as much as mine, and which has been the home of the diocese for 1,300 years. I publish, then, these accounts in no spirit of complaint: if the Church at large decided on the little flat I should go there without a murmur, but while it is considered right for the Bishop to be steward of this property for the Church, I shall continue to use it, as I have tried to do up to now, as I know my precedessors on their own lines have done before me, and as my Brother Bishops are doing in different parts of England, for the good of the diocese at large.

A. F. LONDON.

STATEMENT OF ACCOUNT
May 1, 1903, to April 30, 1904.

	£ s. d.	£ s. d.
Cr.		
Income of the Bishopric of London ..		10,000 0 0
Dr.		
Permanent Charges:—		
Rates & Taxes, Fulham Palace & London House	848 12 6	
Q.A.B. (for repairs executed by predecessors and first-fruits and tenths of the income of the See)	422 4 7	
Income Tax	500 0 0	
Fire Insurance	27 1 6	
Inland Revenue Taxes	20 8 0	
Interest on £5,000 borrowed to furnish houses	135 0 0	
Life Insurance (£5,000) to cover loan	172 16 2	
St. James's Square Trust	4 13 0	
		2,130 15 9
Payments to Legal Secretary for Diocesan work, Household account, Fulham and London House:—		35 6 5
Servants' wages (i.e. four male & seven female), food, entertainment of ordination candidates four times a year, average forty men: Saturday entertainment to working people, average seventy persons (Bedrooms at Fulham 32; London House 17) ..	1,678 9 5	
Caretaker at London House, wages, and Expenses	103 1 11	
		1,781 11 4
Repairs of Houses	1,190 7 3	
Furniture	53 13 11	
Coal, Gas & Electric Light	379 9 5	
		1,623 10 7
Diocesan Entertainments:—		
Two garden parties	347 2 0	
Children's Christmas Party	92 10 0	
		439 12 0

	£	s.	d.	£	s.	d.
Garden & Farm Account:—						
Ten men's wages per annum ..	520	0	0			
Horse for cart & garden work ..	35	0	0			
Garden seeds, coke for stoves, keep of						
horse, pig and poultry	145	17	0			
Fruit for garden parties	20	0	0			
Nets for tennis court	2	11	11			
Stable Account:—						
Hire of four horses in constant use ..	210	0	0			
Wages of three men p.a.	205	8	0			
Carriage repairs	89	4	6			
Liveries	22	7	0			
Forage, shoeing, & tooling	326	5	0			
Stabling of horses when visiting						
Parishes, coal for stables, and sundries	41	15	10			
				1,618	9	3
Subscriptions and Offertories:—						
Bishop of London's Fund, per annum	400	0	0			
E. London Church Fund, per annum	100	0	0			
London Church Schools' Repair Fund	500	0	0			
Other subscriptions & offertories ..	674	7	7			
				1,674	7	7
Education of Nephews	342	17	1			
Personal Account	294	17	8			
Help to individual cases	125	0	0			
Printing, Stationery and postage ..	368	9	4			
Staff salaries:—						
Chaplain & Private Secretary.. ..	277	0	0			
Petty Cash Account	30	0	0			
Books & Newspaper Account	33	7	2			
				1,471	11	3
GRAND TOTAL				10,775	4	2

In January, 1935, the Bishop published another Balance Sheet, from which it appeared that at the end of 1934 he was £500 out of pocket.

To us of to-day the item of Income Tax at (apparently) 1s. in the £ reads like a fairy-tale, but, even so, the outgoings were enormous. The Bishop had at the end of his life some invested capital, but no evidence is forthcoming of the existence of any of it at this time. The royalties on the sale of his books may have amounted in 1901 to a hundred or two a year. He does not seem to have had any other means, except perhaps a modest holding in the Post Office Savings Bank, and he was undertaking great responsibilities.

It is a happy thing for Bishops now that, with the help of the Commissioners, their incomes are being divided into (a) official, and (b) personal. Eventually none of them will handle (a) at all.

Bishop Luke Paget of Chester once said, in the course of a Retreat which he conducted at Watermillock, Bolton, in 1923, how he gloried in his calling. But he added, "I am ashamed of my house, and I am ashamed of my income." "Irks care," said Browning, "the cropfull bird?" It seems not, but it does irk the conscientious diocesan bishop.

Fulham Palace, formerly known as the Manor House, has been one of the homes of the Bishop of London for twelve centuries at least, and the Bishop's tenure is perhaps as old as any in England. It is said that Bishop Earconwald (675-693) acquired it from Tysktal (or Tyrhtel), Bishop of Hereford in 691. In Domesday its value was assessed at £40. There is one break in the tenure. Colonel Edmond Hersey became Lord of the Manor by the payment of £7,000 in 1647 and held it for thirteen years. The fine old barn in the grounds is said to date from his occupation.

It was till lately a summer residence only, the winter being spent at London House. At an earlier date there were also country manors at Much Hadham in Herts and Wickham in Essex, and a hunting-lodge near Highgate, now the tenth green of the golf-course. The mediaeval home of the Bishop till 1749 was the Palace in Aldersgate Street, and before that the "New Pallys" near St. Paul's, on the ground now known as London House Yard. This house, which is described as "new" in 1478, perhaps stood on the site of a still older palace.

The oldest portions of the estate are about half the house, the garden wall and the barn. The Great Court was built by Bishop Fitz James (1506-1523). He was in a time of transition a conservative, what was in those days called a "Trojan", i.e., rather than a "Greek", with little love for the New Learning. He described Dean Colet's foundation of St. Paul's School as "pestilent".

There is a good deal of Tudor brickwork left, and a room in which Bishop Bonner's ghost is said to walk. The Great Hall is of the sixteenth century. In it, though still unfinished, Bonner examined heretics. Howley in 1814 turned the Hall into an unconsecrated Chapel. It is not known with certainty where the ancient Chapel stood. The present Chapel dates only from the time of Bishop Tait. The silver-gilt vessels, the gift of Bishop Juxon (1633-1646) are inscribed with a solemn warning against alienation from sacred use. The present appearance of the house is due to Bishop Howley. His declared aim, which was achieved, was "a regular building without any Gothic nonsense". One of the most interesting rooms is the Porteous Library, with many books given by Bishop Porteous (1787-1809). There are eighty rooms, most of which are now in the "derated" part of the Palace, and have not been restored since they were damaged by blast during the war.

Among the most famous Bishops of London, besides those mentioned already, are Dunstan, Foliot, Sudbury, Courtenay, Warham, Tunstall, Ridley, Grindal, Sandys, Bancroft, Abbot, Laud, Sheldon, Compton, Blomfield, Temple, Creighton. To these names was now to be added that of Winnington-Ingram.

The mediaeval diocese consisted of Essex, Middlesex and parts of Herts. It has at various times also included some parishes in Surrey and Kent. From 1540 to 1550 the county of Middlesex was in the short-lived diocese of Westminster. The diocese of London now covers the City of London, the boroughs of the county of London on the north side of the river, and the County of Middlesex, which is rapidly becoming a built-up area. The population of the diocese in 1901 was 3,610,000 and in 1911 was 3,811,827 and in 1939, 4,500,000.

The Bishop found eventually many ways, of which more will be said later, of using the Palace for the common good, and he was always prodigal in giving money away. But it was natural that a man of simple habits, a small eater, a teetotaller, one of ten children of a country parson, educated at Marlborough and Keble, two institutions which deliberately seek to combine plain living with high culture of the mind, who had lived in the midst of poverty in East London, whose nearest approach to luxury had been the modest comfort of 2 Amen Court, should have been daunted by the prospect of living in a Palace. Perhaps he was comforted by the example of Bishop Westcott. Westcott, himself a pattern of humility, to whom it was acutely painful to be "congratulated" on his promotion to a bishopric, so humble that it was said that he quite often lost his luggage when travelling because he contrived to give the porter the impression that it did not matter what became of it, was nevertheless intensely conscious of the dignity of his office, and proud of his historic home at Bishop Auckland. A perhaps nearer example was Bishop Edward King, of Lincoln, whom Ingram had known and loved and honoured since undergraduate days. Anyhow, he inhabited both houses, London House until the First War and Fulham Palace to the end. And the people of the diocese on the whole were glad—rightly or wrongly, they always are—that it should be so.

His life there was from the first intensely laborious, and he at once formed the habit of never wasting any time. The daily programme here described comes actually from a rather later period, because fuller information about that period is available, but it had not changed much. The chief difference was that he found, as many find, that the longer he remained at his post, the more people there were who seemed to have claims on him, and so the programme became more and more congested. He was called at 7, and took the first bath (there were never less than three) of the day. Holy Communion was celebrated on Thursdays as well as on Sundays and Holy Days at 8. On other days he would be in his study by that hour, and he spent the time until 8.30 at his prayers. This half-hour or the half-hour immediately after breakfast was the time for intercession. He had on the shelf under his prayer-desk masses of letters. He found that the sight of the hand-writing helped him to concentrate on the needs of the writers. His faith in the power of Intercession was simple and intense. He constantly wrote to friends, "I am praying for you"—and he meant it. One who knew him for many years said, "He could as easily be without his food as without prayer, for it is prayer that sustains his whole life." No one knows how often he said in sermons "Man is a praying animal", and went on to develop the idea that man was made with the power of praying and was meant to pray.

Mattins was said in the Chapel, more or less in full, at 8.30, and the household and visitors all came. At Mattins and Evensong there was a hymn, which the Chaplain was expected to accompany on the organ. One chaplain, who was a good musician, but no instrumentalist, demurred when he was first instructed to act, and his first performance justified his modesty, and made some of the domestics giggle. But the Bishop would not yield, "That's all right, old boy. Rome wasn't built in a day." Eventually, after weeks of purgatory for the congregation (this is the Chaplain's own story) he emerged capable of accompaniment. Once, when the same Chaplain was reading the First Lesson, the story of Korah, Dathan and Abiram (Numbers xvi), before he reached the punishment which is recorded to have fallen upon them, the Bishop stood up, saying, "That'll do, old boy; I'll read something a bit different."

At 9.15 the Chaplain came to the study with the letters. After the Chaplain came the Secretary. The average post, year in, year out, was about sixty letters a day, and the Bishop was accustomed to say that they were all answered the same day. The majority were concerned with the administration of the diocese, with making engagements, and with the sifting and sorting of candidates for Ordination, but many were about the difficulties, spiritual, intellectual and material, of the writers, and many were personal letters from friends, especially young friends.

If there were no morning meeting, he would be occupied with interviews from 11.15 to 1, and some of those who came were invited to lunch. Sometimes the pair of scissors which lay on the table would be handed to them, and they would be told to go into the garden and cut some flowers for themselves. What the gardener thought is not known. The cook soon abandoned the habit of basing the provision for lunch on the housemaid's report of the number of beds occupied overnight. There were nearly always visitors, as well as people specially invited to meals. One Chaplain, who served for two years, can only remember two evenings on which he dined alone with the Bishop.

The afternoon was often pledged to a meeting of some diocesan or other Church Committee, or some body of trustees. In the winter there was Squash once a week at the Bath Club, and in the summer tennis as often as possible. When there was no game the Bishop would take a sharp walk along the towpath. He had a great belief in violent exercise. It took his mind off problems, and it kept him young. When he played games, he enjoyed winning.

In the evening there would often be a journey to a parish for Confirmation, Institution of a new Vicar, or a pastoral visit. Then back to the study to finish letters, or to resume the duties of a host.

Friday was the off-day, spent as a rule on the golf-course, generally with a clerical but sometimes a lay opponent. If two clergymen and two laymen made up a foursome, the Bishop would say to the laymen, "The Church will take you on," and he was very pleased if "the Church" won. He would often say, when things looked bad for his side, "The Church never gives up." In later days Eric Hamilton and W. G. Pennyman were among those who were often summoned for this purpose.

On his return, after a bath and tea, he would set himself to compose what he called "the message for the week". Sometimes it was made to last for more than a week, but for a week anyhow it was used, with adaptations and improvisations, for nearly all purposes. To continue to use the same message for say, a Confirmation, an address to the British Legion, a sermon in a suburban Church on Sunday evening, and a Missionary rally, often made considerable demands upon his ingenuity, but the Bishop was never daunted.[1]

After the sermon-making he would spend the rest of the day reading undisturbed in his study. He also read constantly while driving about London. As the car drove away from the door of a Church or place of meeting, the light would be switched on and he would open his book. He was not a reader of big, heavy books. It may be doubted whether he ever made much, for example, of William Temple's longer volumes, but he read a great many of the smaller books, especially on Christian Apologetics. It had in earlier years seemed to academic students of theology that the books he recommended were a little out of date, but as Bishop of London he had always read and constantly mentioned in his Sermons the latest new hand-books.

[1]The list of recipients of the message is quoted from an ex-Chaplain, but I can confirm it in one instance. I had occasion for personal reasons to be present during the same week as the annual Festival Day of Queen's College, Harley Street, of which he was Visitor, and at a Confirmation in St. Paul's, and I also happened to see a short report of what the Bishop had said at the consecration of a Churchyard. The address was the same each time. It began, "What is Life? Life is a mystery. No one can tell us what Life is", and it went on at the College and at the Confirmation to refer to the work of Sir James Jeans and Sir Arthur Eddington.

The Bishop's Engagement-books for thirty-four years lie before the writer of this book. The first, which only begins a week before his Enthronement, is a slim volume, with seven days to a page. It is crowded with entries in small writing, and evidently proved inadequate, because next year and thereafter he had a larger book with a page for every day. Even so he found space to write on Friday, December 11th, 1901:

> 11.30.   Suffragans and Archdeacons.

In later books this often became "Suffs". The entries are very various and for some days very numerous. On Monday, October 21st, 1901, there were apparently eleven interviews, a lunch some-where and engagements at 4.30, 8 and 9. The 1901 Book includes the Fulham Garden Party, which was a legacy from his predecessor, and a pencilled entry on a spare page at the end, "Children's Dance", which looks like the beginning of the famous Innocents' Day Party. A year later it appears on December 28th.

At the end of the 1901 Book there came, as in all diaries, some engagements noted ahead for the following year, and there is one entry of great importance. "K. G. Averill, 11, Cambridge Gardens, Folkestone." Mr. Averill became his Secretary, and was, until he died in 1925, a most faithful and devoted fellow-worker and friend. One more note of less importance is that of a book which someone had evidently recommended him to read. Those who remember it will know that, if he took the advice, the Bishop had in 1902 at least one delightful spell of "innocent merriment". It was *David Harum*.

In the pocket of this book is a paper which seems to come from the author of some children's books, whom the Bishop had known in her young days. It runs:

> "This is for you, because you came
> And played with six small sprats a game,
> And read to us in days long spent,
> And so to you this book is sent;
> The book your grown-up children write
> For bairns who have not the delight
> Of your kind presence, nor can know
> A love that lasts from long ago."

The Bishop won affection because he gave it. But giving meant self-giving. It was not a strain, but a constant draining. All those interviews involved a series of concentrated efforts to penetrate the need of someone, to share joys or sorrows, and to contribute some assurance of faith. It would have been impossible for anyone except a man who had a great deal to give. Even for him it was exhausting. It did not cost him what it cost Terence Mulvaney on that cruel hot night in Fort Amara, because he did it easily. But it was work for all that. To pass, as he passed constantly, from the grave sessions of the Ecclesiastical Commission, or Q.A.B. or the Governors of the Charterhouse, to "Bishop, I'm in such trouble. Can you help me?" taxes a man's adaptability and strength.

All this burden of work he shouldered eagerly. And the reason was that he made it all personal. The work was his way of helping souls. Many of the best bishops have groaned under the burden of correspondence and administration. They have performed their duties faithfully, but it was often irksome. Ingram looked forward to his holidays, but there is no sign that he ever grumbled at his work. Archbishop Lord Lang at the end of the long episcopate recalled "the golden days" of the first decade of the century. In fact the chief difficulty of writing this book is the difficulty of bringing before a generation which has seen Ingram as an old man, rather tired, and apt to remember the past and to diagnose the present in terms of what he had himself been accustomed to do five and twenty years before, the fine picture of the early days. He was then a young paladin of Christian faith, eager, happy and outstandingly successful. The eagerness and happiness remained to the end of his life. The success—the word is used seriously, of that which ought to be the effect of the life and work of a Bishop—was less at the end than at the beginning, but only if measured by the standard that he had himself created.

VI

THE CHRISTIAN LEADER

ALONG one road, which had its ramifications, Ingram represented a considerable drop in the episcopal standard in London. A wise old priest, who had spent many years in the diocese, said about 1904 in conversation that in comparison with those of his two predecessors the Presidential Addresses of the new Bishop at the Diocesan Conference were disappointing. No listener, he said, could ever doubt the power of Temple or the learning and brilliance of Creighton. To his precise and, in point of fact, Tractarian mind, the breezy talks which now came from the President were unsatisfying. Creighton, for example, had said in 1900:

When we look back upon the history of our Church, we see that the Church somehow or other seems to have constantly courted disruption. It is the great fault that can be brought against the Church of England, that it has shewn a very decided reluctance to make room for new exhibitions of the working of spiritual powers. It is to that, unfortunately, that we owe so much Nonconformity as exists at present. The Church of England has in the past been too satisfied with its system, and too reluctant to see that system either changed or explained so as to meet the altering circumstances of the time. I am very sorry indeed for every departure that was ever made from the Church of England in this country, and that I would have wished that those, who regulated the destinies of the Church at each of such crises, should have made many more concessions than they did, and should have been even willing, if it were necessary, for a time to depart from the assertion of principles which were of great importance, trusting that those principles, if they really were as important as they appeared, would have reasserted themselves in view of the experience of the coming time; because we can always recover things, and, if things are eternally true, then the eternal truth must inevitably prevail. But, unfortunately, in my opinion, we have seen in the history of the Church of England a system desperately maintaining itself in its integrity and allowing consequently the growth of a number of bodies outside, whom it made very little attempt to conciliate. An important question for us at the present day to keep clearly before our minds is, whether or not, with the experience of the past before us, we now seriously think that that is the ideal which we ought still to pursue.[1]

Ingram would say cheerfully that in the diocese of London they were a band of brothers, and that he had two horses to drive, who were called Keble and Simeon, and that they went in a pair in perfect harmony.

Of this optimistic diagnosis, one of his clergy, a discriminating admirer, said that "it was true in his study". The fact was of course that in this particular matter, as in others, he was betrayed by his method of generous personal approach. The same writer goes on to say:

> He would talk over something that was causing trouble in a parish, issue no real instructions, assure the man that he valued him, trusted him, and so on, say some prayers with him, and banishing the problem from his mind, turn to the next thing.

Hence his happy belief in the harmonious pair of horses.

And yet it was not only his own cheery optimism, or his own wishful thinking. There was much truth in what he said in a Sermon at St. Paul's on the Sunday after the London Church Congress in 1899, when he was still Bishop of Stepney:

> "I have no sense of superintending a divided Church in East London."

There was, and is, much truth in this view. Only his single and simple eye saw the pattern as more single and the problem as more simple than it was.

But there was more than that. The problems of the capital were not only those of advising the perplexed and controlling the wayward among the clergy. They were larger than that.

In the first place, the Bishop of London should be, if possible, a man who can give an address to the Royal Society, and beat them on their own ground. Or perhaps rather, not on their own ground, for he need not be a scientist, and indeed science is so departmental that not many of the Fellows themselves could lecture on ground outside their own allotment, but at their own level. When

[1] *Church and Nation*, 330-2.

Creighton was appointed Bishop of London, Scott Holland wrote to him:

> My dear Friend,
>   All our arms are open to receive you, as you know well. The old Dome is alive with delight. It knows you so well already.... This big place cries out not only for noble drudgery, but also for a *Chief*, who is at least far enough out of the smoke to see how the battle goes.

Creighton replied:

> My dear Holland,
>   You are a dear man who has the knack of saying helpful things. When I came to Peterborough, you pointed out the usefulness of a bishop saying and doing little things outside his ordinary business; and you said how weighty they were, coming from him. I have often thought of your words and their wisdom—I have been more useful, and have gained more influence, by never being in too great a hurry to do little things, that were not obviously my duty, than in any other way.
>   Now I feel the truth of your warning not to rest satisfied with the drudgery of my office. I have a strong feeling that a bishop ought not to be merely an ecclesiastical official, but a link between various classes and various activities. He ought to try to make all sorts of things converge, so that the standard and efficiency of each is heightened.[1]

Holland could, and perhaps did, write in much the same way to Ingram, and Ingram did many things outside the ordinary routine of his duty, which were of great value. But Holland would not have worded his last sentence to Ingram in exactly that way, and the "extra" things that Ingram did were not the same things that Creighton had done. Creighton could captivate the audience at the Annual Meeting of a Mechanics' Institute or the guests at a London dinner-party by his miraculous power of penetrating to the heart of a topic and expressing profound thought in lucid and epigrammatic words. Ingram at any meeting would radiate faith, hope and charity. At the end of it he would remember the face of a young clerk whom he had seen once before and would ask him to tea at Fulham Palace, or he would stop on the way to a sermon at a suburban Church to pay a sick visit, leaving happiness and quick-

[1] *Life*, ii. 198, 201.

ened faith behind him. Truly God fulfils Himself in many ways, lest one good custom should corrupt the diocese of London.

A man holding a high official position in the scientific world once said to Bishop Welldon that to have a man of the intellectual calibre of W. R. Inge at St. Paul's was a great asset to Christianity in England. There were many ways in which the Bishop was of incomparably greater service to the cause of Christianity in London, and indeed in England, than the Dean, but he never got on terms with the leaders of thought. He would dine with the Judges, or at one of the Inns of Court, or with the British Academy, or may be, with the Royal Society. They would like him, and be all the better for having met him, and he would like them and get on well with them. And the Peers were always glad to see him at the House of Lords. But the leaders of thought did not take him very seriously. They hardly ever do take an ecclesiastic very seriously. It is not exactly one of the chinks in their armour. It is one of the places where there ought to be a chink, but is not. Anyhow the Bishop of London should be one of those whom they are compelled to take seriously. How to find the man, who can do the endless pastoral and administrative work of a Bishop of London and can also win the respect of the intellectuals, is another matter.

An incident in the writer's own early life illustrates the view taken of him in high-brow circles. When he was a young student of theology, a learned, sceptical old gentleman, a man rather like the Squire in *Robert Elsmere*, said to him, "Why don't your leaders tell people about the effect on religious faith of the truth about the gigantic size of the universe and the smallness of the earth?" The young man, being at that time a diligent reader of Ingram's little books, piped up and said, "Oh, but I read only the other day in a book of the new Bishop of London of 'fifty million blazing suns'."[1] He snorted, and said, "I'm glad to hear that such a great missionary leader as Winnington-Ingram is talking such good sense." But it is probable that the old gentleman, who was a friend of the writer's father, took the Bishop of London about as seriously as he took the young man. If such people ever heard him preach, they were edified, because what they want in a sermon is "religion", not

[1] This was a favourite illustration of his. In his Presidential Address to the Diocesan Conference in 1922, it was "one hundred million blazing suns, all greater than our sun".

argument. But they like to feel that the preacher has argued for himself, and could argue with them if he were challenged. Ingram was friendly with the high-brows, as he was with everybody, but he rather shied away from ministering to them. It was not that he was afraid of them. His faith was such that he was never afraid of anybody. One who had heard many of his talks to large audiences at Oxford between 1899 and 1902 said soon afterwards that he had been greatly impressed by the courage of the man, standing up, as it were, on the Areopagus, and offering to answer any question that the Athenians might ask. It was not fear, it was humility, and obedience to the divine leading. It was that he felt that his vocation lay elsewhere. Even at Oxford he felt that his mission was to the undergraduates rather than to the dons.

This feeling had a natural, innocent result, which was not always understood. He had a habit of saying, half in joke, that he had anyhow picked up a First in Mods and a Second in Greats, and at the end of his episcopate, when he talked about Bishop Fisher as his successor in London, he would say, "He has advantages over me, three Firsts instead of one, as well as a charming wife and six sons." It was as if he rather felt that he was being disparaged and dismissed, and could not resist pointing out that he was not such an ignoramus as they supposed. He was fond of saying that nothing that he had ever read in Plato or Aristotle would have taught him what to say at East London sick-beds, though in fact it is probable that most of what he had read of those authors he had by that time forgotten. And who could blame him for that? He had been doing other things. Many a parson and many a layman, who went through the mill with credit at the University, has failed in the pressure of life to maintain his academic studies. He may have thought at the time that he would continue to read his Aristotle or his Homer. He has not done it. But he is the better man for having worked at them once.

The Bishop of London should also be a Statesman. He need not be an administrative genius, with an immense capacity for detail. He can always find other people who will keep the records and analyse the results, and estimate the probable effect of this or that course of action. He will not have, like the Chancellor of the Exchequer, a large staff of trained Civil Servants, but he can have some competent professional and amateur help. He himself ought to be able to do what Richard Hooker expected from a Bishop. Examining the contemporary claim for "parity of Ministers", Hooker said:

> We must note, that it is in this case; he that sitteth at the stern is quiet, he moveth not, he seemeth in a manner to do little or nothing in comparison of them that sweat about other toil, yet that which he doth is in value and force more than all the labours of the residue laid together.

What did Hooker mean? In modern language, *mutatis mutandis*, part of what he meant is surely something like this:

London is a place where Satan has many subjects. It is essential to make it luminously clear that the Church of God is on the other side, the unfaltering enemy of world and flesh and devil, an elect race, a royal priesthood, a holy nation, a people for God's own possession, that they may shew forth the excellencies of him who called them out of darkness into his marvellous light (1 Peter ii. 9). The Church must make no compromise with sin.

On the other hand London is the headquarters of all that general Christian idealism, which is felt in the House of Commons, in the House of Lords, in the Inns of Court, in the City, in the West End, in the East End, in Bloomsbury, in Chelsea, in the suburbs. There are innumerable people in all ranks of life who have a Christian education behind them, who have Christian instincts within them, and, if they are handled in the right way, a Christian future in front of them. Sometimes there comes a crisis in their lives, a point on the road, not to Damascus, but to Athens, or Corinth, or Sybaris, or Brighton, or Nowhere in Particular, when they suddenly look up and see and are converted. But as a rule they must not be hurried. Somebody must discover their vulnerable side, through Art, through Reason, through Social Service, through their children or what not, and approach them in the right way.

Now, how are the two duties to be combined? How is the Church to utter the prophetic cry, "Nineveh, Repent!" and at the same time not quench the smoking flax, not break the bruised reed? It is a problem in every diocese, in every parish, almost in every family, but it is most acute in London. For Ingram it was, as so often, a case of *solvitur ambulando*. He saw his duty and went straight ahead. He was fond of saying, "Take one day at a time, and trust the Holy Spirit to see you through." His zeal made him a prophet, and his kindness and his pastoral heart gave him an instinctive approach to very many lives which was conspicuously effective. But he does not seem to have thought the thing out. And, though it would be quite unfair to say that he did not take long views, they were seldom in any very original or independent direction. His utterances at Diocesan Conferences were generally commendations of the commonly accepted lines of progress. He would speak of the necessity of maintaining the Faith, of the importance of preserving Church Schools, of the need for building suburban Churches, for augmenting the stipends of poor benefices, for resisting vicious influences in literature or Drama. It was all true, and it was all good. And like Macaulay, he had "his own heightened and telling way of putting things". But it was rather obvious. And he occasionally permitted himself to commend that well-intentioned policy, often popular in ecclesiastical Assemblies, but almost always a disastrous policy, "the interests of the Church".

The fact was that he was not a statesman. He was an Evangelist. Mrs. H. L. Paget writes that he was, so to speak, made in East London:

finding himself a kindred soul with his neighbours in Bethnal Green, and thus able to bring to West London and elsewhere something of the glow, the courage, the tenderness and the wit of London East of Aldgate pump. Archbishop Davidson, perceiving this, used his influence to get his appointment to the diocese of London, sending Cosmo Lang, the administrator, to Stepney. The mistake, if there was one, was not Ingram's. Bishop Creighton's premature death had robbed London of a highly cultivated and balanced judgment, and actually the Diocese of London needs an administrator at the centre. London is not only made up of the quick, flashing wit of the back streets—back chat from back streets, it is not picturesque or arresting as a whole; it stretches into wearying suburbs where fine cedars, dying amid builders' materials, mark the green belt that has been lost. London also gathers itself up into the heart and mind—mind of the governing heart, of the centre, the concentration of parliament, business, science, art and fashion, a focus of world opinion and a challenge to the Church. It is true that the clever and critical mind of the centre will never be won by argument and it is a mercy that the Christian religion is again and again expressed by paradox. The human need is essentially simple, the entrance to the Kingdom conditional on men becoming as "little children", but the little child has to grow, and pass, according to St. Paul, from a milk diet to stronger meat.

It would not have been easy to get the Bishop to realize the need of accurate social study or the trend of social work and social thought. Bethnal Green, steadily moving forward in education and becoming yearly more self-conscious, more critical, more independent, remained to the end of life as he first knew it, his early love and his adventure. Women's work and position—if we take that as a symbol of a changing world—did not really enter his mind. It would be difficult to estimate how far he touched and influenced the actual centre in those early vigorous growing years. None the less the "success"—the astounding success of the appointment to London was immediate. . . .

Meanwhile in actual fact the Church in London grew more individualistic and congregational. It was not that the Bishop wished to draw people to himself, but he was actually too busy, too much in request, to harvest his crops. The statesman was lacking in a character that was otherwise so richly endowed and, to those who loved him, it has always seemed tragic that the Church lost her greatest evangelist by placing him in an administrative post too soon. It is true to say that his love of Evangelism almost amounted to an escape from the complicated cares thrust upon him, and he rarely, if ever, failed in those sensitive, sympathetic visits to men and women in sorrow, sickness or joy. Indeed he was never more himself or of greater influence than when following this, his true vocation.

London, of which Cobbett as long ago as 1830 had spoken as "the great wen of all, the monster called the Metropolis of Empire", had grown with terrifying swiftness to terrifying dimensions. It was the business centre of the world. It contained six hundred parishes, each with its company of regular worshippers, its large circle of "occasionals", and its "not even that, but friendly". It contained very large numbers of decent, semi-pagan people, and it contained some human beings almost as savage and barbarous as there were anywhere. There were pools of iniquity in West and West-Central London, as there were round Waterloo, compared to which the unwashed indigence of Bethnal Green was purity itself. Mr. Michael Sadleir has recently described it with a remorseless pen. In 1888 the London County Council, of which Lord Rosebery was the first Chairman, had begun to create some London patriotism, some enthusiasm for the local government of the capital, and the inauguration in 1899 of the twenty-eight Boroughs, each with its Mayor and Councillors and Aldermen, had further localized such public spirit as there was. This nowhere rose to the towering heights of the devotion to Notting Hill which Chesterton attributed to Adam Wayne, but the electors of Westminster, Holborn, Finsbury or Shoreditch had begun to feel on All Hallows' Day that they were helping to govern themselves. And even if the notices posted in the Parks were so worded to suggest that the Parks belonged to the L.C.C. rather than to London, the citizens, if they thought it over, could say that the great city, with its slums and its Hyde Park, was theirs. Nevertheless it was an unwieldy, sprawling giant.

Against this Goliath, or that part of it which was evil, a young David flung himself.[1] He had no elaborate armour. If he had lived a hundred and fifty years earlier, he could, in the worst manner of the eighteenth century, have girded his loins with sloth, having put on the breastplate of respectability, having his feet shod with the preparation of the gospel of ease; he could have taken the shield of rational credibility, with which to quench all the fiery darts of "enthusiasm"; he could have taken the helmet of convention, and the sword of the spirit of that age, which was "the religion of all sensible men"; with all care and moderation, praying at proper seasons, attending continually at the House of Lords, in all perseverance for the best interests of the Establishment. All this he could have done, but he never even thought of the office of a bishop as being anything but the vocation to be a shepherd, to defend his flock against the lion and the bear, and to challenge "this Philistine" who came to defy the armies of the living God. He went down to the brook, and chose five smooth stones and put them in his shepherd's bag.

What were they? They were in effect, as they appeared in his

[1] It was an illustration which the Bishop had used himself in his Pastoral Lectures at Cambridge. He was suggesting ways in which a young curate could be equipped for beginning work in East London, "(i) *Moral Integrity*. It is the old story: David goes out with his sling and his stone; he does not want Saul's cumbrous armour; Goliath comes swaggering against him with his bluster and his brag, and David, with the unearthly strength of his moral rectitude, lays him low." p. 42.

happy, useful life, Faith, Hope and Love, together with Simplicity and Sincerity. But he himself, in his humility, did not know that they were that. So far as he knew, they were Holy Baptism, Confirmation, Holy Communion, the Bible and the Prayer Book. But, because he was a servant of God, and because those things really are of God, God gave him the three Theological Virtues, together with the Simplicity and the Sincerity. And with those plain weapons he smote Goliath a resounding blow. He did not kill him, because what was evil in this Goliath was of Satan, who is not mortal, but he disturbed the throne of Satan not a little. To quote again from Mrs. Paget, "For a very considerable time the inchoate mass of the capital was actually gathered into a sort of unity round him."

And this was not merely by the charm of his personality, or by general exhortations. He was all afire to bring the whole Gospel of Christ to bear on the actual conditions of life in a great city. We have seen how at Oxford House he tackled abuses, and when he reached a higher level of authority, he did not forget his Christian Social Union principles. He knew that abuses must be denounced in the pulpit, but they must be met in the street and in the Council Chamber. In a sermon delivered in St. Paul's at the end of his Stepney period, and published in 1902, he said:

These are His people—His own, part of Himself! The Incarnation gives us hope.

What, then, are we to do? The question comes very near us to-day, for on Thursday next the new boroughs are to elect their representatives. Everyone must realize what a chance has been given to us here. These new Councillors will assess and collect the poor rate, and the rate for lighting and draining: they will have power to destroy houses which they pronounce unfit for habitation, buildings dangerous to the public health, and areas which are overcrowded; they will appoint the sanitary officials and inspectors, and administer all the sanitary regulations and the demands of the Factory Acts in domestic workshops; they will have power to build such hospitals as they think fit, and they alone can adopt the Acts for public libraries and baths and washhouses. They will control the condition and the cleansing of the streets; they will be responsible for the suppression of disorderly houses, and the protection of public decency—in a word, the social and moral life of London will be to a great extent in their hands. The

State has framed this machinery, but the Church must put the moral aspect of it forward—the Church must fill it with the true spirit. These twenty-eight boroughs will be perfectly useless in the attempt to reform London unless they are inspired from the very start by the sympathy of enthusiastic and Christian people.

This Sermon was called "The action of Faith on the Life of a Great city".[1]

The general exhortations at the Diocesan Conference were very moving to the hearers. It was a great thing to have a Bishop of London who in 1922, after twenty years at the head of the most exacting diocese in the world, could speak as Ingram spoke. It was a time of disillusionment, after the First War. He had referred to Russia and Ireland, about both of which he took the view which was at that time common, and, as some would say, conventional. He had dwelt on two matters of diocesan concern, on both of which there was more than one opinion among his audience, the division of the diocese and the City Churches, and then he said:

I come on to what I really have most at heart. I feel that somehow there is something wrong not only about the Diocese, but about the whole Church at large. I have thought over it a great deal, and my belief is that we are snowed under by machinery and are losing the spirit. I ask you to think over what is the object of a diocese, and the object of a Diocesan Conference as representing the diocese. I believe that the object of the whole thing is to create a passion, an enthusiasm, for God among the people amongst whom we live. That is really the whole point of our existence at all. We ought to have, and there ought to be, in the Diocese, and of course through us, in the nation, an enthusiasm, a passion, for the character of God Himself. That I do not find. Think for a moment of how full of this some of the old prophets and the old psalmists are. We have a long string of praises, almost tiring unless we enter into what it really means. Some years ago I read a book, the title of which was "The Splendour of God". Suffer me for a few minutes if I come away from all the business before us and think of what ought, I believe, to occupy and wholly absorb our hearts and our minds—the splendour of the God whom we worship. We talk about not raising £100,000 in London. We really can hardly believe at all in what I call the Eternal Giver. I should like to write at

[1] *Under the Dome*, 53-56.

the back of every Bible the real meaning of the Bible, "God the Eternal Giver, who lives to give". That is what the Bible is "about", as the children say. They say, "What is the book about?" It is about God the Eternal Giver. He gives us life, He gives us the beauties of Nature, He gives us the birds, He gives us the flowers, He gives us the prophets, He gives us the Son, He gives us the Spirit, He gives us the Church, He gives us the Bible, He gives us everything that we have got that we love. He gives us the Sacraments every day; He eternally lives to give.

> "He lends not, but gives to the end,
> As He loves to the end. Does he seem
> To take back a gift? Comprehend.
> " 'Tis to add to it, rather amend,
> And finish it up to your dream."

We ought to be absorbed in the Diocese, in every village, and every parish, in the spreading of this idea of the Eternal Giver.

Truly, it might have been said of the speaker, in the words of the Queen of Sheba:

Happy are thy men, happy are these thy servants, which stand continually before thee, and hear thy wisdom.

And this despite the fact that both the wisdom and the character of the Bishop differed at almost all points from those of King Solomon.

The Bishop was at his best at Diocesan Conferences. He was alert, knew everybody, and was eager to be fair to all shades of opinion. He sometimes revealed his own preference, for or against a resolution or an amendment, and in those cases the Conference generally went with him.

He was always in great demand at Church Congresses, which used once to be held every year. He generally spoke at the Men's Meetings. These meetings were crowded, and he always received a great welcome when he stood up. He would begin with a little compliment to the Bishop of the Diocese, who was presiding, and would make the most of some old association at Oxford or in East London or elsewhere. Then he would talk to the men in vigorous, telling words, not sparing their weaknesses, declaring the whole counsel of God. At Northampton in 1902 he said:

The Congress speaks, first of all, to your reason, and it comes down here to thunder in your ears the question whether or not you are applying to your reason the greatest possible object for the reason—and that is God. Are your minds in Northampton thinking upon God? God forbid I should not say and admit the great difficulties that there are in religion. It is perfectly true that, in some senses, and in one true sense, we are all agnostics—we all only know in part. St. Paul said so himself. There are tracts of truth we do not know, and shall never know. But the question the Congress asks Northampton is whether it is accepting or rejecting the only Lamp that has ever come to light up the darkness of the world. Don't you see what it has to say to your intellects about God allowing suffering in the world? If I did not believe in Jesus Christ I could not believe in a good God. The difficulties would be too immense. If He really had been, while little children died in the slums and 30,000 people were blotted out in a moment on some island, careless of mankind, I could not have believed in His goodness at all. I ask you to look in the direction in which the Church Congress points its finger, and that is to the Cross of Jesus Christ. I believe it with all my soul that in that Cross we have the answer to the awful doubt about God's goodness which comes upon our intellects. . . . Secondly, the Congress has a message to your hearts. I have seen a great congregation of free people almost sobbing with excitement and pity and enthusiasm as they have seen a fireman creep up a ladder into a burning house, and out with a child. I have seen it on the part of men who would pretend that they had no emotion at all. And what humbugs some of you are. You pretend you have no heart and no feelings. There is a soft heart and tender feeling when you get beneath the surface. Your feelings are stirred by real heroism and real distress. I have been with a working man on Sunday morning while all his three children died one after another within an hour. I have knelt with him hand in hand by his dying wife; and I know you have hearts. Look and see if any rescue by any fireman ever was so gallant as the rescue of the suffering, of the poor and of the sinful by Jesus Christ Himself. . . . Thirdly, the Congress has a message to your consciences—those consciences which we know exist, in spite of all argument to the contrary; and the Congress says this to you: Be honest with yourselves, be honest with that conscience. Do you put five shillings on a horse to improve the breed? Do you really not go to Church because you are afraid you would be turned out of a pew? Is it really the reason when you stick, some of you, to the drink, that it is because those fanatical teetotallers are trying to rob a poor man of his beer? I am a teetotaller myself, but I say that the old Church of England Temperance Society is perfectly right to rally all in the temperance cause, whether teetotallers or not. The Church Congress says: Be honest with yourselves, you have got to stand before God. What a very short thing life is after all. I went away for a few weeks' holiday this year. When I got back, four clergy had died and three people I intimately knew in London. Life is a passing thing, and you have soon to stand before the God of Love, Who planted the conscience in you. Be honest, be honest with yourselves, is the message of the Church Congress to your consciences.

There were some who thought that in these addresses he spoke too much of himself and his own work. It was a habit which grew upon him in his later years, and became a little wearisome, but there is this to be remembered. There were some among his contemporary Bishops, and there had been Westcott in the generation before, who had thought far more deeply about theological and social questions, and Westcott, shy scholar as he was, became at Durham the miners' friend, revered and trusted. But unlike some of his fellow-Bishops, Ingram had, so to speak, worn the overalls and gone through the shops. He had actually done the work in the mean streets. He knew the work by experience. In fact, it was the only thing he knew. To extract its evidence was his specific contribution to the Christian study of social problems. If he was egoistic, it was, at least in his middle years, with the egoism of St. Paul, who said, because it was the thing that needed saying, and no one else was in a position to say it so effectively, "I laboured, and yet not I, but the grace of God which was with me."

This is how a well-known journalist of that period, Mr. Raymond Blathwayt, described the Bristol Congress:

And then came the Bishop of London, in a very different way no less impressive and remarkable than the Bishop of Bristol. Also very tall, with thin, wiry, well-shaped figure, a clean-cut handsome face, with a clever humorous mouth and a delightfully winning mode of speech.

Dr. Ingram, as is well known, is at home with everyone, and his personality is acceptable alike to the gracious lady who sits beside our king and to the hard-headed, hard-working artisans and mechanics of industrial England. As it has well been said, Dr. Ingram's greatness and most probably his claim on posterity lies and will lie in the fact that he more than anyone else has commended the Anglican Church to peer and peasant alike, and so has, with the magic of his inimitable personality, knitted together the East and West of our great metropolis.

And the men of Bristol recognized this, and hearty, even overwhelming, was the reception they extended to him.

"Has the Gospel failed?" that was the question he put to his enormous audience, a question which he handled with characteristic skill and daring.

He pictured a secularist urging an affirmative reply and backing it up with the case of unavenged Macedonia, or the chaos and tumult of the Education Bill or the empty condition of our Churches and chapels. "And yet," said the Bishop fearlessly enough, "I do not think the Gospel has failed," and with great tenderness and wonderful power of illustration he depicted a brokenhearted father or mother hanging over the bed of a dying child.

What else but the Gospel could comfort them or bring balm to such aching hearts? Could Plato, or Socrates, or Shakespeare? No, only the Gospel of Jesus Christ, and that has not yet failed and it never will.[1]

It was not this address but it was something like it, that caused Dr. R. F. Horton, the distinguished Congregationalist leader, to write from Amsterdam:

Easter Monday, 1911.

My dear Bishop,

I hope it will not seem to be an intrusion, if I send a line to thank you for what you did on Good Friday. I read about it this morning in a foreign country, and I thanked God for it.

It was such a noble and beautiful testimony for our Lord, and must have preached to multitudes who do not enter Churches.

What a glorious position you have gained for testifying to Him! I cannot help rejoicing in it, and praying that you may have still further inspiration for reaching the vast indifferent masses of London.

As I get on—and near the end of the brief opportunity—I wish that I knew how to promote the union of all Christians in Christ's name, that we might present a common front, and a common testimony to the unchristian world. How remarkable it was that *Watts, Toplady and Charles Wesley* were the mouthpieces of your praise on Good Friday! I wonder whether we could find in the hymns, and in the devotional

[1] The Men's Magazine (Organ of C.E.M.S.), Jan., 1904.

attitude the union which we seek in vain on lines of doctrine and policy.

May God give you a rich sense of blessing in this latest effort for London.

Believe me to be with warm esteem and gratitude,

Yours most truly,

ROBERT F. HORTON.

This chapter could not end better than by quoting the words written by Henry Scott Holland under the title of "Arthur of London":

> "God who created me,
>   Nimble and light of limb,
> In three elements free
>   To run, to ride, to swim:
> Not when the sense is dim,
>   But now from the heart of joy
> I would remember Him:
>   Take the thanks of a boy."

Somehow that is the verse, with its fresh freedom, with its buoyant charm, that is in my head as I think of the Bishop of London. He was a boy just like that when I first saw him:

> "Nimble and light of limb,
> In three elements free
> To run, to ride, to swim."

He used to be brought up by his Keble Dons to an odd little gathering which we called Pesec, because it was a tiny, political, ethical, social, economic sort of club, made up of a few dons and some favoured Undergrads, who met at Arthur Lyttelton's, in his rooms over a chemist's shop in St. Giles (known therefore as "the Pill-Box") to talk about Cities and the Poor, and Social Problems, and all that we have heard so much of since. We thought ourselves rather in "the forward movement" in those far-away days. We were burning with Ruskin and Carlyle: we read together "Unto this Last": we discussed: we railed at the dry bones of the older Political Economy: we clamoured for a breath to come from the four winds and blow upon these bones till they might live. And there, silent, and amused, probably, at the heat of the Dons—lay curled up in some armchair the lean, keen, active boyish figure, looking very young, with the face that we knew.

He has learned a good deal, since those happy times, of the grim City and its swarming Poor. He had smelt the fish-shops in Bethnal Green Road. And into it all he has carried the soul that gives life to the pages of "Unto this Last".

And he has felt, too, how the Vision is yet for a time, and a time, and half a time. He has waited in vain for the Trumpets to blow, and for the sealed Thunders to speak. We thought it would come so quickly and so surely, as we debated in the "Pill-Box". And yet, here we are, drawing to the end of our time, and he has all this sad London to shepherd and to feed: And is anything achieved at all? Is the cloud lifted? Is the dawn any nearer? Who knows? He must feel sick, again and again, at hopes deferred. But, nevertheless, as I look at him, back floats the beautiful boy's prayer; and I seem to see that he has never ceased to be the same boy, "nimble and light of limb", who lay curled up in the low chair. He has retained the heart of a boy. No weary years can stifle it: no burden break it. He is a boy still: keen, generous, cheery, hopeful. He flings himself into his work with the spirit that revels in the joy of a football scrum. He faces difficulties as a boy riding at first fences. Nothing daunts: nothing can defeat him. He goes forward with a cheer against impossible obstacles; he is convinced that he will tumble over somehow. The one thing is, never to look back. It is bound to be right, if only you go straight on. So he can bound in upon any Meeting, and give it the call which promises victory. Why not? Are we going to be beaten when God is on our side? Poor old Experience may sit in a tight corner, shaking its silly head, and doling out dismal facts. What are facts? We are going to conquer facts. We are creating a new experience. So we all believed when we were boys. That is what makes our boyhood so glad and triumphant a vision. Why is our boyhood vanished? Why have we let our best possession slip through our fingers? Why have we grown old, and downhearted, and bald?

Here, at least is one man who has kept himself a boy. He is "nimble and light of limb" as ever; he is in every element free; he still "hopes all things: believes all things: rejoices not in evil, but rejoices in the truth". He is not going to stop for aught, for anything. "Running, riding, swimming": by any method that comes to hand: he is ready to go forward; while we, poor old dotty crocks, must pull ourselves together and totter faintly after him. For who can refuse? Who can resist his optimism? Who can keep cool as he listens to his "View-halloo?" The blood wakes; the old stir of the Chase is alive in us: we are almost boys again ourselves, under this infectious gaiety. We find ourselves waving our hats round our heads, and tally-ho-ing like mad.

The heart of a boy! Could there be a better boon to bring to the service of God in this worn and tired City? What a power, what a glory, to spend in freedom and mirth, without stint, without reserve, as he spends it! Is there any gift that we more sorely need?

In its strength he moves about, bearing a glamour with him of hope and joy which is irresistible. We yield to it, we know not why, before we know what we have done. He is so winning. He wins the Costers and he wins the Peers. For all have been boys once: and he touches the common ground. So he could feed the Oxford House from out of the two Universities. He attacked them both, and the young responded to the appeal of one who could enter so intimately into the heart of "Youth with the star above his hair".

Inarticulate Blues have, before now, become positively vocal on platforms in the Town Hall at Oxford, in front of their fellows, for love of him.

Nor is it only the Undergrad who is drawn out of himself down there. Weird old creatures, known as Doctors, Proctors, Heads of Colleges, and such like, crawl out of their hidden lairs under his spell, and sit in St. Mary's listening, wondering, while one wipes away a tear and another feels a funny sob in his throat; and none can tell you why. Only, they look up at his face: and the breath of another world, somehow, blows upon them, borne in upon them through the soul of a boy.

> "Not when the sense is dim,
>   But now, from the heart of joy,
>   I would remember Him:
>   Take the thanks of a boy."

So Canon Beeching's boy sings his Prayer. So, of old, in Oxford days, our Bishop prayed to give thanks to God out of the heart of all that was joyful in his keen young life.

Now he cannot, always, keep the joy. The sense must be dimmed a little. The years have done their work. The cares of the bewildered Church have weighed him down. The sorrows and terrors of London have passed into his soul. He has sung, with face set as flint, with lips drawn hard in resolution, with eyes aflame, the further verse of the prayer.

> "Jesu, King and Lord,
> Thine are my foes to fight:
> Gird me with Thy sword,
> Swift and sharp and bright:
> Thee would I serve if I might,
> And conquer, if I can,
> From day-dawn till night:
> Take the strength of a man."

It is a dire tragedy to watch the grey, strained look that is coming into the face which ought to be so young. Now and again we tremble lest the boy-heart should be broken, and have gone under and should never again be dancing about us with its rippling glee, with its dauntless daring. But God is good: and he trusts himself to God with rare simplicity: and the Spirit of God, if he will keep close within its friendship, will for ever renew the wastage, and breathe over him the breath of the new Day. The Spirit comes and goes as it listeth; it can never grow old: and "so is everyone that is born of the Spirit".

We will commit him whom we love to this Regenerative Spirit, to be sustained and cherished; that, so, at the very last, he who was created of God so nimble and light of limb, may still be able to surrender back to God a spirit unhurt, unsullied, undefeated; and be enabled, even though the sense be at last dim, still to claim that out of the heart of a joy that has never been taken away from him, God may yet

Take the thanks of one who is, to the very last, a boy!

H. S. HOLLAND.

VII

THE LENT MISSIONS

THE Bishop felt very acutely the spiritual burden of his cure.
There were all those millions of people in London, increasing in
number by many thousands every year, not indeed wholly un-
shepherded, but multitudes of them still deaf to the shepherd's
voice, or beyond the sound of it. And he was the chief shepherd.
It is an ancient principle of the Church that the Bishop has the
pastoral charge of all the souls in the diocese. He is of course compelled to delegate his authority to the parish priests, but when he
institutes a priest to a benefice, he says "your cure and mine". To
a Bishop at his Consecration is said—Be to the flock of Christ a
shepherd, not a wolf; feed them, devour them not. Hold up the
weak, heal the sick, bind up the broken, bring again the outcasts,
seek the lost."

Ingram found, with St. Paul, that the care of all the Churches
came upon him daily. His method of discharging his episcopal duty
was characteristic, and Pauline. He had of course his diocesan
organizations, and he devoted not a little time and strength to the
raising of the necessary funds, of both which things more will be
said later. But the special contribution which he felt constrained to
make to the building up of the Body of Christ in London was
preaching.

He loved preaching, and always, to the end of his life, he could
say, as he said to a group of his clergy at High Leigh in 1934, "My
brothers, I have been preaching the Gospel for fifty years, and even
now I never go up the pulpit stairs without a thrill of eagerness to
proclaim the Good News." He believed, with St. Paul, that the
Lord had sent him to preach the Gospel. He might have added,
again with the Apostle, "Woe is me, if I preach not the Gospel."
He did this, on "Occasions", when something of a pronouncement
was expected, by constant visits to parish churches, at Confirma-
tions, and, above all, by his Lent Missions. Year after year he chose

in Lent some area of the diocese, and preached in the larger Churches on Wednesday or Thursday evenings, on Sunday evening, and, to men only, on Sunday afternoon. The services for men were an essential part of every Mission. He said at Highgate in 1906:

> I look on no Mission as complete unless, at any rate for a time, I get my brother men round me, and speak to them heart to heart and soul to soul. Over and over again I have found that there is something in the life of my brother men which is choking their spiritual life. Sometimes it is simply indifference . . . sometimes it is unbelief. . . . Again and again in Missions up and down England have I found that the difficulty lies in some moral failure . . . at such services as these in a Mission the soul is pulled up—"Where am I going?"[1]

The Bishop was an experienced Missioner. His custom at Oxford House had been to conduct a Ten Day Mission, generally in East London every November, and sometimes more often. This was partly that he might himself take his share in the Mission-work of the Church, and also that the young men of the House might have the experience of visiting the streets of the parish in preparation and in helping at the Mission itself.[2]

On the last morning there would be Holy Communion at a very early hour, perhaps at five, so that all who had been moved by the Mission might give thanks and make their final act of self-dedication.

A chapter of *Work in Great Cities* gives a number of valuable counsels to young men who might be called upon in after years to take part in mission-work, and also, as was inevitable, many reminiscences:

> I shall never forget the services in the Beckton gas-works during dinner-hour. Standing on a tub in the middle of three hundred or four hundred men, who were devouring the last remnant of beef steak by the lurid light of two or three furnaces, dressed in the rough clothes, which even the well-to-do among them put on during their working

[1] *Mission of the Spirit*, 12.

[2] An old friend writes, "He took me to Limehouse when he was about to take a Ten Day Mission in the Parish Church. He was given a very small bedroom and he was very tired. I lit his fire, and he said, 'Keep quite still. I want companionship, but I must be quiet.' He sat right on the fire with his head on his hands for over an hour. Then he was his bright self. He began his sermon for his first service of this Mission, 'I speak to dying men and dying women'."

hours, and yet listening with all their ears to what we had to say, it was hard to recognize those wild-looking figures as the same men who, washed and changed, might be seen in the church in the evening at the mission-service, or, in cases where the "shifts" did not permit, on Sunday afternoon at the men's service.

About individual work for souls he says this:

Be faithful: probe home: it is the most merciful thing to do, whatever pain it gives, and it is absolutely essential in a mission, which is nothing if not "charged with reality". Get the whole burden of the conscience told out to God: there can be no healing till there is frank and full confession to God; then lead up to the Cross, valued at last when we know ourselves sinners, that so the soul, receiving pardon and peace, may go forth to serve God with a quiet mind. Then build up in the faith. Find out what is lacking: perhaps the man never prays, has never been baptized, never confirmed, never a communicant. Help him to form a resolution, thus running the molten ore of his emotion into a mould before it cools, and get him to go to the missioner and take a mission resolution-card, on which the resolution he makes before God is solemnly inscribed and attested.

Elsewhere he recalls many incidents of Missions, which shew how exacting the work was, and what calls it made on the faith and wisdom of the Missioner:

After my first sermon at a mission a boy came into the vestry and flung himself down in a paroxysm of grief because he had been guilty once of breaking the seventh commandment, and I could not convince him that he could be forgiven until I took him by the hand and knelt with him in front of the Cross; and then the truth of God's pardon in Christ at last flashed into his soul. On another occasion there was a girl who had been made to sin against her will, and she found it hard to believe that she could be forgiven. It took me half an hour to convince her, and it was not until she knelt at the foot of the Cross that the truth of God's forgiveness dawned upon her, and into her face there came a look of most wonderful peace and joy.

The Bishop of course knew very well that the London Lent Missions of his episcopate were not real missions of this kind. In fact if the Missioner had been anyone except himself, the thing would have been a failure. But he could count on crowded congregations, which would be up to a point continuous from week to week. And he had a mysterious power both in the pulpit and in private talks of getting on terms very quickly with his hearers.

It was, in the circumstances, all that he could do. The message of each Mission was continuous, and there were actually many hearers who followed him from Church to Church and so heard it all. Some of these were godly women, who valued the Mission and were of course welcome participants in it, but in point of fact they did often occupy seats which might have been more profitably occupied by someone else. Some of those were no doubt what St. Paul calls "silly women", but some were such women as are the backbone of the Church of England, its chief workers and its chief pray-ers. They deserve all that they get, and more. Here are the recollections of one such woman:

If I may I should like to send a memory of the ordinary person to whom the name of Bishop Winnington-Ingram means a very great deal. I am one of many to whom he has brought an uplift and hope that has lasted through a lifetime.

Those of us who followed him during those wonderful Missions of his in the West End of London know that he gave us a message and an anchor that has held us fast through all the troubled years which have followed. Always he was the same; utterly patient, unsparing of himself, ever ready to help and answer the doubts and fears of the humblest who appealed to him. We knew, as we listened, that we were not moved by oratory, nor even by a wonderful personality; rather that we were listening to a voice which was handing on to us the message of love and forgiveness from God Himself. Not one member of those vast crowds who followed him round—waiting patiently outside each Church till the regular congregation had taken their seats and the general public were admitted—could doubt the sincerity and the eagerness of the men and women who would not miss one word of that divine message.

Especially I remember that first Mission, "Jesus of Nazareth passes by". In it we learnt, through the selfless teaching the Bishop gave us, that actually and truly Jesus was there giving His message to suffering mankind through our Bishop, the culmination being that outstanding Three Hours Service at St. Mary Abbott's Church. There, in those days before shop-queues were known, the line of people at 9 a.m. stretched far up the hill, waiting to go in to early Mattins and stay on to the

Three Hours Service. The congregation was hushed, expectant, filled, perhaps for the first time, with a realization of the wonder of the Cross, and its saving grace.

This was the testimony of one of the many women who listened. The men often stroll in when everything has been made ready, and are rather inclined to pat themselves on the back because they have come at all. The majority of listeners, it may be supposed, heard only one or two sermons. That was of course a weakness, inevitable if a large area must be covered. On the other hand each sermon was more complete in itself than a single sermon of an ordinary Parochial Mission would normally be. The Bishop was, not with that particular intention, but in fact, to some extent a follower of the old Evangelical tradition of the eighteenth and early nineteenth centuries, that every sermon shall unfold what was called "the plan of salvation", so that a casual hearer, coming in, would learn the gist of what the Christian religion had to say about the eternal destiny of man.[1]

They were great Mission services. The Church was full from end to end. Many of the congregation had been waiting for as long as an hour beforehand. The prayers were very simple, an invocation of the Holy Spirit, and then, for the most part, petitions which had been sent in. "Pray for a son, that he may want to be confirmed"; "For a girl in great temptation"; "For me, that I may know what to do"; "For my boy, who is going with bad friends"; "For my husband, to give up the drink". Or, like this:

One touching message, among many others, from this vast congregation, which I must notice, and must answer. It is a note without address and without name—just a cry from the deep: "A man who has been tempted above his ability to bear temptation, and found no way of escape, humbly and respectfully asks your prayers. He is one of the thousands who are hanging day by day upon your words, and begs for a word of comfort, which, by the help of the God he has denied and betrayed, may bring to him true repentance, without which it must be impossible to obtain the grace of the Holy Spirit towards the amendment so eagerly—oh, so eagerly!—desired—"

[1]Those who were Calvinists, as many were, had their own emphasis and terminology. An old gentleman of ninety-five said to a young relative shortly before he was ordained in 1902, "Young man, every sermon of yours must contain the three R.s" (Ruin, Reprobation and Redemption).

the simple *cris du cœur* which every missioner knows. And the Bishop had his own brotherly way of laying them before the Heavenly Father, and upholding them with all the spiritual power that he and the congregation could bring to bear.

Then he would answer the questions which had been sent in. This was of course an inducement to the Sunday congregations to come to the other Church on the Wednesday following to hear the answers. The answers were always confident, simple and easy to understand. Sometimes, he would say, "There is no answer to this question. No one knows," and some thought, as some had said in Victoria Park, that he was over-fond of the word "mystery".[1] The critic could complain that the answer did not go very deep, and it was no doubt often true. But what is certain is that they supplied the kind of solution for which the questioner was hoping. An Origen, a Hooker or a Westcott, eager to do justice to the subject, might have answered more scientifically, at far greater length, and much less effectively. Pastors who have to do with simple people, who are themselves accustomed to live by a few simple formulas, like "Mustn't grumble", or "There's a good time coming", are driven by force of circumstances to hand out simple formulas. It is a risk, but if they are theologians enough, and honest men enough, to know what they are doing, it is a risk which must be taken. One critical hearer, himself an accomplished theologian, said of one answer that he heard that it was "an ultra-facile way of handling the subject, and that it appeared entirely to miss the point of the question". He sometimes skated lightly over difficulties, and on points of scholarship he was sometimes deficient or misinformed, but his answers were direct, simple and satisfying to the questioners.

It is quite easy to pick holes. Every now and then the Bishop was not familiar with the best theological opinion on a subject, but for the most part such weakness as there was arose from lack of time to deal fully with a large matter. Sometimes a supplementary question, had it been asked, might have landed him in difficulties. Thus, he was asked at St. Pancras in 1906:

[1]"In East London, when fighting for the truth of the Christian Faith, I used often to have said to me, when some particular difficult question had been asked: 'Now, sir, don't say that this is a mystery'—as if saying a thing was a mystery was the common refuge of every Christian apologist in a difficulty."

In fact, he constantly explained the word as bearing its invariable Pauline sense, a thing that was once hidden, but is now revealed. See e.g. Romans xvi. 25, 26, Ephesians iii. 4-6.

124

St. Matthew xix. 16, 17: What is meant by Christ's saying, "Why callest thou Me good?" How is that consistent with the fact that He is said to be the Son of God?

and answered:

If you look at the Revised Version, which explains so many difficulties, because, of course, it is the more careful and accurate translation, you will find that the young man asked our Lord, "What good thing shall I do that I may have eternal life?" And our Lord says, "Why askest thou me concerning that which is good? One there is who is good." Therefore, if you refer to the Revised translation, the difficulty of the questioner who sends up this question falls to the ground.[1]

If the questioner had known that in St. Mark x. 18 and in St. Luke xviii. 19 the Revised Version has, "Why callest thou me good?" a supplementary, though of course not unanswerable question, might have been asked.

A characteristic answer, which brings out a favourite, and valuable, thought of the Bishop was this:

Now, this is a question that touches one of the great mysteries of life, but I think there is only one answer. It is all part of a great scheme that the sins of the fathers are visited on the children: that the wickedness of the wicked man who has misused his free-will is not interfered with at the time, even when he injures others, but that GOD has chosen that we shall be in one another's hands for good or for evil. If you come to think of it, if we were not bound together by these ligaments and ties, Christ would not have saved us. This is an important thing to remember. Unless we were a family connected with one another, Christ's glorious death and life would not have been able to save us. If you were to argue that everyone must stand by himself on a platform in a state of perfect individualism, then you have got to save yourself. What we seem to see is this: that, just as mischief goes through the body of the family, so good flows through the family: and it was because Christ saw the corrupting influence in the human family that He came down and made Himself head of it, and thus through the ligaments and connecting links sprang a new life. Therefore we have to face the other side. When you go into a children's hospital, like that in Great Ormond Street, and see ward after ward of children suffering from disease which they have inherited from others, it is an

[1]*A Mission of the Spirit*, 100.

awful thing. You must remember that, if GOD allows this, on the other hand, He used that very fact of mutual interdependence that He might thereby save us; and we should therefore help one another. And, then, we have to remember that the whole Christian Church has, as a loving society, to walk shoulder to shoulder, and guard these little ones. These men must be punished, and our business is to make life a hell to them till they repent. I would harry some of these men and women out of London. And if the Christian Church rose to what was said to the men on Sunday afternoon, if they would bind themselves to destroy the works of the Devil, we should get rid of a great deal of mischief. We want more moral courage and co-operation in our Christian work in fighting evil.[1]

Others are:

How can I prevent myself from falling into utter indifference from time to time? In spite of myself, I am drawn away from Christ; something comes between Him and me, and prayer is so unreal.

If it is simply a cloud which has come to try your faith, then it has not come in between Christ and you at all. You must not mistake faith for feeling; it is a very common thing to do. When the sensible joy in religion seems to go, many imagine all is gone; it does not follow at all. You are not told that you will always have sensible joy in religion. Nothing can really come between you and Jesus Christ, except sin. Ask yourself—Is there something that I am doing, and will not give up? And if you know that something is wrong, and you will not give it up, then there *is* something between you and Jesus Christ. The whole object of the Mission is to remove that; but if that is not so, then do not mistake faith and feeling. There is nothing at this moment between you and Him, and if you follow on through the darkness, you too will come to the light.[2]

and:

I cannot feel as if God is a real Person.

That, my brother, or my sister, is why God became incarnate. The Incarnation is God's answer to the doubts of His children. Of course, we could not feel that God was a Person if there had been no Incarnation, and therefore, as Dr. Liddon says, "my Christianity safeguards my Theism". But now that God has come into the world in the Person of Jesus Christ, cannot you feel that God is a Person? "He that hath

[1] *A Mission of the Spirit*, 153.
[2] *ib.*, 30.

seen Me, hath seen the Father," Christ says. As I kneel down at my prayer-desk in the morning, I feel I am praying to someone like Jesus Christ—loving, gentle, drawing, winning. Surely, after the Incarnation, we can think of God as a Person.

A theologian to-day would prefer to say that "God is Personal", or that "there is Personality in God", on the ground that "a Person" suggests the limitations which restrict the life of a human person, but it may safely be concluded that the answer given met the questioners' actual needs.

In 1905 the Mission was to West London, and the centres were Holy Trinity, Sloane Street; St. Paul's, Onslow Square; Christ Church, Lancaster Gate; St. Peter's, Cranley Gardens; Kensington Parish Church; St. Peter's, Eaton Square. In Holy Week he preached at St. Paul's, Knightsbridge; St. Andrew's, West Kensington, and on Good Friday at Holy Trinity, Brompton, but the Services of that week were not reckoned as strictly part of the Mission. He felt what he called the "temerity" of undertaking such a Mission, but he also felt that powerful influences were at work making the West End a greater wilderness of unbelief than even the East End, with results far more widespread and disastrous. When the time came, the Churches were crowded to the doors, and many could not gain admittance. An eye-witness has recorded that at Holy Trinity, Sloane Street great numbers of men were standing in the gangways, when the Bishop went into the pulpit. There was a titter when he announced the text, "Make the men sit down". It was in point of fact impossible. There were no seats, and scores of men stood all through the service. Such a thing had not been seen in London since Liddon's time.

Later, at the end of Lent, the *Church Times* summed up the Mission in this way:

> The Bishop of London is nothing if not a shepherd of souls. It is a sad comment on the history of Christendom that the fact should be noteworthy. An equally striking comment, and one more hopeful, is the eagerness of men and women—in present circumstances, of the men more especially—to hear his gospel. He has not the gifts which go to make a popular orator. He has a fair amount of learning, and no more; he has a fair capacity for ready speech, and no more; no torrent of eloquence issues from his lips; he has no majestic presence, no

dominating charm of voice or manner; he condescends to no tricks of rhetoric or sensational displays. In the pulpit he is just a plain Christian man, of earnest thought and earnest delivery. There are many such who draw no crowds. But there is more behind. He is the Bishop; he is the pastor of souls in this vast city; he is conscious of it, so simply, obviously, and unashamedly conscious of it that he communicates the consciousness to others. Men know that their pastor is come to speak to them; he has a more than personal message, a more than personal authority. The effect is great.

He himself describes the result, preaching in Wakefield Cathedral at the Dedication of the Walsham How Memorial[1] in April, thus:

> As for the humble efforts they had been making among the West End Churches during the past few weeks, he could only say that the astonishing response had been a rebuke to his own weak faith. To quote the words of Canon Body, "There has not been such a Lent in London for twenty-five years."

The contents of the sermons were always a mixture of evidential argument, Prayer Book teaching and Evangelical appeal, with not a little reminiscence of pastoral work in East London. He would be saying at one moment that Professor Huxley had acknowledged to Canon Gore that there was a sense in which the mysteries of the Christian religion were child's play compared with the mysteries of science, or that the world could not have made itself, any more than millions of letters, thrown out of boxes, could form themselves into one of Shakespeare's Plays. In the next paragraph he would be pleading with his hearers to break the chain of sin which held them in its grip:

> There is an old story I often used to tell in Missions—in fact, I remember telling this story at the very time when the man of whom I shall speak to you was present, and the story is this: The devil gave a soul once the task of making a chain. The soul went on making this chain—a horrible chain of habit—year in, year out, month after month; and when he brought it there was always the same reply, "Take it away and make it longer—take it away and make it longer!" After receiving that answer six or seven times the chain was brought, supposed

---

[1] The connection was that Walsham How, before becoming Bishop of Wakefield, had been Bishop of Bedford, as the East London Suffragan was then called.

to be finished at last, and then he got his reward; "Take him and bind him hand and foot—bind him with his own chain, and cast him into outer darkness." I remember that a man—a respectable man, well dressed—sent for me after that Mission Service, and as I went into his dining-room he looked at me and said, "You had your eye on me all the time. This is my chain and you knew it"; and he put his hand on a decanter full of brandy on the table. He said, "You were speaking to me, I know, but thus I break my chain!" He dashed it down, bottle, brandy and all, on the floor. Now, it is possible—and quite as possible for the most respectable-looking man here as for the poorest—that a secret chain, either of drink or gambling, or both, has been gradually woven round some soul here for years. This is the afternoon on which that chain is going to be broken; or, if not, this is the afternoon on which God in Heaven has stretched out a hand which will enable that chain to be broken. If not broken to-day, probably it never will be.

Next he would be pointing out that the liturgical and sacramental worship of the Church was emancipating rather than limiting, that it gave a spiritual security which could not otherwise be obtained, and that Holy Communion was not a thing intended only for a few:

Do you really suppose, for instance, that the Holy Communion was given for a few select clergy and Sisters of Mercy? The first communicants were working people, and the great mass of working men and working women of to-day were meant reverently and earnestly as a regular thing to receive within themselves the fruits of Redemption, the means by which the living PERSON, in the closest, nearest way, comes within our souls. Do not despair of yourself. Yes, even if you have not come to church for years, you were meant to arrive at that, and to be prepared and to come to it. You cannot possibly divorce all those words about Christ dwelling in us from those other words, "He that eateth Me shall live by Me." Use all means of fostering and encouraging and giving scope to the life of CHRIST in you which the Church brings you and offers you in CHRIST's name.

A few minutes later he would be describing some death-bed scene:

I found Jane Crease and Dick Ede in the slums in the East End. Jane Crease had been in pain for something like fifteen or sixteen years, and she was left absolutely alone, except for a hard-working father and

I

mother, who did their best for her, but with no friends, and nothing to do all day, lying there in the little street in which she lived. I can remember my first visit, and how she welcomed me when I took on the parish work, as Rector of Bethnal Green. I raised up people to go down and bring hope to that poor girl. After about twelve months I remember going in—of course I had been in every week to see her; but on one particular visit, when some friends had been down to cheer her up, and read to her, I remember her waving her hand round to her photographs, and saying with a smile on her face, "It is a changed life to me, Mr. Ingram. You see I have all my friends here with me. My life is changed now, and I owe all these friends to you." Now the last five years of that little woman's life was a different thing, because she was surrounded by hopeful people who came with bright faces to tell her about this and that. We used to carry her into Bethnal Green Church for her Communions when she could not move; and by the Hope of the Church her life was changed. She died about five years afterwards, bright and happy to the last.

Dick Ede was long dying of consumption in that slow way which lasts for years. I took into him my young brothers from the Settlement at Oxford House. Many a young clergyman to-day has been educated by Dick Ede! Many a one has, at his first pastoral visit, learnt from that boy his patience and other lessons which he has never learnt elsewhere.

One of the best of them was the North London Mission of 1910. The centres were: All Saints', Harlesden; St. Andrew's, Willesden Green; Hornsey Parish Church; Tottenham Parish Church; Edmonton Parish Church; Enfield Parish Church; and on Good Friday evening the Paragon Theatre, Whitechapel, lent free of charge. The book, which also includes an Address to West End Ladies, given during that Lent on "The Weakness of West End Christianity", is called "The Mysteries of God". The original owner of the copy from which the extracts here given are copied has written in pencil at the beginning of the second sermon, which was given at All Souls', Harlesden, "My Church. I heard this". The text of the sermon is, "Sir, we would see Jesus". The preacher's first point was that the nearly four million non-Christian people or less than Christian people in the diocese of London will not see Jesus until "We", the Christian people, have seen Jesus ourselves. It is rather naïvely assumed that "Socialists" are hostile to the Christian Faith, and also, it would seem, that the Christians are to be found among the possessing class, but it is a plea for what the preacher calls "real Christian Socialism". Here is a part of it:

"I am quite certain of this, that the real cause of the bitter Socialism of the present day is that Christians—we who are in the minority, and have all the good things in trust—have been such faithless stewards of our trust. If there had been a real Christian Socialism, in the true sense, a real understanding by everyone who had intellect, or wealth, or leisure, that he had those things simply in trust for the others, we should never have had throughout Europe this bitter cry of the Socialist who would hew down everything. And that is absolutely true with regard to the Christian faith. Do you really suppose that you can attain real success by having in a few selected churches of West London crowded congregations and beautiful music, unless all the churches in this growing London, and all the churches in the slums of the East End, are also prosperous and successful? It is, I believe at the bottom of my soul, the want of faith and true Christianity among the Christians of London which is the bar to the conversion of the rest. Still only one in ten go anywhere, to church or chapel. Why? Because they cannot see Jesus, until those who are the professing Christians of London have seen Jesus much more clearly than they do. If we see Jesus, they will see Jesus."

A little later comes:

There is no monotony in the company with Jesus. His presence makes a romance of every day.

The reader here has pencilled in "I like that", and at the end of the sermon, which is:

If from now you make this glorious object your aim in life, and start on your real vocation at last, you will live in the sunshine, and when you are called to die, you will die in the sunshine of a happy faith.

there is the word "Beautiful". These simple tributes are only a specimen of what thousands were saying.

Many a preacher has longed to help his hearers to love God. Not all of them are so simply persuasive as this:

I want to try to help you to love GOD. How do we start when we want to love someone on earth? Why is it—if I may take someone who is lying very ill to-day, whom I greatly love and honour, the Bishop of Lincoln, why is it that everybody who knows him loves him? Suppose that I did not love him, and yet wanted to love him, should I sit down and say, "I must try to love him; I must make myself love him, I must lash myself up to love him," as we often do about GOD? No; I should first of all get to know him. Then I should notice all the different things in his character; I should look to see what he did, what he said, how he acted. And when I had been with him a long time, I should grow to know him and grow to love him, because of what he was, because of what he did. I can remember gradually getting to know him—looking back over the last twenty-five or thirty years— gradually getting to know that very great and honoured man. And that is exactly what it was. Everybody used to say to me: "Canon King"—as he then was—"how good and lovable and saintly he is!" Well, it was all nothing to me for a time. I did not know him. But then the time came when I was introduced to him, and attended his lectures as a young man, and then later I got to know him as an intimate friend. When he admitted me to his friendship, all those traits about him of which I had heard sank into my mind, and, without making myself love him, I did love him.[1]

or this:

How can you have Christ in you and be dishonest in your work? How can you have Christ in you and be harsh and unkind to your wife at home, never inquiring how the children are getting on with their Bible-lessons, or bringing them up in GOD's love and fear? How can you have Christ in you if you are caring nothing how the Church progresses down here? All that apathy, that harshness, that dishonesty, that besetting hidden sin, has got to be sold—to use the expressive phrase—got rid of, and then you can buy the treasure of the ages for nothing. Now, will you do it? I have a feeling that it is a very solemn thing to ask that question. Will you do it? I am making you the offer of the ages. Oh, my brother, my sister, as you love your children, as you love your wife, your family, as you hope to leave the world a little better than you found it, take your first step, and do not hesitate for a moment. If it is the right hand, cut it off, and cast it from thee; if it is the right eye, pluck it out, because you have offered you to-night the treasure of the world.[2]

[1] *Mysteries*, 87, 88.
[2] *ib.*, 41.

Or this at a Men's Service in Enfield Parish Church:

Will you then—that comes to be the question—share the triumph of the Cross to-day? It is not enough to believe in it, not enough to be convinced by the arguments I began with; it means a conscious, wholesale, and lifelong surrender to the Cross, if the Cross is to triumph for you and in you. Why not make it this afternoon? Give up this pagan life, give up this carelessness, this never coming to GOD's house; give up that sin that crucifies your SAVIOUR again, and be the clean, honourable, godly gentleman that you were born to be. You were never born to a life like that—half animal, half pagan; you were born to be men of GOD, to carry the Cross as your banner, to help to save the world. Why be contented with such a miserable existence compared to what you might have? Rise up to your true heritage to-day, and claim your right in the triumph of the Cross. The Cross is in the field, and under that banner you have got to win Enfield for GOD. And what a life it will be! the Cross triumphing more day by day; tempers subdued, bad ties removed; more and more influence over others—what a triumph of the Cross in you, after you have received absolution and pardon at its foot! "Lift up your heads, O ye gates: and be ye lift up, ye everlasting doors," and the ransomed sinner shall come in. Another soul saved for Enfield, and the trumpets will sound on the other side.[1]

It is difficult to believe that the readers of this book will not be touched and stirred by such a plea, though it reaches them only in cold print after forty years.

In the Preface the Bishop says:

I wish that the book could convey one-tenth of the earnestness and reality of those Mission services, the fervour and swing of the hymns, and especially the sight, every Sunday afternoon, of often more than a thousand men on their knees after the service, singing, "In the Cross, in the Cross, be my glory ever"; or, "O my Saviour, lifted on the Cross for me"; or "O for a heart to praise my GOD".

One of the leading clergy who was present, and who will forgive my recording this if I do not reveal his name, dashed the tears from his eyes one afternoon, and said, "Forgive me, Bishop; I am a Welshman!" Certainly it was often a sight touching even to tears, and one which might well fill with hope anyone who was despairing of the evangelisation of the men of London.

[1] *Mysteries*, 297.

Truly in those Missions he did "the work of an evangelist"; he made "full proof of his ministry". And it was an apostolic ministry. He was, says Mrs. Paget, "one of the rare evangelists produced by the Church of England." She goes so far as to say that "it has always seemed tragic that the Church lost her greatest evangelist by placing him in an administrative post too soon."

Nevertheless, the Church did not altogether lose her greatest evangelist. There were the Lent Missions, there were the innumerable heart to heart talks with individuals, and to the end of his life he was always glad to hear of a Mission in any of his parishes. He never failed to emphasize the necessity of careful preparation.

In his own later Missions the appeal is less compelling. Very few men, except perhaps some of those who devote themselves wholly to the work, can go on being Missioners all their lives. The later Missions drew large crowds of listeners, and did much good, but the books do not read so well. All the books are repetitive. The same stories and the same reminiscences recur many times. In the later books he seems to have found an increasing difficulty in thinking of fresh things to say, or fresh ways of saying the old things. That did not matter at the time. The hearers did not know it, and would not have minded if they had. The sermon was what they needed. There is a story, perhaps quite untrue, that a famous missioner of some generations ago, Canon Hay Aitken, preached at a Mission the sermons which had not only been preached before, but were printed in a book, and moreover some of the congregation actually had the book in their hands as they listened, and followed every word with great delight.[1] So the congregations at the Bishop's Missions were content. And in any case it remains a wonderful thing in the first place that the Bishop of London should feel the call to preach a succession of Lent Missions in all parts of his diocese, in the next place that he should do it with such eager and effective simplicity, and in the third place that he should continue to do it, effectively, if with reduced effect, for so many years. He was not an orator like Edmund Burke, Daniel O'Connell or Charles Spurgeon. He was not "a public speaker of extraordinary merit, who had at his command an unceasing flow of perfectly-modulated sentences",

---

[1] Hay Aitken was a man of intense faith, a great lover of souls, and there are other stories about him which suggest that with almost any method he would have made good.

like William Pitt (of whom the words quoted were used), or William Temple. But he had two gifts which not all orators possess. He utterly believed what he was saying. He believed nothing else. That was the creed that inspired every hour of his life. And in the second place he had the pastoral heart. He passionately desired to win souls for God. This gave him the power of an orator. It was said of his audiences by a shrewd observer, "They hang on his lips. They do really want to know what he will say next."

It is not to be supposed that all who listened and were moved by his words remained steadfast. A far greater evangelist, much nearer to the convert than a preacher can be to a thousand people at one service in a Church, once had to write, "Demas hath forsaken me, having loved this present world." And doubtless there were many who contrived to stifle their uncomfortable conscience and to forget their embryo conversion in a few weeks or in a few hours. Yet the Bishop's Lent Missions had the touch of greatness. They were creative in the lives of others. "So we preach, and so ye believed." As a Missioner, if it be remembered that he was a Bishop of the Church, and accordingly could not spend his whole life in roaming from place to place, he may be compared to John Wesley, or perhaps even to St. Francis. There are certain sermons of Wesley which are for Methodists the standard of doctrine. Ingram would have been startled and distressed to think of his sermons being adopted as a standard of anything, but it is a fact that, if anyone wants to know what Church of England piety and moral teaching is like, there it all is.

VIII

ORTHODOXY

INGRAM was an orthodox divine. He had, as we have seen, a period of dubiety at School and at Oxford and for a time after Oxford, but he faced it in a sensible and constructive way. In the end Christian faith took strong hold of him, and thereafter he never seems to have wavered. He rejoiced all his ordained life in a bright, untroubled serenity of belief. He said to Ordination Candidates at Fulham in October 1911, "After twenty-seven years, in spite of all my difficulties and shortcomings, I believe twenty times as strongly as I did twenty years ago." And he could have said at least as much in 1940. At the centre of it was an intense devotion to our Lord, together with a firm belief that He had founded a visible Church, of which the Church of England was a true part.

It is indeed the best way for orthodoxy to develop, from Christ to the Catholic Faith and the Catholic Church. An orthodoxy beginning at the other end, or arising from the cool reflection that the Catholic Church is not likely to have been mistaken all these years, or perhaps even that things generally are in the melting-pot and here at least is a coherent and edifying system, would be barren and unsaving. An orthodoxy, developing, as did that of Saul of Tarsus, from the conviction that Jesus is Risen and is the Saviour, to the full glory of the Pauline mystical, Christ-centred theology, is living and fruitful and regenerating. In point of fact, it seems not unlikely that the germ of St. Paul's doctrine of the Catholic Church as the Body of Christ came to him with the momentous words heard by him on the Damascus Road, "Saul, Saul, why persecutest thou *me*." Ingram's conversion, so far as the manner of it can be ascertained, grew out of faith in the Resurrection of our Lord, but it held all the promise of his churchmanship. It could perhaps be expressed in the Pauline words, "That I might know him and the power of his resurrection."

That Ingram's religion, when it came to maturity, was Christ-centred, is utterly certain. Bishop Eric Hamilton, one of his "boys", later ordained by him, and Vicar of a London parish, said of his first acquaintance with the Bishop, "I had never known anyone to whom our Lord was such a real Person." The Bishop was fond of quoting John Wesley:

> I saw an ocean of light and love flow over an ocean of darkness and death, and in that I saw the infinite love of God; and the day that the ocean of light and love flowed over the ocean of darkness and death, was Good Friday.[1]

A short statement of his faith is:

> I tell you frankly that I could not believe in God at all if I did not believe in Jesus Christ. As Dr. Liddon said, "My Christianity safeguards my Theism," by which he means that his belief in God depends upon his belief in Jesus Christ being the Son of God. And when we see the Son of God—and never forget that "the right faith is that we believe and confess that Jesus Christ the Son of God is God and Man"—when we see the Son of God Himself on the Cross, when He says "I thirst," "I thirst with this poor man left three days and nights on the battle-field," that is the answer to the problem of the suffering of the world.
>
> > His are the thousand sparkling rills,
> > That from a thousand fountains burst,
> > And fill with music all the hills;
> > And yet he says, "I thirst."
>
> If He were only a *man* dying on the Cross, well, it would be only another good man done to death. But it was God who suffered on the Cross, and He suffers with those brave men at the front.[2]

The Bishop in his preaching always felt that he was charged with the duty of defending as well as expounding the Christian Faith.

> The theory of evolution makes the Incarnation more probable than the old "Carpenter" theory of Creation did. The illustration of the impossibility of a box of letters throwing themselves into a play of Shakespeare, which I found made such a great impression on the crews of the battleships of the Grand Fleet, is all the more forcible if the atoms which constitute the world were gradually moulded into the

[1] *Addresses in Holy Week*, 57.
[2] *The Church in Time of War*, 167.

world as it is to-day. It is only the crazy who can imagine that the world, as we see it to-day, could be made by accident. There is as clearly the mark of the Mind in the play presented by Nature as in the plays presented by Shakespeare. God, then, on any shewing, took an immense amount of trouble with the world, and by whatever method the world was made, man is clearly the crown of Creation. What, then, is it likely that God would attempt to do next, after taking all this infinite and age-long trouble in producing man? Surely He would attempt to reveal Himself to man in some intelligible form. The sunrise, the sunset, the sky, the flowers, have no object unless there is someone to appreciate them, and hence the creation of man. Man himself has no object, from God's point of view, unless he can respond to God's love and appreciate His character, and be fit to be His companion through all eternity.

How could God make Himself known to man?

Now the moment one has realized that God would be sure to reveal Himself to mankind, the Incarnation becomes probable. How do we get to know anyone except personally? How can character be revealed except through a person? If, therefore, it was possible for revelation to come through a Person, this would clearly be the best and most efficacious means of revelation.

It was not so much to be noted that Someone appeared; it was the character of that Someone which did appear which was so important. This character has been subject to the scrutiny of men for two thousand years, and has well stood the scrutiny. The following are well-known quotations, but nothing can better them, as they come from such unexpected quarters. It was not some fervent Christian, but the sceptic, John Stuart Mill, who said to the young men of his day, "Live so that Jesus Christ would approve of your life." It was not a bishop or a Christian father, but Lecky, the author of the *History of Rationalism*, who wrote, "The record of those three short years has done more to regenerate mankind than all the disquisitions of philosophers and all the plans of statesmen." Jesus Christ, then, is a unique figure Who stands upon the plains of history to-day, dwarfing all the puny race of men which stands around Him. The greatest and the best who have lived since then have attributed to Him what grace of character or particular virtue they may seem to have possessed.

At the same time he always clothed his theology in practical dress. Thus in a sermon at St. Paul's, exactly in the manner of St. Paul himself in the great passage of Philippians ii, he uses the doctrine of the Incarnation as a motive for some moral duty. St. Paul had used it to teach the Philippians unity and humility. The Bishop used it to teach the spirit of service.

In order to get to the point of view from which we can see these things as they are, away from the Gospel-hardened state in which we find ourselves listening time after time to the most moving facts, yet utterly untouched by them, let us picture how these three scenes presented themselves to the watching, waiting band of angels who are, according to the literal translation of the passage in St. Peter, ever "straining" to look into the extraordinary mystery and glories of the Incarnation.

The first scene which illustrates the manner in which Christ came rises before us when we remember how our Lord Jesus Christ, after supper, laid aside His upper garments, took a towel and girded Himself and went round and washed the feet of His disciples. Now, you and I have heard that story so often that it seems to us to be almost a matter of course. But the angels, when they saw that marvellous Being, their supreme Captain, Lord of the Heavenly Host, at whose whisper their legions would spring to service, kneeling at the feet of Judas, and washing the traitor's feet, must have thought this the climax of the extraordinary drama which they were watching, and which alters, whenever it is accepted, the ideals of men. We are expected to descend to the lowliest service, to be ready to live in the background, unnoticed by anyone; nay, even to do what the world calls the dirtiest work in the cause of Christ. That is what Christian service means, and this thought of it has been stamped in some measure upon the conscience of man.

Then comes the second, hardly less striking, scene. A toil-worn, patient, hard-worked, weary figure moving up and down the valleys of Palestine, set upon one thing only—doing good. "He went about doing good." Other men might have comfortable homes, but the Son of man had nowhere to lay His head; other men might have leisure, but he had no leisure so much as to eat; other men might reasonably take some measure of rest, but the message ringing in His ears from morning to night was this, "Work while it is day; the night cometh when no man can work." And as He passed from village to village He gave new significance to the motto, "I am among you as one that serveth." People had been kind-hearted, doubtless, before; the human instincts of family love have always asserted themselves; but when it became the ideal of the slave of Christ that he should ask himself from morning to night, "How much good can I do before night-time, and how many people can I help in these hours? How much sympathy can I bring to those who mourn? How many in danger can I warn in time? How many who are going wrong can I bring back?"—this was a perfectly new revelation to the world. But even in this life of constant service the climax was not reached until black against the sky there stood at last the Cross, and those watching angels saw the Being they loved so well make that last surrender of Himself for men. Even to them it was a revelation of what service meant, a revelation of service so utter and devoted that it has been stamped for ever upon the consciences of mankind. It has given an almost terrible meaning to the motto, "I am among you as he that serveth." "This commandment I give unto you, that ye love one another, as I have loved you."[1]

Here is something a little more specifically theological, but still very simple:

You remember the plea of one of His disciples, "Shew us the Father and it sufficeth us." And he replied in words that are to my mind the most precious words in the New Testament, *"He that hath seen Me hath seen the Father."* Therefore the reason that I am a Christian is (i) because Jesus Christ declared that He was the Way, and (ii) because He has proved Himself to be the Way.

(i) First of all, He said, *"I am the Way,"* and that is what I have got to prove to you to-night, and it is very much more important than it appears at first sight. Why do I say that it is of vital importance that Jesus Christ said of Himself that He was the Way? In my young days I had my doubts, as I dare say some of you young men and women have your doubts, when you wake up from a child's faith, and ask yourselves, "Why do I believe this? Why do I believe that? Why do I believe these things that have been taught me by my parents and teachers?" I passed through a very long and painful time of doubt when I was a young man, and the book that helped me most was a book which I still believe to be one of the greatest books ever written, and that is Liddon's *Bampton Lectures*, and that book put this very clear question to me as a thinking young man, Did Jesus Christ speak the truth or not? What did He say about Himself? I studied the New Testament to see what He said about Himself, and I found that He declared, "I am the Light of the World"; "I am the Bread of Life"; "Come unto Me, all

[1] *Under the Dome*, 101-106.

ye that labour and are heavy laden, and I will give you rest"; and I said to myself, "I have got to choose; either the One who made these solemn declarations is a deceiver, or He is the eternal Son of God, He is the Word of God, He is the revelation of the Father. He is the One prepared from the foundation of the world to come down to us, and that is what St. John said. "In the beginning was the Word, and the Word was with God, and the Word was God, and the Word was made flesh, and dwelt among us."[1]

From time to time, when he judged that it was necessary, he would make a more careful and thorough declaration of his faith. One such was made at the London Diocesan Conference in 1904:

> There is one subject on which I wish to speak to you to-day at greater length than on any other, on which I think that it is time that some, at any rate, of the Bishops should speak out with greater clearness than has yet been done, although I have every reason to believe that they are all of one mind in the matter. I allude to the question of the Virgin Birth of our Lord. How pressing the question is may be illustrated by an extract from a correspondence with an able and honest man of thirty-five, who was ready to give up a lucrative profession to be ordained. He was a man of blameless character and exceptional powers, but when it came to his account of his views, this is what he writes; and if he sees the allusion in print he will know that I am quoting it with nothing but honour and respect for his honesty and straightforwardness, whatever I may think of the views themselves:
>
> (i) I do not believe in the Virgin Birth of our Lord as a piece of historical fact, and that sort of miracle seems to me unnecessary in the light of the much greater wonders that are occurring unceasingly.
>
> (ii) I do not believe in the Incarnation as a unique fact, but I do as a general fact; I believe that God is incarnate in all the universe.
>
> (iii) I do not regard Jesus as differing in kind from other great prophets and teachers.
>
> (iv) I do not think that the holding of any particular belief or faith has any bearing on the future welfare of individual souls.
>
> There is nothing specially remarkable in the views themselves; but what is remarkable is the belief with which he prefaces his answers: "My opinions do not differ materially from those held by many distinguished men now in Orders, but I might not conceal them so care-

[1] *Why I am a Christian,* 57.

fully as they mostly do"; and coupled with this his clear conviction that there was nothing the least inconsistent in his holding those views and taking Orders—for which he was prepared to make great sacrifices—in the Church of England.

Now, if this idea is at all widespread, it is time for someone in authority to say very clearly that this is not the Catholic faith of Christendom, but that the Incarnation, however consonant with the great truth of Divine Immanence, is an unique fact; that JESUS CHRIST does differ in kind from other great teachers and prophets; and that the Virgin Birth of our Lord is neither unhistorical in fact nor unnecessary as part of the Gospel for the salvation of the world.[1]

Preaching at the Ely Theological College Festival in the same year he referred to "the apparently unrebuked attacks on such sacred articles of the Faith":

It must pain many to be taught by ordained and responsible teachers of the faith that "it may well be the case that the idea of resurrection could lay hold on the popular mind only under the form of carnal resuscitation. . . ." And again, "The tradition of Christianity has certainly fastened on the more materialistic statements of the Scriptures, and woven them into literature and liturgy"; or when we come to the fully developed form of the argument in an explanatory essay to read, "Is the resurrection really inconceivable apart from the materialistic notions which current Judaism contributed to the earliest literature of the Christian Church? Is an honest belief in the Resurrection really inconsistent with a reverent agnosticism as to the historical circumstances out of which in the first instances that belief arose? Is the faith of the Church in a Divine Christ, living, present, active, really built upon an empty tomb?"

It is difficult to know what the writer really means; the plain interpretation of his words is that the body which was buried in the tomb remained there to perish by dissolution, wholly apart from the Risen Lord. If this be his meaning, then he plainly questions any resurrection of the Lord's body whatsoever, and sets aside such cherished and early accounts of the Resurrection as the words to St. Thomas, "Reach hither thy hand, and thrust it into My side" (St. John xx. 27); and again, passages like the following, "He shewed unto them His hands and His side; then were the disciples glad when they saw the Lord" (St. John xx. 20). "And the angel answered and said unto the women, Fear not ye, for I know that ye seek Jesus which was crucified; He is not

[1] *Faith of Church and Nation*, 3 f.

here; for He is risen, as He said. Come, see the place where the Lord lay" (St. Matt. xxviii. 5, 6). "Why seek ye the living among the dead? He is not here, but is risen" (St. Luke xxiv. 5, 6). "He stooping down, and looking in, saw the linen clothes lying, and the napkin that was about His head not lying with the linen clothes, but wrapped together in a place by itself" (St. John xx. 5, 7). It is clear that the view thus put forward contradicts the Resurrection-story in some of its most important particulars, and is definitely different from the faith in the Resurrection of Jesus Christ which has been held by the Church from the beginning.

The writer has assured me that he believes with all his soul in the Incarnation, and he can say in another passage, "Jesus Christ, who was crucified under Pontius Pilate, survived death in no impoverished ghostly state, but in the fulness of personal life, enfranchised from terrestrial limitation; and He made His presence known to His disciples by convincing evidences"; but we are surely entitled to ask what these convincing evidences were, other than those recorded; and therefore the idea that Christ's body perished in the grave must be repudiated by the Church, as I now repudiate it publicly, in this representative gathering from different dioceses of the Church, as Bishop of the diocese in which some at least of the statements quoted were made.

"The resurrection of the body!" says Bishop Creighton. "There was a time when science rather mocked at the possibility of it." That is changed now. I think, at least, I have heard the utterance of a great biologist, who said, 'If there is a Resurrection it must be a resurrection of the body. Body and spirit are so intimately connected that the one cannot be conceived as existing for ever in a perfect state without the other.'" And finally, on this point, have we priests of the Church of England any right, without any formal leave from our Church, on our own responsibility, to set aside the express declaration of our Fourth Article: "Christ did truly rise again from death, and took again His body with flesh, bones, and all things appertaining to the perfection of man's nature, wherewith He ascended into heaven, and there sitteth until He return to judge all men at the last day?" Whatever may be the inevitable difficulties of the Gospel story, the reality of our Lord's resurrection body and its continuity in a glorified state with His earthly body, "may be proved by most certain warrants of Holy Scripture," and are essentially involved in the faith of Christendom.

Does this justify "a spirit of fearfulness"? That some half-dozen priests at the most, in their—as I hold—mistaken efforts to make the faith easier to believe to themselves and others, or, as they no doubt

quite honestly believe, to get nearer to the truth, are belittling to-day
what the Church has always believed to be the historical accounts on
which that faith is founded, is that to fill with a spirit of fearfulness the
"one Catholic and Apostolic Church", which has survived heresy
after heresy, which, like some gallant ship after a voyage of thirteen
hundred years and more in this country alone, through apathy, through
unbelief, through apostasy, through persecution, has come to us with
its treasure safe, in Creed, in Sacraments, in unbroken Orders, and in
stately Liturgy? As well might an Atlantic liner fear the ripple in the
Channel, or the cross-currents in the Solent! No; it is needful to notice
these things as we pass, but, if the Diocese of London be any criterion
of the Church of England, of which it is a part, then the one unbroken
voice which welcomed a few weeks ago the repudiation of the attack
upon the Virgin Birth will welcome the restatement of the Creed of
Christendom that "Jesus Christ died, and was buried, and rose again
for us", and rose again in such a way that He could say, "Behold My
hands and My feet, that it is I Myself. Handle Me and see, for a spirit
hath not flesh and bones as ye see Me have" (St. Luke xxiv. 39).[1]

This was one of the causes of his immense popularity with the
clergy, but only of his own diocese, not of all. He "contended
earnestly for the faith once delivered to the saints".

A much shorter and more popular statement of the same ideas
occur in *Why I am a Christian*:

> Some of you may say, But does it matter whether I believe in the
> Virgin Birth, or not? Well, I should not think of excluding from the
> communion a *layman* who felt a difficulty in believing in the Virgin
> Birth, but the teachers of the Church must be true to the teaching of
> the Church and of the Creed. That "He was born of a pure virgin",
> has been the teaching of the Church from the beginning. You say it
> does not matter. But I think of the young people to-day who are
> fighting with their passions. Is it nothing to have a new manhood
> created? The great entail of sin was broken by the birth of a second
> Adam. There is nothing, I believe, which helps the young man or
> woman in the midst of their struggle with the passions of life more
> than the realization that they can stretch out their hands and lay hold
> of the power that is theirs in Christ, and which has been brought to
> them through the Virgin-born.

[1] *Faith of Church and Nation*, 14-22.

Thou didst leave Thy throne and Thy kingly crown
When Thou camest to earth for me;
But in Bethlehem's home there was found no room
For Thy holy Nativity.
O come to my heart, Lord Jesus;
There is room in my heart for Thee.

That is a beautiful prayer, and it goes right to the heart of the matter.

Into Biblical Criticism he did not go very far. He was never a "Verbal Inspirationist". To the people of Christ Church, Lancaster Gate, and also of St. Margaret's, Westminster, he said:

What are we doing, for instance, about the Old Testament controversy? Are we on the one hand snatching at the new discoveries, to throw over the whole book as a patchwork of legends and inaccuracies, glad to be at last rid of a thing which has puzzled us so long? Or, on the other hand, are we—which is equally bad—without taking the trouble to inquire into the truth ourselves, handing over to unjust clamour the students, some of whom are the most Christlike men on earth, who are trying in an earnest and devoted spirit to discover and tell us the truth?[1]

To ordinands at Leeds:

It is sometimes thought that by becoming Christian ministers we give up our love of Truth. Nothing could be more unfounded. The Christian minister who has not an intellectual delight in Christianity is not worthy of the name. The creeds, when accepted, merely put us on a plateau, as it were, where we can be personally fed with Truth by the Good Shepherd Himself. Every year that we see the Gospel in action, every book that we read about the faith, every time that we meditate upon the New Testament, nay, every study that we make in history, philosophy, astronomy, we get more and more food for our minds, and it comes from Christ Who is "the Truth".[2]

At another time:

I think I might call myself an Orthodox Modernist, for I try to study everything that has been written from a Modernist point of view, and

[1] *Men Who Crucify Christ*, 24.
[2] *Good Shepherds*, 32.

all that the best scholars can put before us about the Bible, and I am prepared to believe that our Lord acquiesced in the popular view of the Davidic authorship of the Psalms.[1]

Yet he was at times uneasy about the results of criticism. To the clergy at a Quiet Day he said:

I find, in going round the diocese, that a good many men have received harm from their reading. They have soaked themselves in critical literature. Several of them have said to me—I have had lately many private interviews and informal talks all round the diocese— "My reading has whittled down my faith. The joy has gone out of my work, the charm has gone, the power has gone." They have read so many books of a certain kind that they have lost their belief in the Incarnation. And if we lose our belief in the Incarnation, where are we? Therefore you should read Dr. Swete's book on this Last Discourse. Dr. Swete is one of the greatest scholars in Europe. In reading his books you hardly realize how great a scholar he is; they are so devotional, and so simple. You will be reassured by hearing one of the greatest scholars of the day assert that in this last discourse we are listening as literally as it is possible to do to the actual words of Jesus Christ. We can hear it in the beating of his pastoral heart. We are watching the pastoral heart of Christ disclosed to us in His last prayer.[2]

The last extract illustrates a characteristic readiness to jump at any "favourable" verdict of a critic. We all do it. We all quote the authorities which support us, and only in a book intended for students is it usual to quote extensively from opinions on the other side. But Ingram did it more than most. He read the books in which he was likely to find ammunition, and he had a *flair* for making the most useful quotations from them. It is easy to criticize this habit.

But what could be felt about him was that he was utterly sincere. Those really were the arguments which had satisfied his mind.

The two major utterances quoted above are from the earlier years of his London episcopate. Here is an illustration of his orthodox zeal in the middle period. In 1914 there was a war of books and pamphlets about clerical subscription. In 1911 a young Oxford don had published a minimizing book called *The Miracles of the New*

[1] *Good News from God*, 78.
[2] *Church in Time of War*, 75

Testament. In 1912 came *Foundations* and Canon Henson's *The Creed in the Pulpit*, both books of a definitely "Liberal" tendency. The Bishop of Zanzibar denounced Streeter for his essay in *Foundations*, and also the English Bishop to whom he was examining Chaplain. The Bishop of London was asked by a number of his clergy, mainly Anglo-Catholics, to invite Convocation:

> to repudiate the claim of some clergy to reject the miracles of Our Lord's birth of a Virgin and the actual resurrection of His body from the tomb, because we believe that these truths lie at the very centre of the faith, and that the statements of the Bible and the Creeds with regard to them are perfectly plain and unambiguous.

The story of what followed is told in Bishop Bell's Life of the Archbishop. The Bishop of London presented the Memorial of the clergy to Convocation in February and announced that he would move a Resolution at the next Group of Sessions. There was a storm of pamphlets. Those which remain most clearly in the mind of the present writer were the work of Gore, Bethune-Baker, and Sanday. There were also a great many largely-signed petitions, mostly, though not all, on the Conservative side. Bishop Gore drafted the Convocation resolution, and Ingram was to propose it. The Archbishop was convinced that it would never do as it stood. Other bishops were consulted. Chase of Ely advised that it seemed to probe too far into the inner regions of personal belief.

His advice was taken, and in the end Ingram moved as follows:

> Inasmuch as there is reason to believe that the minds of many Members of the Church of England are perplexed and disquieted at the present time in regard to certain questions of Faith and Church Order, the Bishops of the Upper House of the Province of Canterbury feel it to be their duty to put forth the following Resolutions:
>
> 1. We call attention to the Resolution which was passed in this House on May 10, 1905, as follows:
>   "That this House is resolved to maintain unimpaired the Catholic Faith in the Holy Trinity and the Incarnation, as contained in the Apostles' and Nicene Creeds, and in the *Quicunque Vult*, and regards the Faith there presented, both in statements of doctrine and in statements of fact, as the necessary basis on which the teaching of the Church reposes."

We further desire to direct attention afresh to the following Resolution, which was unanimously agreed to by the Bishops of the Anglican Communion attending the Lambeth Conference of 1908:

"This Conference, in view of tendencies widely shewn in the writings of the present day, hereby places on record its conviction that the historical facts stated in the Creeds are an essential part of the Faith of the Church."

2. These Resolutions we desire solemnly to re-affirm, and in accordance therewith to express our deliberate judgment that the denial of any of the historical facts stated in the Creeds goes beyond the limits of legitimate interpretation, and gravely imperils that sincerity of profession which is plainly incumbent on the ministers of the Word and Sacraments. At the same time, recognizing that our generation is called to face new problems raised by historical criticism, we are anxious not to lay unnecessary burdens upon consciences, nor unduly to limit freedom of thought and inquiry, whether among clergy or among laity. We desire, therefore, to lay stress on the need of considerateness in dealing with that which is tentative and provisional in the thought and work of earnest and reverent students.

The Archbishop, summing up the debate, which was on a high level, said that the Resolution had no intention of prescribing to students "conclusions beyond which you must not go":

I should agree that it would be a mockery to tell them to study, and then to arrest them in such a manner. I do not say anything of the kind. Rather I would say to every honest student of these matters, "Follow the truth; do your utmost to find it, and let it be your guide, whithersoever it may lead you."

He went on to emphasize the special and peculiar responsibility of the clergy as accredited teachers of the Faith:

When a child is brought to be baptized, the minister is called upon to ask the godparents clause by clause to go over the Creed, and to ask them whether they steadfastly believe it. For such ministering it is surely essential on his part that he should believe it himself and boldly stand by it. But even towards men who do hold that trust and responsibility, who are among the clergy and who are students of these subjects, we desire with earnestness beyond words to shew to them throughout their investigations and inquiries a considerateness, a respect, a patience, a hopefulness, and an encouragement to the utmost of our power. We are bound to do so on the ground of our fatherly relation to those whom we want to help and stimulate as fellow-students, and whose difficulties we are eager to smooth, and whose path we want to guide aright where we may. We value with them the love of truth, and the liberty of thought; we value the close friendship which links them and us. Some of us have our own ample personal experience of such difficulties, and therefore we should extend a sympathetic and considerate hand to them. To such men we are not inquisitorial. The Resolution does not say, "If you feel that at present you do not steadfastly believe this or that!" The man's present position may be anxious, unhappy, hesitating, and for that very reason temporary. What do we say to a man who distinctly maintains, "I recognize that the Faith of the Church of which I am a minister rests on a great basis of historic as well as doctrinal statement, and part of that historic statement I deny?" To him we deliberately say, "Hold; consider your position as an accredited spokesman claiming the Church's authority to teach."

The Resolution was carried *nem. con.* Gore wrote to the Archbishop on May 2nd, 1914:

> Thank you indeed for your very kind and satisfying letter. I have ventured to send it to London in confidence.

In this way the zeal of two bishops, the prudence of another and the many-sided wisdom of the Primate carried the Church of England through another crisis. It was so serious that at different times both the Archbishop and Bishop Gore were considering the possibility of resigning.[1]

To return to the general subject of the Bishop's orthodoxy, he constantly preached about the Atonement. One of the Chapters in *Why I am a Christian* is entitled "Why Jesus Christ had to die". A characteristic treatment of the great subject, about which he always said that all the books were unsatisfying because they all dealt with an event that is beyond human understanding, is to be found in *Good News from God*:

> When during my days of doubt I was nearly kept from being

[1] See *Life of Archbishop Davidson*, 41.

ordained, I was greatly helped by dear old Dr. Dale, the Nonconformist —and I do not think his book on the Atonement is at all out of date to-day. *He says that somebody had to keep the broken law of God, for nobody had kept it.* If there was no prosecution for crime in England, and a man was let off directly he said he was sorry, where would the standard of morality be? God had to keep up the moral standard of the world, and somebody had to keep the broken law of God; and the Son of God, to whom all judgment was given, came to do it. "Lo, I come to do Thy will, O God." He perfectly fulfilled it by His life, but in fulfilling it, because He came up against the cupidity of Caiaphas, the worldliness of Herod, the treachery of Judas, He went down before it. It meant death for Him, but it is because we are bone of His bone, and flesh of His flesh, that we can plead His sacrifice; and, therefore, it is not a morally degrading thing to say in the words of the hymn I have already quoted.

> "For, lo, between our sins and their reward
> We set the passion of Thy Son, our Lord."[1]

A Sermon delivered in St. Paul's at the end of the North London Mission shews how he was accustomed to think and speak of the Resurrection of our Lord. Among his points are:

Now it is quite clear that this Good News, if it comes at all, comes on Easter Day; but a great deal hinges upon what happened on Easter Day, and it is in order that I might guide you rightly as to what happened on Easter Day that I have been examining very carefully the last few days all the accounts again, and weighing to the best of my power, the arguments in Frank Morison's new book, *Who moved the Stone?* and Mr. Dobson's book on *The Empty Tomb and the Risen Lord.*

To go straight, then, to the point. I am more and more convinced that the Empty Tomb, *so far from being a legend, contains the heart and soul of the whole revelation.* ...

But it may be said: *Does it make so great a difference whether the tomb was empty or not?* To my mind it makes *all* the difference.

The fact that the Ressurection, and other events in the Gospel-Story, are "miraculous" presented no difficulty. He rejoiced in the miracles. He knew of course that Paley's old argument had been reversed, and that Christians do not now believe the Gospel because of the miracles, but believe the miracles because of the Gospel. And

---

[1] *Good News from God,* 79.

on this ground, viewing the miracles as the natural fruits of the supernatural Gospel, he rejoiced in them. Preaching in a London Church in 1904, he said:

I want to-night, so far as I can, to fortify those who have to fight the battle by at least one message that will help them, and I have selected this particular miracle because it is narrated no less than four times in Holy Scripture. If the attack, which from so many quarters tries to sweep the faith from under our feet, does away with the miracle of the feeding of the five thousand—the only miracle recorded in all four Gospels—what other miracle could be considered safe from a similar attack? So I ask you, first of all, Did this thing happen? Dr. Liddon pointed out long ago that we shall all of us cease to pray if once our faith is undermined in the Being to whom we pray; we shall soon cease to practise prayer for its subjective influence upon ourselves if once we lose faith in the supreme loving Being who hears our prayers. Therefore, before I seek to point out what seem to me the deep, the certain, the most comforting lessons which spring from the story, I face with you this question, my people: Did it happen?

I believe it first because it is told me by truthful, plain, unimaginative men.

Then, again, I believe it because I find myself now in a world of miracles. I see that you still have up round your church the decorations for the harvest festival, still the loaves and the flowers. Do not those remind us of what a world of miracles we live in? It is a very dull man or a very uninstructed man who imagines that he understands the world in which he lives. The appearance of life was the greatest miracle that ever took place. There must have been a point in the history of the world at which there was no such thing as organic life, and there never was such a break in the uniformity of nature as when that life appeared. After all these thousands of years no one knows what life is. No one can define the difference which stands between the living people who sit in the church at a funeral and the dead body carried in. They know that there is the difference that one is alive and the other has no life, but no one can define it. I opened a medical book the other day in a hospital, and the first words that I read were these, "Sleep is as great a mystery as ever." You see the golden stalk of corn, and you know that it was a little seed; but how the one became the other no one can possibly explain. Therefore, the second reason that makes the mirac- ulous believable to you and to me is that we live in a world of miracles, in a world of wonders; and it does not surprise me at all that One who could bring in (and we will see in a moment why He could) a law higher than the laws that I see working to-day would do so if He saw occasion when face to face with a hungry crowd.

In this insistence on the miraculous nature of Christianity, and of acceptance of the miracles as an essential part of the fabric of Christian faith, he made great use of Cairns' *A Faith that Rebels*. It was an instance of his quickness to seize upon any work of scholarship which was of use to him. So in former days he had quoted Sir William Ramsay on St. Luke and the Acts. In one of his last books *The Secrets of Fortitude* (1941) he quoted from one of the Sign Post series, and said:

> It is a very striking thing that these young men who write the "Sign Posts" have all come round to the old orthodox presentation of the Catholic religion, which some of us older men have had to uphold for years against a too liberal theology. They all believe in the Virgin Birth of our Lord and His actual Resurrection from the dead.

The series is one upon which academic theologians of the 'older school look with an occasionally doubtful eye, as taking rather too much for granted, but it was eagerly read by many of the younger clergy. And it was grist to the Bishop's mill.

Sometimes he was led astray by his enthusiasm. He publicly commended a rather flamboyant book *When it was Dark*, because it depicted the terrible results of some fraudulently-engineered discovery that the Resurrection of our Lord was fictitious. The results were that the morality of the world crumpled up. The publishers were not slow to take advantage of his praise, and later editions of the book had a quotation on the outside cover. The Bishop was not daunted. In a charge to Ordination-candidates in 1904, he said, "Now, although, of course, as in all books of that sort, the effect is highly coloured, yet I hold that the story contains a great truth."[1]

Constantly, in popular articles contributed to the *Sunday Graphic* (in 1935) or in some other paper,[2] he would say that the Gospel miracles are illustrations of a higher law. Writing at a time when

[1] *Faith of Church and Nation*, 108.
[2] Among them were "God and the Poor", "God in Society", "God and the Business Man", "God and Miracles", "God and the Sinner", "Can we trust the Bible?"

all England was following the progress of a Test Match in Australia, he would picture the ball swiftly approaching the boundary, or falling towards the ground. Suddenly, an arm shoots out and a sure hand grasps the ball. Its natural course has been arrested by the act of man. So in our Lord's miracles the natural progress of a dying child towards death is arrested by the Hand—at once natural and supernatural—of the Lord of Life.

To a certain extent, He "rationalized" the miracles, not always very successfully. He did this, not in the old way of Strauss or Paulus, but by bringing them into line with other accepted events. Thus, the Feeding of the Five Thousand was miraculous. But so is the Harvest. He wrote in the *Sunday Graphic* on March 3rd, 1935:

> Despite the fact that every day provision in some mysterious way is made for the needs of people here on earth, there remains grave doubt concerning the miracle of the loaves and fishes. The real miracle is that 115,000,000 people are fed every day by sowing a few grains of wheat.
> The multitude was fed because Jesus understood the divine laws governing supply and demand. We call that definitely a miracle, but are there not examples all about us of needs being met to-day in equally remarkable ways.

This is not very convincing. But in the main he took his stand on the sure ground that if our Lord was the Incarnate Son of God, His presence in the life of earth may be expected to be attended by phenomena which do not occur at other times. In this he was more up to date than perhaps he knew. There is no sign that he was familiar with what is called Barthianism, or with that form of it which has come through to English readers in such a book as Hoskyns and Davey, *The Riddle of the New Testament.* Yet Karl Barth has called the attention of Europe to the fact that the original Christianity was not, as nineteenth-century "Liberals" supposed, a mild system of ethics, upon which dogmatic additions have been super-imposed by St. Paul, and the Evangelists, or some of them. The Figure of our Lord, as now seen by historians, is tremendous, prophecy-fulfilling, Messianic, Apocalyptic, supernatural.[1] The picture is not particularly congenial to our tired, prosaic, comfort-

---

[1] In order that I may not incur the reproach of mentioning only those authorities to which I am most inclined to defer, I will add, although this book is not intended for students of theology, that some of the exponents of what is called "Form-Criticism" take a different view.

loving age, but there it is. It is the New Testament picture, and Barth rejoices in its "otherness". Those who would still have us pick out the startling, overwhelming parts of the story and throw them away, are throwing away the Gospel, and are a century behind the times. Dr. E. W. Barnes' *The Rise of Christianity* is a credulous and old-fashioned book.

It does not seem necessary to quote largely from his teaching on the doctrine of the Holy Spirit. It was abundant, but not distinctive. His frequent appeals to congregations to yield themselves to the power of the Spirit, the fact that one of his Lent Missions was "A Mission of the Spirit", and that his favourite maxim was, "Take one day at a time and trust the Holy Spirit to see you through"—are evidence of his scriptural and evangelical belief in the presence and power of the Divine Paraclete. The Cambridge (and Oxford) sermon quoted at the end of chapter four contains a carefully reasoned application of the doctrine to the conditions of undergraduate life at the University.

This gave him his churchmanship. It was his belief in Christ, and his, not equally personal—that could hardly be—but warm, living and indeed intense belief in the presence and work of the Holy Spirit that made him a great Churchman. Whereas to-day the question, "Did Christ found the Church?" is generally answered by saying, "No, because He took over the old Israel of God, and recreated it," he answered simply "Yes." He was fond of referring to Scott Holland's great sermon on the Rock of the Church, in which he had shewn, with convincing eloquence, that a secure edifice could not be built on the shifting sands of popularity, but only on the firm faith of the pledged, believing company. It seemed to him quite incontestable—as indeed it is—that our Lord surrounded Himself deliberately with a company of believers, in the first instance, twelve men, and that His desire was that this company should grow and develop. To this end He devoted much time, as is shewn in Latham's *Pastor pastorum*, another book that Ingram was fond of quoting, to the training of the chosen instruments. He often used a figure, which is part of the conception of the Church as the Body of Christ, the reminder that we are the Body, we are the members, we are all the hands, or other visible organs that the Ascended Lord now has, and if we do not carry on His work, it will not be carried on.[1] Another illustration which he often used was that the Church is like the Gulf Stream, which goes through the cold ocean and produces fertility wherever it goes.

He took for granted the continuity of the English Church. He was the hundred and eighth Bishop of London, and the Bishops of London had always lived at Fulham. In 1904 there was a great commemoration at St. Paul's of the 1,300 years of diocesan life. It was announced as a "Service in commemoration of the consecration of Mellitus as Bishop of London by St. Augustine and in thanksgiving to Almighty God for His mercies to the Church in London during 1,300 years." The Service was stately, the Litany in Procession, and then Evensong and a *Te Deum*. The preacher was the Bishop of London.

The Service was a striking illustration of the continuity of the English Church, about which the Bishop never had any doubt. Of the Reformation he would say—varying in his homely way the seventeenth century Bishop Bramhall's well-known metaphor of the weeded garden or the pruned vine, "a man is the same man still, even if he has washed his face".

Somebody once asked him, "Bishop, are you happy in the Church of England?" It was a wholly unnecessary question. To begin with, he was always happy. But of the Church of England he would have said with Sir Thomas Browne that:

"there is no Church whose every part so squares unto my conscience, whose articles, constitutions and customs, seem so consonant unto reason, and, as it were, framed to my particular devotion, as this whereof I hope of belief—the Church of England, to whose faith I am a sworn subject."

A Canon in the north of England will perhaps remember the appreciative chuckle with which he heard for the first time as a Cambridge undergraduate in 1908 a favourite saying of the Bishop, "Why am I not a Dissenter? Because I don't dissent."

His view of the Church of England is set out clearly in a sermon given at Hendon Parish Church in 1930. These were his points:

[1] He says that he heard this first in a speech by the Reverend W. E. S. Holland at the Guildhall.

(i) The Church of England respects human reason.

(ii) It holds quite firmly to the historic Catholic Faith of Christendom.

(iii) There is no branch of the Christian Church which so loves the Bible as the Church of England. Dr. Liddon used to say that the Church of England had two letters from heaven read in the morning and two letters from Heaven read in the evening.

(iv) "I love the Church of England because she is comprehensive in a true sense. Three distinct schools of thought find a place within the fold of the Church of England. We have the Anglo-Catholic, we have the Evangelical, and we have the Orthodox Modernist. We have the Anglo-Catholics. How much we owe to the Oxford Movement, for bringing back to our Church order and discipline and rightful ceremonial, and the constant use of the Sacraments! We have only to compare the Church of England to-day with that of a hundred years ago to see how much we owe to the Oxford Movement. Then we owe a great deal also to the Evangelicals. They have always kept us keen about Missions; they have always kept the Missionary spirit well to the fore. We owe a great deal also to the Orthodox Modernists. You cannot read the latest Commentary on the Bible without realizing how much we owe to them; as you know, Bishop Gore and Canon Goudge, two of the strongest Anglo-Catholics in the Church to-day, are the joint Editors of that Commentary, and so you may be quite certain that there is nothing which undermines the Christian's Faith in a Commentary for which they are responsible. It is a great thing to know that we have been able to bring the light of modern knowledge and modern criticism to bear on the Bible without affecting its great message. It is a great thing when a Church can hold within its bosom such men as Prebendary Hinde, Prebendary Mackay, and the Dean of St. Paul's—and yet to be able to learn something from them all. Naturally, we who hold strong Church principles hope that they will prevail. There is, I know, a small party that is almost over the edge towards Rome, and there is another section which could almost be described as Nonconformist, but when you get to the main stream you find comprised within this one Church those three great parties.[1]

He was fond of quoting Bishop Lightfoot's famous saying, which he heard himself as a young man at a Church Congress Sermon:

[1] *Good News from God*, 45-7.

> Under a Church which holds the historic orders in one hand and the open Bible in the other, Christendom will one day be reunited.

Of this it may fairly be observed that the word "under" since the Lambeth Appeal of 1920 has become out of date. For the rest it stands.

Of sin, his faith and his wholesome, blameless life gave him an intense horror. He was familiar from his East London days with many forms of wickedness, and he often spoke with great plainness to West London audiences. He could be sympathetic with struggling individuals. It is probable that he was never stern with anyone, perhaps often not hard enough. His principle was that ascribed by Hosea to the Lord, "to draw them with cords of love, with the bands of a man". Yet he hated sin. He repudiated it with the instinctive repulsion of the saint. He often advised confession in his sermons as a thing which was available and could be used. He heard many confessions and he practised confession for himself. He was one of those who welcome and understand the emphasis of the Book of Common Prayer on penitence. His teaching on sin, as on everything else, had an Evangelical root. He looked forward to the time when he would meet his Master face to face and account for the way in which he had used a redeemed life.

He was never tired of preaching about prayer. He would often quote Trench's famous sonnet:

> Lord, what a change within us one short hour . . .

He would begin a sermon like this:

> We are born to pray. We are *praying animals*. As the fin of a fish demands the water and the wing of the bird demands the air, so the instinct of Prayer demands God. People who do not pray get restless and unhappy. They get what Canon Newbolt called "THE INSOMNIA OF PRAYERLESSNESS". They are not fulfilling an elementary law of their being. Perhaps some of my readers feel like that. Do let them ask themselves, "Is it because I have given up my prayers?"
>
> But secondly, it is not only because it is natural to pray, but it is because *we are told to pray* by the Highest Authority in the world.[1]

Or like this:

[1] *Secrets of Fortitude*, 16.

Why then pray? Because prayer is the access to this friendly unseen world, it is bringing down unseen forces; it is invoking the unseen wind to move the seen leaf; it is living in the eternal which can never pass away. *"Heaven and earth shall pass away, but My words shall not pass away."*

Is it not worth while then to enter together the unseen world, the only real one, and call down all the love and power waiting there to descend upon our country in its difficulties, on our Church, on those we love, and on ourselves? For while all that we see passes away, God is eternal and Heaven is eternal.

There is behind this shifting pageant which we all know as life, One Eternal Governor and Ruler of the World, Who is so deeply interested in human life that "not a sparrow falls to the ground without His noting", and by whom we are assured "the very hairs of our head are all numbered".

Then he would go on to speak of the power of intercession:

There is a kingly, priestly power put into the hand of every Christian —that every baptized and, still more, every confirmed Christian, is the Lord's remembrancer. It is a kingly power, because it gives us the right of saying like a king, "I will." When any young man, nay, any child, kneels down and simply and earnestly prays for another, that prayer is countersigned by Jesus Christ and swept into His intercession, and avails with God. On the other hand the power is priestly, because it means this—that just as Abraham pleaded for Sodom, just as Moses pleaded for God's people in the battle, just as Aaron ran in between the living and the dead, so—O awful yet glorious power!—we may plead for the guilty: so we may help to decide the battle: so we may run in between the living and the dead. That is the first thing which comes out as certain.[1]

There is a necessity for times of prayer:

We who live in crowds, we must make a solitude if we do not find one; we must get up into our watch-tower, and be alone with God; no fellow-curates, no number of workers, no pressure of engagements can take away our responsibility—one by one—to God, for our individual work; we each have our little bit of the wall to watch, and not all the busy rushing to and fro in the world will atone for our bit of the wall being neglected.[2]

[1] *Banners*, 86.
[2] *Messengers, Watchmen and Stewards*, 33.

And there is a sense in which we must "prayer without ceasing".

Does it not come out perfectly clear that just as the atmosphere which surrounds the earth in which we live stops the friction of it, and makes life possible, and catches the meteors as they fall upon the earth and burns them out into thin dust, so every single one of us, from the cradle to the grave, has to surround the soul with an atmosphere of prayer. That is the sense in which we are to pray without ceasing—Prayer is to be an atmosphere of the soul, an attitude of the man, a position of the whole man, that we are never to do anything in life without asking, "Is this God's will?"—never to do any work or spend a single day without living in that atmosphere of prayer, and having the sense of the covering presence of God. And if we do this we carry out the Apostle's command, "Pray without ceasing." Go back, then, my brothers and sisters, go back into the battle of life from which you have come for your Sunday rest, go back determined to be men and women, boys and girls, of prayer. So, whatever happens—trouble, worry, or disappointment—you shall have the peace of God which passes all understanding, and whether your lives are great or humble, those lives will not be lived in vain.[1]

And, once more, of the extreme difficulty of recovery after years of prayerlessness:

You find it very difficult work, my friends, do you not? and perhaps you are inclined to give it up in despair. You say, "It is so hard to pray again; I cannot remember the words; I cannot remember what to say." What it is like is this: it is exactly like recovering a man from drowning. You put him down on the ground, you imitate the signs of life, you expand the lungs, and as you imitate the signs of life, if there is life in him, the life comes back and you say with relief after your anxiety, "Behold, he liveth!" So exactly is it in trying to recover men from prayerlessness, for yourself or anyone else; you are working back to nature, just as you are working back to nature with a drowning man. But it is painful for that drowning man to come back; it is with effort, almost with sobbing, he comes back to life. So do not be discouraged, my brother; though you find it hard work, you are working towards nature, you are coming back to life; and if you persevere, if you bend those stiff knees again, and make those dry lips utter a word of honest prayer, the angels will cry with joy and relief, "Behold he prayeth!"[2]

[1]*Banners*, 74-5.
[2]*ib.*, 66-7.

And behind this, was his own prayer-desk, under the top of which were stacked masses of letters, from friends for whom he prayed morning by morning. He believed that the sight of their hand-writing helped him to enter into their need and to bring them before God. Of the power of intercession he never had the smallest doubt.

His was a very simple faith. Some of the more learned, and thoughtful among his hearers often longed to say, "But, Bishop, it isn't really so simple as all that." But they never did, and it would not have been any good if they had. He was using the arguments by which he had himself been convinced.

It is probable enough that the faith came first, and the arguments, or most of them, came later. That this is far from being illegitimate is urged with great force by Bishop Gore in the Prefaces to *Belief in God* and *The Holy Spirit and the Church*. Ingram was a long way behind Bishop Gore in intellectual power and theological and other learning, but in his own way he followed the same course. He was a believer because there had been given to him the Gift of Faith, and he had cherished it, and it had developed, as its does. "Lord, thou deliveredst unto me five talents; lo, I have gained other five talents." The arguments which confirmed his faith were simple, but he was addressing the common man, and for the common man it was all right. Lady Blennerhasset, a politically Liberal but theologically orthodox Roman Catholic, said once about Father Tyrrell, "I know he must be wrong, because my washerwoman could never understand him, and I must have the same religion as my washerwoman." It does not follow that Tyrrell was wrong. Still less does it follow that Gore was wrong. Or, for that matter, St. Athanasius. But there must be somebody who speaks to the washerwoman in something like her own language. And for the washerwoman, or perhaps still more for the clerk at Golders Green, for the workman in Stepney, for the undergraduate, for the public school boy, Ingram was the man.

He said once to the Physicians and Surgeons on St. Luke's Day at St. Paul's:

> Do you make enough allowance for our practical difficulties in teaching? You go into some country Church, and you hear some simple explanation of the Gospel of the day addressed to the simple village folk who may be present; it touches none of your difficulties,

and you make up your mind that the parson of the place is a man be-hind the times, who could not possibly help you in your own difficulties, whereas, if you gave him your confidence, you would often find that he would only too gladly give you by yourself strong meat for men, although, well educated and intellectually keen as he was, he had perforce to give in church milk for babes.[1]

"All things to all men" is a difficult and even dangerous ideal. But "plain things to plain men" is a good working principle.

[1] *Under the Dome*, 213.

161   L

IX

ADMINISTRATION

BISHOPS have different gifts and different methods. Samuel Wilberforce in the nineteenth century had been so ubiquitous, so versatile, so efficient, that he revolutionized the whole idea of a Bishop's life and work. It was commonly said that he "remodelled the episcopate". One of his brother-bishops wrote to him, "You have introduced such a system into the episcopate that one has time for nothing." Not all had his ability, but his example was infectious. Gone were the spacious days in which an eighteenth-century Bishop of Lichfield and Coventry was pleased at his elevation to the Bench because he would now have time to arrange his library and correspond with his friends.[1] Gone too were the days in which a distinguished Member of Parliament, commenting on the pleasantries of some witty prelate, said that, if he were paid what a Bishop gets for doing what a Bishop does, he would find sufficient cause for merriment in the credulity of his fellow-countrymen.

Nevertheless, not all Bishops conformed exactly to the Wilberforce pattern. There were the scholar-bishops, like Lightfoot, who somehow contrived to pursue their studies. Good Bishop Edward King of Lincoln, as Scott Holland put it, "did not attempt organization, beyond the actual diocesan necessities." He was content to spend day after day travelling by slow trains up and down his huge diocese, happy if he could confirm a few of his beloved ploughboys in a village at the end of it.

Ingram, a loving disciple of Edward King, inherited from him, amid the different conditions of London life, a truly pastoral conception of his office. Yet King had been driven at the end of his life to throw himself into a scheme for Church Extension at Grimsby. Ingram, throughout his episcopate, was driven by necessity to organize. But it was not his forte. The *Church Times* said in a leading article on May 8th, 1946:

[1] I owe this to Prebendary Boggis' interesting book of reminiscences, *I Remember*.

162

Lack of administrative firmness was, it is true a weakness in a greatly beloved bishop. Dr. Winnington-Ingram was also often over-worked, and in consequence the quality of his preaching suffered. But these were disabilities which men and women in their tens of thousands were thankful to overlook because London had a bishop who cared personally for them.

Would it be untrue to say that, except for a few rare souls, who are both clever at affairs and also able clearly to discern the pastoral and evangelistic significance of Church Finance, administration is seldom the forte of the best pastors? There are some who can combine the Way of Martha and the Way of Mary. But not very many. Ingram was not a Mary who tried to add the work of Martha to his own. He gave what time he could to sitting at the Master's feet and spent the remainder of his strength in "much serving". But he was never "cumbered" with it. He was "careful" but never "troubled". If he be compared with the Twelve, of whom he was one of the successors, he had in him much of Peter, and much also of Andrew.

He gave himself to the task which fell upon him, of administering his great diocese of 620 parishes. And one of the things he brought to it was an immense power of work. He had always been methodical at Lichfield; he had always cleared his table before he went to bed.[1] At Oxford House interviews had been timed almost to a minute. At Amen Court the double duty entailed even more careful planning of the time. Later, he took good holidays, during which he found time to read a number of books and to write a great many short and very illegible letters, but at Fulham he wasted no time. A few hours each week were spent in exercise, which he regarded as a necessity, and all the remainder of the time he was hard at work. One of his later Chaplains describes the organization of the work and life at Fulham as "a masterpiece of method" which made on him "a never forgotten impression". Even when, in 1933, the Bishop had been dangerously ill—he just missed having double pneumonia—and was still so weak that the doctors forbade letters and "work", he rejoiced in the opportunity of reading, and planned his day accordingly. "In the morning a good solid book of Doctrine

[1] Into my own humble admiration for the far-off excellence of this achievement, there creeps a doubtless unworthy suspicion that the result is sometimes attained by sweeping everything off the table into a drawer.

to feed my mind, in the afternoon *Liturgy and Worship* to send me to sleep." It was just published, and "he read it all," says the Chaplain, "but found it a bit heavy, and with his unquenchable cheerfulness rejoiced in the soporific qualities." (There is surely an almost Franciscan touch about this.) "After tea light reading to wake me up, and then before lights out a devotional book to close the day."[1]

Sometimes, as he went out on to the tennis-court, he would chuckle and say, "But we do a spot of work sometimes." Every now and then, says a Chaplain:

> when the pressure was at its worst, the car waiting to take him to some important engagement, a room full of people waiting to see him individually, and the telephone-bell ringing interminably with urgent messages, he was quite unmoved. He just smiled and said, "Oh, this is nothing; it's an idle life here at Fulham."

If some imperative sick-call had robbed him of the time he had intended to give to prepare some speech or sermon, he never resented it. He hardly even regretted it. He made the best of it. As schoolboys put it, he would "go on unseen". More accurately, it might be said that he recalled the substance of some old address, and used it. Yet there was more in it than that. Of him it might be said, as was once said of Bishop Wilkinson when, a sick man, he had to drag himself to a Confirmation, that "he threw himself on the authority of his office". The way in which Ingram put it was, "Trust the Holy Spirit to see you through." Or, "If I use all the time I have, I must have faith in God for the rest."

He trusted his assistants, but expected everything to be done right. A Chaplain would not dare to leave a job half-done, and he was, as one records, very wide-awake, though good-tempered if anything went wrong, and constantly willing to take the mistakes of others on his own shoulders. There was a time when one of his Suffragans inadvertently and through a misunderstanding might have got himself and the diocese into a difficulty. "With unruffled calm and little but a smile for rebuke the Bishop cleared up the mistake and all was well, and forgotten, so that mutual trust was

[1] He always had one such at hand. A favourite book was Father Congreve's *The Spiritual Order*. When wanting it, he would say to the Chaplain, in the words that Cyprian used when asking for a volume of Tertullian, *Da magistrum.*

never shaken. There was no reaction of worry or of irritation, though the matter was troublesome and even anxious at the time."

The work was all on familiar and (the word is used without intention of disparagement) conventional lines. Keep the parishes going, more clergy, more ordinands, more confirmation-candidates, more communicants, better subscription-lists, more churches, schools and halls, and keep everybody happy. He never had time —and indeed he was not the man—to sit down and think out new ways of presenting the everlasting Gospel to the changing generations. He always put the Gospel in the same old way, and saw before him the same old people. He never quite realized that East London was no longer the shabby, cheerful, uneducated place which he had known in his Oxford House Days. With some priests who believed that there had come about a radical change in the outlook of the East Londoner, and that new and more political methods, or at any rate more politically-conscious methods, of applying the Gospel were essential, he was in imperfect sympathy. Personally most friendly, as always, he would say, "I knew East London, my boy, before you were born." True, but was it still the old East London? And those priests, whether they were wise or foolish, who wanted to go into the political movement and attempt to convert it from within, were not encouraged. It is possible that he was right, but it is certain that he reached his conclusion on old evidence. Apart from politics, he did not allow enough for the movement of history. The incorporation, for example, of Queen Mary College, formerly the East London College, into the University of London as a constituent College would have seemed to Samuel Barnett a sort of crown to all his work. The Bishop would visit the College, if invited, bear his witness and make a cheery speech, and give them a pat on the back, but he would not appreciate to the full the importance of what had been done.

Another matter in which he had not moved with the times was Women's Work. There had been women at work in Bethnal Green, whose services he had greatly valued, but of late years an immense amount of organization has been done by Diocesan Boards of Women's Work. In early days it was almost all done by amateurs, and it was sometimes even supposed by them that "Church Work" consisted of distributing half-crowns. Further, no one seemed to realize the disastrous conditions of employment for those who were paid. There were, says Mrs. Paget, "cases of real hardship and even privation", and lack of training often made the work ineffective.[1] Great care is now taken that a licence shall be issued only to trained and qualified women, and that they shall have enough to live on. Good training and examining is available, and women are turned out well qualified to do educational, moral welfare, social and parochial work. The Bishop, though there was an excellent Board of Women's Work in his diocese, never appreciated what was being done. One woman writes that:

> Women's work and position—if we take that as a symbol of a changing world—did not greatly enter his mind.

Another, who had first-hand experience, writes:

> I do not think that the Board of Women's Work had any significance to him. He was personally kind and friendly so far as I was concerned, and he was glad that someone was looking after the "dear old Bible women",[2] but beyond that I do not think he took the work seriously.

At the same time it ought to be said that the Bishop was an early believer in Votes for Women. A correspondent, who is "in no way a supporter of the Church, to which I have long attributed the principal cause of the deep degradation and subjection of women", testifies that, when a deputation of Suffragettes went to Fulham:

> They were invited inside, to wait till he could see them. He, although naturally not approving of their tactics, listened attentively to their statement and ACTED!! He went to Holloway to see about it. All honour to him!! . . . The sequel I do know about, and honour him for it.

[1] In 1916 it appeared that of 402 women working in 253 parishes, 10 were paid £90 or over, 14 from £80-£90, 40 from £70-£80, 99 from £60-£70, 130 from £50-£60, 53 from £40-£50 and 45 from £30-£40. Eight received less than £20. The salaries of three are not stated. The average was just under £55. It should be remembered that this survey was taken at a bad moment. From that time things began to improve.

[2] This name was no doubt a survival in his mind from an earlier period. There was at one time an association of workers who did excellent work, but laboured under the title of "London Female Scripture Readers". It was part of the duty of the Boards to transform, gently and with due appreciation of long service rendered, the devoted but unqualified worker into the devoted and competent worker of to-day. It is ceasing to be true, but it was true once, that the Church of England regarded women workers much as it regards the Apocrypha, as useful "for example of life and instruction in manners, but not to establish any doctrine".

The "sequel" was this. There is an educational institution in London, where, according to this correspondent, "the atmosphere is very proper and religious." Soon after the interview at Fulham, the Bishop visited this Institution, and:

> To the amazement of the audience (who of course looked upon the Suffragettes as a species of mentally deranged hooligans, as the Press had universally designated them, and could not see any spiritual object in the movement), the Bishop, in his address, dwelling on the growing selfishness and egoism in the population, said, "I should feel a little hopeless, had I not seen the spirit of self-sacrifice, and willingness to suffer for an ideal, of the Suffragettes. . . ." The very proper audience was simply petrified that their Bishop should ever mention such women, let alone approvingly.

The correspondent is in error in supposing that the Bishop was "practically alone among clergy" in the matter, but it was a courageous act. Even so, it came from a warm heart rather than from a long head.

These limitations represent defects in statesmanship, which it is easy for the onlooker to perceive and criticize. Of course he had not the capacious mind of William Temple, to have knowledge and to know mysteries, without lacking charity. Who had? But Ingram's personal sympathy was so rich and so unfailing that one wishes that he could have added to it an intellectual sympathy in which he was deficient. Yet there it is. No one can be equipped at all points. The Dean of St. Paul's, reviewing in the *Sunday Times* (21st July, 1940) his *Fifty Years Work in London*, writes:

> We have no insight given us into the development of his thought. Indeed, it may be doubted whether there was much development of that kind. What Dr. Winnington-Ingram believed and was when de became the youthful Bishop of Stepney, that in all essentials he believeh and was when he retired after forty years of strenuous episcopal labours. But what a splendid thing that was! I do not think that we would have had him change.

What was true of his theology was true also of his ecclesiastical statesmanship. Nevertheless, in the business of the *ecclesia* he "laboured more abundantly than they all".

Much of the work consisted in raising money. At this he was

superb. He was better at procuring, in the earlier and middle periods, donations for East London and for special cases,[1] than he was at meeting the continual large financial needs of the diocese. The claims of the constant expansion of London were very great,[2] enough to make mincemeat of any budget, and there can be no thought of blaming the Bishop for the comparatively low position of London in the annual list of diocesan quota-payments. In 1926, thanks to the skill and energy of the Reverend C. E. Curzon, later Bishop of Exeter, the full quota was received, but the figures in other years were not so good. In most years it was seventy per cent, though in 1934 it rose to seventy-five. It must be remembered that the actual amount was large. In 1934 the Diocese agreed to regard £75,000 as the quota of ambition and £55,000 as the quota of obligation. Also, it is noteworthy that during Ingram's episcopate the sum of £1,038,000 was given by the parishes to the Diocesan Quota.

Apart from the Quota, which consisted wholly of contributions from the parishes, a great deal of money was raised from outside London. In early days Torquay was a hunting-ground. Ingram, as Bishop of Stepney, visited the town every year, and often came back with as much as £500 from a single week-end. Brighton and Eastbourne were also worked, and sometimes played off one against the other, but the great source of extraneous income was Bournemouth. Mrs. Winnington-Ingram lived there from the time when she became a widow in 1891 to the time of her death at the age of ninety-six in 1924, and it was known that the Bishop always spent his winter holidays with her there. From 1897, with one or two exceptions, until the year of his death he preached there, at first for the East London Church Fund, and later when the East London Church Fund, like the Bishop of London's Fund, had been merged into the Diocesan Fund, for that Fund, every year. The peak period

[1]An appeal in St. Paul's for an aged and poverty-stricken East London clergyman once produced £1,300. The Bishop used to say that the happiest day of his life was in 1918 when, in response to a letter in the *Times*, he was able to send cheques of £200 or £100 or £50 to four hundred London clergymen. As Bishop of Stepney he preached one day in a West London Church, and had £1,000 sent to him for East London. Next year he preached again in the same Church and mentioned the gift. A like cheque came. The third year he again, after some hesitation, did the same thing, and received a letter, "You shall have it to-morrow, dear Bishop." He thought he had identified the giver and thanked him. The man at first denied, and then admitted, in confidence, that he had sent the money.

[2]The population of the diocese rose between 1901 and 1911 from 3,610,000 to 3,811,827, and by 1935 to 4,025,247.

was about 1910. A number of the East London clergy went with him, and preached in the Churches, and there was a crowded Meeting in the Town Hall. Often the amount given would be over £1,000.

In matters of finance the diocese had the help of some laymen of first-rate capacity, who laboured at the preparation of estimates and reports, and gave wise counsel. Among them were Lord Justice Bankes, Viscount Sankey, Sir Montague Barlow, Chancellor P. V. Smith, the Hon. Evelyn Hubbard, Sir Edward Thesiger, Mr. G. A. King, Sir Lulham Pound, Mr. Guy Paget Bowman, Mr. J. A. Longley, Mr. R. C. Nesbitt, and a very competent permanent staff, which has been housed for many years at 33, Bedford Square.

To what end was all this labour? He would have said himself that it was all for the building of the Kingdom of God in London, and, so far as was possible, beyond. It actually consisted in the oversight of the affairs of many hundreds of parishes and of occasional concern with the private affairs of many thousands of people in those parishes. Incumbents have perplexities about which they want the Bishop's advice. They want to do, or have done, something for which episcopal sanction, or indemnity, is required. Assistant curates occasionally become restless, and think that a change of work would make for happiness. Someone has got into trouble, and needs to be reprimanded or comforted, or both. A man is entering or leaving the diocese, and there must be a welcome or farewell. A new district is springing up, and a likely young priest has been selected. He must be told what the place is like, and how he had better begin. An undergraduate picked up at Oxford on a recent visit is a certain or possible ordinand, and must be advised about Cuddesdon or Wycliffe Hall or Cheshunt. A young wife has written to the Bishop: "My husband is unfaithful to me, and my friends tell me that I ought to divorce him. What ought I to do?" and she must have some counsel. A priest ordained a dozen years ago, who had joined a Bush Brotherhood in Australia, is at home on furlough, and has been invited for a few days to Fulham. The Bishop must have one or two talks with him, and hear all the news and give him some encouragement. Once a month there will be the Staff Meeting of Suffragan Bishops and Archdeacons. Theoretically, the Staff was consulted about all appointments, and no doubt always in fact about the more important. But sometimes it was not possible to wait for the monthly meeting, and sometimes the Bishop went ahead by himself, occasionally, it is whispered, with the result that duplicate promises were made to two different men. Once a clergyman of standing in London, in whom the critical faculty was strongly developed, was at Fulham. "You don't like me, X," said the Bishop. "Why not?" "My lord, I don't agree with your appointments." "Which, for example?" "Well, you appointed —— to St. ——. I said at the time that he would empty the Church in twelve months. I was wrong. He emptied it in six." "Well, you can't pick a winner every time, old boy." This was perhaps one of the times described by a Chaplain:

> A vivid little picture of him will always remain in my mind of an occasion or two when he had been "caught out" in some mistake—he would look at you with a half-guilty, half-mischievous look of a small boy "discovered in the act".

And all the time there were the constant visits to parishes, four a week. This is the recollection of a friend:

> "Of course I know that people think that I ought not to dine with the Vicar—he is poor, etc. But it gives them a chance to tell me their troubles." From dinner to the church—the same old cracked voice, and same old sermon. Then coffee with the Church Council in the Parish Hall. There, standing in his purple cassock, with the Vicar, he kept them in roars of laughter, pulling the Vicar's leg.

Much of the difficulty of administering the diocese of London arose from the vagaries of the clergy. One of the really difficult cases that he had to handle was that of St. Saviour's, Hoxton.[1] In 1907, the Bishop appointed to the benefice the Reverend E. E. Kilburn, a former curate at St. Saviour's, then serving in a Midland parish of "English" Catholic tradition.

Kilburn was a very good and holy man, devoted to God and his people. He soon became greatly loved. Ecclesiastically, at St. Saviour's he developed in a remarkable way, and before many years, except for the fact that the parish was one of the parishes of the

---

[1] I am indebted for nearly all my knowledge of this to Mr. Lawrence E. Jack, who is preparing a History of the Parish, and has generously placed a large quantity of information at my disposal. Passages between inverted commas are quotations from his pages, not necessarily his own observations, but emanating from the parish.

diocese of London and not in actual communion with the Pope, it was completely "Romanized". Perpetual Reservation on the High Altar, Benediction, the Rosary, Shrines of the Sacred Heart, of Our Lady of Victories and of St. Joseph, Corpus Christi processions through the streets, the complete disuse of the English language, the regular use of the Latin Missal, Rituale, Vesperale, Ritus Servandus, and for the people the "Simple Prayer Book" of the Catholic Truth Society and the Westminster Hymn Book gradually became the order. The Bishop had preached in the Church at Solemn Evensong on November 29th, 1910, a date when all this had only gone a very little way, but he was afterwards compelled to put the parish "under discipline". It appeared that the full programme was very attractive to parishioners and others. Services and Meetings of Confraternities and Sodalities were numerous, and the Church was always full.

In 1917, the Bishop, who was incessantly bombarded with complaints, not from the Parish but from Protestants outside, sent Archdeacon Holmes, who was as sympathetic to St. Saviour's as an Archdeacon is ever likely to be, to visit the Church and report. He reported that there had been on Corpus Christi a Procession through the streets, and that the Vicar would not give an undertaking not to repeat it.

The Bishop replied:

Dear Archdeacon,

I am grieved at receiving the report you send me, except upon the point of reverence of the procession, as it leaves me no alternative but to take the steps which I have so long tried to avoid.

You will agree with me that prosecution should be avoided if possible, especially in this time of war, and until the long-proposed reform of our Church Courts is carried out, but the Vicar of St. Saviour's has now placed himself, as far as it is in his power to do so, outside the number of the Churches which maintain a proper relation on Catholic principles to their bishop. You must therefore tell Kilburn that I cannot visit his Church, or allow the Suffragan Bishops or yourself to do so; nor can I license curates thereto nor sanction any diocesan grant being made to the parish, until such times as he undertakes to observe the regulations as regards Reservation which have been accepted generally throughout the diocese.

I feel sure that all in the diocese who know the long patience with which I have treated Kilburn will understand the necessity of the step which I have been forced by him to take now that my constant and fatherly admonitions have failed to take effect.

Yours very sincerely,

A. F. LONDON.

The parishioners were simple people, who had been converted to the kind of religion that was practised in the parish. They were happy in it, and that was all they knew. The belief of the Parish, or anyhow of the clergy, was twofold.

(a) "St. Saviour's, Hoxton, for some years had been quite indistinguishable from a Roman Catholic Church. There was nothing in either the building or the services to suggest even any remote connection with the Church of England. The position held by the clergy was (briefly) this; That they rejected State control of the Church in any shape or form, and regarded the Book of Common Prayer as an alien method of worship enforced by Parliament. They held that only the old Latin services had any canonical authority, and they hoped that eventually the small but vigorous pro-Roman movement would so leaven the whole Anglican Communion that there would come about a spiritual *anschluss*, as it were, under the Holy See. . . . The secret of St. Saviour's popularity with the laity seemed to lie in the fact that if anyone inquired as to why this or that is done, the clergy would not preface their explanation by starting to say, 'Well, we do that because I . . .' —thereby shewing it to be something that is done because the Vicar personally approved of it. St. Saviour's clergy would simply say that it was done 'Because the Church orders it' meaning, of course, the Holy See. . . . There is only one Catholicism, that of the whole Western Church, so there can hardly be such peculiarities as 'sane Catholicism', 'Prayer Book Catholicism', 'moderate Catholicism', or any other kind of Anglican 'isms' which seem to be so desirable on the part of clerical advertisers in the Church Times columns."

About this there is nothing to be said except that it is a point of view, which may conceivably in course of time become more widely adopted, but it is completely inconsistent with the position of the Church of England, accepted at the Reformation and formulated in the Book of Common Prayer.

(b) Everything which is said in the New Testament about the presence of our Lord in His earthly life can be said quite simply about the presence of the Blessed Sacrament. Vespers are sung "*coram SSmi*".

"The day has dawned for better processions than those which terminate in bishop or priest as principal figures. In this procession God was evident . . . such a procession as was in ancient use, and reaches back to the day when our Lord proceeded to Jerusalem—Either the Blessed Sacrament is God—or it is nothing. Catholicism knows no *via media*. Either the Church of England is Catholic, or it is not."

"Can anyone doubt for a moment that if all the Churches of the Church of England were Homes of the Blessed Sacrament, and the full faith taught and practised within them, there would not be the lamentations we hear on all sides to-day? If, for example, St. Paul's Cathedral were open day and night and our Lord duly enthroned there, if priests could be got at at any hour of the day or night to hear confessions, would not that Cathedral be a greater power in London than it is to-day? Would not the scene in the house of the Pharisee be enacted over and over again, and the sinful women of the streets (ay, and the men who cause them to be there) turn in to water His feet with their tears of devotion and penitence? Yes, the faith has mightier powers than Acts of Parliament, and it is a battle well worth the fighting, if only we prove worthy of fighting it."

In September 1919 the Bishop of Zanzibar paid a visit to St. Saviour's, which, as the parish was under the ban of the diocesan, was a very irregular thing to do. He had scruples, but apparently overcame them. He led the congregation in the veneration of a relic which a young soldier had picked up outside a Church in France which was bombed while he was passing it.[1] The following morning he celebrated. "He could not very well use Latin, and, as English was taboo, he celebrated in the Suahili dialect according to the Zanzibar rite!"

There seems to have been a good deal of discussion among the Bishops about the St. Saviour's Case. There was a time when Bishop Gore is said to have leaned over the table towards the Bishop of

[1]The soldier, who was a St. Saviour's man, had recognized that it was a sacred object, had brought it back to England and had handed it to one of the clergy, who "saw at once that it was a major relic of St. Cornelius".

London, and sternly demanded, "How long do you mean to allow a Hoxton Curate to pull you along by the nose?"

There is no record of what passed between the Bishop of London and the Bishop of Zanzibar, but when the Bishop of London suggested to the Vicar that he should resign and go to Zanzibar, "where these things are allowed," the Vicar said he had no intention of either resigning or going to Zanzibar and added, shrewdly enough, "If the Monstrance be wrong in London, I cannot understand how it can be right in Zanzibar."

The Bishop and the Vicar remained good friends, and each defended the other against false accusations, but the Bishop would not concede what the parish wanted. In 1923 the Vicar, worn out, it is said, by strain, and pastoral labours and by financial anxiety for the parish, determined to resign. One of the assistant Priests was about to become a Roman Catholic, but it is believed that at the time the Vicar had no intention of following him, though he did later. He asked the Bishop if he might nominate his successor. The Bishop, "who had really no desire to see the place smashed up but only a toning-down," agreed. One of the assistant Clergy was suggested, but he was unable to accept the Bishop's requirements, and it was agreed to appoint another priest. He came, having apparently accepted the conditions, but in fact there was little change. The Services were still in Latin. In fact, the new Vicar always affirmed that "it was solely due to the wonderful witness of St. Saviour's Hoxton, that the Roman authorities sanctioned the opening of the Malines Conversations".

In August 1923, the Bishop of Zanzibar again visited the parish. He confirmed in the Church and, "it being the Sunday within the Octave of the Assumption, preached after the evening Vespers, presided at the great procession in honour of our Lady, and gave 'Pontifical' Benediction". The organist of the Church remembers the Vicar saying to him that there had been "an awful row with the Bishop of London over the Confirmation".

The Vicar died, and a new appointment became necessary. Two deputations from the parish approached the Bishop about this time. One was from the boys of the parish. There is no record of its reception, except that it was "very kind". The other consisted of the Churchwardens. Here there was an amusing incident:

"The Bishop was apparently determined to be very firm and also very stern on this occasion. The conversation at first was decidedly formal, and before very long his Lordship broached the problem of the Latin. He thumped his hand on the table and said, 'as the 108th Catholic Bishop of London, I WILL BE OBEYED.' To this Mr. John Charles Denis Hurly, the senior churchwarden, replied that the greater number of the Bishops of London had themselves said Mass in Latin (Hurly was an Irishman. He belonged to St. James' Clubs and knew the Bishop very well in social circles in the West End of London). At this retort the Bishop looked at him, and there was an awful silence, and then he went into fits of helpless laughter at the utter cleverness of Hurly's retort. The conversation from then onwards became warm and cordial, and all three parted amicably."

The new Vicar was instituted on October 2nd, 1927, and from that time the use of Latin in public services ceased, and in other respects the order reverted to what it had been up to 1919. "When the Bishop had announced his resignation, the Vicar asked him if, as a gesture, he would preach at the Dedication Festival in May 1936. He came, and while he was being vested, he suddenly looked up and said to us all, 'Do you know I saved this Church thirty years ago. People forget that sometimes!' He preached in a homely, conversational way, and was not well heard. One of the sentences that were heard and remembered was, 'So I said to that dear old lady, Well, mother, have you asked the Lord Jesus to help you?'"

In October 1940 the Church was wrecked, and much of the parish destroyed. What remains of it is combined with St. Michael's, Shoreditch, under the Vicar appointed to St. Saviour's in 1927.

In all the mass of detail a few larger things stand out, matters of policy. One was the proposal to divide the Diocese. This had actually been suggested at the Diocesan Conference as early as 1901, Ingram's first Conference, and the Bishop had then expressed himself "not in favour of it at present".

Later two schemes were put forward. One was that there should be a Province of London, with an Archbishop. It need hardly be said that this was not the same as Pope Gregory's original plan in

597, because that would have involved the dethronement of Canterbury from its ancient primacy.

Nor was it so extensive as another proposal which William Temple as a young man had suggested in a Life and Liberty Tract in 1917, that the Province of Canterbury (which at that time included Wales) should be divided into seven provinces, having centres at Canterbury, London, Winchester, Exeter, Lichfield, Ely and St. David's. This never became popular, and, so far as is known, Temple in his later years did not develop, or perhaps even retain, the idea.

The new plan was more realistic. It was to create a third Province of London, including the dioceses of Southwark and Chelmsford, but it never got very far. The Bishop disliked it, as did the Bishops of both Southwark and Chelmsford. Nor did it commend itself to the Archbishop of Canterbury. The present Archbishop of York, then Bishop of Southwark, writes about it (1947):

> After the four-year war there were any number of schemes for the re-organization of the Church of England, produced by ingenious minds, which some of us regarded as quite impracticable, however desirable they might have been if there had been a clean sheet to start with. ... I do not think that any of us took this proposal very seriously.

At all events, it collapsed.

Another, less sweeping, but still considerable scheme was for the division of the diocese of London. It had been divided before. Not to speak of the vast overseas areas which had at one time been reckoned as within the jurisdiction of the Bishop of London, or of the Diocese of Westminster, including almost the whole county of Middlesex, which was created in 1540 and only lasted for ten years, the modern creations of St. Alban's (1877) and of Chelmsford (1914) had relieved London of large areas in Hertfordshire and Essex. Of course that only involved lopping off outlying portions of Greater London and beyond. The proposal now was to re-arrange all London in three (or four) new dioceses, a much bolder thing.

It came up at the Diocesan Conference in 1920, when the Reverend A. S. Duncan-Jones, now Dean of Chichester,[1] moved:

[1] It had originally been intended that the resolution would be moved by William Temple, or, failing him, Canon Bullock-Webster, but they were both prevented from being present. Some of the advocates of the proposal found it hard to separate it from the other proposal for a Province of London.

That the overgrown size of the diocese of London calls for speedy sub-division, and that the Enabling Act affords a new and welcome opportunity for facilitating such division.

He was supported by Mr. Douglas Eyre, of Oxford House, Mr. Clifton Kelway, Lieut. General Sir A. F. Codrington, the Reverend R. Webb Odell and others. All the speakers for the resolution dissociated themselves from any suggestion that they wished to escape from the jurisdiction of their present Diocesan, or that he was not doing day by day all that man could. As Mr. Kelway put it:

While the present state of things might be altogether delightful, they had to look at the matter not from the point of view of the present moment but as affecting the Church in the future and its organization in the perhaps greater days that were to come.

The general idea seems to have been that the new Diocese of London should consist of the City of Westminster. It was pointed out that the diocese contained about four million people and 1,629 clergymen. The next largest diocese, that of Winchester, had 1,300,000 people and 1,000 clergymen, and there was a movement to divide it.[1] London was an impossible burden, and the provision of Suffragan Bishops, admirable men as they were in themselves, and everybody's friends, was not the best way of solving the problem. In the Dominions and in U.S.A. they did not believe in Suffragans. If a Bishop, generally by reason of age or infirmity, needed help, they procured the consecration of an Assistant-Bishop, generally *cum iure successionis*. Further, the proposal would lessen the peril of bureaucracy, and, as a move away from prelacy, would conciliate Free Churchmen.

The Bishop was not in favour of the plan. The late Mr. Firth, who was Secretary of the Additional Home Bishoprics Endowment Fund, once said to a friend that every bishop favours the movement for dividing dioceses, but says, "Not mine".[2] In his speech at the Conference he praised the work of his Suffragans and Archdeacons, and explained the system of close consultation and co-operation which obtained between himself and all of them. If he were to

[1] This has since come to pass. The Dioceses of Guildford and Portsmouth were created in 1927.
[2] Prebendary Boggis, *I Remember*, p. 158.

remain in charge of only a portion of the diocese, he would no doubt have an easier time, but he would not like having no voice in the appointment of the Bishops of East or North London. London was, and would in any case remain, a unit, and it would cause great perplexity if the Bishops of Stepney and Willesden were men of widely different standpoints. And could East London, the poorest part of the diocese, be left alone in its poverty? West London would not continue to feel, as it had done hitherto, responsible for helping East London, if they were not under the same Bishop. Then, who would have, or how would you divide, St. Paul's Cathedral? No Londoners would accept St. Pancras or Hampstead Parish Church as their Cathedral. Finally, how could he begin to raise the £250,000 which would be required to finance the scheme, while the parochial clergy were still so underpaid?

There were rejoinders to some of these points. It was said at the Conference that the argument about the appointment of Bishops of East or North London was really a criticism of the way in which diocesan bishops (and other dignitaries) are appointed now. And it was suggested that for the money Fulham Palace might be sold. Outside the Conference it had also been suggested that the City Churches might be raided.

The resolution was carried by 212 votes to 122, as was also a rider:

> And, in order that this division may be carried out in the wisest and most efficient way, the Bishop be asked to appoint a Committee to go thoroughly into the matter and report within a year to the Diocesan Conference.

The Committee was appointed, under the chairmanship of Lord Justice Younger, who presided over no less than eighteen meetings. The Report was signed by all the Members of the Committee. Their proposal was not to divide the Diocese there and then, partly because of the complexity of the matter, the necessity of maintaining the unity of London, and the cost of division (though they believed that the financial difficulty was not insuperable), and partly because the Church Assembly had created a New Sees Committee, the first report of which had just been published. In it the New Sees Committee said that the problem of the Diocese of London could not properly be solved without consideration of the complete Metropolitan area. This made it a larger thing than could be decided by the London Conference alone.

The resolution:

> That the Report of the Division of the Diocese Committee be adopted, and that the Conference, having considered the Draft Report of the New Sees Committee, forward the Report of the Committee on the Division of the Diocese to the Bishop of Manchester, as an interim Report, for the consideration of his Committee—

was carried by a large majority.

The New Sees Committee seems to have desired to go forward in the matter, and their Report was on the Agenda for the Church Assembly in February and June 1922, but through lack of time it was not considered. Meantime, it appeared that the Bishops of the Dioceses concerned were opposed even to the idea of having a Conference about it. The Bishop of London consulted the Rural Deaneries and reported that a majority in the ratio of 8 to 5 were against division. He said at the Diocesan Conference in 1923 that he did not intend to append his signature to any resolution of the Conference on the subject,[1] until he had been satisfied on the points which he had previously mentioned as grounds of hesitation. In this way the project lapsed. One of the promoters said, "The Bishop was the deadly foe of our proposal."

Another controversial topic which flared up at about the same time as the question of dividing the diocese, but had also been a matter of debate before and has been a matter of debate since, was that of the City Churches. Built at a time when many people lived in the City, they had lost nearly all their resident population. Not many had parsonage-houses in the Parish, and the City clergy were compelled to live in the suburbs. The cost of maintaining clergy (£40,000) and choirs and virgers (£14,000) was considerable, and, so far as Sunday Services were concerned, there was little to shew for it.

On the other hand it could be urged that many of the Churches were ancient and beautiful, that City men and women were proud of them, and that all or nearly all of them were well used during the

---

[1] By the rules of the Church Assembly the signature of the Bishop is required to make any decision an act of Conference.

week. Some of them, having special connections with some group of people (e.g., Australians, London Students, friends of the Church Army, etc.), or making special efforts, were well filled on Sundays. Could not a long view be taken? It was perhaps not likely that the population would flow back into the streets where John Stow, Thomas Cromwell, John Milton, Isaak Walton, Samuel Pepys, Samuel Johnson, Oliver Goldsmith, Charles Lamb and many other famous men had lived, but there were some who thought that even this might happen. Yet, apart from that, let us have, it was said, some imagination, and envisage the time when a Church tower or spire in the next street will really mean something in the life of the workers in the City. Further, it must be remembered that, whereas people living in the suburbs do not mind walking a mile to Church on Sunday, there is not time in the City, during a lunch-interval or within the limits of a business call, to visit any Church unless it is near at hand. A census of persons using one City Church (St. Edmund, Lombard Street) revealed the fact that, apart from services, 120 persons per day, that is 600 per week of five days, entered the Church. Most of those remained from five to fifteen minutes, to say their prayers.

Of many others like things could be said. To mention a few only, in one City Church where the present writer often worshipped between 1930 and 1935 (St. Nicholas, Cole Abbey), there was a good regular congregation on both Sundays and weekdays. In another Parish, All Hallows, Barking by the Tower, the large income of the benefice was used by Dr. A. W. Robinson and his successor, the Reverend C. E. Lambert to maintain a staff of mission-clergy, while the parish itself was well served. The latter Church is now the Headquarters of Toc H.

The Bishop's policy was, on the whole, one of sacrificing a number of City Churches in order to build Churches in the suburbs. He did not carry it to extreme lengths. A Commission, consisting of Lord Phillimore, Bishop Browne, Archdeacon Holmes, Lord Hugh Cecil (now Lord Quickswood), Sir William Collins, Sir Rowland Blades, Mt. A. F. Buxton, the Hon. H. C. Gibbs, Sir Francis Green, Sir Lulham Pound, reported in 1919.[1]

[1] The Report was unanimous, with some reservations by Lord Hugh Cecil and Sir William Collins.

There had been a like Commission in 1899. At that time the resident population, which in 1861 had been 113,000, had sunk to 35,000, and by 1919 to 13,000. The day-population was estimated in 1911 to be 304,000, and had no doubt increased since then. Excluding St. Paul's and certain non-parochial churches, there were 47 Churches in the City, with a total benefice-income of £40,000.

The Report of the Commission was very drastic. The recommendations were:

1. That the benefices should be grouped together into four great new parishes, each with a Rector, four Assistant Clergy and Wardens, and in each Parish a Rectory.

2. That there should be ten Lecturers, who should devote themselves to study and the promotion of theological learning in Greater London.

3. That nineteen churches should be pulled down and their sites sold, and that nine of the thirteen parsonages should be sold.

The Report had a very bad reception in the City. Resolution after Resolution was passed condemning it. The Bishop protested against being supposed to be responsible for it:

I have been pilloried as an iconoclast from one end of the City to the other, as though it were my Report. You might as well say that the King is in favour of divorce because he appointed a Commission to go into it. The difficulty remains where it was, only added to by the furore which the Report has produced. It is a terrible thing to pull down a consecrated Church, for a beautiful Church is a sacred thing; but it is also terrible to see 10,000 people without a church at all. . . . Strongly as I feel about pulling down a consecrated Church, when you come to deal with a Church, for the site of which over half a million is offered, and you can move that Church stone by stone, say, to Tottenham for £20,000 or £30,000, you have to ask what is God's will, when you can build twenty-five Churches out of the money. It is a question to be asked on one's knees.

And, two years later:

We have got to look at both sides of the question. I hate to pull down a single church, but we have got to face the matter as it stands. . . . Can anyone defend forty-nine City Churches with forty-nine Sunday

Services, attended by a few people or perhaps none at all? It is ridiculous to go on with that. I have given leave for the closing on Sunday of a good many of them, while keeping them open on week-days. It otherwise seemed a ridiculous waste of man power. I do not, however, want to proceed in this autocratic way, but according to some perfectly well-organized plan.

The Diocesan Conference in 1920 seems to have felt that the proposals of the Commission were much too drastic, but that some rearrangement was urgently required. A resolution "that this Conference cannot approve any further secularization of consecrated buildings and sites within the area of the City of London" was lost by a large majority, and the resolution finally carried had the effect of leaving the matter in the hands of the Bishop.

He was in fact in favour of pulling down a certain number of the Churches, and it was because he was a pastor, and moreover a pastor who lived in the present and saw very clearly the present situation. He saw the thousands of people in the new suburbs and that outweighed with him both the historical associations and the possible future of some of the City Churches. He was far from being the reckless destroyer that in some circles of the City he was said to be, but he consented (at least, it was done during his episcopate, and it could hardly have been done without his consent) to the pulling down of five Churches: St. Bartholomew, Moor Lane (1900); Holy Trinity, Gough Square (1908), St. Alphege, London Wall (1920), St. Catherine, Coleman Street (1925), All Hallows', Lombard Street (1937).

The case of All Hallows' is instructive and shews that the Bishop was no mere iconoclast. All Hallows', which had become a rallying-point for the Student Christian Movement, and London Students generally, was one of four churches within a distance of a hundred yards from one another, St. Edmund's being actually in the same street fifty yards way. The heavy traffic which came from London Bridge along Gracechurch Street had caused serious cracks in the East Wall, and there were also cracks in the North and West walls. Repairs would have been very costly. Barclay's Bank was built all round the Church, and the Bank was willing to give a large sum for the site. The Lord Mayor, who was one of the Wardens of All Hallows', proposed a resolution asking for the union of the two benefices, All Hallows' and St. Edmund's. In two years this was done. The site was sold for £303,000. The Rector of St. Edmund's, an elderly man, was pensioned. The Rector of All Hallows' became Rector of St. Edmund's. All the woodwork of All Hallows' was put into a beautiful new Church at Twickenham. The new Rector of St. Edmund's was given £10,000 to rebuild St. Dionis Hall, a place much used by Students. The remainder of the money was put into the hands of the Ecclesiastical Commissioners to make a special fund to build churches in and around the dioceses of London. The released stipend is used for the payment of clergymen at All Hallows', Twickenham and elsewhere. It was generally agreed in the City that this matter at least had been handled in a sensible and business-like way.

The Bishop summarized his own attitude in the general matter of Churches "redundant" in one region and needed in another at the Conference in 1929, when he said:

> I am looked upon as the worst iconoclast in England. You will perhaps remember the picture in *Punch* on the occasion of Wren's Bicentenary, and below the words—"Let's keep the occasion by pulling down some of his churches." That was just a joke, but as a matter of fact I had to stand the racket of all the City churches discussion, and if ever there is a church to be pulled down in Central London, all the indignation is turned on the poor Bishop of London for daring to touch that sacred building. Now you have committed yourselves to the policy of looking round and seeing whether there is any church in Central London which is unwanted, and backing me up in trans-ferring that church to a place where they have no Church. Do not forget that you are committed to that policy, and I am going to lay the blame on you.[1] As a matter of fact, we have five Commissions going, and if they report that a church is unused and certain parishes should be amalgamated, that church shall be pulled down. When I tell you that one important firm has offered £50,000 for the site of one church into which seven or eight people go on Sunday, and the incumbent is willing that it shall go, there is something that we can do at once. That £50,000 will build four or more churches in Hendon, or where they are wanted. I am going to claim your support for this policy.

[1] The reference was to a Resolution passed at the 1928 Conference in favour of uniting benefices and removing unnecessary churches, and related only to churches outside the City area.

Referring to the case of St. Andrew's, Wells Street, which was removed stone by stone to Kingsbury, Middlesex, the Bishop said:

> I hope that once for all it will silence those people who say we are pulling down London's Churches.

The Archdeacon of London (E. N. Sharpe), writing to the *Times* on 25th July, 1937, indignantly denied the allegation that the chief interest of the Bishop and the diocesan authorities in the City Churches was in their value as building sites.

A great event in the history of the diocese was the keeping of the thirteen hundredth anniversary of the consecration of Mellitus as Bishop. There had been a British Bishop of London named Restitutus, who attended the Council of Arles in 314, and was one of those who were so poor that their expenses had to be paid for them out of continental funds, but after him the Christian faith was utterly stamped out, and there was no succession. Mellitus, a monk from Italy, was sent over to join Augustine in 601, and was made Bishop of the East Saxons in 604. They were a heathen people, and though the Bishop had some success in converting a number of them and built a Church of St. Paul on the site of the present Cathedral, and set up his episcopal stool there, the East Saxons drove him out and returned to their paganism. It was Mellitus who refused to give the East Saxon Princes the "white bread" of the Eucharist unless they submitted to the laver of Holy Baptism. On the death of Laurentius, who had succeeded Augustine, Mellitus became the third Archbishop of Canterbury. He suffered from gout and is said to have been a man of great spiritual power. Bede says that, though he could not walk, he could soar into the heavenly regions.

The great Service of Commemoration was held at St. Paul's on May 5th, 1904. There were present the Archbishop and many Bishops of the Province, 800 clergymen of the Diocese, and a great congregation of the laity.

The following Prayer, written by Canon Newbolt, was said during the Service:

> Almighty God, Whose ways are from everlasting and Whose

counsels are faithfulness and truth: We yield Thee hearty thanks for that Thou didst in mercy vouchsafe to raise up into this city Thy faithful servant Mellitus to be the shepherd and guardian of Thy sheep who were scattered abroad in the cloudy and dark day. And humbly we beseech Thee to grant that we Thy servants and children of Thine inheritance may shew forth our thankfulness unto Thee by holding fast that apostolic faith and discipline thus delivered to us; so that, rooted and grounded in love, we may grow up unto Him in all things, Which is the Head, even Christ, Who liveth and reigneth with Thee and the Holy Ghost, ever one God, world without end. Amen.

Another event was the re-opening of the restored St. Paul's nearly thirty years later. Wren's Church had been founded and built on difficult ground in just the right way, but Wren could not foresee the shaking which traffic, above and below ground, would cause in after years. The great Cathedral was in danger.

The story begins in 1914. Canon Alexander, whose name will go down in history as the preserver of St. Paul's, after a year of engineering experiments, issued in the name of the Dean and Chapter a first appeal for St. Paul's as "the Church of the Empire". In response to it, and to further appeals, a total of £400,000 was collected from all parts of the world. The famous "Dangerous Structure" Notice was served on Canon Alexander in 1925. It was actually a mistake. The structure had been dangerous, but the work had been done, and the engineers were just about to issue their final report. The Treasurer, however, seized the opportunity of making his third appeal. The dome-area was closed from 1925 to 1930, and the public supposed that St. Paul's was in danger. It was not so at that time, but the closing of the area meant that the remainder of the process could go forward more quickly. The actual work was one of engineering. The foundations were and always have been solid and intact. Nothing was done to them either then or since. The eight huge piers that carry the dome had to be reinforced with steel rods. Eventually, to safeguard the foundations, the "Sacred Area" round the Cathedral was formed, and provision for it was made part of an Act of Parliament. The work thus done saved the Cathedral twice over, because, if it had not been for the reinforcement, the piers could not have stood up at the bombing of the North Transept during the Second War.

There was a great Thanksgiving Service on 25th June, 1930, which was attended by the King and Queen and many leaders of the national life.

The cause that was really after the Bishop's own heart was the provision of priests and churches for the ever-increasing population of Outer London. For the whole period of his episcopate the official figures of Mr. Dashwood, the Diocesan Registrar, are, New Churches consecrated, 79; Churches re-built or enlarged, 38. Total, 117.

There were in his life three stages of this sort of Church Extension. There was in early days the provision of men for the East London parishes. This he did by attracting—there is no other word for it—undergraduates from Oxford and elsewhere, as well as such priests as were considering a change of work. The number of young men whom he drew by his magnetic power into a desire for Holy Orders is incalculable. There must have been many thousands. Some of them sought Ordination at his hands, and some elsewhere. "I knew that I must be ordained, and, if possible, in London" is a common testimony.

The second stage was the provision of Churches for Suburbia. Here his plan was actually an anticipation of that put forward after the Second War by Sir Patrick Abercrombie, units of about 10,000 people. The ecclesiastical centres of the new districts were the old village churches, Harrow, Hendon, Finchley, Willesden and so on. The areas had been fields a generation before, and were now covered by red-brick houses. Soon the tide flowed much farther out than that, until by the end of Ingram's episcopate nearly all Middlesex seemed to have been covered with houses.

The last lap was the effort known as the Forty-Five Churches Fund. The Bishop spoke in 1936 of the growth of London as "one of the most difficult problems which have ever confronted the Church of God".

It is a little difficult to record the actual progress of the fund, because the Bishop's optimism sometimes led him to use figures in what grammarians call a proleptic sense, in which the future is mingled with the present and it is hard to distinguish what is hoped for from what has been achieved. The Fund was launched in 1930, with an Appeal for £250,000. By 1933 a quarter of that sum had been given with some further promises, but fresh needs had arisen, and a sum equal to the original £250,000 was still needed. In 1936 the Bishop of Willesden reported that they had built or were building fourteen churches and twenty-six halls, most of them strong centres of worship and fellowship. In 1938 Prebendary Eley, Secretary of the Diocesan Fund, reported that there were now sixty-three districts, and in sixty of them sites had been secured or were being negotiated, in fifty-three there were halls, in sixteen permanent Churches had been consecrated, and in eight others Churches would be begun within the next twelve months. The cost had been £380,000, of which £20,000 was borrowed money. He added that, over and above this, since 1921 no less than £150,000 had been spent by the London Diocesan Fund on manpower. In the same year the Vicar of St. Paul's, South Harrow, gave convincing testimony to the value of the work done. Each stage, the appointment of a Missioner, an Assistant-Missioner, of a whole-time lay-worker, of a second curate, had visible results.

> "There is an amazing contrast between the older part of my parish and the new part. Visiting the older part, you are up against it. They have been there for ten years or more and have been accustomed to doing without a church. In the new part they are prepared to consider coming into the fellowship of the Church."

Among the stronger centres of Church life in the new districts were Kenton and the John Keble Church at Mill Hill.

It was all rather a desperate struggle, but the Bishop was always hopeful. In 1933 he said:

> I feel we mustn't listen to the pessimists; we must take to heart the exhortation of Caleb and Joshua—"Let us go up and possess the land; we are well able to overcome it."

And in 1936 he said:

> I can only say that I myself face all these problems with a good hope and unafraid, because, as we look back, we see even greater difficulties in the past surmounted, and I believe if "He smote the stony rock

indeed that the waters gushed out and the streams flowed withal", that He can "give bread also and provide flesh for His people".

It is worth remembering that the last verses of the Psalm (lxxviii) from which these words are taken are about David, the shepherd-boy whom the Lord chose to be His servant, "that he might feed Jacob His people and Israel His inheritance". And it continues: "So he led them with a faithful and true heart; and ruled them prudently with all his power."

X

THE ANGLO-CATHOLICS AND
PRAYER BOOK REVISION

THIS is a chapter which will be of interest to some readers. Others may decide to skip it, and from their point of view will lose very little. Nevertheless, it must form part of the book, because the matter of it occupied much of the Bishop's time and attention, gave him in the eyes of many a not wholly deserved ecclesiastical label, and caused him much anxiety. In order to make the situation clear, a little history is essential.

The original leaders of the Oxford Movement or Catholic Revival in the Church of England were content to re-affirm the divinely-created nature of the Church. The Catholic Church was the Body of Christ, and the Church of England was a true and apostolic part of it. The Establishment was accepted as a fact, not intolerable, but incidental, accidental, non-essential. For ceremonial they cared nothing. It did not occur to them to make any change in the accustomed method of worship. Newman stood at the North End when he celebrated Holy Communion during the whole of his Anglican life. Pusey continued the custom at Christ Church for many years after 1845. They believed and taught high churchmanship and high sacramental doctrine without any attempt to express it in external form.

This was because the Movement was in the first generation intellectual, appealing to the University of Oxford and the readers (mostly clerical) of Tracts for the Times. The next generation was different. After Newman's secession in 1845 the Movement ceased to be of Oxford. A few heroes, notably Church and Marriott, carried on in the University, and there was always Dr. Pusey in the background, but for the most part the cause lived on in the slum-parishes. Men like Lowder in East London, Mackonockie in Holborn and the brothers Pollock in Birmingham, were able and intelligent, but not intellectuals, not scholars, not profound theologians, any more than the much-loved Father Stanton in the third generation. They carried the teaching of the movement into the courts and alleys of great cities. They converted thieves and prostitutes. By day and night they were good shepherds of the flock. Father Lowder in his Dockland parish would think nothing of picking up a cholera-stricken child in his arms and carrying him to the hospital. This caused them to be loved, but what they chiefly wanted was to be believed. To reach their parishioners and arouse faith, Ear-Gate was not enough. Eye-Gate must also be called into use. Accordingly, they built great churches, with dignified and richly-furnished chancels and sanctuaries, and surrounded the altar, which was the focus of their worship, with all the dignity of ornament and ceremonial that they could think of. It was essential, not only to say, but also to exhibit in action, what they meant.

They were commonly called Ritualists. This was a misnomer. A rite is a liturgical service, like Evensong or the Churching of Women after Childbirth. A ritualist is properly a scholar like the late Dr. Brightman, who knows about the history of liturgies, Eastern and Western. These men should properly have been called Ceremonialists.

The method, backed, as it was by devoted pastoral labours, succeeded. People began to confess, to communicate more frequently, and to hear Mass, as they were taught to call it, every Sunday. Even those parishioners who were but lightly touched by the religion of the parish would not hear a word said against "the Fathers". "They're all right, they are. And if anyone says different, I'll black his eye."

It was the ceremonial which was the trouble. There was in actual fact a stately and dignified English tradition of ceremonial, which was in a condition of suspended animation, but was authorised by the Ornaments Rubric.[1] They did not know this, and the Bishops, and also the secular judges before whom at that time such matters often came, not only did not know it, but denied that it was so. The slum-priests knew that they must have some way of expressing their teaching, if it was ever going to mean anything to Doll Tearsheet and Bill Sykes. They turned accordingly to what seemed to

[1]This will be found in the Book of Common Prayer, just before the Order of Morning Prayer. When the English Use was revived in its exactness, as for example at St. Mary's, Primrose Hill, it was called by its critics "British Museum religion".

them the only source, the living customs of another Church. They imitated the Roman Catholics. They were not in any other respect "Romanisers". It was a great distress to Mackonockie, the inflexible leader of the group, when some of his friends from time to time became Roman Catholics. They described their practices as following Catholic custom. A more common title for their successors in this generation is "Westernisers" or followers of the "Western Use". They carry their imitation of Roman Catholic customs to an extreme and, as many think, absurd point. Many of them are eager for the reconciliation of England with the Papal See, and a few seem definitely out of place in the Church of England, but the ugly word "disloyal", often thrown at them, is in the great majority of cases quite unjustified.

To return to the pioneers. In many respects their appropriations were harmless enough, and resulted in practices which have spread throughout the Church of England and are considered by most people to be uncontroversial. Retreats, Parochial Missions, the Three Hours Service on Good Friday and the use of green as a liturgical colour at Ferial seasons, are all Roman in origin. But there is nothing in them that is alien to the Anglican tradition, and the borrowing has been happily and profitably made. Other innovations, which were in point of fact revivals rather than borrowings, were more controversial. The complaint was at first about such things as lighted candles, Eucharistic vestments and genuflexions, and even, here and there, about the use of the surplice rather than the black gown in the pulpit, and in the background there was a deep Protestant distrust of the practice of Confession. As time went on, it appeared quite clearly that the main points of controversy were:

(1) The right to make, or at least the desirability of making, changes of order or additions in the Eucharistic service.

(2) The right to reserve the Blessed Sacrament continually in the Church, and the manner of Reservation.

There was a time when the use or non-use of incense was thought, very oddly, to be a third decisive point, but to-day, while preferences remain, for or against, the use of incense is commonly allowed to be (a) scriptural, and (b) not doctrinally controversial. The two matters mentioned above remain hard points of controversy.

By 1889, when Ingram came to Oxford House, the Judicial Committee of the Privy Council, which was legally the supreme tribunal even for cases of Church doctrine and ceremonial, had been discredited in the public mind as a court for such purposes. It was being left to the Bishops to restore order, if they could. Bishop Frederick Temple, while he was in London, had rather given the Anglo-Catholics their head. They were workers. He himself was a great worker. He liked and respected workers, and so he did not interfere with them very much. The result was that the diocese of London became, in a liturgical sense, undisciplined. At Creighton's accession, it was said to be "in a state of chaos".

Creighton was an intense believer in the Church of England. He never for a moment doubted that it was part of the Catholic Church, but he emphasized its Englishness. He knew ten times as much history as the Anglo-Catholic clergy, or as anyone else, and he had a strong sense of the duty of obedience to law. He hated anything like persecution, and he could not adopt the dragooning methods which Sir William Harcourt, Protestant Colonels and Mr. Kensit pressed upon him, but his whole influence was in the direction of moderation. He found the Anglo-Catholics rather a nuisance. He reasoned with them patiently, but his flashing wit was sometimes unpalatable to them. One of his jokes was said at the time to "have lost him St. Peter's, London Docks". There was a conference about incense, and one of the priests said, "But it must be remembered, my lord, that we have the cure of souls." "Yes," said the Bishop, "and you think that they must be cured with smoke, like herrings."

Ingram succeeded to a diocese in which there was very great variety of practice. Islington, as always, was a strongly Protestant Evangelical area, secured for ever by its Patronage Trusts, and the West London parishes of Prebendary Webb-Peploe, Canon Webster and Canon Fleming were Evangelical centres. Broad churchmen were not numerous. Dean Stanley had died in 1881, Llewellyn Davies and Page-Roberts had left London, Edwin Abbott was no longer at the City of London School. Haweis had just died. Most parishes were of that rather undifferentiated complexion which was then called "mod-High".[1] There were a good many of the

---

[1] The great proof of the "success" of the Oxford Movement is not the existence of St. Alban's, Holborn, or churches of that kind, but the fact that in the great majority of Parish Churches the service is what it is. It is everywhere, with very few exceptions, very different

type which was beginning to be called "Anglo-Catholic" and of these some were more "advanced" or "extreme" than others.

One of the really difficult cases was that of St. Michael's, Shoreditch, which arose in 1903. The Bishop thus spoke of it at his Diocesan Conference:

> You will readily understand that to disturb a parish priest in his work among the poor is a distress to any Bishop, and especially, perhaps, to one who has learnt by long experience to love the poor himself, yet who knows how touchingly they follow those who teach them, and reward them for their work with a loyalty and affection which is their only earthly reward.
>
> It was only, therefore, from a stern sense of duty, that I decided that I must prosecute Mr. Evans for his teaching and practice at St. Michael's, Shoreditch. All pastoral remonstrance and episcopal monition had been disregarded, perhaps not unnaturally by one who had persuaded himself that what he taught and did was part of the Catholic faith, and that no Bishop had a right to interfere.
>
> Such action, in any similar case, I shall certainly take again. I draw the clearest line between those who during the past forty years were led to suppose, by silent acquiescence, that some use of incense, if not actually contemplated by the Ornaments Rubric, was at any rate a harmless adjunct to Divine worship, and those who with their eyes open introduced such services as I have described into their churches.

Another, even more difficult, case, which arose later, that of St. Saviour's, Hoxton, was described in chapter IX.

Meantime, there was the Prayer Book, which was the authorized manual of worship and standard of doctrine, and there was a nation, and also a Parliament, which were in the main Protestant. And that not Protestant in the old Elizabethan sense of "Anglican", in the sense in which Hooker was a Protestant, but Protestant in the sense that most of them disliked and distrusted the word "priest", and thought that excesses and what they called "Popery" ought to be controlled by the strong hand of law.

It was unfortunate, and unfair, that the charge of law-breaking should be used one-sidedly. There was a great deal of lawlessness among the Evangelicals. The direction to say Morning and Evening

from what it was a century ago. The late Dean of St. Patrick's once said to me that the one result of the Oxford Movement in the Church of Ireland was the introduction of the use of the black stole.

Prayer daily throughout the year was constantly disobeyed,[1] and liberties were taken with the Liturgy. Nevertheless, omission in these matters always seems to English people less blameworthy than excess. More particularly, when there is a claim to supernatural authority, and what are sometimes called "priestly pretensions", and above all, when what is done is, or even looks, at all like Rome, such practices as the locking of the Church from Sunday to Sunday, except on Wednesday or Thursday evenings, and the saying of the Words of Administration to a railful of Communicants at a time, seem to them small things in comparison.[2] Thus "the lawless clergy" in common speech were the Anglo-Catholic clergy. Moreover, it was not realized that conditions of life had everywhere changed so much since 1662 that complete conformity with every rubric would have been pedantic and most unwelcome to congregations.

Ingram was not, in the generally accepted sense of the word, an Anglo-Catholic. In reply to the question "Why are you not a Roman Catholic?" he was accustomed to say cheerfully, "Because I am an English Catholic," but this was in the sense in which any Cathedral Canon of Tractarian lineage, believing the Apostles' Creed, might have used the expression. He was in the first place an Evangelical, with a great passion for the conversion of souls. In the application of this to personal needs and pastoral work, he was a strong Churchman, devoted to the Prayer Book, with a clear sense of the intensely sacramental nature of the Christian religion. He did not, as some Bishops delight to do, make a practice of celebrating Holy Communion every day. Sundays, Thursdays and Saints' Days were his occasions for Communion. One of his Chaplains (he generally chose an Anglo-Catholic for Chaplain), before being appointed, asked if there would be any objection to his making arrangements to celebrate elsewhere on certain weekdays, as he had been accustomed to celebrate on most mornings of the week. His

---

[1]The Royal Commission of 1906 reported that, out of 622 Churches in the Diocese of London, in 232 there was no daily service, in 114 no service on Holy Days and in 1 no service on Ascension Day. The proportion in most other dioceses was a good deal higher.

[2]It must be remembered that the time spoken of is nearly fifty years ago. To-day toleration (or indifference) has increased. Parishioners are not now unwilling to speak of "Father So-and-so" if his congregation so speak of him, and they do not as a rule accuse him of being "a wolf in sheep's clothing" or "eating the bread of the Church of England, and teaching the doctrine of the Church of Rome." They are content to say, "Oh, well, you see, he happens to be very High Church."

reply was, "Of course not," and he went on to explain that "From a boy I was brought up to regard Holy Communion as a treat, and one does not want treats too often." He promised to pontificate at the "High Mass" in the open-air at the White City organized by the Anglo-Catholic Congress in 1933. In reply to protests he explained that to pontificate only meant saying the Absolution and the Blessing as is prescribed in the Prayer Book. Further protests followed. He patiently ascertained the reason of the objectors. "Having narrowed the grounds," his Chaplain writes, "to contra-vention of Prayer Book rubrics",

he secured a promise from those responsible for the Centenary arrange-ments that there should be some Communicants. In face of this promise the Kensit party promised to call off all protests at the Service. Five stalwart men, duly fasting, made their Communion, and no organized unseemliness occurred. True, in the distance a noise was made but it was by irresponsible individualists, and Mr. Kensit wrote at once to say how grieved he was that it had happened.

He had many friends among the extreme Anglo-Catholics. At Oxford House he had been on intimate terms with the clergy of St. Peter's, London Docks. In fact it was during that period that he first became aware of Anglo-Catholicism. "London," he said to Evangelical clergy in 1911:

was a revelation to him in more ways than one. He came across a body of people who spoke of the Sacrifice of the Mass, were very anxious to introduce prayers for the dead, felt that the Saints had been very much left out in our too Protestant Church, talked a great deal about private Confession, very much disliked being called Protestants, felt that the Church of England had drifted away a good deal from any real tangible doctrine of baptismal regeneration; felt that many Churchmen had made Confirmation not much more than a mere repetition of the bap-tismal vows, and desired to see more preaching and teaching of the Real Presence of our Lord in the Holy Communion. These were at that time an absolutely new set of ideas to him, and he at once set to work to try and understand them.

The effect of this study was not to convert him to all the beliefs, but to make him understand them better, and to like the men who ministered devotedly on those lines.

In June 1902 he took part in the Burial Service for Father Dolling of St. Saviour's, Poplar, and spoke movingly of Dolling's love for mankind. The *Church Times* said, "Not yet has the Church of England, so far as the bishops are concerned, ceased to act the part of the 'stony-hearted stepmother', to her noblest children. But as far as Mr. Dolling is concerned, the Bishop of London has wiped out this reproach." One of the last things he ever did was to dictate from his dying bed an affectionate tribute to Father Wainwright of St. Peter's to be included in his Memoir.

He knew that the Anglo-Catholic clergy were hard workers, and it seemed to him during his earlier years in London that they, more than anyone, shared his own Evangelical passion for conversion. In later years, whether because they went back a little in this respect or because others went forward, he came to think that they had less of a monopoly of this grace. He was always ready to visit their churches, except in a few cases where he felt obliged to impose a ban, and he allowed himself to be piloted through a good deal of unaccustomed ceremonial, which he neither liked nor understood. His chief aim in early years was to keep the different schools of thought together. At the Diocesan Conference in 1903 he appealed to Anglo-Catholics not to use the word "Mass".

At all events, he always liked the Anglo-Catholics, and believed in them, and was always disposed to trust them. A certain amount of confusion arose from time to time through his inveterate habit of saying to a man, "All right, old boy, I know you only want to do the best you can for your people. Go ahead on these lines." This would be said with real fatherly sympathy, but there was often nothing on paper, and the moderate policy which he had desired to commend sometimes in course of time "suffered a sea-change into something rich and strange". People said sometimes that the Anglo-Catholics "had him in their pockets". The writer can remember once commenting to a friend on something that the Bishop had said publicly. "Ah, yes," was the caustic reply, "that is because what Mackay whispers to him in his bed-chamber, the Bishop proclaims from the house-tops." One who knew him well says, "It was not that he was afraid of them, but he liked them, and desired to stand well with them." And they knew how to approach him on his more impressionable side.

196

In 1906 there was a Royal Commission over which Sir Michael Hicks-Beach, later Lord St. Aldwyn, presided, on Ecclesiastical Discipline. The Commission heard masses of evidence. Among the witnesses was the Bishop of London.

It appeared that incense was used in about forty churches of the diocese, and this use had been customary in these parishes for a number of years. The use was "a restricted use", and was believed to be in accordance with a compromise arrived at with Bishop Creighton and continued by himself, which was referred to by witnesses as "the compromise".[1]

In the matter of Reservation the Bishop said:

> I draw a clear difference between reservation for the sick and reservation for purposes of adoration.

There was naturally a certain difficulty in maintaining this distinction. For example, a locked chapel might have gates of open iron-work, through which a Pyx or Aumbry was clearly visible. In any case, the six churches which were under discipline for their ceremonial use of incense, declined to modify their existing use of Reservation.

The Bishop further said that he had required the discontinuance of the Mass of the Pre-Sanctified on Good Friday at St. Columba's, Haggerston and St. Clement's, City Road.

The Commission recognized that the law of public worship was "too narrow for the religious life of the present generation. It needlessly condemns much which a great section of Church people, including many of her most devoted members, value, and modern thought and feeling are characterized by a care for ceremonial, a sense of dignity in worship, and an appreciation of the continuity of the Church, which were not similarly felt at the time when the law took its present shape." There were a number of irregularities, practices which "lie on the Romeward side of a deep cleavage between the Church of England and that of Rome", defended as "Catholic custom—an allegiance which is found in practice to

[1]This may have been so, but it appears from the Life of Archbishop Davidson that the Bishops were rather taken aback by the announcement of Ingram's policy, and felt that it rather forced their hands. Later, in more important things than this, there is evidence that other bishops were embarrassed by his readiness in particular cases to concede what in theory was not permitted. He would perhaps have replied that some of his cases were more difficult than any of those in other dioceses.

involve assimilation to some of the most distinctive methods of Roman worship", which they believed "Should promptly be made to cease".

The nineteenth century method of procedure, of which the earlier stages were ecclesiastical diocesan or provincial courts, but the final court of appeal was the Privy Council, a secular Court, was in their opinion useless, because thousands of clergy, with strong lay support, refused to recognize the jurisdiction of the final court. Ingram had, very unwillingly, initiated proceedings in two cases, which were stopped by the resignation or submission of the incumbent, but, with one or two exceptions, the Bishops were extremely reluctant to use the secular arm. The Commission reported that:

> Confronted by a state of things in which ritual divergencies of very varying importance were prevalent, and in which the removal of all divergencies and the universal establishment of the standard of the Acts of Uniformity was plainly impossible, Bishops Creighton and Ingram, in London north of the Thames, and Bishop Talbot in South London, in an exceptionally difficult position, have been driven to attempt a solution of the problem by forbidding some and tolerating other irregularities. But it is not surprising that this course, which has been adopted more or less by other Bishops also, has led to results which must be regretted.

The advice of the Commission was that Letters of Business should be sought for the Convocations to revise the Prayer Book. Such Letters were sought and obtained, and the long task of revision began. It took twenty years.[1]

In the meantime the Bishop of London had to administer a difficult diocese,[2] and the difficulty, as least as it was seen and put before him in indignant letters by the Protestant public, was mostly on one side. An indication of the line taken by him can be seen from the following letters to the Vicar of St. Peter's, London Docks:

[1] In 1907 the London Diocesan Conference carried by a large majority a motion proposed by Prebendary Webb-Peploe that "this Conference does not consider the present time to be opportune for any alteration of rubrics". It also appeared in 1911 that all the deaneries were opposed to the idea of Revision. The Bishop spoke at a Diocesan Conference in that year in favour of proposals which had been made by Dr. Walter Frere.

[2] A London schoolboy wondered, like Miss Prattle about Dr. Jenkinson in Mallock's *New Republic*, whether the Bishop was High Church or Low Church. His mother took an opportunity to ask the Bishop. He replied, "Tell him, my dear, I have to father them all."

July 10th, 1907.

Dear Wainwright,

As I promised at our interview yesterday, I put on paper the terms on which I should be able to visit St. Peter's.

(i) If all extra services, not in the Prayer Book, or not sanctioned by me or by my predecessors, were discontinued. I have no reason for thinking that there are such services.

(ii) If the Reserved Sacrament were removed from the Church, either into some locked chapel where no services are held, except a weekly Celebration of the Holy Communion, or into some other safe place which I should have seen and approved.

(iii) If the use of Incense were restricted to those Festivals upon which I should agree with yourself. Although I cannot of course in any way bind my successor, I should hope that this would prove a permanent settlement with your Church, and it would be a great pleasure to me again officially to visit St. Peter's.

On January 27th, 1909 he wrote:

Dear Wainwright,

All your services and prayers and hymns have now been submitted to me or my predecessors, and approved. I understand, moreover, that you are prepared to use no hymn or prayer of which I do not, as Bishop, approve.

There remain therefore the two questions of Incense and Reservation.

(i) With regard to Incense, in view of the fact that Incense has been used in your Church for 40 years or more, I make no order.

(ii) With regard to the Reserved Sacrament, I sanction its being used for the purpose of communicating the sick, but direct that it shall be reserved in the mortuary chapel pointed out to me at my visit this morning, instead of the side-Chapel where it is now reserved. I feel sure that you will comply with this direction.

On December 20th, 1920.

Dear Father,

You have been so loyal about the Reserved Sacrament that I should like you to remove it from the Mortuary this Christmas, if you can find some suitable place in the Church. It might be in any side-Chapel, but not on the High Altar. God bless you in your faithful work.

Among the post-scripts in a bundle of correspondence are:

"All this is a great sadness to me."

and:

"Who is the brother who sends these things to the Press? He ought to have his head put in a bag."

And, in regard to some emendations which he was requiring in a parochial manual:

"You see I want to defend myself everything I sanction."

To his Diocesan Conference he said in 1902 that he was between the upper and nether millstone. Speaking of the thirty-nine "difficult" Churches, he said that:

> they consisted of the clergy and a large and enthusiastic body of laity . . . an often infuriated and at any rate sensitive congregation. The upper millstone was the opinion clearly expressed by those whose opinion has to any Bishop of London a very strong moral force upon him, though it has not legal binding power upon him . . . and that is the opinion of their Graces, the Archbishops. Therefore when you picture to yourselves a Bishop of London thinking to himself how he is going to steer his way between these two difficulties, how he is going to deal between the action of the upper and nether millstone, you will see, I think, the difficulty he is in, and you may perhaps wonder why it is that after such an experience I am alive this morning, and apparently well and cheerful to tell the tale.

It has not been possible, and would in any case be tedious, to trace in detail the history of the Bishop's dealings with the practice of the extreme wing, but there is no doubt that disorder, in the sense of the Report of the Royal Commission, increased, and not least in the Diocese of London, during the twenty years between the Report and the issue of the Revised Prayer Book. The London Evangelicals sorrowfully ascribed this to the policy of the Bishop of London. Some of it may have been due to lack of policy, but for the most part it just happened, in London as elsewhere.

The 1914-1918 War made a difference. In 1917 a thousand clergymen presented a memorial to the Bishops saying:

> "that the denial of the right of access to the reserved sacrament for the purpose of devotion would be understood to involve denial of the duty

200

to adore Christ whenever and wherever His sacramental presence might be vouchsafed. Compliance with such a restriction cannot rightly be demanded and will not be given."

Such rebellious language filled Gore "with something like despair".[1]

In Convocation that year the Bishop of London frankly admitted that the plan of locked chapels had broken down. Human grief and anxiety had overwhelmed it. The bishops "might just as well have

> stood in Palestine in the path of fifty thousand people who thought our Lord was in a certain house, as resist what is at least the same number of people who wish to lay their burdens at His feet to-day."

Gore always maintained that the Bishops had lacked prescience and had acted too late, and ineffectually. He also thought that many of the clergy had been very headstrong. Before he was a bishop he had written to another priest:

> We might have got a reasonable use of incense and a reasonable use of reservation, if people had made any genuine attempt to keep within the reasonable limits of the Prayer Book. As it is, we shall have to submit to being cut backwards, I fear, but assuredly it is very largely our own fault. Of that I do not perceive very much recognition, and yet to me it appears quite indisputable.[2]

Ingram's kind-heartedness, his affection for the Anglo-Catholic clergy, and his light-hearted way of considering that a friendly interview, a prayer and a blessing had settled a question for ever, did not promote the discipline which was being demanded in many quarters, which he himself really desired to see.

It was felt on all sides that the new Prayer Book, when it appeared, would either settle everything or at least bring everything to a head. During the long process of the work of revision, there was debate and experiment. The semi-official drafts, which prepared the way for the 1927 Book, were the work of representations of a more or less central or Cathedral type of churchmanship. Looked at from

---

[1] *Life of Bishop Gore*, 391. The comment of the Archbishop on this was that "it would have been not only surprising, but repellent to Lancelot Andrewes, or William Laud, or E. B. Pusey, or John Keble. *Life of Archbishop Davidson*, ii. 798.
[2] *Life*, 184.

another point, the Drafts embodied what such men as Bishop Walter Frere and Bishop Guy Warman thought might fairly be required of everyone. Meantime there were unofficial books, the Green Book (Church Union, Anglo-Catholic), the Orange Book (Alcuin Club, the "English" liturgical school), and the Grey Book (rather "Life and Liberty") published to persuade and guide the Church. The Evangelicals put out no Book. They announced themselves content with 1662. Most of them gradually became willing to see something on the lines of the semi-official drafts. The ultra-Protestant wing were opposed to all revision. They maintained, with great sincerity, and even greater inaccuracy, that they, and they alone, obeyed the Book.

When the Revised Prayer Book was at last published in 1927, the Bishop was on his World Tour, and only at a later date became aware of the atmosphere which its appearance produced.[1] He had of course taken part with the other members of the Upper House in its formulation, and like the other Bishops, with four exceptions, he defended it and spoke for it. It was in fact the Bishops' own remedy for disorders in the Church. It was approved by large majorities in all three Houses of the Church Assembly (Bishops, Clergy and Laity) and in all or nearly all, the Diocesan Conferences.[2] Most of those who voted for it had a few qualifying regrets. Bishop William Temple, then of Manchester, wrote: "A genuinely good book." Canon Quick said: "It is the only tangible hope."

The central body of Evangelical representatives voted for it, with some qualms. They thought that it was a not unreasonable compromise. Opposition came from some of the Anglo-Catholics and some of the more definitely Protestant Evangelicals. The Protestants opposed it because they thought, quite erroneously, that by it the Archbishop of Canterbury and his brother Bishops had sold the pass to Rome. To them the restoration of the Canon or central Eucharistic prayer to something like the form of 1549, the express authorization of Eucharistic vestments, and the permission in certain circumstances to reserve the Sacrament, was flat Popery.

It may be difficult for many readers of these pages to understand

[1] One of his clergy, reporting an interview, says, "It struck me that the Bishop knew very little about the final form of the Measure."
[2] The voting at the London Diocesan Conference: The Bishop, For: Clergy, 138 for: 83 against, Laity, 186 for: 178 against.

the strength and sometimes the bitterness of Protestant feeling and the hatred of Popery in some quarters. There are, or were at that time, those who spoke of "bread-worshippers". There is, or was, such Protestantism in Northern Ireland, in Lancashire, and perhaps elsewhere. The disciples of it adopted every means to discredit the Book and to procure its rejection by the House of Commons. As everyone knows, the Prayer Book is part of an Act of Parliament, The Act of Uniformity of 1662, and cannot legally be changed except by Parliament. It had been originally the work of the Church, and the House of Commons, then consisting wholly of Churchmen, had forborne to criticize or amend it, but had given to it legal sanction. Under the provision of the Enabling Act of 1919, Parliament, while not competent to amend any Measure of the Church Assembly, had still the power of saying "Yes" or "No". When the new Book appeared, Members of Parliament were diligently circularized, and were informed that, in spite of the Archbishop's pledge to the contrary, a change of doctrine in the Romeward direction was involved.

Many of them believed this, and in spite of excellent speeches in the House of Commons by Mr. (later Earl) Baldwin, Lord Hugh Cecil (now Lord Quickswood), Sir Boyd (now Lord) Merriman and others, the Book was twice decisively rejected. It is the fact that there was a majority of representatives of English Constituencies in favour of it, and it is therefore true to say that a Revised Prayer Book for the Church of England was thrown out by the votes of members whose constituencies were not concerned. To that, however, it may fairly be replied that our Parliament is a British Parliament and has authority in all national matters. A possible rejoinder is that many even of the English members were very far from being members of the Church of England. Some readers may recall a letter from Lord Birkenhead to *The Times* after the rejection, in which he made great play with the recurring refrain "always including Mr. Saklatvala". But all that again is part of the burden of "Establishment".

Some of the speeches delivered against the Book had a bearing on the diocese of London. Provincial Members of Parliament, discovering, very likely with a good deal of reluctance to handle such matters in Parliament at all, that it was their duty to become acquainted with the circumstances, took counsel with one another, and some of them were informed that London was the headquarters of the new-fangled High Church ways. Some of them visited Churches where there were rumours of strange goings-on, and one Member, a Scottish Presbyterian, held the House breathless while he described, with an eloquence worthy of a better cause, what he had seen and what he inferred:

"Why did they wear clothes? Because something was going to happen. Why did they take a wafer? Because something was going to happen. Why did they consecrate it? In order that something might happen. Why did they put it away in a little tabernacle? Because something had happened. What had happened? Would the right hon. gentleman who said that this Book did not contain any change of doctrine at all, tell him what had happened? Why did the priest wear his garments? That something might happen through him and through nobody else. What did he, in the faith of his heart, anticipate, by the grace of God, might happen? What did he understand to have happened when he placed the Elements in a special little tabernacle for the faithful to see or to feel even the mystical presence of? He understood, and there was not one of them who was so casuistical as to deny it, that the mystery, which to others might be magic, but to him was one of the most sacred mysteries in the whole of the living universe, had happened—God Himself, through him as the instrument, had come down upon the material manufactured by man. That was Transubstantiation, and that was the dividing principle between the two Churches. If the Church of England wanted that, then let her have it. Let her go on her own journey, and God be with her; but if she did not want it, then she could not pass this Book."

It is the fact that the diocese of London contained many "extreme" parishes, and that the Bishop had been gentle with the clergy of such parishes. When the news came at midnight on December 15th, 1927 that the Book had been rejected by the House of Commons, he was startled. An eye-witness reports that:

He was quiet for a moment, and then said in a low voice, "It was my fault."

He must have meant that his own lack of success in controlling difficult elements had given to Members of Parliament a false impression of what the Church of England really was.

Meantime, a body of Anglo-Catholics, not largely represented in the Church Assembly, but fairly numerous in the Church, disliked the Book for quite different reasons.

(i) The Book restored a large part of the Eucharistic Canon, that is, it set the Prayer of Oblation and the Lord's Prayer immediately after what had since 1552 been called the Prayer of Consecration. This was to be followed by the Communion of the People. So far, so good, though many would have preferred the further step of putting the Invocation, Confession, Absolution, Comfortable Words and Prayer of Humble Access between the Consecration and Communion. But the Epiklesis, or Invocation of the Holy Spirit:

> With thy Holy and Life-giving Spirit vouchsafe to bless and sanctify both us and these Thy gifts of Bread and Wine, that they may be unto us the Body and Blood of Thy Son, our Saviour Jesus Christ.

now came, as in the Scottish and American Prayer Books, *after* the Recital of the words "This is My Body. . . . This is My Blood". There had been an Epiklesis in Cranmer's 1549 Book, but it had come *before* the Recital of the Words. The position of the Epiklesis was defended by pointing out that Consecration is the act of God, in response to the prayer of the Church, and that it was not to be thought of as occurring at any precise moment, however solemn, but was the divine response to the whole prayer, sealed by the congregational "Amen", at the end. It was also said in defence that the new Canon followed what might be called the divine order of events. The Commemoration of the Institution was now (rightly, in the opinion of all liturgical scholars) followed by mention of the Resurrection and Ascension of our Lord, the Divine Events which give reality to the Sacrament, and make it not merely a remembrance of what was done in the Upper Room and on Calvary, and what could be more suitable after that than commemoration of Pentecost and an Invocation of the Holy Spirit. And there were also of course the Scottish and American precedents.

Against this there was the fact that it involved some rather difficult theology. Moreover, English communicants had been taught for years and had come to believe that Consecration was effected by the recital of the words. The Church of England had been tied by its

Prayer Book since 1552 to a narrowly Western view of the manner of Consecration. "More Roman than Rome itself," Bishop Frere used to say. This had been marked in Anglo-Catholic Churches by genuflexions, often after each half of the Words, and by other symbolic practices, and in the congregations by a silence which could be felt. It was disturbing to have a different view thrust upon them which invalidated, or made otiose, much of their treasured practice. "Why," they said, "should we have an Invocation of the Holy Spirit when the Consecration is already complete." This was a real difficulty, not only to Anglo-Catholic theologians but to a very large number of simple and devout people.

(ii) Reservation of the Blessed Sacrament for the purpose of communicating the sick was now definitely permitted, but it was hedged round with what they considered to be un-Catholic and exasperating conditions.[1] The desire of the Bishops was to prevent the Services of Benediction, Exposition or Devotions before the Blessed Sacrament from being held. It seemed to the Bishops (and to many others) that such services encouraged an unduly and untruly local conception of the divine Presence.[2] Accordingly, Reservation was to be strictly for the purpose of communicating the sick, and, further, was only to be allowed even for this purpose if the Bishop of the diocese considered that in the circumstances of the parish it was desirable.

This was very unwelcome to the Anglo-Catholics. Comparatively few of them desired to have the extra-liturgical services which were ruled out by the Book, but very many resented the idea that in what they deemed to be a simple matter of pastoral duty they were to be at the mercy of the veto of a possibly quite unsympathetic bishop. They also desired liberty to give Communion outside the service to persons who were prevented by their daily duties from coming to Church at the time of service. The learned Dr. Darwell Stone put a weapon into their hands. He discovered

[1] The Bishop of London said to a priest (I have a full report of the conversation made the same day) that he regarded this point as the worst thing in the book.
[2] Bishop Gore said that these practices were "devotionally very attractive" but could not be justified on theological grounds. The author of the standard book on the history of the subject, W. H. Freestone, *The Sacrament Reserved*, concludes his inquiry—"The original purpose of official Reservation (i.e., Reservation in Church) was purely practical (for Communion). The development of any *cultus* of the Reserved Sacrament was the direct outcome of the acceptance of the doctrine of transubstantiation as the orthodox belief."

that Archbishop Peckham had said *ex cathedra* in the thirteenth century that it was the duty of the parish priest to reserve the Sacrament in the parish church, so that it might be always available. It was claimed that injunctions of this kind, if not definitely repealed, were still binding. This was a good weapon, which they used with vigour. Between December 1927 and the second approach to Parliament in 1928 Anglo-Catholic opposition to the Book hardened a good deal.

The Bishop of London's reaction to all this was as follows. His reply to those who said that the new Prayer Book betrayed the Church of England to Rome was expressed in a letter to Sir William Joynson-Hicks, leader of the Protestant party.

First of all, you seem to ignore, not only in your letter, but in all the speeches I have heard and read of yours, the fact that the Old Prayer Book can be used unaltered by those who wish to use it. This point is fundamental, yet is often left entirely out of sight in recent discussions. . . . Your next point relates to disorder in the Church; but do you find it so very easy to produce order in the State, even with the most efficient police in the world? You promised some of us who came as a deputation on January 26 a year or two ago, to deal in some way with night clubs and drinking clubs, but so far as I know you have done nothing with regard to either. I do not blame you; I know the difficulty of the question.

You next come to Reservation for the Sick, and ask would it not be fairer to have said that the object of Reservation was to placate that section who believe in some form of Transubstantiation? No! It would not have been fairer, for it would not have been true.

What you do not seem to me to see is that there is another way to regard the Holy Sacrament besides yours, which is not Transubstantiation, and is quite as legitimate in the Church of England as your own. This is a doctrine of the real and objective Presence of Christ in the Sacrament which has been pronounced as tenable in the Church of England as you, of course, know, both at the Court of Arches, and the Judicial Committee of the Privy Council.

I do not believe that you realize how many of our people hold this view, or how much consideration we owe to them in this matter of Reservation. If the sacred elements are the Body and Blood of Christ to you in the morning, when you receive them, so they also are to the sick person in the afternoon.

Cannot the people on your side be generous enough, not only to keep within the Church of England, but make happy in the Church of England those to whose work and devotion we owe so much?

I quite admit that there are a handful of people, both priests and laity, who would really be happier in the Church of Rome, but to antagonize the whole body of Anglo-Catholics who are perfectly loyal to the Church of England is not the way to deal with them. Your present policy, if successful, can only lead to a disruption of the Church of England. This, I feel sure, no one would deplore more than yourself.

Yours faithfully,

A. F. LONDON.

Fulham Palace, May, 1928.

To the Anglo-Catholics he was disposed to say (with Bishop Gore) that the Book gave them a great deal more than might have been expected, and more than some of them deserved. It is probable that to these two Bishops together, in their different ways, much of the credit for the gains in the new Book were due.

The rejection of the Book by Parliament, which did not of course mean that in the eyes of Parliament all parts of it were to be condemned, but that, in view of the controversial nature of some parts of it, it was not to become the law of the land, elicited a notable declaration of spiritual independence. The Archbishop had never been enthusiastic about revision, the New Book was not precisely what he would have chosen, and he was always rather disposed to listen to important laymen at the House of Lords and the Athenæum. Nevertheless he had guided the Church, and its Assembly, through the difficult years of revision with conspicuous wisdom, and he now boldly declared that in the unanimous opinion of the Bishops:

> It is a fundamental principle that the Church—that is, the Bishops together with the Clergy and the Laity—must in the last resort, when its mind has been fully ascertained, retain its inalienable right, in loyalty to our Lord and Saviour Jesus Christ, to formulate its Faith in Him and to arrange the expression of that Holy Faith in its form of worship.

The Bishop of Durham (Henson) said that the situation was definitely intolerable, and that the only remedy was Disestablishment. Most of the Bishops, though it was a hard blow to have their own prescription for disorder rejected by Parliament, and then still to be expected to restore order and be blamed for not doing so, determined to make the best of a bad job. They said in effect that they would carry on as if the Deposited Book had received State sanction. It would not of course be the official, legalized Prayer Book of the Church, but they would allow deviations from the order of 1662, if they came within the limits of what was permitted in 1927. Some of them added that the larger changes, such as the use of the long Eucharistic Canon, should not be made unless the good will of the Parochial Church Council had been secured. The new Prayer Book had no legal sanction, but it had been approved by the Church and might be used.[1]

The Anglo-Catholics had one more shot in their locker. It could not be denied that the Book had been approved by all three Houses of the Church Assembly, and it was the fact that the two clerical Houses consisted of exactly the same persons as the four Houses of Convocation of Canterbury and York. Nevertheless, by reason of the rejection of the Book by Parliament it had not gone back, as it would have done, if Parliament had assented, for final adoption by the Convocations. There is no doubt that it would have received final adoption, but in fact it never did. From one point of view this is a technicality, from another a constitutional defect. Thus, when Anglo-Catholics speak, sometimes rather contemptuously, of the "abortive" 1927-1928 Prayer Book, they mean that it was never finally approved by the Convocations, and so has no Synodical authority. When Protestant Evangelicals so speak, they mean that it did not receive the approval of Parliament. There is reason to believe that the Protestant Party would have withdrawn their opposition between 1927 and 1928 if the controversial points of the Book had been excised, but the Bishops could not agree to this, because the Book at those points was actually their remedy for disorder.[2]

The Book has in fact been very widely used since 1928. Many parts of it are used almost everywhere, and in some places all of it. In some matters, e.g., the alternative prayers provided for use after the Third Collect, in the Baptism and Marriage Services, congrega-

[1]The Bishop of London said at his Diocesan Conference in 1929, "Of course in this Diocese we shall follow the lead of the Province, and as the Province has decided to allow any deviations which do not go beyond the Prayer Book of 1928, they are allowed in the diocese. But I would like anyone who starts the new Canon to let me know . . . If the Parochial Church Council is willing, it is allowed to be used.

[2]See Life of Archbishop Davidson, ii. 1348.

tions have been most grateful for the improvement, sometimes not knowing whence it comes. The language of the Book has been a good deal criticized by competent judges, and there is no doubt that the next attempt, whether or not it proves able to bring together different sections of ecclesiastical conviction, will be a better liturgical production.

There was for these reasons a measure of uncertainty about the authority of the Book which made it difficult for the Bishop of London to regulate extra-liturgical devotions. He made an appeal to the Anglo-Catholics: "I shall look upon you and your friends as a general looks upon soldiers who desert him in a great battle if you do not support me now"[1]—but it was not very successful.

Then came the Synod of the Clergy, the first to be held in the diocese for some centuries, in 1928. It proved a disappointment for the Bishop. His proposals were defeated. 1,066 voters were present. Two questions only were answered in the affirmative:

(i) Are you willing that the Bishop should allow Reservation of the Consecrated Elements for cases of known sickness until the known sick person can on the same day be communicated? (Majority 82).

(ii) Are you willing to support the Bishop in endeavouring for the sake of peace in the Church to secure that practices which are consistent neither with the Book of 1662 nor with the Book as amended in 1928, shall cease? (Majority 36).

To all the rest the answer of the majority was in the negative. Some called it an "unholy alliance". One of the leaders on the Anglo-Catholic side is content to say that "Catholics and Evangelicals (for quite opposite reasons) voted No to all but two of the questions which the Bishop asked us to answer in the affirmative." One of the clergy present described it as "a most humiliating experience".

The Bishop got over his disappointment, as he always did.[2] He issued Regulations about Reservation which led to the "Revolt of

[1] In a private letter.

[2] He was sometimes rather exasperated by some of the Anglo-Catholics. Some years before this he received a telegram from some Anglo-Catholic signatories, urging what a witness of the incident calls "some drastic action". As he read it, "a rather impatient look of disapproval momentarily shadowed his face but he said nothing till afterwards. His remark later was, 'I just can't be bothered with them. If they think like that, then let the whole lot go over to Rome.'" In 1936 the Bishop complained at the Diocesan Conference that in a Church which had been "under discipline" for twenty-five years, an assistant priest, who had been appointed to succeed his Vicar on condition that he gave up Benediction with the Monstrance, had now written to say that his congregation were slipping away to

the Twenty-one". The response of the majority can be seen in the following extracts from the Parish Magazine of a London Parish:

> The Bishop of London has made it clear that he is not attempting to forbid adoration, but only a particular method of adoration. We very much regret his decision, and to obey it involves great sacrifice, but we feel that he is acting within his rights and should not feel justified in refusing obedience. The Bishop is willing to allow another service to take the place of "Devotions" provided it could equally well be used if the Reserved Sacrament were not present. He cannot and he does not attempt to control the mental intention of the worshippers, but he desires the service to be of such a kind that any one present who does not share our view of the nature of the Eucharistic Presence would not regard the proceedings as meaningless.

A later number of the same Magazine (September 1931) records that the prohibition of Devotions was afterwards withdrawn, and that "the service, with the consent of the Bishop, recommenced on September 19th".

The twenty-one incumbents addressed to the Bishop an Open Letter, in which they stated their case against independent action by "two provinces". He drafted a reply, and submitted the draft to the Archbishop (Lang), whose answer was:

My dear Bishop,

I have now tried to give further consideration to your letter, recognizing as I do its very great importance in the present situation and the way in which it will be scrutinized by those on both extreme sides who wish no well to the Bishops at the present time. I am bound to say that the more I think of it the more I adhere to my own opinion that you would have been wise, after characteristic personal words, to have declined to enter into public controversy with clergy in your Diocese to whom you had issued your directions, stating that you would have been willing to talk matters over with any of them and that doubtless opportunity would be given to you to deal in a more fitting way with the large questions which their letter had raised. If you had wished to go beyond this, I still think it would have been sufficient to say that you were not able to agree with either of the main premises on which their argument was founded—namely that the Church of England is nothing

other Churches, whose Clergy, without saying anything to the Bishop, had started Benediction. The Bishop added, "This is most unfair to him and most unfair to me and I want it to be distinctly understood that Benediction with the Monstrance is forbidden in this Diocese."

more than two Provinces of the Western Church, saying much what you have done in your present letter. Secondly, that your regulations do not in any way impugn any doctrine of the Catholic Church about the nature of the Presence of Our Lord in the Sacrament of Holy Communion, and there you might have put in what you have said in your point (2). But, as I said before, you have your own responsibility and you must view the situation in your own way and will probably think it right to issue for the most part unchanged the letter whose draft I now return. Only, even so, I beg you not to put in . . .

Forgive me if I seem too critical. But assuming that you put out your draft much as it is, I am sure that the latter points which I have mentioned are of real importance. You know how earnestly I pray that in your immense difficulties you may be guided and strengthened.

The Bishop adopted the detailed suggestions, and his reply, as sent, is as follows:

In my opinion your letter contains five fallacies:—

(1) In the first place let me point out that it is a mistake to suppose that all intercessions and prayers and hymns are forbidden in every church in which the Sacrament is reserved. On the contrary I should be extremely sorry if those informal little services of meditation and prayer which many, including the very poor, love and understand more than they do the statutory services, should cease to be held.

All that is forbidden is Devotions *directly connected with* the Reserved Sacrament. All I have forbidden you to do is to move the Reserved Sacrament from its appointed place, to open the Aumbry or Tabernacle, to cense it, or to allude to the Presence of the Reserved Sacrament in your prayers.

Out of the 170 Incumbents who have Reservation in this diocese and who are as strong Anglo-Catholics as you are yourselves, with a few exceptions, you 21 are the only ones who have not seen your way to obey this regulation.

(2) The second fallacy is that the Doctrine of the Real Presence *depends* upon such devotions directly connected with the Reserved Sacrament.

It is a matter of common knowledge that for 800 or 1,000 years such Devotions were unknown. You surely cannot contend that the whole Church, including the Church of Rome, during that period did not hold the doctrine of the Real Presence.

(3) Feeling, I think, a little uncomfortable on this ground, you then

take your stand upon the method of the appointment of Bishops. No one feels the possible danger which underlies this method more than I do myself, and I was Chairman of a joint Committee of the Convocation of Canterbury, which suggested a better method. This was turned down not by the House of Bishops but by the House of Clergy. But can it really be contended that the fact that the State has a voice in the appointment of Bishops, which it had (as you acknowledge) long before the Reformation, really frees us as priests from the obligation of our oath of Canonical obedience.

Remember we knew all about this method of appointment when we were ordained, and still better when we were instituted to livings; in the service itself we promised Canonical obedience to our Bishops, knowing that they were nominated by the State. Is it not too late now, when we are placed in important positions on this understanding, to turn round and say that we repudiate the obligations which we solemnly took with our eyes open?

I feel sure that the conscience of the Laity of the Church will not support you in that contention. By all means meanwhile agitate in Convocation and eventually in Parliament, if necessary, for some constitutional change.

(4) The fourth fallacy is that a National Church has no power to regulate its own customs and ceremonies. Pope Gregory, to whom we owe so much for sending us St. Augustine, took a very different view; he told Augustine to respect any local traditions and customs which he found.

What you speak of a little contemptuously as "Two Provinces" really means what is now the world-wide Anglican Communion which I have recently visited, spread throughout the world. One can hardly call the Church of England with its great daughter Churches in Canada, the United States, Australia, New Zealand and South Africa, "merely two Provinces" of the Church.

(5) But the greatest fallacy of all in your argument is the belief that because things have been obtained by disobedience in the past, therefore they will be in the future.

By all means agitate in Convocation and convert the Church, if you can, to your view, and then start upon the Nation, but for the time I would ask you to consider what harm you are doing by open disobedience to "admonitions" which no fair-minded people could call either unreasonable or "ungodly".

Yours affectionately in Christ,
A. F. London.

It would be difficult to investigate and tedious to record what happened in all the parishes concerned, but the result was that, speaking broadly, the Anglo-Catholics in London got what they wanted. The Bishop listened with friendliness to all the deputations of any kind that ever came to him. Sometimes the Evangelicals would wait upon him, and suggest that men of their school were not often appointed to livings in episcopal patronage. To this he was inclined to say that they were provided for by their Patronage Trusts in North London. That said, he dismissed them with kind words and a blessing, and went on as before. His excellent Suffragans, while they could not be classed as Anglo-Catholics, would not have been claimed by the Evangelicals as of their party. He appointed the Reverend E. N. Sharpe to be Archdeacon of London, and thereby secured not only an admirable Archdeacon but a sober and liberal exponent of Evangelical opinion. Yet this could not be called a characteristic appointment.

The Evangelicals, who were loved by him and loved him in return, were rather sad about their standing and prospects in the diocese. It seemed to them that their place in the sun—according to most of them, a place with others, but, in the opinion of some of the more inflexible, the only lawful place—was being reduced. In so far as this was due to the policy of the Bishop, he might have replied that he was only registering at his own level a movement in the Catholic direction which was taking place in the Church of England. The Bishop had said in 1907 in a sermon at St. Matthew's, Westminster, that:

> There is only one principle in making appointments in the present state of the Church of England, and that is to maintain something like continuity in the doctrine and practice of each parish; otherwise you wound consciences and distort the minds of the young, and drive people in disgust from the Church altogether.

To this principle he always intended to adhere, but (a) it is very hard in making appointments not to have a bias, and (b) there was, as is said above, during his lifetime a movement all along the line. The London parish in which the present writer was brought up and confirmed, which is in the gift of the Crown, has become very different from what it used to be.

One of the Evangelical leaders puts it in this way:

> In his readiness to encourage zeal wherever he found it, the Bishop seemed to lose sight of the fact that he was changing the current of ecclesiastical thought and practice in London. He was putting into strategic positions men whose teaching was cutting at the root of the principles of the Reformation, fidelity to which seemed vital to Evangelicals.
>
> The Bishop was unable or unwilling to perceive the full effect of this upon his diocese; nor would he acknowledge that there was considerable discontent among his clergy. In his view everything was all right in the best of all possible dioceses; and his charm of manner, real goodness and saintly life did much to hush the murmurs of those who could not bear to be in opposition to one who, notwithstanding his own preferences and opinions, was beloved by all. In any case the Bishop pursued his own happy course unmoved by the representations made to him.

To Anglo-Catholic deputations he listened more effectively. Partly because they explained to him what a Catholic Bishop ought to do, and partly because they put their case as a matter of pastoral care, with which he sympathized intensely. It may look like weakness, but his chaplain at the time writes that "his attitude towards these priests was not so much one of weakness as of sympathy with priests whom he knew and believed to be working with all their heart and soul to the Glory of God and the Church".

He gave a great deal of time and attention to the questions raised by them. Was it too much? In one sense it was not, because from one point of view it could be said that the character of the Church of England depended on the answer given to such questions. In a deeper sense it was. Time was spent on arguing about Rubrics which could have been given to the conversion of souls, as well as to other more general work of the Church. A London incumbent, in his youth a famous athlete, said, "Relatively, he gave too much time to placating unruly parsons, but he was so much liked by his friends that he could give them a miss without losing them."

In dealing with men, he was shrewd, and not ignorant of the devices of controversialists:

> Once he seemed to think that I was pulling wool over his eyes. He

chuckled and remarked, "Never make the mistake, my dear boy, of thinking a Bishop is such a fool as he looks."

Another time he was talking about a very extreme clergyman who, it seems, had told Arthur Foley that there was a growing demand among his people for Communion in one kind. "What nonsense! I know perfectly well what has happened. The curate, probably encouraged by the Vicar himself, has been telling them that it is the right thing to want, but they never thought of it themselves—of that I am quite sure."

Yet he loved them, and to a considerable extent he gave them their head. Let this chapter end with a tribute from a priest who was at one time on the staff of one of the extreme parishes in London, and has since had some remarkable wartime experiences:

Arthur Foley—now that's someone. I admit London diocese was chaotic, but where else was there so much religion? I wish I could find words for it, but there seems to me, even now, a quality about the religious life of church after church in that diocese which is very uncommon anywhere else. A quality of which the very liability to abuse proves the worth. A sort of Christian vulgarity which was— still is—productive of immense overflows of love. I've never really thought about it much—besides my trouble is that I can see things but am too ignorant to express them. But I am sure that the typical Anglo-Catholic priest of the Arthur Foley generation in London seemed to "have something", as the Americans say, which I have rarely found outside that diocese. Even in —— it was quite different. One was back in the C. of E.! Yes, yes, of course. But what a lot one missed.

A bit bitter at times? Yes, they were that, and not to be wondered at, since they had not only to fight in the vanguard but to guard against the stab in the back from those who followed to make sure of being in on any properly consolidated territory. Yet how often that bitterness was transformed by grace into pure naughtiness—so disturbing to the righteous, so winning to the sinner.

XI

FRIENDSHIPS

O NE of the difficulties of writing this book arises from the fact that the Bishop's life was made up of innumerable personal contacts. He had, as everyone must recognize, an extraordinary gift for friendship. Often it made him think that he could settle a knotty problem with a few kind words spoken to a controversialist. The kind words were utterly genuine, and, from the side which was at the moment in question, they did penetrate the impasse. He concentrated on the needs of the person to whom he was talking, and he had, for that purpose, a very sure touch. He extracted from people what they had not thought that they were going to say.[1] And it was, to use words which he often quoted from Hosea, "by the bands of love, by the cords of a man". There is a story of Bishop Gore, going up the stairs at Lambeth to have a talk with Archbishop Davidson, and telling himself, "Now, Charles, you know you must not agree to that," and then, as he came down again, "Now, Charles, you know you never meant to agree to that." Bishop Gore fell, if it be conceded that it really was a fall, a victim to statesmanlike persuasion. It was not that with Ingram's friends. Charmed by his loving smile, they yielded up the secrets of their hearts. This, to them, brought happiness and peace, but, at times when statesmanship was needed, the Bishop would often sail off on the magic carpet of his buoyant optimism, and leave the problem incompletely solved. An East London clergyman (the Reverend Kenneth Ashcroft) reported to the Bishop that some men in his parish had been abusing the Bishops. He says:

I was working in Poplar in the difficult days between the two wars. There was a great deal of extreme left-wing activity. Indeed at one period a "Red Army" (only about 40 or 50 of them, it is true) used to parade round the streets every Saturday evening, and groups of young

[1] It need hardly be said that this refers to conversation, not to auricular confession. He did hear a great many confessions, especially of the clergy.

enthusiasts used to spend the night painting slogans on the pavements. When the clergy tried to do anything in the way of outdoor speaking, they were subjected to continuous heckling. Gilbert Shaw was running a club for unemployed men and did quite a lot of outdoor speaking as well, and soon we got to know some of the interrupters, and good fellows they were too. But they were firmly convinced that the Church of England was hopelessly reactionary and "in the pay of the capitalists". "What do the Bishops care about us? They sit in their palaces while we go short," etc.

In one of our many arguments—in which both sides always said the same thing again and again—one of the more vocal revolutionaries said once more that the Bishops just did not care. We denied this. Then he said, "Well, anyway, none of them would see us and let us put our case." I remember saying that I would bet my shirt that if any of them asked Arthur Foley for an interview they would get it without difficulty. "Well, you ask him," said they.

I wrote to him and told him what had happened, and he replied, telling me to come and see him. On the appointed day I went to Fulham. Arthur Foley had got it all clear in his mind, "I'm going to ask you to bring ten of them to tea next Saturday afternoon," he said.

We discussed arrangements and at one point someone, I can't remember who, asked where the Bishop would receive these men. He snapped out, as he could when he was irritated, "In the drawing-room of course—where do I usually receive guests?"

He was obviously filled with glee at the prospect of once again getting into contact with East End hecklers.

What an afternoon it was! We arrived, and were shewn into the big drawing-room, from which his study opened. Our ten revolutionaries were a little overawed by its size. In a few moments Arthur Foley came in looking alive, and splendid, in his purple, and in a few more he had everyone at his ease. Then the talk began. Some very hard things were said, to which the Bishop listened, delighted and unshocked. When he spoke, he talked with disarming candour and friendliness, telling his guests where he thought they were right and where he felt they were wrong.

At 4.30 we had a very jolly tea party then some more talk, then he blessed us and sent us home. Coming out of the Palace, one of the men said to me, "What a bitter cold place—ain't it got no central heating?" I was apologetic, but "it ain't us I'm thinking about," he said, "but it's a disgrace that that dear old gentleman should have to live in this cold place." A little later he said, "you mustn't think that we would want to turn him out of here—it's sort of right for him."

That afternoon made a lot of difference to Poplar, and we no longer heard the old, old story that the Bishops didn't care. In fact, the ten were somewhat uplifted and took the line, "He's a friend of mine"— and they never said a truer word.

It is intensely characteristic. Of course it did not resolve the social problems nor redress inequalities nor remove scandals, but for once it brought East and West together in a human and Christian relationship, and it gave to a Christian bishop ten friends, and, through them, many more.[1]

It was in the same spirit that he used to say, "When I go to Harrow for the Confirmation, I think it is most important that the parents would be made to feel responsible for helping their boys to carry on. So after the Confirmation I get the parents to stay behind by themselves and give them a little talk." It was no doubt a very winning talk, and probably did more good than the same number of words from any other person in England would have done, but there was always the half-suggestion that after such a talk there would be no more trouble in the homes. It was not vanity. It was simplicity and boundless optimism, and a belief that personal friendliness would unlock every door. And perhaps it will for the time being. But there are winds, cold winds and hot winds, which slam the doors again. Nevertheless, the man who could so easily open doors into the hearts of Harrow Parents and of Left Wingers from East London was both loving and versatile.

This chapter is made up from letters and reminiscences, only a part of what was actually available, and no doubt representing only a thousandth part of what the Bishop was always doing all his life. He did it to all sorts of people, but above all, to the young. Let us see him first with children.

He liked nothing better than to be surrounded by children. There are among the books of newspaper-cuttings which friends have diligently preserved many photographs of the Bishop sitting among groups at the Princess Christian Day Nursery, Hammer-

---

[1] It should perhaps be added that another East London priest, who was not the Vicar of the parish but knew something of the circumstances, is of opinion that the ten men were not in fact completely satisfied.

smith, the Heritage Craft School, Chailey, the Marine Hospital, Tidemills, St. Nicholas and St. Martin Hospital, Pyrford, and also with Guides, Scouts, Church Lads' Brigade and child-actors in *Where the Rainbow Ends*.

An East London Vicar writes:

I remember opening my front door one night in —— Street, when he had come to preach for us, and finding him on the step surrounded by a choice collection of small East London children. Of course they collect pretty easily; but other people succeeded in arriving without them. His critics thought of him as a showman, and, of course, no one could know him at all well without seeing plenty of signs that would bear just that interpretation; but no one would know him at all well without being quite sure that he really did like people.

He captivated children in the pulpit. Like other speakers addressing adult audiences, he was sometimes unable to reach the children at the same time. There was a little girl who said towards the end of his sermon, "Mummy, I'm tired. Can't the Bishop go back to Heaven?" Doubtless quite often he triumphed even over the desperate problem of the mixed audience, as a clergyman once did, preaching in a church in Exeter. A little boy, whom his parents had with some hesitation kept with them during the sermon, sat patiently listening, and clutching his penny in his hand. At the end he suddenly said, "That's jolly good. I'll give him twopence." The Bishop must have had many experiences comparable to that. There is in actual fact no record of his sermons to very young congregations, but his general habit of arranging his teaching, under five heads, or giving six reasons for a belief, would have made his meaning very clear to them, and his fatherly affection always charmed them.

The Dean of Gloucester remembers an instance of his effectiveness with a rather older audience. It was at the Public Schools Military Camp at Aldershot, sometime before 1910. "The Bishop preached in the open-air at 7 a.m. His sermon lasted exactly two minutes, and it was divided into four heads, each of half a minute. It was excellent. The amount of good teaching which the Bishop contrived to pack into that miniature sermon was the admiration of us all."

In their own homes, and as often as possible in his home, he took them by storm. When preaching in a London church, he would go into the Vicarage for a meal, and would make friends with the children, if they were old enough to be still up. If not, he would go upstairs and see them in bed. Here is one such incident:

He came over to a Confirmation at St. —— and had supper with us. Of course, we were very hard up, but on account of the children we usually had some kind of help in the house. Still, this was a time when we hadn't any, and my wife was looking after everything. After supper he insisted on seeing the children, who were asleep in bed, and blessing them. Then before we went into church he said some prayers with us two, blessed us, kissed my wife, and that, so far as we guessed, was that. However, next morning, my wife got a letter from him enclosing £10 and giving an invitation for us all to come to Fulham Palace for a fortnight, where she and I would be free, and someone would entirely look after the children. We couldn't go, but there it was.

The evidence of Miss Pearce, who was often summoned from her brother's house at Westminster Abbey to help in the entertaining of some set of visitors, is that among them at any given time:

There would probably be a clergyman's wife and child who were staying at Fulham for a few days after the child's tonsils had been removed.

On one occasion:

As always, I was called into the study to be told about the people who would be at dinner. That evening the story was amazing. A Bluecoat boy, whose mother was a widow living in Fulham, had been badly kicked at football. The result was a sarcoma in the leg, and the boy had about two months to live, and needed constant trained nursing. The Bishop had realized that the widow could not possibly pay for a nursing-home, and so the mother, nurse and boy were installed in pleasant rooms, looking out on the garden, for the rest of the boy's life. It was the year that the Bishop paid a visit to Canada, but he was able to lay the boy to rest in Fulham churchyard about a week before he started.

Miss Pearce adds:

I suppose his constant joyfulness arose from the fact that he could constantly shew his love for his Lord by loving his neighbours as, or even more than, himself.

There were some who took advantage of his kindness. Here is a picture of the more seamy side. Some trouble, of a personal rather than an ecclesiastical kind, had arisen in a parish, and the ex-Vicar and his wife, then no longer in the diocese, were asked to come to Fulham to help the Bishop in the matter:

There was a pretty odd crowd at dinner, but I can't remember who they were. Before dinner and the appearance of the Bishop, conversation was very sticky, and one felt that it was intended, almost by the method of direct question, to discover why we were there. After dinner, interviews began, so there must have been, I suppose, some people who weren't residents. When I was sent for M. was left with the rest. She was subjected to a pretty solid catechism on the lines, "What do you want from the Bishop?" the assumption being that no one came who was not trying to get something from him. In the end she had to stop it by bluntly refusing to answer, and when I returned the atmosphere was very sticky. They seemed to be partly just inquisitive, but partly self-appointed guardians, unfriendly, making her feel that "we know you are only spongers like the rest". It was all a bit too much a party of adorers of the dear Bishop. He never, by the way, succeeded in doing anything to solve the St. —— problem but he wanted to try.

This was no doubt a bad patch. One shrewd lady, who had opportunities of observing, says that "The circle at Fulham narrowed pitifully", but testifies in the same letter that the Bishop's forbearance with dull people, and doubtless sometimes unpleasant people, was unending. And it is probable enough that some of those who were present on that sticky evening had ailing children, whom the Bishop was helping to heal. The hard-up parents of sick children are tempted to be acquisitive.

Here is a happier reminiscence from the Dean of Hereford:

My earliest recollection of Bishop Ingram is in the nineties. I was away at School but I shall never forget the talk about his visit to Godalming, Surrey, where my father was Vicar, to speak at a men's meeting. Surely no other man has been so constantly talked about in

Vicarage homes as Arthur Foley, in his younger days. His coming was like a breath of new life which I can still feel, though I was not there when he came, and which had made a difference in the home.

What he did, how he played football in the attic with my sister aged eight, what he said to the men, what encouragement he left for the Vicar in his work, and what he was in himself, was felt for many a long day afterwards. The two boys at school felt they had missed something by not being there, and hoped that they would yet get a chance of meeting him. What if that was the impression that every Bishop left as he entered the homes of his people! In those days he was Bishop of Stepney.

But our chance was soon to come. The whole family was thrilled with the news that he had been made Bishop of London. I cannot remember whether it was for the first or the second great Children's Party at Fulham on Holy Innocents' Day, that my sister Molly and her two brothers were bidden to come. At any rate I very well remember walking round the garden with the Bishop, and his telling me (a boy of fourteen at Charterhouse) that he had published his balance sheet as Bishop of London, to shew that he spent more on his job than he received.

A strange conversation to a small boy, but I remember being rapidly caught up into the interest of his life, and feeling mentally that if he did save a penny or two on the income I should feel he very well deserved it. The thrill of that first party at Fulham! Part of the excitement was that we came without our parents. We had no claim to be there; my father was not a London Incumbent. But the Bishop had retained a memory of my sister, and of his welcome at Godalming, and the boys were asked to come as well.

The great event at Fulham every Christmas was the Children's Dance. Year by year the children of the London Clergy, the Choristers of St. Paul's, his own little nephews and nieces, some other children, and some ex-children who were invited as stewards, assembled on Innocents' Day. There was a band, dancing, Adults' Supper and Children's Supper. The following authentic dialogue, overheard in a Vicarage, illustrates the abundance of the material provision:

"Pig!"

"Pig! I like that! Who ate seven ices at the Bishop of London's Party?"

Here is the recollection of one favoured guest:

I remember the grand old house, and the great bedroom to myself, with a roaring fire of coals. It was plain, but spacious, and there was no stint in the necessaries of comfort. First came the high-tea at 5.30, and such a good one. Then we changed, the great company of guests assembled, and waited for the thrill of the evening, the voice of the Bishop on the landing above, looking perfect in the black (not purple) evening dress of a dignitary, waving his gloves, greeting his guests, signalling to the Viennese Band to start the music. It was a fine band in those days. Then for several hours joy reigned. I remember noticing how beautifully the Bishop danced himself, usually with one of the smallest mites. For three or four years we went regularly to that dance, and as we grew older we were roped in as stewards. I must have been at the first four or five dances. And I took my eldest girl to the last one in December, 1938. It was an unforgettable experience. The same ritual was observed, the same high tea, the same band, though the uniforms were a bit faded then. Everywhere the Bishop was the cynosure of every eye—wearing all his Orders and Decorations!

Another experience from a parent:

The Christmas Children's parties at Fulham on the Feast of the Innocents must have their due place in any record of the Bishop, for then the old Palace rang with laughter and music, and was illuminated by sheer happiness. The local fly, the occasional motor, the chartered bus or even the hurried walk that hastened to a run from the nearest Underground, brought the crowd of invited guests from all the Vicarages and Rectories in the Diocese. From chattering with excitement the children warmed to chattering as if at home, the Palace literally hummed. And the Bishop who received them all ("and you must remember to be very polite to the Bishop, when you see him") soon became the leader in everything and the friend of all—he was the child among children, one of themselves.

One little boy was staying with his mother at the Palace. The mother went up late in the evening to see if he was all right. When she returned, the Bishop asked how he was. He had been found wide awake. "I'm too happy to sleep."

The Bishop himself was always happy and he slept well by night, and sometimes as he grew older even in the day-time.

For here is one more snap-shot, and this not of the party, but of the street outside. The car, returning home after a heavy day's work for the Bishop, had stopped at the corner by Fulham Church. The Bishop was asleep inside. A tiny ragged child, holding an even smaller and grubbier one, cried out excitedly, "Look! 'Erb, look, There's the Bishop, asleep in his pram." Does not the author of Proverbs say that "The sleep of a labouring man is sweet"?

Parties of boys and girls were constantly asked to come to Fulham. To the girls of Miss Soulsby's famous school at Brondesbury the annual visit to Fulham was an event. And not to them only. An old girl of St. Margaret's, Bushey, writes:

> Every year my school used to be asked to a garden-party at Fulham. It was certainly one of the events of the year to us, and the first Tennis VI always played Tennis with the Bishop. He must have been about 80, or anyhow a goodish age then, but he really played a wonderful game, three sets on end. We always had a Service in the Chapel before returning home and he always talked privately to each of the girls who were leaving School that term.

He wrote to a schoolboy who was about to be confirmed:

> Just a line to say that I shall be thinking and praying for you in your preparation for Confirmation. It is a great time for making a deciding turn in your spiritual life, and getting a real hold of spiritual things. God knows you and loves you. I shall pray that you may make Him your great Friend for life at your Confirmation.

One of his boy-friends, who later attained to a distinguished position, writes:

> I first met him at London House in 1907 and I stayed with him in his Bournemouth hotel a few weeks before he died, and in all those years he never changed—gay and optimistic as ever to the end. His personal love for our Lord was a revelation to me as a boy, and it was always the most real thing in his life.

The Bishop wrote to this friend in 1941:

Dearest,—

It is a real pleasure to hear from you again, and I answer through

225   P

Freddie, who sends you his kind regards, to save your eyesight, as one of my letters was returned as "illegible".

I often think of you and pray for you. You are the only one of my boy friends who has become a ——. I take a special interest in you, and I love you as a dear son. I hope my very little godchild is going on well. Let me know how she is, and love to dear ——.

Yours,
A.W.I.

Visits to Boys' schools were a regular part of his programme. Marlborough was of course an annual engagement. There was the Confirmation at Harrow every year, and at Merchant Taylors' School every other year. Winchester, Wellington College, Radley, Cranleigh and other Schools were constantly visited. There was a time when he made a regular pilgrimage to a number of Public Schools, preaching on "Why should I not be ordained?" a suggestion which led to the discovery and eliciting of many vocations to the priesthood. That, and other sermons of his, were long remembered at Schools. The Earl of Selborne recalls that at Winchester the Bishop:

was in a class by himself in his influence on the boys. He was the only preacher who really cut ice with them. My recollection of his preaching on Advent Sunday in Winchester Cathedral is extremely vivid.

Canon Spencer Leeson writes:

He was a regular visitor to Winchester during my time there as a boy from 1905-1911, and I can well remember his extraordinary youthfulness and vitality, both as a preacher in Chapel, and in the way he mixed with us during the week-ends. Some of his phrases still stick in my mind, with the familiar and well-loved mannerisms; the drawing of the hand over the head, and the loose throwing-out of the left arm. Few men have had a greater power of throwing themselves into any society that they visited for a few hours.

The Sermon counted for much, but the talks to boys counted for much more.

One of the leaders of the younger Evangelical clergy writes:

He had a very formative influence in my life, and it was largely through him that I was led to Ordination. He used to come every July to my old School, and would preach in the School Chapel in the morning, and sit on the cricket-field in the afternoon in a deck-chair, having invited any boys who like to come and talk to him. I recollect that there was always a queue, and probably as many as a hundred were seen and blessed by him. He would talk to us about our homes, our future careers, and anything else we like to ask him about. He always used to invite me to play in one of his hockey teams in the Christmas holidays, and to Tennis in the summer at Fulham. He used to invite us to go and see an Ordination at St. Paul's, and to join the newly-ordained after for a meal in a near-by Restaurant. I have many books he gave and autographed for me, and, when I was ordained by him, a signed photograph. He used to have two by him, one in his cope and mitre, which he jokingly said he kept for his Anglo-Catholic friends and the other of just "an ordinary person" for his Evangelical friends.

The visit to Marlborough gave him special pleasure. He spent a week-end there every year for forty years, at first during the summer, and later in the Michaelmas Term. He would arrive on Saturday afternoon, play Tennis with a selection of Prefects, and liked various old friends to be invited to meet him at dinner that evening. On Sunday he celebrated Holy Communion at eight, preached at the later Morning Prayer and spent the rest of the morning talking to boys whose parents or relatives he knew or boys who wanted to talk to him. In the afternoon he would visit various friends in the town, and in the evening he always made a tour of his old House, B.2, and presented half-a-crown to the boy who happened to be occupying his bed.[1] This practice was discontinued because there was a time when he found ten boys piled on the bed, each claiming to be the rightful owner. He also used to entertain Marlburians at Fulham, especially for an annual game of hockey, at which he played Centre Forward and was always allowed to score at least one goal. He did not know (at least it may be supposed that he did not) that this was arranged, but it was always a matter for careful planning between the two captains. After his death one of his pectoral crosses was given to the College, and it is now set in the new Processional Cross which was dedicated in the Chapel on 26th June, 1947 by the Archbishop of Canterbury, him-

[1]There is a *varia lectio*, "a sovereign", but the evidence of the great majority of MSS is for "half-a-crown."

self an old Marlburian, in memory of the Bishop. There is also a Memorial Tablet to him in the ante-chapel. The Archbishop said of him at his first London Diocesan Conference in 1939, "He first captivated me thirty-eight years ago when I was a small boy at Marlborough and he came to pay his first visit as Bishop of London."

The Bishop of Mauritius at the Jubilee Meeting in 1934 recalled three Marlborough Sermons, "David and Goliath", "The Shadow of a Great Rock in a Weary Land" and "Launch out into the Deep". The Bishop of North Queensland in *The Bush Brother*, 20th June, 1946, recalled:

One memorable Sermon about the prospects of life after death. It so pleased the boys that it had to be reprinted again and again to satisfy their requirements. When new boys arrived, older boys used to say to them, "You'd better get the Bishop of London's Sermon."

He once said in a Sermon, "I have been all round the world, and wherever I have been I have found the highest administrative posts filled by Old Marlburians." Then he suddenly remembered that he was preaching in Harrow School Chapel. He tried to make the best of it by adding, "Of course the same is true of Old Harrovians," but it was too late.

One old Marlburian has a very charming recollection, which he has "proudly cherished for thirty-five years":

In about 1911 Dr. Ingram came to preach the Speech Day sermon. I was then about 15, and was proud to think that so fine a man had himself, as a boy, passed along the same paths of School-life as myself. After the Service was over, boys and parents gathered in the Court outside the Chapel to talk and meet friends, before moving off to the mid-day meal. I remember, so well, feeling rather lost and forlorn on that particular Speech Day. I had no parents or relations to enjoy the festivities with, and standing alone, watching the various groups of boys with mothers, fathers, sisters and brothers, I was suddenly startled from my dreams by a kindly voice, and a friendly grip on my arm saying, "Can you shew me the way to 'Upper School', my dear young friend?" Very proudly I escorted him across the big Court, and as we went, he plied me with all sorts of questions such as:

What form was I in?

Who was my House Master?

Where did I live?

Have you any brothers and sisters?

He shewed intense interest in all the answers, and then when we had reached the entrance to Upper School and I said, "Here you are, Sir," he smiled in a delightfully roguish way, and said, "Yes, my boy, I really knew all the time, but I thought I would like to talk to you for a moment. I was a boy here myself many years ago, and I shall never forget my way about the old place.

This is a simple story of a very dear person, whom I have loved ever since, though I never met him again.

Was there anybody, not only among the Bishops, but anywhere, who would have done this, and done it so well?

And why has all this about Schools been included in the Chapter called "Friendships"? Because that was his weapon, at the Schools, as everywhere.

There are innumerable stories of his kindness to people whom he met by chance:

I was a private in the London Rifle Brigade and the Bishop was Chaplain. It was his custom, during his August visit to the Camp, to spend much of his time in the lines chatting with the men, and I think the Officers' Mess did not see a great deal of him.

On one of these occasions I was talking to Dr. Ingram alone and he discovered in the course of his friendly inquiries that I was employed as a clerk in an office in St. James' Street, S.W. "That is quite near me," he said, "you must come and have tea with me one afternoon." Taking him at his word, I subsequently arranged an appointment and presented myself at London House. He sent an apology by a Chaplain to say that he was engaged on an important interview, but that tea would be served to me, and he would see me afterwards.

After I had had tea, the Bishop came into the room, informed me that this was the time of the day when he always took a little exercise and suggested that we should go for a walk in St. James' Park.

It is too long ago for me to remember details of the conversation during that half hour's stroll. Sympathetic inquiries about my work, my family and of course my religion, I know were made.

The amazing thing to me and why I shall never forget the occasion is that the Bishop of London, with his heavy burden, was willing to make time to take a real interest, without condescension in the life of an obscure young man. There cannot have been many like him.

The congregation waited outside the Church to give the Bishop a send-off, and a friend of mine and I were standing together. He came along looking at us all with his friendly smile, came up to me, and said, "I know you, don't I?" "No, my Lord, I am afraid not." Turning to my friend he said, "Well, I know you, don't I?" "No, my Lord, I am afraid not." Then noticing that we were both in mourning, he said, "What's the matter? You're both in mourning." I replied, "I have just lost my mother." And my friend added, "I have lost my father." He took both our hands, and said, "You poor dears." The little action was typical of his sympathy, and we treasured it very much.

These are passing incidents, though if all such could be recorded, they would number many thousands. More important was the way in which he could take trouble as a result of such an incident and do something. This happened thirty years ago:

I was trying to run a girls' club in a very rough neighbourhood, adjoining a well-established Boys' Club. Ours was an off-shoot, allowed to continue so long as it was properly run. The girls crowded into our small quarters and, though utterly wild and untrained, valued their Club-Life, such as it was, good fellowship, a piano, sewing and laughter; but I was unable to get sufficient help to keep the Club running every evening without outside assistance. The Club meant much to those girls (there were no picture-houses then) and the streets or crowded dirty rooms were their only haunts when not at work. This cottage-club was friendly and therefore grew larger and larger in membership, but its life seemed doomed unless more workers were forthcoming, and its prestige was established.

I was unknown to the Bishop, and did not come from a clerical family. I ventured, without telling anyone of my purpose, to write to Dr. Winnington-Ingram, stating our case; and by return of post I got a letter from his Chaplain asking if I could come the following day to London House, and then the Bishop would see what could be done.

I went and was received by him with great kindness; his sympathy dispelled all fear. He listened to further details and then at once sat down and wrote a letter which he told me to take to a friend of his. After he had given me his Blessing, I left, rejoicing, with the letter. When I gave it to the recipient, after reading it, she replied, "My Bishop tells me to go and help. I will be with you to-morrow night."

And so it was for years of to-morrows. She came and brought many others with her. Money flowed in, a big new building was erected, and the Boys' Club too gained much by the development of their one-time smaller neighbour.

Both buildings are now bombed to the foundations. In their time they did their work and fulfilled a purpose which, but for the Bishop's quick perception and real sympathy, would not (so far as the girls were concerned) have grown, and become the important factor which it did become.

Memories of him remain very vividly in my mind. Once we took the members of a Girls' Club to Fulham Palace. They were wild girls, shouting and careering about on his lawn. The Bishop came out of his study, looking at them; then he turned to me and said, "Dear things—how I love them." That love was his secret.

A friend of mine (the Principal of a Women's College) asked him one day, "Bishop, I wish you would tell me the secret of your influence over people?" He looked surprised, then smiled and answered, "I only just love them all."

It was his secret and the answer was the love that others gave him. I have two pictures of him which I shall always remember. One shewed him laughing and amused in his car, almost hidden by the crowd of young factory hands to whom he had given a lift. The other was of two young priests peering through a gap in the hedge outside Fulham Palace, one eagerly saying, "You can get a glimpse of him here sitting at his desk in the study window—just as he did when I had an interview last week—once I saw him playing Tennis." That was very typical of the enthusiastic love which his people had for him. It was through his love that many of us came to an awareness of the love of God.

A very dear relative of mine had committed suicide and I was filled with despair, feeling that it might be the unpardonable sin. I could find no relief anywhere. After one of the Bishop's Mission Services at Holy Trinity, Sloane Square, I determined to try and see him. Very fearful and afraid that I should be refused, I went to the vestry door and asked. In less than a minute the Bishop came to me and led me into the dimly-lighted Choir Stalls. There was no hint of weariness or rush in his manner as he listened. He said a great deal which brought comfort, but what I would like to hand on is the one sentence which rang in my ears for days, bringing complete relief from my fears. He looked at me with that smile, the healing power of which only those who knew it could realize, then laying his hand on mine he said, "Get this—God loves the dear fellow as much now as he ever loved him."

When one saw the kindness in those eyes, and heard the answer in his voice, one knew that he had given the complete answer to all doubts and fears.

Here is another of a different kind:

In 1910 I was assistant curate at St. ——. The Scout Movement was just getting into its stride and, as it seemed to me to be a good method of training boys, I started a troop in the parish. I soon met a very keen Scoutmaster who was running another troop in the same town. I will call him Smith. He was a married man with three or four children and an engineer by trade. He was a good fellow with the sort of wistful shy goodness one sometimes finds in the intelligent artisan class. His job was a good one and he earned a reasonably good salary. He was devoted to his wife and family and to his scouts. Indeed, he and his wife were honorary father and mother to the boys of the troop.

Suddenly he was discharged from his job. It was one of those mean tricks which it is impossible to expose. His manager had tried, some four or five weeks before, to induce him to acquiesce in some dishonest deal in connection with the firm's fuel and Smith had refused. Nothing was said at the time but just over a month later he got the "sack" on some entirely different pretext.

In those days, when there was no provision for unemployed workers, anyone who fell out of work had to worry along as best he could, first spending his savings and then selling his possessions. Gradually Smith went financially down hill. He could not get another job, perhaps because his former manager took care not to give him enthusiastic recommendations. It was a heartbreaking business. Very gallantly he went on with his scout work in the evenings and looked for work by day. He got thinner and shabbier and more and more worried-looking. He was a proud man and his friends did not know what to do. The only thing we could think of was to send anonymous parcels of food to his house after dark.

About eighteen months after he fell out of work he came to see me one day and said it was no use pretending any longer, that his family were beginning to starve and that he was desperate. Then he just sat and cried. I felt pretty bad too, I remember.

I knew that Smith had been one of the Bishop of London's boys in

Bethnal Green, and it suddenly occurred to me that our last hope was Arthur Foley. By the way, he was always known to his clergy and talked about by that name and I still think of him like that. I told Smith what was in my mind. He was horrified. However I told him that, whether he liked it or not, I was going to write to the Bishop. I did so and by return got a note telling me to arrange that Smith should be at Fulham Palace on the following Tuesday at 12.45 p.m.

With some difficulty we fitted him out for the expedition. If I remember rightly I lent him some shoes and someone else a pair of trousers. And on the appointed day we sent him off—very shy and nervous.

In the late afternoon he came back to my flat. I have never seen a man so changed and transfigured in so few hours. He was on top of the world. His confidence was restored and he was his own man again.

This is what he told me. He had been shewn into the Bishop's room and greeted with Arthur Foley's usual matter of fact friendliness "as though it were only yesterday I saw him last". After a short chat the Bishop said, "Well, Smith, we had better go along and have a wash before luncheon." Smith was flustered and protested that it wasn't for the likes of him to lunch at Fulham Palace. "Don't be a snob," said the Bishop, "haven't I had tea with your mother many a time?"

After they had washed the Bishop took Smith by the arm and led him along to the dining-room. There was a fairly large party. Smith was placed next the Bishop, who introduced him to the guests as a "very old friend of mine". Everyone was charming to him and he was soon quite at his ease, talking about the old days in Bethnal Green, the scouts and so on.

At the end of the meal Arthur Foley said, "I hope Smith won't mind what I am going to say," and went on to tell the guests of his misfortune and how it had come about. Then he said, "I want you to help me send him and his family to Canada." In a few minutes they had promised enough for the plan to be carried out—as it was a few weeks later. Everyone who knew the Bishop will remember how he insisted on being quiet for a few minutes after lunch, so he took Smith to his study, gave him his blessing and—this was what made the tears run down Smith's face when he told me the story—"he sent me back to Liverpool Street Station in his own car and the chauffeur called me 'Sir.'"

This last touch was characteristic, writes the priest. "When he did this kind of thing—as he often did—he always did it

233

beautifully. There was a lovely finish about his compassion. Like our Lord, he would have *touched* the leper."

Here is an illustration of his genius for turning casual contacts into something deeper:

Just before he gave up the Diocese the Bishop arranged to dine with a group of the "Friends in Council". This group dined every month at the City Livery Club, which occupied the top part of the old St. Paul's Chapter House. We used to meet before dinner in an upstairs lounge looking out on the Cathedral. The Bishop arrived on time, looking young and well. At dinner he was full of good stories and amusing talk. As we left the dining-room a page asked me to speak to the Manageress. I went along to her office and she asked whether I thought the Bishop would mind the staff having an opportunity of saying good-bye to him. "We all love the Bishop of London and we shan't get another chance." I told her I was quite sure he wouldn't mind. I asked him if it would be all right and he said, "Of course, dear boy."

I went back and told her what he had said and that as the Bishop would leave at 9 p.m. she had better have the staff lined up on the stairs. It was a lovely thing to see. On the stairs of that historic house the Club staff stood waiting to say good-bye. Arthur Foley came to the top of the stairs. He said a few words to the effect that it was nice of them to want to say good-bye to their old Bishop, and then, as though it were the most ordinary thing in the world he said, "Now, dear children, kneel down and I'll give you my blessing for the last time." I shall never forget that picture—the club servants kneeling on the stairs and Arthur Foley—his love for people shining in his face—looking a Prince in his purple, the jewels in his pectoral cross catching the light and his hand uplifted in blessing.

Then with his light boyish walk he went down the stairs.

There were smiles on the Club servants' faces and tears in their eyes as they went off to their various jobs.

It was a beautiful thing to do and it was beautifully done. Not that the Bishop thought about it like that. It was the most obvious and natural thing to him and it sprang from a simplicity which was child-like but not in the least childish. He was the Bishop of London, the latest of a long and illustrious line, what more natural than that his spiritual children should kneel for his blessing when they said good-bye.

As an example of his selfless charity a priest recalls this incident:

In 1922 my father died, after much suffering. We were living in Addison Road at the time. The Bishop knew of my father's illness, and when he died I rang up Averill in the morning to tell him. The Bishop was out and Averill told me that he would not be back until late in the evening; he said he would tell the Bishop. At about 10.15 p.m. the Bishop, who had only just got back to Fulham, came round to Addison Road, to see my mother and us. "His coming into the room," said my mother, "was just like a burst of sunshine."

The same writer also remembers:

It was Confirmation Day at Harrow School (where I was a Master), and the Bishop came, as usual. It happened that on that day my wife gave birth to twins. The Bishop, without any hesitation, went straight after the Service to our little house, walked into my wife's room (she had been for some time a great friend of his) and said, "I shall be god-father to both of them," and was. And the last time these two god-children saw him was just before his retirement, when they played tennis with him for more than an hour in pelting rain.

An eye-witness recalls an incident:

A characteristic picture left in the mind of a very tired man, coming after a long and hard day's work to the evening meal at London House, his first question an inquiry as to the wife of one of his clergy who was dying. The Bishop had hardly sat down before the telephone rang, and as the Chaplain returned he signed silently that she had died. "You will forgive me," said the Bishop, rising from the table at once; "I must go to him." The whole incident seemed to pass into a certainty and silence that was in sharp contrast to the crowds and cheering that met and followed him elsewhere; but here was the great Bishop.

An old St. Paul's Chorister, now Vicar of an important parish, writes of the time when Ingram was Bishop of Stepney:

It was a case of hero-worship. When he occupied his stall, the service seemed to be alive. When he occupied the pulpit we listened. This is saying a lot. The hum-drum, the conventional simply did not exist when he was there. During his visits to the Choir-School he radiated good humour, and life became one jolly joke.

The serious side of the Bishop was recognized by all, and his influence was very deep. Some of us felt we wanted to be like him. My own vocation was largely due to his unconscious influence.

High spots were reached during his occasional appearances on the playing-field at Willesden Green, which we shared with the Merchant Taylors' School. There he would change and take part in a Soccer game. And what a part! Rules were flung to the wind, and, in a veritable whirlwind of banter and merriment, the game proceeded. Everyone must be made happy and was. Then the journeys home on the smoky, smelling Underground. Life was endangered in the scramble to crowd into his carriage, where the fun was fast and furious.

One annual moment was awaited with immense pleasure both by present and past choristers. This was the Old Boys' Reunion Dinner at the Choir School on St. Paul's Day after Evensong. As he appeared through the doorway leading to the dining-hall, with that never to be forgotten smile, everything ceased until he had been welcomed and himself had greeted everyone.

He never forgot us. Seven years after I had left he came to Cambridge to speak at a Men's Meeting. A crowd of us saw him off at the station on the Monday morning. I pushed my way through the rest, and to my immense pride, and to the astonishment of the others, he called me by name. I asked him to write in a little book. "What are you going to be?" he asked. I replied that I was going to be ordained. He said, "Ah! that's the best adventure of all," and wrote, "Be not weary in well doing." The little book, *Papers for Working Men*, is before me as I write. As the train moved away, he called out, "See that you fall not out by the way."

I have been looking through letters from the dear old Bishop. They illustrate his extraordinary power of personal individual sympathy for people, and especially young men. My father was Vicar of X for thirty years, and my recollections of those days are of the Bishop coming down frequently to play golf, and nearly always on Easter Eve. He was wonderfully helpful to my father and mother and all of us. Through him I was introduced to Mrs. Y., who found £100 for me to go to Keble as an Ordinand. He married me. Hundreds of people have been able to say that they were his friends. In the midst of his busy life this seems to have been his special gift.

I first knew him when he was Bishop of Stepney. I used to ride on his back up the stairs to bed (I am now 52). Later at the end of 1914 when I was in the Life Guards and he was living at London House I frequently dined with him, and in fact I did so on the night before I went to France. Later, when he came to France early in 1915, he came over and, I believe, conducted the only mounted cavalry service in his experience. We were mounted in the form of a square, and he stood and addressed us from a farm-cart in the middle.

I once had an argument with him in the private Chapel at Fulham. He wanted me to play the organ, but I have never played, and I had the greatest difficulty in persuading him that I could not.

Here is a simpler tribute:

He was my god-father when he was in charge of the Stepney diocese. He had many lady workers, and one who was appointed to visit my mother, who was poor and had eight children. He was very good to send her away and got my brother and I into a good home to be brought up in the right way, to fear God and honour the King. I cannot send any letters as I never received any, but this is my remembrance of life. I hope his soul is at rest in peace.

Yours faithfully,

Miss ——

Here is a little series of letters which tell their own story:

Dec. 30th, 1916.

Dearest ——,

I am simply *delighted* with your news. If there is anyone who deserves such happiness it is you. God bless you, dear, again and again and give you years of your life. Of course you must bring him up to see me as soon as possible. I am putting in a little note for him. I dare say you see him *sometimes*. How Wonderful God is in his dealings with the children of men.

Your loving old friend.

On the occasion of an operation:

(Undated).

Dear ——,

I have been praying for you every day and I am thankful you have come through so well.

To the husband in sickness:

(Undated).

I am sorry to hear from —— of the terrible time you have been having. The whole question of pain in the course of a useful life like yours is most puzzling but I think when we know all it will be clear.

I quite expect to have a time of suffering before I finish my earthly career and I must try to bear it with the same patience and fortitude with which —— says you are bearing yours. When we meet Christ we shall be glad to have had some share of His suffering with Him, but I do hope it will pass at last and you will take up your useful work again.

November 20th, 1942.

Dear ——,

Thank God he did not linger too long. Now he is at peace. No more trials and suffering until you meet him again. It was a perfect marriage and you made him a perfect wife. I prayed for him every day, night and morning, and "we asked life for him; He has given him a long life even for ever and ever."

Yours in loving sympathy.

I am just going to have Evensong and I shall thank God for him.

And here is another set:

May 31st, 1944.

Dear ——,

I am sorry that the charming wife I remember so well has been taken from you for a time, or rather only her visible presence, for I am sure she is with you constantly in spirit.

I have always admired her from the day I married her to you, and I am glad she had an affection for me.

I can well imagine how lonely you will feel without her, but you must remember the truth of that blessed belief in "The Communion of Saints", and you will always have a loving example before you till that great day when you will meet again and have her for ever.

Yours in most affectionate sorrow,

A. F. WINNINGTON-INGRAM.

1945.

I well remember how your dear wife *always* remembered my birthday. I don't wonder you miss her sweet presence, but no doubt she is with you invisibly in spirit. It was such a happy marriage.

1945.

Thank you so much for your Christmas Greeting. It used to be from *her* too.

A.F.W.I.

He had, says a Vicar, an uncanny knack of finding links with people:

> That well-known trick, which I have often seen him play, of finding out something personal about anyone to whom he was just going to speak, one's organist, virger, anyone, and then talking to them on the personal footing that the bit of knowledge gave him, wasn't, I am sure, only so as to make them think what a wonderful man he was, but because it was one method, and one that he knew he was good at, of putting across the Gospel. He was so expert that he could talk to someone, fail completely to place him, and leave him quite sure that he knew exactly who he was and all about him.... Showmanship, if you like, but not with Arthur Foley as its end.

And here, to end the Chapter, are some of a long series of letters to the same correspondent. There are said to be some three hundred in all. The recipient was the daughter of a London Vicar. She says:

> I can remember the Bishop, then Bishop of Stepney, coming to confirm there in April, 1898, and to the Vicarage afterwards. I possessed a Birthday Book in those days, so of course asked the Bishop to write in it, and he laughingly said, "You must send me a present." I replied that I did not feel sure about a present, but that I would write him a letter. Being only a child at the time, I was almost counting the days till I could send him my best wishes (he had quite won my heart, as I think he did the hearts of *all* children). Then when the day came, it happened to be the day of my father's funeral, and he had come to take the service. Ninety-nine bishops out of a hundred would have been in the vestry till it was time to begin, but not so *our* Bishop—he was at the West end of the Church and came down the steps to meet my Mother and opened the carriage-door for her, and gave her a little word of sympathy. So I had my opportunity to fulfil my promise and wished him "many happy returns" at the Church door—and every year since then I have never failed to write or to see him. He always said that he was so touched that I remembered his birthday on such a sad day, and afterwards he sent me a book, *Voices of Comfort*, and wrote my name in it and "In memory of January 26th, 1899". Ever since then he has been a second father to me and I used to go and see him both at London House and at Fulham, at the latter often for tennis. I remember once playing with him in pouring rain, he was so keen to get the exercise.

We used to see him in Bournemouth after his retirement, and one of my latest memories of him is walking down the East Cliff with him and stopping to look at the sun setting over the sea. He said it always made him think of the text, "The path of the just is as a shining light, which shineth more and more until the perfect day." This was also the motto he gave to my husband when he married us.

The letters tell their own story. The first child died a day after birth, and after a second child was born it soon appeared that he would have a life-long delicacy.

September 21st, 1920.

Dearest M.,

It does seem a long time since we met or corresponded, but the Lambeth Conference was quite absorbing, and I know you had to lie up for the great event. I shall pray hard that it may be all right this time, and I will book November 2nd, 3.30 "on spec". I am afraid it cannot be the 1st as I shall be in Oxford, but it will be in the Octave, and "it" will duly be enrolled among the Saints.

October 15th, 1920.

Darling M.,

I don't think anything has given me greater sorrow for a long time than this fresh disappointment. It was my prayer for you to have "your heart's desire". But "whom the Lord loveth, He chasteneth". He must be going to bring you to a state of perfection of character vouchsafed to few of us by calling you to bear so much. Try to remember that Eternal Love is behind all. . . . I shall come up just the same in the afternoon. . . . It makes me love you all the more.

Your loving Father-in-God.

November 28th, 1920.

Dearest M.,

I am *so* glad that you are better and write so much more happily. I am pleased, too, that you want to see my dear old Mother. Yes! I shall always pray that you may have your heart's desire.

Your loving old friend.

September 21st, 1922.

Dearest M.,

This is just to welcome you at the hospital and say that I shall be thinking of you all right on Saturday morning. I am glad you remembered the verse, "Underneath are the Everlasting Arms". Let them tell me when you are visible after the operation, and I will look in and see how you are. . . . Don't be a bit afraid of anything. God will take care of you, and it may make *all* the difference to the future.

Your loving "Father".

August 29th, 1924.

Dearest M.,

It is lovely to hear of your happiness with your child, when we remember the past and I do feel, with you, much gratitude to God for giving you at last your heart's desire.

The next letter is omitted as too private: a later one says:

——Don't worry too much over little ——. He is God's child, and He loves him.

The moving story behind these letters would have touched any-one. It touched the Bishop, but whereas many would have been content with a transient feeling of sympathy and "I wish I could do something", he, like the devoted Persis, "laboured much in the Lord". And, as the present writer happens to know, in this case, as in many, he was "creative in the lives of others".

R

XII

THE UNIVERSITIES

To the Universities Ingram turned as to his own home. There is no record of contacts with the University of Durham or with the institutions which a modern writer has called the "red brick Universities", which are a large and increasingly important part of English life, but in the two ancient Universities he was a familiar and beloved figure. Oxford had been his happy hunting-ground ever since the Bethnal Green Days. At Cambridge he became known to ordinands through his Pastoral Theology Lectures, "Work in Great Cities" in 1895. As Bishop of London he visited both the ancient Universities every year. Sometimes it was to preach the University Sermon. More often it was to give the "popular" sermon at 8.30 in St. Mary's, and in both places, but especially at Oxford, there would be a Monday night meeting as well.

Of the years before 1914 Canon Spencer Leeson writes:

> The two greatest draws in those days were he and the late Archbishop Lang. Their style was utterly different; the Archbishop, grave and measured, a born orator, and the Bishop of London, unconventional and racy, seeming to enjoy flouting a congregation that thought itself very intelligent and advanced, by the simple, homely method of his appeal.

The Dean of Hereford's recollections are of:

> The magnetic leader of young men. The pulpit of St. Mary's with him in it is a memory that remains. The simplicity of the message! One saw the truth, not through the argument but through the conviction, felt and experienced, that Christ is the power of God unto salvation. I heard many preachers at Oxford, Cosmo Lang, Gore, Henson—none of them drew men to St. Mary's in the same way as Ingram, or in such numbers. Year after year it was the same.

The Bishop of Bristol, an ex-Vicar of the University Church of Oxford, writes:

The astonishing thing was that, though he was already past his best by 1933, he continued to draw enormous crowds. The church was probably fuller for him than for anybody else except William Temple. How much people heard of what he said towards the end, or indeed what they thought of it, I don't know. A certain amount of it was apologetics of a surprisingly naïve type, and the more intellectually quick-witted may well have scoffed. The fact remains that beyond all question virtue went out of him, and I have no shadow of doubt that the effect left by many of those sermons was a convincing impression of the vitality of Christian faith and goodness.

Nearly all the reminiscences dwell on the fact that he insisted on giving what in technical language are called "Apologetic" sermons, though there was no hint of "apology", in the English sense, about his preaching. He was always confident and happy. Speakers who are not familiar with the Universities often exaggerate the necessity of having a "high-brow" approach. There was a "South London Week" at Cambridge soon after the first War, and the Rt. Hon. J. H. Thomas, M.P., was the principal speaker. He thought it necessary to quote from Aristotle and Saint Augustine in the course of a stirring, but over-intellectualized appeal to the post-war undergraduate. The audience was refreshed after him by the Bishop of Woolwich (W. W. Hough), an Old Cambridge athlete and Corpus Missioner, who won their hearts. He was obviously, what Ingram himself was at many such meetings, the old war-horse, worn and battered by many years of toil, yet with the ever-fresh attraction of a burning faith. Ingram knew the undergraduate, and did not make the precise mistake of J. H. Thomas, but as one old Oxonian says, "I think he never got over his picture of himself as an intellectual champion of the Faith." This was the result of his years in Bethnal Green, with Sunday afternoons in Victoria Park.

For the most part he was quite unaware that the thing, the very great thing, that he was really doing was not the thing that he was trying to do. The Dean of Hereford goes on to say:

The sermon was followed by the talk in Christ Church Hall, when the Bishop dealt with difficulties that had been put up to him.

It was here of course that one realized that the Bishop had lost the habit of intellectual approach to a problem. A very able, shrewd man, no mean scholar at the University, the Victoria Park had done its work, and he never lost the direct appeal *ad hominem, ad populum*. A contemporary of mine, a scholar of Oriel, was very interested in the Bishop's intellectual presentation of problems. He used to say that the Bishop was the most striking example he had come across of the mystery of the Kenosis! There was a complete self-emptying of the higher thought of scholarship, in the interests of humanity.

Sometimes he seems to have perceived it. Canon R. A. Edwards remembers an occasion about 1910:

> It was the hey-day of his popularity, and St. Mary's was crowded—as was also the Hall at the House for his Monday evening meeting about East London. The sermon—I forget its text—was an attempt to prove "that the God of the Old Testament was the God of the New". No doubt, I was young and had all the cock-sure criticism of youth, but I was disappointed with him, and felt that he was sliding away from every difficult issue and was generally making very heavy weather of the subject. I can't remember the detail, but I sat there in the gallery feeling that he had started a lot of hares that he couldn't catch, and must be doing more harm than good. Then, with that characteristic gesture that shot out his prodigious shirt-cuffs, he waved the whole thing aside, presumably aware, as a preacher of his kind would be, that he had not carried his hearers with him, and suddenly said, "But I know it's true," and for the next few minutes to the end of his sermon abandoned his labouring apologetics and preached straight out of his experience. It redeemed the whole thing. You remember those Missions when he answered questions. But in fact he was never quite up to the rôle, didn't sufficiently grasp the strength of the case he was attacking, tried to cover a wide subject in a few words, and so forth. Whereas his real strength lay in his own personal faith, and his success wasn't, as he thought, in argument, but in conveying that faith to his hearers, and even in his later years when he was all but inaudible he still conveyed it.

With a London audience of public schoolboys he had the same power. In 1912 there was founded the Cavendish Club, intended to promote among young men of good education, with social advantages, a sense of responsibility for the welfare of their fellow-citizens.[1] The basis was to be Christian principle, but there was to be

[1]Another like effort was the establishment of Liddon House, just off Oxford Street. To it the Grosvenor Chapel was afterwards attached. Bishop Walter Carey said at the time, "If you know any Guardsmen with doubts, send them there." The Bishop of London said in 1907, "I should like to say publicly now how great a debt not only St. Matthew's (West-

only one clerical member, Dick Sheppard, who was to be Chaplain of the Club. It proved, for a time at least, to be of great value. There was in connection with its launching a great meeting at the Queen's Hall. It was an appeal to the older boys at Public Schools, who were there in large numbers, to interest themselves in social service. One who was present and has since occupied very distinguished positions, writes:

The Bishop spoke with immense authority of his days in East London. Certainly I date from that meeting something of a revolution in my life and there must be many like me. It was on the day before the Coronation of George V, and you can imagine what use both speakers (the other was Archbishop Lang) made of that as a symbol of what they wanted us to do.

Many of those present went on to the University, where they came once more under his spell.

The visits to Universities were occasions for making a great many personal contacts. The present writer was himself a witness of what he has always considered a very remarkable feat about 1907. The Master of Gonville and Caius (Mr. E. S. Roberts) was Vice-Chancellor. The Bishop came to preach at Cambridge and stayed at Caius Lodge. Mrs. Roberts, the friend of all members of the College, invited a large party, consisting of the leading characters of the College, and two or three resident M.A.'s, to meet the Bishop. He was very friendly, and then came the amazing thing. There was a little alcove just off the drawing-room. He sat there and saw all, or nearly all, the men in turn for about two minutes each, and won all their hearts. Only a very few of them were ordinands, and they had not been selected for their piety. He found out about them, asked a number of them to stay with him at Fulham, and made them all his friends.

It happens that there is another witness of this. One who was then an undergraduate at Caius, and has since been Fellow of a College and the occupier of an important position, has sent his recollection of the evening. It differs in one topographical respect from the other

minster), but the whole Church of London, owes to the self-sacrificing life, the devoted work and the saintly character of Mr. Trevelyan; and I rejoice to think that the life of the new "Liddon House" will begin under his leadership and inspiration." (Sermon at St. Matthew's.)

story, but it is probably more accurate, because it is from within. He writes:

> I carry, after the lapse of many years a very clear recollection of one episode, illustrating his possession of the "royal" faculty of remembering names and people, and of knowing just what to say to each of them.
>
> The Bishop had come up to preach the University Sermon— and incidentally I can think of nobody else in my undergraduate days who could ever fill Great St. Mary's to overflowing with undergraduates for the University Sermon, as he invariably did. He was staying with the Master of Caius (then E. S. Roberts); and some fifty undergraduates were bidden to the Lodge after Hall to meet the Bishop. He stood by the fireplace, and we were detached singly for about two minutes' conversation with him. I remember that within one minute he had elicited from me the fact that I was struggling for a "Blue" at Rugger—though I'm quite sure that I hadn't been bursting to tell him so; and I learned from several others afterwards that he had managed to get straight at their chief concern of the moment.
>
> When it was time to disperse, the Bishop stood by the door and mentioned the name of each of us as he shook hands to say good-bye. After thus naming correctly some twenty of those who had been total strangers to him an hour earlier, he laughingly remarked, "I don't think I'd better go on like this in case I should get caught out—though I don't think I should be!"
>
> I realize that this is a very trivial incident which may quite well fail to deserve a mention in your forthcoming "Life"; but the fact that I remember it so vividly after forty years is perhaps a sidelight on the Bishop's personality, and how it "got across".[1]

Sometimes the contact was very transient, but somehow it was always used. A Major writes:

> It happened to me to row Bow in my College "First Togger" in 1914. The Bishop was on the College Barge (he had been a keen rowing man when up) just before we went down to the start of the first day's racing. We were all seated in the boat, and he came down from the top of the barge to the pontoon to see us go off.

[1] Memory recalls another occasion at Caius, when Bishop Gore was the University preacher, and stayed at the Master's Lodge. At Mattins on that Sunday it was the turn of a certain eminent oarsman, then a resident B.A., to read the Lessons. It was his custom on such occasions to fortify himself with a whisky and soda, to enable him to face the ordeal. This time he said to himself: "That old Bishop will be there, listening," so this time he had two. And then it happened that the Bishop spent the morning finishing his sermon (and doubtless saying his own Mattins) in the Master's study. And so the prophylactic was, so to speak, wasted.

I suppose that I looked as frightened and nervous as I felt. He spoke to me and said, "I rowed in that place when I was up, and I felt terrified. You need not be. If you do your best, it will all come right in the end." We made a bump.

When there was a little more time, the contact would be more vital. A friend of the writer, a Roman Catholic doctor, remembers being taken by another young man, many years ago, to lunch at Fulham. At lunch the Bishop, looking into his face, and lifting his finger, said, "Remember, throughout your career, that Christ is God." And this man has remembered it. It was a bold and effective way of touching the spot.

The Universities, especially Oxford, were not ungrateful for his help. In 1905 a deputation of twenty Oxford undergraduates, headed by Mr. K. Cornwallis, a famous quarter-miler, President of the O.U.A.C., waited upon the Bishop at London House, and presented him with a pastoral staff on behalf of the junior members of the University. Mr. Cornwallis, in making the presentation, said that it was a token of the affection and esteem in which the undergraduates held the Bishop. A book contained the names of four hundred subscribers, at 5/- each, and the balance that remained after the purchase of the staff was represented by a cheque for the East London Church Fund. The gift was a complete surprise to the Bishop. He said in his reply, alluding to a recent visit to Oxford, that there had been "an attempt in some quarters to make out that two thousand high-spirited young men had been offended by a little plain-speaking." His own belief always was that what undergraduates liked from him was plain-speaking. What he thought before, he knew that day. As he carried the staff about his diocese, he would seem to hear the voice of his old University repeat to him the charge of the Consecration Service, "Be to the flock of Christ a shepherd, not a wolf; feed them, devour them not; hold up the weak; tend the sick, build up the broken; bring again the outcasts, seek the lost." He would go on with his often difficult work cheered immensely by the love and sympathy of his young brothers.

When there was time for a longer interview, he drew many young men to thoughts of Holy Orders. It is no doubt the ideal thing that all young Churchmen should believe that the *best* thing for them is that they should be ordained. They should all, ideally, be willing, and the Church should then be able to choose those who are truly called, and best suited to the life. The Bishop seems to have believed something of that kind, as is proved by his oft-repeated sermon, "Why should I not be ordained?" At any rate, he elicited many vocations by his talks and by his sermons.[1] In *What a Layman should believe* (1938), he said:

> One year I was elected Chairman of my old College Association, and when I was receiving the guests at the Annual Dinner, I saw two young clergymen come up, evidently recently ordained. I said, "I am glad to see you have been ordained." "Yes," said one, "it was your sermon in St. Mary's about 'the polished shaft', that did it." "Same here," said the other.

One young man who was helped by the Bishop to feel this summons was Dick Sheppard. He wrote in his diary on 2 June 1902, "I have been to hear the Bishop of London preach. He hit me between the eyes. I must be ordained."

In 1901 a young Indian Civil Servant, not long from Oxford, was in the Sindh desert when he read that the Bishop of Stepney had become Bishop of London. His first thought was, "Now the poor will have a chance." His second thought was, "Will he accept me for Holy Orders?" Telegrams and letters passed, and the result was that J. C. Pringle resigned his position in the I.C.S., went to Cuddesdon in 1902, was ordained to the parish of East Hackney, under Algernon Lawley, and eventually became Secretary of the Charity Organization Society, an acknowledged expert on all problems of poverty. Pringle was not the only man of that calibre in whose ears the Bishop had sounded the call of London. There were several in his year at Cuddesdon, and doubtless of other years and in other places, of whom the same could be said.

Here is a reminiscence from Bishop Mark Carpenter-Garnier:

> Possibly the following note about the beginning of my long friendship with the Bishop may serve to illustrate (though I feel sure you will receive an abundance of such illustrations!) the generosity and spon-

---

[1] A Cambridge sermon, which has dwelt in one memory for many years, is one on the text, "Come, for all things are now ready." The theme was one which he often used, God's patient preparation of the world for the coming of Christ, and His no less patient guiding of the world, and the Church, and you, since then, in preparation of *this* moment in *your* life.

taneity of his kindness and friendliness. I first heard the Bishop preach in Holy Week 1899, to a crowded congregation in Holy Trinity, Sloane Street, when I was about to leave Winchester and go up to Oriel. He made a deep impression upon me, and I was greatly attracted by him. But, while I lost no opportunity of hearing him preach when he came to Oxford, it was three years before I was brought into personal contact with him. In March, 1902, however, an old Marlburian, a freshman at Oriel, was invited to stay with the Bishop at London House, and I asked him, if he got the chance, to put in a word for me. Term ended, and we both went down, when I got a telegram: "Come to dinner to-night, London House"; and after all these years I remember still the thrill that telegram gave me. I had only a few words with the Bishop at dinner, but later in the evening he called me into his study. Perhaps only those who knew him in the great days of his apostolate can fully appreciate now what was the charm of his attractiveness and the quality of his influence. He had the gift not only of putting a shy man at his ease, but of making him feel completely happy, even exhilarated, in his presence, and of attracting him not only to his own person, but to the deeper things for which he stood.

That first interview was not a long one, but it had an astonishing conclusion. The Bishop invited me there and then to go with him on Easter Eve to Bishopthorpe, to stay with the Archbishop of York and Mrs. Maclagan for a week; and that memorable week, when I shared the holiday of this enchanting companion, proved to be the foundation of a lasting friendship.

With young women he was just the same, attractive and inspiring. There is no record of visits to the Women's College at Oxford or Cambridge, or to Bedford or Westfield or Holloway, but one who was Secretary to the London Girls' Diocesan Association writes:

It often fell to my lot to arrange the various conferences and week-ends, etc., that took place at Fulham, and in which he took such an active interest. He was remarkable in knowing the varied interests, family affairs, troubles and joys of the many young girls who gathered there. They never failed to get fresh inspiration for the work they were carrying out—I think I may venture to say that his addresses at that time no longer carried the weight that they had at a former time, and that he inspired by his absolute goodness. The celebrations in the Fulham Palace Chapel which were taken by himself made a very great impression—and most of all I think I carried away with me the Peace and Faith that came to us in the simple Evening Service of Compline—

"Keep us O Lord as the apple of an eye"—comes to me often as said by him at that time. . . . This may shew one aspect of a diamond that had many facets.

I feel compelled to say what I know in loyalty to an old and kind friend.

He enjoyed the society of young women. There was an occasion in 1935 at the Master's House at the Temple, now unhappily destroyed. The Master and his wife, on leaving London, gave an evening party. The Bishop accepted an invitation. He greeted his hostess and the judges and barristers who were present with his usual friendliness, but presently he was observed through an open door in another room, leaning back in an easy chair, with the only four young girls who were present sitting either on the arms of his chair or in adjacent chairs engaged in pleasant conversation. They were Veronica Carpenter, Ursula Laidlaw (the Master's Secretary), Margaret Blunt and Betty Hindley. Judge Sir Alfred Tobin remarked, "Look at the Bishop of London, lying in state."

To return to the young men, there was one very great occasion in 1902, when Oxford was stirred to its depths. Bishop Carpenter-Garnier's recollection of it is that:

In a letter written to me early in October the Bishop asked me whether it would be worth while having a meeting on "Work in Great Cities"—in a big hall, when he came to Oxford to preach in November, and suggested my going to see H. N. Bate, Dean of Magdalen, and M. Furse of Trinity. The idea at first was that some senior member of the University should be asked to preside, while others should be invited to support the Bishop by their presence on the platform. Then H. F. B. Mackay, of Pusey House, suggested that we should have an all-undergraduate platform, with one of ourselves in the Chair. This idea won the day, and a committee was formed of representatives from every College, with Mike Furse as Chairman. We took the large hall of the Town Hall, advertised the meeting widely, persuaded William Findlay, the Captain of the Varsity Cricket XI, to preside and gathered together a platform of Blues and other social lights. The meeting was an outstanding success: it was said that over a thousand undergraduates were present; and the Bishop held us all spell-bound. But it was his meeting! No amount of organization could have produced such a result, and in all probability no other man in England at that time could have attracted so large a company of young men, and not only held their attention, but aroused their enthusiasm.

It was characteristic of the Bishop that he never forgot that meeting, but even as lately as December 1944, referred to it as "that fine meeting" I had got up for him; as if he had not been himself the secret of its success.

The Monday evening meeting was thus reported in the *Church Times* of 21 November 1902:

The Bishop of London (Dr. Winnington-Ingram) attracted an immense congregation of University men to St. Mary's on Sunday evening last. Every available space was occupied, and even standing room was not to be found in the spacious edifice, the congregation overflowing into the porches.

Dr. Ingram met with a splendid reception at the Town Hall on Monday evening, and his address on "Work in Great Cities" was followed by a large gathering of University men.

Mr. Findlay, of Oriel College, presided. In welcoming the Bishop, the Chairman said he had always been given to understand that London ought to have twelve Bishops; he thought they would all agree that they had on the platform a Bishop who was equal to twelve. (Applause.)

The Bishop of London, who was enthusiastically received, thanked them for coming in such tremendous numbers to back up and welcome an old Oxford man. (Applause.) He said he was born neither in Belgravia nor Bethnal Green, and brought a perfectly unbiassed mind to this great problem of great cities. He was a country boy, and spent his summer holidays shooting and fishing, and he thought, if anyone had told him then that he would have spent nine years of his life in the greatest slum in the world he should either have put his fishing-rod down his throat or peppered him with his gun. (Laughter.) They never knew what was coming to them, and when he was in Oxford little did he think what his life was going to be. He came that night with no Cockney prejudices. Speaking of the extraordinary fascination of work in a great city, he said as he went day after day rushing from end to end of the great diocese, of which he was the spiritual head, of three millions and a half, and saw the thousands and thousands of people who were passing every day, he felt at the centre of the world-problem. There was a kind of fascination in thinking of this great, mighty multitude of souls, all busy about their work, and in thinking of their eternal future, and, as he went home late at night, driving under the stars, and thought of all those thousands asleep under the silence of the stars—let them remember that every eight minutes a soul left this world for eternity from London alone—as he thought of all the sorrows, of the horrible things that were happening, of the hearts that were broken, of the joys and sorrows of a great city like that, it seemed to draw one's heart down to it, and one was content to serve a great city like that—it drew them out of themselves, and made them forget themselves altogether. Besides the fascination, there was almost the terror of it. Had they all realized that London increased 40,000 every year? The whole transport of London was breaking down. They had to open the churches of the City because girls came up by the six o'clock train in the morning, two hours before their work began, and they thought it was a good use for the old mother church of the country.

Besides the ever-growing size of London, as William Cobbett said, like a great wen growing every day, they had to think of the over-crowding. It was almost impossible to speak of what overcrowding meant. When they saw a whole family all brought up in one room, the only place to eat and sleep in, when they thought what that meant for the decency of the boys and girls, how they saw and heard things they ought never to see and hear, how it meant the stunted growth of the children, it was a most intolerable evil, and of all evils it was the most impossible one to overcome. The County Council had played a noble part in many ways in trying to remedy overcrowding. The over-crowding of London was still terrible, and had an enormous influence on character. Let them think it over; they wanted their intellect in these things, for they were going to sit on their County Councils in days to come—think what a problem it was they were going to try and help them to solve. It was an awful thing to think of 80,000 women and girls roaming over London like lost spirits every night. If there was one body of men who could stop a thing like that it was the body of men he saw before him. He proceeded to point out on the top of his rather black picture marks of hopefulness of the problem. The first thing which was of extraordinary hopefulness, especially during the last ten or fifteen years, was the way the working-men were rallying round the Church, and were beginning in consequence of the effort made amongst them really to understand, and give a hearing to the Gospel. The working-men began to see that there was some reality about people who stuck to their work in the way the clergy of London did, and they were just beginning to see the results of years of patient work. (Applause.)

What did the dons think of it all? It is not always realized that

University dons, with their varying degrees of personal adherence to the Christian Faith and the Christian Church, are nearly always anxious that religion shall be properly represented to the undergraduates. They take great care to provide what they think is the right sort of Dean or Chaplain for their own College, and they are glad that the University should have visits from preachers who will attract. When Ingram came, the Deans and Chaplains welcomed him with both hands. They knew that he would make things much easier for them in their difficult and delicate work, which is both pastoral and evangelistic. The lay dons, with the exception of a very few who were hostile, welcomed him as one likely to help the young men to be Christians, or at least as likely to do good. Those who came to listen—and they were not a few—were sometimes startled to find how much they were moved by a very simple Gospel sermon. Non-episcopalians welcomed him as an evangelist who had the root of the matter. "Did you see —— there?" said one young cleric to another after one of Ingram's Cambridge meetings, naming a well-known Presbyterian. "No, was he there?" "Yes, and vigorously applauding all the more Catholic parts of what the Bishop said."

Sometimes, of course, they were critical. There was an occasion, not at a University, but it happened that, for a special reason, a good many academic pundits were present. The Bishop, who was getting old, and had not expected the congregation to be particularly learned, preached on his reasons for believing in God. As they went out, one philosopher, who was certainly on the side of the angels, said to another, "According to the latest pronouncement of science, the Supreme Being is a very long way off. Perhaps it's a good thing that it will be several million light-years before He hears that!"

In spite of occasional failures with the intellectuals, the result of unfounded assumptions or uncompleted syllogisms, those visits to Universities were great adventures and great victories. There had been a time when Ingram, as a young man, had gone out like David against Goliath. Now he was come to his maturity, and to his royalty, and, even though his enthusiasms had sometimes been extravagant, like that of David when he danced before the Lord with all his might, and though he had been too easy with his Absaloms, it was the simple truth that the young clerical dons who were doing their best to be theologians and priests, could have said of him, as the people of Jerusalem said of King David, "Thou art worth ten thousand of us." And the older men, the Professors and Heads of College, who were approaching the end of their time of service, could have said, if they were on the Lord's side, with old Barzillai the Gileadite, "Thy servant would but just go over Jordan with the King. But behold, thèy servant Chimham; let him go over with my lord the King; and do unto him what shall seem good unto thee." (2 Sam. xix. 36, 37). And so they encouraged their young men, if they seemed to have the vocation, to be ordained, and to work in London.

Many hours during these visits were spent in interviews, and during those interviews momentous decisions were often made. There is a possibility that he was over-eager in encouraging men to seek Ordination. He took the view that everyone is called, and those who are fit ought to respond.

There may be some young man here who is wondering what to do with his life, who has been kept back from thinking of being ordained by all kinds of misunderstandings or excuses, or because he is waiting for a call. Here is the call:—"I thirst—I thirst for your devotion. The offer of your service to-day will enable me to quench the thirst of others. I will send you forth with the water of life into some parish where there are thousands who never pray, and whose souls are thirsting for life, and I will use you to quench their thirst! Is not that worth giving your life for?"[1]

It is all true, and if there could be a perfect system of selection for the Ministry of the Church, it would work well. But the Bishop's optimism made him over-easy in accepting candidates, and though it is probable that it deceived him more often with older men—and in recommissioning men after some failure—than with undergraduates, he accepted some lame dogs. It was not, however, in London but in another diocese that the Bishop, who had succeeded a very soft-hearted man, described the staff of part of his diocese as he had inherited it, "The blind, the halt and the lame, a veritable Pool of Bethesda!"

Ordinands who consulted Ingram, or men who with his advice

---

[1] *Addresses in Holy Week*, 88.

and help became Ordinands, were directed to Theological Colleges. He himself had not been at such a College. He somehow picked up unaided all that is learned at them. These things are chiefly how to pray and that Christians are brothers. A raw student arrives, full of fears, and begins to be taught—happy is he if it be for life—just those lessons. There was a time when the Colleges were suspected, and spoken of as "hot-houses", but now, in general, the necessity of professional training is universally recognized, and, in particular, it is now admitted that the life of the priest is so exacting that some kind of intensive training for it is essential. And, to meet another unfounded objection, so far from the Colleges being melancholy places, the life there, apart from the sacredness of the Chapel and the serious duties of lectures and private studies, is so joyous that a rather unsympathetic observer has gone so far as to refer to "the fatuous hilarity of the Theological College."

The *ethos* of the Colleges is known to all old students, but it has never been better described than in Scott Holland's picture of Cuddesdon in the old days under Edward King:

I suppose that Cuddesdon men will always say that, whatever else came out at Christ Church and Lincoln, still there was never anything quite so full of thrill as the old days on the blessed Hill, when King was Principal. The whole place was alive with him. His look, his voice, his gaiety, his beauty, his charm, his holiness, filled it and possessed it. There was an air about it, a tone to it, a quality, a delicacy, a depth, which were his creation. He could draw love out of a stone: and there was not a man of any type or character that did not yield to his sway. Great burly chaps, arriving alarmed and unshaped, keeping their portmanteaux packed ready for a bolt, were at his feet before they knew where they were. There was nothing of the forcing-house, of the seminarist pose, as was popularly supposed. All was human, natural, free. "Here is one of my hot-house plants," I remember him saying at one of the annual luncheons, as he laid his hand on the enormous shoulders of a man who had stroked the Oxford boat to victory for four years running on the Putney course. It is hopeless to try to tell the wonder of those old days. All over England there are men who look back to them, as to a heavenly vision—to which, by the infinite mercy of God, they have not been wholly disobedient.[1]

[1] *A Bundle of Memories,* 81.

Ingram sent men to all Colleges, according to his view of their particular needs. There was one for which he had a special affection, because it was to a certain extent his own Diocesan College, and he was one of its founders. The Dean of Carlisle, formerly Principal of Cheshunt College, writes:

A.F.L. always spoke of the foundation of the College as one of his greatest acts of faith. It was through the munificence of Canon Fox Lambert, then Vicar of Cheshurst, that the College came into being. But once started it had to travel on its own legs, and none could have worked over it more devotedly than did A.F.L.

St. Andrew's Day was always ear-marked in his engagement book to be spent at Cheshunt. He drove down on St. Andrew's Eve, dined in College with the men, and after dinner came into the Common Room and talked. Afterwards the Principal's study was placed at his disposal, and he interviewed one by one all the men in the College. I was always impressed by his power of summing up a man's character. It was, I think, largely instinctive, and, of course, the fruit also of a long experience of young men. Many a man has spoken to me afterwards of the help he received from the Bishop on some point that was troubling him.

Much of the fruit of all this labour was apparent in the loving enthusiasm of the two thousand men (or those of them who were able to be present), whom he had himself ordained, at the great King's College meeting in 1934, which will be described in another chapter.

The Ember-tides at Fulham are always spoken of as indescribable. There was, says one chaplain, "a sort of sparkle" about the October Ordination, which "made the occasion, never dull, even more exhilarating for all concerned". The Bishop was just back from his holiday in Scotland and was full of life. He would say to the priest-candidates in his study, "What has been the chief difficulty in your work during this deacon's year?" And sometimes he would add, "Don't say it was your Vicar." But there was much more than this. It was in the study at Fulham that two thousand men found him what he most of all wanted to be, a Father-in-God to his own clergy.

A few notes have been preserved by one who heard the Bishop's Ember-tide charge in October, 1922.

The Pastor must have:

Diakonia, Ministry. "I am among you as one that serveth."

Semnotes, gravity, not flippant; careful in holy things.

Tapeinophrosyne, humility.

Sophrosyne, discipline in ordering of whole life.

You must remember you are the only Body that our Lord now has: you are His hands, to bless and heal; His feet; His tongue to speak His words.

Dangers—Swank, self-love, giving occasion of offence, insincerity.

Helps—Humility.

> Tenacity of purpose—the single eye.
>
> Sympathy—Capacity for being really interested in other people.
>
> Tact—sense of touch.
>
> Sense of humour.

Readers of this book will have little difficulty in perceiving where this came from. It came from God, but it came through the devoted life of the speaker, one to whom the famous words of Chaucer can justly be applied:

> He wayted after no pompe and reverence,
> Nor maked him a spyced conscience,
> But Cristes lore, and his apostles twelve
> He taughte, and firste he folwed it himselve.

XIII

OVERSEAS

THE great journey round the world was undertaken in 1926–1927. By that time the Bishop had already been twice across the Atlantic. He had visited U.S.A., and Canada in 1907, and Canada in 1910, and he was to go again in 1931 and 1936. There were other journeys which will be mentioned later in this chapter, though not in exact chronological order, as minor events.

The purpose of his 1907 visit to U.S.A. and Canada was twofold. He was to take part in the laying of the foundation-stone of the Washington Cathedral, a noble modern building in the Norman style, to address the American bishops at a great Commemoration Service at Richmond, Virginia, and to present a Bible, given by the King, to the Presiding Bishop at Bruton Parish Church, which is believed to be the oldest church in the United States.

I exhibited the actual documents, with great seals attached to them, making the early appointments in the history of the Episcopal Church in the United States, and I was able to give to President Roosevelt the original document, signed by Cromwell, and sealed by Bradshaw, appointing one of his Colonels (who for twenty years had turned out the Bishops from Fulham) the first Governor of Rhode Island. The document had been left behind by the Colonel in Fulham Palace, and with the leave of the King and the Dean and Chapter of St. Paul's I was allowed to give it to the President, who was a great admirer of Cromwell. I was told by the Bishops afterwards (fifty of them were on the platform), that this lecture or popular talk had done much more permanent good than I imagined at the time.

In New York he was invited to give a talk in, or rather, on Wall Street, the Stock Exchange of the City. He spoke from a platform in the open air. The Street was filled, and every room within hearing was crowded to the ceiling.

The following letter was sent to the Bishop from some representatives of the congregation:

VOTE OF THANKS TO THE BISHOP OF LONDON

At a meeting held this date, at noon, the Rev. William Wilkinson, Minister, presiding, it was moved, seconded and passed, by a standing vote unanimously:

That the thanks of this Meeting be given to the Lord Bishop of London, for his kindness in coming and preaching here; and this meeting expresses to his Lordship its sense of the religiousness, the appropriateness, the usefulness, and the power of his sermon, which realized the ideal of what a Christian teacher ought to teach.

Wall Street, New York,
    October 21, 1907.

It was signed by the Bishop-Coadjutor of New York, the Rectors of St. James', Grace Church, St. Thomas' Church and by six laymen. There dwells in the memory of the present writer a recollection of a possibly over-cynical description of the scene by Charles Maasterman. It was something like this:

The Bishop of London addressed the business men of Wall Street. At the end they crowded round him, shook him warmly by the hand, and said, "Well, good-bye, Bishop. We've enjoyed your talk. It's done us all real good." After which, they cheerfully went back to their business of rooking their neighbours.

The other purpose of his 1907 visit was to see his numerous nephews and nieces. An elder brother had settled in Canada, and had had nine children, all of whom eventually married and had children.[1] On the way to the farm near London, Ontario, where his brother lived, he visited Toronto, and spoke there and elsewhere, at "Canadian Lunches". These are occasions when you pay a dollar for your lunch and then enjoy, or endure, a twenty-minutes talk from an invited speaker. He chose such topics as "Old London and New London", and "John Bull and his little foibles". It is not known whether he told the story of the British soldier, who being required in U.S.A. to give his birth-place said, "London." "Do you mean London, Ont.?" "No," he said, "London, the world."

The Bishop found the people of Ontario intensely British, as they always are, but at that time a little inclined to think that Old

---

[1] He said once to the Prime Minister that a Canadian Government ought to put up a statue to the Winnington-Ingram family because they had done so much to increase the population of Canada, a much-needed work. There were thirty-seven of them.

Britain was rather "played out". He reassured them and explained that the home people had a habit of understatement, which sometimes caused them to be misunderstood in Canada, or other countries where the trait was less marked.

The Bishop himself wrote home to Mr. Gillson, his chaplain:

> I am fairly taken aback by the storm of welcome which I have received, and it all seems so genuine that it has been cheering, if a trifle wearing.
>
> Toronto makes your mouth water after the slums of East London. Every child is straight as a dart, and well fed : every street with beautiful shady avenues and a nice breeze off the Lake. 350,000 people—and no poor!

He also said publicly:

> I am firmly of the opinion that Canada is going to be the greatest country in the world.

and

> Some day this country is going to have a population of a hundred millions.

This visit made a great impression on the Dominion. Lord Grey, the Governor-General, wrote from Government House, Ottawa on 10th November 1907, a long autograph letter describing his Battle Fields Scheme for Quebec, thanking the Bishop for a donation towards the cost of the scheme and his blessing on it, and concluding:

> Come back to us soon. The heart of Canada, which you have captured, is aching for another sight of you.
>
> > Believe me,
> > Ever yours most gratefully,
> > > G.

The Bishop records that Lord Grey punctuated his sermon in Quebec Cathedral with "Amen, Amen" and "Quite right, Bishop," more than once.

Sir Robert Falconer, Head of the University of Toronto, wrote inviting the Bishop to accept the honorary degree of Doctor of Laws, which, owing to the Bishop's engagements elsewhere, would have to be conferred in absentia, and added:

I have been watching with great pleasure the enthusiastic reception
which you have been having,

and in another letter:

The inspiration of your visit to Canada will, I am sure, be remembered by us for many years.

He paid another visit to Canada in 1910. The purpose of that was
to attend the Consecration of the new Cathedral at Halifax, Nova
Scotia, and to take part in the keeping of the two hundredth year
of the use of the Book of Common Prayer. King George V sent
by him a beautiful copy of the Prayer Book, made for the occasion
at the cost of £50. It was depositied in the Church of Annapolis
Royal, a place which had been taken from the French two hundred
years before, and it was at the Thanksgiving Service after that battle
that the Prayer Book had been used for the first time in Canada.
Ingram was accompanied by the Bishops of Glasgow and Washington, representing two sister-churches. Among other things he
noticed, as all visitors to Eastern Canada must notice, the perfect
satisfaction with which French-speaking Roman Catholic Canadians
live under the British Crown. "Tell the King," said a French
University President, "how 'appy we are!"

The 1926 visit was a much more elaborate affair. It was nothing
less than a tour round the world. It was no small thing for a man of
sixty-eight, who had been Bishop of London for twenty-five
years, to embark on a journey of 25,000 miles, but it was arranged,
and accomplished, and it was, beyond all question, a great success.
The actual journey was in the end much longer than had been intended. And every waking hour of it was strenuous.

The beginning was a request from the Protestant Episcopal
Church of the United States that the Bishop should be the first
holder of the newly-founded Turner Scholarship, instituted for the
purpose of making "a Christian appeal" to the American Universities. At first the Bishop was unwilling, for more than one reason.
The appeal had to be made in the autumn, and so could not be disposed of during the normal holiday months of August and September, because the students would not then be in residence. This was
one difficulty. It would mean leave of absence from London during
an important part of the year. There was, in the Bishop's own view,

another obstacle. He said that he was not a Lecturer, and there were others who would do it better. But the Americans were persistent. They knew what they wanted. They did not want a Lecturer. They wanted the Bishop of London. They wanted the man who had lived at Oxford House, and knew East London, and was accustomed to handling young men at the English Universities and boys at Public Schools. They were even willing to wait two years until the twenty-fifth years of Ingram's episcopate made some sort of break natural, and at last, finding that the London Suffragans and Archdeacons were willing to carry on, he consented.

Then the plan grew. Why not go first to British Columbia, that most British of all the provinces of Canada, to which the Bishop as Chairman of the British Columbia and Yukon Association, had sent out £240,000, and visit the young Church there? And then, after the U.S.A., why not come back round the world, and see something of those often lonely Bishops, who are consecrated in St. Paul's or Westminster Abbey, and sent out, as some put it, "to sink or swim", in the Far East. After all, the Bishop had been Chairman of the Corean Mission for twenty years, he had both ordained and helped to consecrate the Bishop of Kobe and the Bishop of Colombo, he had met very many overseas Bishops and other clergymen, and had talked over their problems with them in London, and he had innumerable contacts with the Missionary Churches. So Eastward Ho!

The programme was already formidable, but there was still something more to come. The Bishop had always been a champion of the cause of "Empire Settlement", and the Church of England Council for Empire Settlement had been blessed by the Church Assembly. He was urged from many quarters to add another three months to the tour, and visit Australia and New Zealand. And then Ceylon could perhaps be taken in on the way home. So, on the principle that "you may as well be hanged for a sheep as a lamb", and trusting that the carry-on organization which would last for six months would last for nine, he determined to face the risk of being called an absentee Bishop, and set off.

There was a certain appropriateness in the discharge of such a duty by *episcopus Londiniensis*. Up to 1787, when the diocese of Nova Scotia was created, everything across the seas was reckoned as in the

Diocese of London. This came from an Order in Council, obtained by Archbishop Laud in 1634. In 1840 Bishop Blomfield of London had been startled by a letter from a clergyman on the far side of British North America, complaining of the little attention which his lordship paid to "that part of his diocese". Since 1787, Nova Scotia had been followed by Quebec, Calcutta, Jamaica, Barbados, Madras, Australia, Bombay, Newfoundland and Toronto, but in 1841 Blomfield instituted the Colonial Bishoprics Fund, and things began to move quickly. In fifty years the Fund, with the help of S.P.C.K., S.P.G., C.M.S., and private donors, collected and expended £840,000 in founding fifty-five new dioceses. In this way the old "diocese of London" was effectively sub-divided. But he was still the ex-Bishop of these vast regions. Further, the Bishop of London is traditionally "Bishop of the High Seas", and every child born and baptized at sea is by custom enrolled in the Registers of Stepney Parish Church, the Mother-Church of the Port of London. Thus Ingram added to his natural fitness for the work a constitutional right to act as an Imperial ambassador "in things pertaining to God".

The party consisted of Mr. Ormond Blyth, who, besides bearing more than half the expenses of the expedition, undertook the whole arrangement of trains and steam-boats, the Chaplain, the Reverend H. G. Thomas, who prudently kept a Diary, and Mr. Blyth's chauffeur, Will Smith, who acted as general factotum and indispensable handy man. They set off from Liverpool on Saturday, 31st July, and at 8 a.m. on Sunday the Bishop celebrated Holy Communion in the ship's Dining Room, using the portable altar which had been given by the Church of All Saints', Margaret Street. Later in the day came tragedy. A heavy swell developed. Mr. Blyth and the Chaplain were driven to retire. The Bishop, who had once been terribly sea-sick on a short voyage to the North of Scotland and had had his hours of discomfort on earlier Atlantic voyages, "kept going wonderfully". In fact, only once on this journey was he seriously affected. And even then not quite defeated. It was on launching out from San Francisco into the Pacific. On that Sunday morning the Diary records:

Rough weather, wind rising and heavy swell. Bishop sick 10 a.m. Took the Service at 11.

The Chaplain was completely down and out. The Bishop, "cast down but not destroyed", arose from his bed at the call of the Steward, and said Mattins and preached. His subject was "the Nearness of God". No one knew that he had been sick, and a Christian Science lady on board said afterwards that it was "the best Christian Science sermon she had ever heard". In his comparative immunity from sea-sickness the Bishop was only surpassed by Will Smith, whose *dura ilia* felt no twinge at all.

They travelled everywhere in Canada in the "Ottawa", a private car put at their disposal by the Chairman of the National Railway. It containined a dining-room, a sitting-room, four bedrooms, and crowning mercy—a shower-bath. This car was later taken over by the Canadian Pacific Railway, and was their home for several weeks. In the States the President of each Railway in turn lent his own private car. This enormously increased the comfort of the journey.

They visited Quebec, Montreal, Ottawa, where it happened to be the centenary of the City, and the Bishop preached on Sunday to a large congregation in the Cathedral in the morning, and (through a microphone), to some 20,000 people in the afternoon, and then Toronto. At Toronto there was a great meeting on "Empire Settlement", and the Bishop said to 2,500 people that, "If we let North-West Canada get filled up *predominantly* by an alien population, we should find it hard to keep it British in sympathy and interest. It was quite right to be open-hearted, but we were filling up the Middle West with people from Galicia, Poland and God knows where." It was a remark which caused some indignation in England, and the Bishop was told to read the New Testament before he went round the world again. He said much the same thing later at Winnipeg, where the Mayor of Winnipeg and the Archbishop of Rupertsland put it even more strongly. The mixed population of the Dominion is indeed something of a problem. The writer heard himself in a great Canadian City of the Middle West in 1937 a story which illustrates the extent to which people of other races are filling Canada. There had lately been a census, and the teller of the story, a University Professor, was asked his name by the official, a man of non-British origin, who called at his door. He gave his name, which may be called for this purpose William Wordsworth. "Vordswort, Vordswort," said the official. "What nationality is that?"

"British." "British? There's not many of them round here." At Edmonton it was said that five and twenty languages were spoken.

After Toronto came Hamilton, London (Ontario), Winnipeg, Edmonton, and then over the Rockies to Vancouver. Everywhere there were great congregations in Church, great meetings in Public Halls and visits to Schools. The Bishop calculated that he had obtained some 200 half-holidays for Schools in the course of his entire journey. Even when he spent a few quiet days with his brother on the farm in Ontario, there had to be a meeting. People came to it from fifty miles round in every kind of vehicle, and one man, gazing at the stream of traffic on the road that led to the farm, and not knowing what else to compare it to, said, "Why, it's like a funeral!"

The great event of the visit to Vancouver was the laying of the foundation-stone of the new Cathedral, a ceremony which was attended by four Canadian Bishops and four Bishops from U.S.A. He met the Provincial Synod of British Columbia at Vancouver.

The Bishop had for a long time been the very energetic and successful Chairman of the British Columbia and Yukon Church Aid Society, and he never missed presiding at the Annual Meeting for twenty-nine years. He knew personally many of the clergy of the diocese. When in 1926 a generous donor gave a peal of eight bells for the Victoria Cathedral, and there was to be a ceremony of naming the bells at Messrs. Mears and Stainbank's Whitechapel Foundry, he wrote, "Of course, I *must* come." He came, and one who was present says:

> We can see him now standing among the bells in his robes, in the blackened walls of the two hundred year old Foundry, delivering one of his rousing addresses with the vigour of a man in the thirties.

At Victoria the ceremony of "breaking the ground" had been performed in May 1926, and the Foundation Stone was to be laid in September. It was supported on twelve smaller stones that had come from Canterbury. These had originally been part of the ruined "Ethelbert Tower". The North-West tower of the new Cathedral was called the "Bishop Winnington-Ingram" Tower. It contains the eight bells, which are the same in size and weight as those of Westminster Abbey.

At New Westminster the Bishop was entertained to dinner by

sixty clergymen. It is reported that the orator who proposed his health said, "At last we see the man whose sermons we have preached for so many years," and it seems that there was some self-consciousness in the laughter which greeted the joke. The story was told at the table that the only man who was ever "found out" was a young curate, to whom his Vicar had suggested that every now and then he should read one of the Bishop of London's sermons instead of his own. He electrified the congregation by his opening words, delivered without any warning. They were "When I was Bishop of Stepney."

It was in British Columbia that the Bishop saw Miss Hasell, whom he had met before at Fulham. Miss Hasell's "Sunday School by Post" is famous. It has been the means of imparting the elements of religious knowledge to thousands of children living in remote places, who would otherwise have been completely cut off from the Church.

On 21st September came a nasty accident, which nearly wrecked the remainder of the tour. A cauldron of scalding water from a ship's boiler on the Arrow Lake went over the Bishop's bare arm. It produced what the succession of surgeons who eventually dressed the wound at various stages of the journey called the worst arm-burn they had ever seen, a septic sore from wrist to elbow. He nearly lost his arm. It was happily arranged that a surgeon became available (none of them would take any fee) at every 400 miles or so of the journey for the next fortnight, and though the arm was very painful for a long time, no engagement was missed. Least of all was there any intermission of the daily prayers and of Holy Communion (in the train or on board ship) on Sundays, Thursdays and Holy Days. This was primarily for the spiritual needs of the members of the party, but others constantly came and were grateful for the privilege. On board ship there is often a priest, but on trains the opportunity is less common. It need hardly be said that very many passengers came and had private talks with the Bishop on Sundays and at all sorts of other times. He, as always, was most accessible, and it is probable that all of them went away after their chat comforted and encouraged.

The next Chapter of the tour was in U.S.A. It seems unlikely that anyone had ever before visited all the twenty-two Universities of the States, and it seems quite certain that no one had ever spoken to all of them within the space of six weeks. The Bishop was not without some trepidation over the task beforehand. He knew Oxford and Cambridge and the English Public Schools, but would the American Universities be the same? There were, of course, great differences. One was that no Church has any official status in the American Universities. There are Chaplains, provided by the denominations, whose work is recognized and valued, but they are not "on the strength", like the Dean or Chaplain of a Cambridge College. There are other differences into which it is not necessary to enter now. But so far as the quality of the young life in them is concerned, the answer is that in all that matters most they are the same as ours.

The arm, which was eventually cured by an oil discovered by a surgeon at the University of Michigan, was still very painful, and one of the results of the accident was that the Bishop could not for some time have any of the golf and tennis which he loved, but there were compensations. As he put it himself:

> I have often thought that there is some connection between Pain and Power, and certainly there must have been some Influence at work, for I knew of nothing in myself to account for the way those dear young people of America thronged to hear that appeal, listening in their thousands for nearly an hour without moving, and came in queues to ask me questions afterwards.

One of his main lines of preaching was that contained in the published Book of Sermons called *The Sword of Goliath*. The text was, "Give me that: there is none like it," and the subject-matter consisted of the four reasons (the Bishop's sermons were always divided into a number of simple and easily-remembered points) which made the Gospel of our Lord Jesus Christ unique. They were its teaching of the love of God, its power to change the heart, its hope of a fresh start and its sacramental teaching.

Another, and even more profitable line was found to be an attempt to answer the question, "Why am I a Christian?" This was a simple handling of big topics, the preparation of the world, among both Jewish and Gentiles, the Advent of our Lord, His claim, the meaning of His Death and Resurrection, and His challenge to mankind. Then would follow strings of questions about Miracles, the supposed failure of the Church, War, the Divisions of Christendom, Church and Labour, and so on. An American paper said:

> "The Bishop of London talked for fifty minutes to 8,000 students of the University of Iowa, and held them spell-bound while he told them what it means to be a Christian," writes a correspondent, who adds: "The President of the University, commenting upon the Bishop's talk, said he had never seen a student audience so intensely interested in a speaker or his words."

Britons talk more interestingly than most Americans, not for what they say, but for how they say it. The American is charmed by the cultured Englishman's conversation, although nine times out of ten the Englishman may be talking platitudes and spilling "bromides". But he is talking distinctly, explicitly, intelligently, resonantly, doing full justice to the noble language of Shakespeare, Milton and Macaulay.

It is perhaps a little surprising to those who remember the *timbre* of the Bishop's voice, which we always supposed to be an irremovable and indeed a deliberate and treasured legacy of residence in East London, that the writer should continue:

> They heard English "as she is spoke" in London's best circles with the nasal twang, the bark and the bite removed, and a mere suggestion of cockney accent added. It was a lesson—not only for our young students of both sexes, but for our friends, the University professors.

But the Americans are deeply intrigued, and easily pleased, by our "English voices".

At all events, they listened, and it may be imagined that great numbers came afterwards and shook hands with the Bishop, saying, to borrow words heard by another speaker on another occasion after a talk given to Canadian students, "I liked your talk. It gave me a new slant on how Christ comes into the picture."

The American tour did not end with the Universities. There were gatherings of the Pilgrims, the English-Speaking Union, and a number of those gigantic lunch-parties of anything from 100 to 1,000 men, with a speech after lunch, which are a feature of North American life. The Bishop was bold enough to take as his subject at two of these gatherings, "The Debt, what ought to have been done about it?" and "Why not join the League of Nations?" He carried his audience far more with him on the first than on the second subject. A leading soldier said to him as he sat down, "Whatever happens, Bishop, whether we join or not, you have always got us behind you at a pinch."

Whenever it was possible the Bishop played golf or tennis. Once he played with Miss Helen Wills. The Californian newspapers had a headline, "The Bishop is a dandy player, but he can't beat our Helen." In fact he never played a single with Miss Wills, and he could hardly have expected to win if he had, but he played in two doubles, once with Miss Wills, and once against her, with two famous American men-players to complete the four, and got up to 4-6 and 5-7 in two sets. The games were played between an Armistice Service at California University in the morning (it was 11th November) and an address to Mills College for Women at five, but from the attention which it received from the Press it might almost have been supposed that the Bishop had visited America for the purpose of the matches. A year or two later the Bishop had the pleasure of entertaining Miss Wills and her mother at Fulham Palace. It was the day after she had won the Women's Championship at Wimbledon. The Bishop sums up this part of his tour in his Fifty Years as "my arduous but delightful visit to the United States".

From San Francisco their ship steamed out across the Pacific for Yokohama, calling at cosmopolitan Honolulu on the way. The Bishop wrote to Miss Catton:

The Pacific is a fraud as a name. We have had it very rough. Mr. B. has been quite bad, but we have all three been sitting in the sun to-day. We are getting to the tropics.

Here is £150 for the London Account,[1] a "douceur" for baptizing the grand-child of the richest man in America, with whom we stayed in San Francisco. You had better put it on deposit as it may earn a little before I return. The other is from a friend for the same account.

We find the journey very boring even when we are not ill. We have the Royal suite, so we cannot complain.

On reaching Japan, the visitor's first request was for a bath, and it is reported by a priest who was there that this piece of news some-

[1] The "London Account" was kept for charity.

how leaked out, and the non-Christian Japanese expressed high approval of the holy man who must take a ceremonial bath of purification before beginning his holy work. In Japan he met for the most part the Churchmen, missionary and Japanese, and observed with interest how thoroughly Japanese the Nippon Sei Kokwai (Holy Catholic Church) is scrupulous to be. He was treated with great respect by the authorities and entertained at a very elaborate official luncheon by Prince Tokogawa. All the Japanese were emphatic in protesting their friendship for Britain. It would be profitless to attempt here to estimate the genuineness of this. Let us attribute to it the maximum of *bona fides*.

There are some very discreet remarks about the "rather natural unpopularity of Japan, as the governing and conquering race, with the Coreans", and the Bishop adds, "Yet no one can deny the much increased efficiency with which everything is carried on now that the clever Japanese have taken the country in hand." It is enough to say that the Bishop's misgivings and his wish to be polite to the Japanese were shared by almost every Englishman at that time.

In China there were visits to Shanghai and Hong-Kong. It was from Shanghai that he sent his famous telegram, when the retirement of Dick Sheppard created a vacancy at St. Martin-in-the-Fields:

> "Appoint McCormick.
> Bishop, Shanghai."

At Hong-Kong they spent Christmas. On Innocents' Day the Bishop thought rather sadly of his accustomed Children's Party at Fulham, but instead he gave an address to the Mothers' Union on the problem of reconciling their duty to their husbands in China and to their children at home, and then had a game of tennis with Mr. Copley Moyle. A day or two later came dinner with the Oxford and Cambridge Society and the Old Marlburians, and a real Chinese dinner, chop-sticks and all, with a large party of Christian Chinese.

Thence to the Malay States. It was an ordeal at Singapore, the place where at least seven races meet, to learn on arrival that he was advertised to give a talk in the Victoria Theatre on "Christianity and the British Empire", but it is reported to have been "well received". There, and in Java and the Celebes, they had a taste of real tropical weather;

To sit perfectly still and to have the perspiration start out of the back of your hand, and a hand of which you are rather proud, that it is always hard and dry, and not that worst of things—a moist hand. That only happens in the tropics.

They had the same experience in North Australia, which was the next stage.

At Brisbane, for which the Bishop had in his early years wanted to volunteer, the programme was:

A visit to the Church Grammar School, a great discussion on Emigration with the Church of England Council (of which Canon Garland is the Secretary), a reception by the Senate and Professors of the University in the Botanical Gardens, followed by tea, and more tea with seventy clergy of the diocese, whom I addressed afterwards in Church, and finally a dinner at Government House, where I was introduced to many of the Labour Ministers.

During the time at Sydney there were many visits to Schools. At King's School, Paramatta the Bishop spoke on "How to keep young all your life". The secrets were:

(1) Regular exercise—not too much of anything.
(2) Keep your *mind active*, e.g., Reading.
(3) Keep your *heart young*, e.g. Sympathy.
(4) Keep your soul in living touch with the living God, e.g. Daily Prayer.

So "those whom the Gods love die young" i.e. are young when they die.

A Sunday at Bathurst, a great Church-centre, was notable for the attendance of 700 communicants, men and women in equal numbers, some of whom had come hundreds of miles to the service.

In New Zealand the party felt what so many travellers have called the peculiar charm of the Dominion. For one thing, the weather is generally fine, and moreover it is not too hot. The only qualification in the Bishop's eulogy of New Zealand is a plaintive note about the unsteadiness of the trains. The Chaplain's brief notes on Auckland are:

Fine Harbour—lovely scenery—glorious sunshine—nice House—delightful people. The Bishop's own description of New Zealand was,

"The best climate in the world, the best fishing in the world, and certainly some of the most delightful people in the world."

At a great Meeting of 3,000 people in the Town Hall of Auckland the Bishop writes:

I took the subject of National Sins, not those of New Zealand especially, but those prevalent at home:

(1) National Selfishness, as exemplified by a man who said, "We have got a nice bit of God's earth and mean to keep it to ourselves."

(2) National Softness, illustrated by the saying already quoted from Vancouver: "Send out as many *serfs* as you like to cultivate our land—our young people don't mean to do it!"

(3) National Gambling, as illustrated by a mother who said to her daughter, "If you want any new clothes, my dear, go to the races: I can't afford to get you any."

This address, so far from offending people, seems to have been very much appreciated, and I find all over the world, that what people like is plain speaking, if done with charity and personal humility, and not as if the speaker was setting up to be himself a superior person.

This was one more of the triumphs—easy-seeming, but really the product of long labour and experience—which he owed to the happy combination of nature and grace that was in him.

During the New Zealand visit occurred three days' holiday, in one day of which the Bishop caught seven rainbow-trout, weighing together forty pounds. One actually weighed nine pounds by itself. The nine-pounder was caught at 5 a.m., the fishermen having risen at 4 in order to take advantage of the best fishing-time of the day.

The people of New Zealand are well aware of their debt to the heroic labours of George Augustus Selwyn in the nineteenth century. A governor-General of the Dominion said once to Prebendary Cash (now Bishop of Worcester), "My work to-day would be impossible without your work a hundred years ago." And a ship-captain, when someone spoke against Missions, said, "Well, they do that much good anyhow; a hundred years ago if you had come to this part of the world, you would not have been *at* the table; you would have been *on* the table."

Back to Australia again, they visited Melbourne, Adelaide, Perth,

and then it was high time to leave the Continent if they were to get
to Ceylon in time for Easter. Palm Sunday was spent on board
ship, and nearly the whole ship's company came to the morning
service. Ceylon was reached on Wednesday. The Bishop preached
on Maundy Thursday at Colombo and on Good Friday at Kandy,
and on Easter Day at Nuware Eliya, the Simla of Ceylon, a cool
hill-station, 6,000 feet above the sea-level, where Europeans escape,
when they can, from the heat of the plains. One congregation during
Easter week comprised 1,500 Anglican churchmen, who were of
four races, Cingalese, Tamil, Burgher (Dutch) and British. Bishop
Carpenter-Garnier, then Bishop of Colombo, writes that:

"in spite of the visit being at the end of a world-wide tour and occurring
in our great heat, he was amazingly alert and vigorous and made a
profound impression wherever he went. We who lived and served
overseas were immensely cheered and encouraged by his visit, and we
were convinced that could people in England realize the value of such
a missionary tour as he made, there would not have been one to grudge
his absence from the diocese.

At another time the Bishop gave Communion to members of
five different nations, all meeting before one Altar.

At the Welcome Home Meeting in the Central Hall the Archbishop of Canterbury said:

London desires to welcome back from a world-enterprise one of the
most beloved of all Londoners: a man who, as brother to all in joy and
sorrow, as a teacher gifted with tireless devotion and resource, as a
Christian of buoyant and quiet persuasiveness, has been so dear to us
all for years and years past. When we found this journey to have been
planned, we wondered how, at a difficult time, we should put up with
his absence. At an hour strenuous, and laborious beyond measure to
the bishops, there were some who said he ought not to go. Surely a
healthier view finds expression when we say that our keenness about
overseas work and the overseas work of the Church of God is so great,
so dominant, that, even at the most strenuous of times, we should
encourage one of our foremost messengers to go, possessing the amazing gifts that he does for such a purpose and for such a task.

The Archbishop quoted from many letters that he had received.
Among them was a tribute from the Bishop of Chicago:

We all feel that the Bishop's visit and his addresses to thousands of students, and his closer contacts with smaller numbers, has been very stimulating to the whole religious life and a real benediction to us all.

The Archbishop of Canterbury's own summing-up was that "no man in history ever gave the Christian message to so vast a number of different men and women in so short a time."

What was the result of it all? There were some who asked the Bishop if he had enjoyed his holiday, and hoped that he felt better for the rest. "You go round the world, my friend," he replied, "and preach, speak and lecture five hundred times and then come home and talk about your holiday." It was a fair retort. The trip had been very strenuous. Nevertheless, there is no doubt that the Bishop enjoyed it. He was always ready for fresh human contacts, and this time he had had them by the thousand. Further, it confirmed him in many of his strongly-held convictions. It is always a great thing when a man can say of an experience, "It has shewn me that everything that I believed is true." It is a reward that comes to many a priest from Confirmation-work, when he sees faith dawning in the eyes of the candidates, and beginning to be manifest in a changed life. It is a corroboration of his own belief. Thus, the Bishop had always felt sure of the value, indeed the necessity, of Overseas Missions. In China he found that while the Chinese respected the business men in Hong Kong and Shanghai, they could not be said to love them. They love the missionaries, "I have seen the affection, the confidence of the Chinese in missionaries." He said that he had come back with this conviction, "that it is Christ or chaos, Christ or nothing."

Another of his convictions was of the spiritual value of the British Empire, and of the importance of maintaining its British character. The United States have had extraordinary success in welding together an immense variety of races. But they were less prejudiced about it. No doubt those who were themselves of British origin hoped that the States would not become too German, too Polish, too Scandinavian, too Italian. But the result of the official policy of encouraging immigration from all parts of Europe was to produce a new nation.

It was a brave experiment, which has been astonishingly successful. It is one of the things which renews a man's faith in Divine Providence. It shews that a great and free nation can be built out of heterogeneous and not always originally very freedom-loving units. Our object was to make a Greater Britain. It was not, in the main, political ambition, or a means of acquiring military glory, or wealth, or prestige. The object was to see what British people could do on virgin soil. Would they be able to settle there, and grow into nations, the new nations which were essential to do justice to the new lands, but nations which had not lost the old inheritance? It was not quite the "Let come what will" which has produced the United States. It was more like "Shall we be able to make good on the new soil, and in the new air?"

This also has been a great success, another new and good thing in the history of the world. Nations have grown up in the new lands, which are completely independent, but the independence only means that the affectionate co-operation of sons is passing into that of brothers. One of the two best things that has happened in the lasty fifty years was the creation of the Union of South Africa after the Boer War.[1] The Bishop of London had not studied the problems of Empire with the acumen of Mr. Lionel Curtis or with the range of Field-Marshal Smuts. He brought to bear on them his robust optimism, and his belief in the Christian Faith and in British manhood, with the further conviction that such manhood was the best possible raw material for such faith.

Nevertheless here, as always, the result of Ingram's work must be sought in persons. His breezy dismissal of obstacles may have been superficial, but there is no doubt about his effectiveness as an evangelist. Of the many who rise up and call him blessed, a large number are among those who listened to him in the three continents which he visited in 1927. Audiences at meetings, congregations in Church, stewards and sailors on board ship, railway-officials, domestic or hotel servants, liked him, and were disposed to listen to his message, and believe it, because they felt that he loved them.

He did a great deal of work for the Church of England Council for Empire Settlement, and, by personal monitions and exhortations, to turn the minds of home people outwards. All his life he encouraged emigration. There is perhaps more than a touch of his habitual optimism, and occasional exaggeration, in words which

[1]The other was the Appeal to All Christian People that issued from Lambeth in 1920.

275

he used at a conference at which Australia and New Zealand as well as Canada were represented:

> The point of the whole thing is that the Church of England, which is by far the most powerful thing in England, has placed its whole organization of 14,000 parishes at the disposal of the Government. All the clergy are agents for emigration. Instead of the old system, where men went to emigration-agents who only wanted their money, they now go to their clergymen. We have our head-quarters at 39, Victoria Street in London, and we are in touch now with the Anglican Church in the Dominions.

The spiritual needs of those who went, especially to the less settled parts of the Dominions, were constantly on his heart. "We must look after them," he would say. To the Canadians he said:

> What are you all doing, my friends, sitting at home here and allowing your people to become pagans? There are English women to-day who are going through the West to try and redeem the paganism of your Canada.

One of his achievements, though not for Canada, was the sending out together of fifty young priests to join Bush Brotherhoods in Australia. He once had a visit at Fulham from three of them, just about to sail, three very tall young men. "Hullo," he said, "eighteen feet of Bush Brotherhood,"[1] and he stood on a chair to shake hands with them. But Canada was his chief love. For the Church in British Columbia especially he did much. The two Englishmen to whom the Church there owes most are the Bishop and Dr. Jocelyn Perkins, of Westminster Abbey, who for many years has been the devoted Hon. Secretary of the British Columbia and Yukon Church Aid Society.

His last visit to Canada was in 1931. He found the Vancouver Cathedral almost finished, and a newly-built Theological College. At Toronto on his way back he had to answer some difficult questions. It was the year of what then was called the financial crisis, and people asked him, "Is it true, Bishop, that the Fleet are in mutiny and that the Socialists are going to have the Bank of England." Having been away for six weeks, the Bishop was not very

---

[1] This was an understatement, a thing unusual with the Bishop. The exact total was 18 feet, 4½ inches.

familiar with the state of affairs at home, which had in fact developed, so far as the public were aware, very suddenly. He cheerfully replied that he thought it would be all right. When he returned he wrote in the Press:

> I think it worth while before I settle down to my work again to let my fellow-countrymen know how affectionately and whole-heartedly Canada is with them in facing their difficulties to-day and in trusting them to surmount them. *We must not betray her trust.*

There had been other journeys in earlier years. In 1908 he visited Moscow and Petrograd. The Anglican Churchmen in Europe (North of the Mediterranean, which is in the Diocese of Gibraltar) are within the jurisdiction of the Bishop of London. The area is administered by the Suffragan-Bishop of Northern and Central Europe, who had been called in recent years the Bishop of Fulham. The Chaplains were invited to Fulham Palace for a four-day Conference every other year.

The Bishop was very warmly welcomed by the prelates of the Russian Church. He had taken the precaution of providing himself with his best cope and mitre, so that he was not outdone in magnificence. He did not risk the embarrassment which Liddon had once felt, when the Patriarch of Jerusalem shewed him two photographs, one of Archbishop Tait:

> I think, in full-blown magpie, and another of a Scottish bishops, gorgeous in cope, mitre and staff; and the Patriarch observed that they appeared to be differently dressed. Liddon carefully examined them, and said that it certainly was so. "How is this?" asked the astonished Patriarch. Liddon observed that we had two traditions as to how a bishop should be dressed, and these were examples. The Patriarch looked at him as if he hoped that he was speaking the truth, and said, "Is not that very awkward, to possess two traditions?" "Yes! It certainly was." "Would it not be better to settle on one, as soon as possible?" "It would be most advisable." At last to his intense relief, the photographs were laid aside: but he felt his reputation had been shaken.[1]

At the ancient Troitza Monastery he was kissed on both cheeks by

---

[1]Scott Holland, *Personal Studies.*

the only Bishop present ("I said, to get out of more kisses, that in our Church only a Bishop was allowed to kiss a Bishop"), he was presented with an eikon ("the picture of the one Master of us all"), which stood thereafter on the altar in the Fulham Palace Chapel.

He was summoned to an interview with the Tsar, who was most friendly and encouraged the Bishop to talk of his impressions of Russia. The Bishop, boldly and perhaps rather indiscreetly, indicated what he considered to be one or two joints in the armour. The Tsar listened most good-naturedly, and then said, "And how are you getting on in Ireland, Bishop?" On the same occasion he had a talk with the Tsarina, and was captivated by her charm.

One of the lighter episodes of the journey was a luge-ing and ski-ing party, arranged by the Reverend A. M. Cazalet, who was his Chaplain and his interpreter throughout the visit in French, German and Russian. The Bishop, to whom this sport was new, was instructed on no account to cross his skis. Thus would he be saved from the humiliating fall for which thirty amateur photographers were eagerly waiting. He proved an apt pupil, and the photographers were disappointed. There was on this holiday expedition a well-meaning lady, who insisted on discussing with him the relation of the Russian and Anglican Churches. At last he said, "I say, Cazalet, get rid of this woman. I can't stand her any longer."

War-time visits to France and the Salonica front are described elsewhere.

XIV

WITH THE FIGHTING MEN

I NGRAM was always intensely patriotic. It was partly his affection
for the men in the Services, but it was also something that went
deeper than that. There was for him a sacredness about England
which was beyond argument. Of course, he said "Britain" whenever
he remembered, but it was England that he meant. He would never
have had any scruples about joining in "Land of Hope and Glory"
with its refrain of "God, who made thee mighty, Make thee mightier
yet". His instinctive judgment was that the national cause must be
right. The South African War was for him "a fight for freedom".

"They would give the same answer to-day. Look at the volunteers
who were a few days ago crowding this cathedral before starting for
South Africa. Is it not true that through their young hearts there is
spreading something they had not known before, something far beyond
a man's mere love of fighting? I believe there is; I believe that many of
these men are tasting now, perhaps for the first time, the joy of sacrifice,
and it is uplifting them to a height which they have not known before.
They feel the joy of being called as a labour of love from their desks
and offices to volunteer for the honour of their country. Then, again,
is it not true that as a nation we are feeling the joy of fighting for a
great ideal? I know full well that some of the nation may have tainted
motives. This is no place to enter into a question of politics, but this
we may surely say, that as a people the English are not wishing to make
mere gain of all this warfare; that, with a perfectly honest conscience,
we are battling for what we believe to be a question of freedom. Our
forefathers fought for freedom, and we and our brothers from distant
colonies, who agree with our ideal, are fighting for the freedom we
have fought for before."[1]

He was moreover an Imperialist, and he was impatient with some
of his clergy who disliked and distrusted "Imperialism", but, like

[1] *Under the Dome*, 72.

nearly everybody else, he had not completely thought the matter out. One of his clergy was arguing with him once about small nations. "Oh, yes," he said, "small nations ought to be free." "All of them?" "Yes, all of them." "What about Ireland?" "Oh, well, that's a very difficult question. You see, Ireland is so close to us."

His judgment about the South African War was, politically, a simple judgment, with which not all Christian people agreed at the time, and some who did have revised their opinion since. But his judgments in these matters were never in other respects undiscriminating. Speaking of people at home and of the spiritual temper which should possess a nation in time of war, he was unfaltering. He said in the Lent of 1915 in Islington Parish Church:

> Have we got anything to repent of as a nation? What about our drink bill, what about the night clubs, what about the way the Age of Consent Bill was talked out in the House of Lords? And—mark you—what about the things that underlie these things: the love of self-indulgence, the love of luxury, the carnal passions which are indulged? We have to go down on our knees, we have to induce the nation to go down on its knees, and repent of these things, and ask to be forgiven. "Purify us from any share we may have had in the cause of this present strife," is the prayer I pray in my chapel every day. If as a nation we are to have victory, we must be a penitent nation, and if we as Church-people are to bring the nation to penitence, we must be penitent too. Do you think we have nothing to repent of? I am not here to speak flattering words to you, though I do thank God for your spendid enthusiasm and your missionary zeal up here, and the good work you have done as Sunday-School teachers, district visitors, sidesmen, and Church-workers. I thank God for you all. But I am here with you under the Eyes like a Flame of Fire. We have not come together to congratulate one another. We have come to ask to be made better men and women.[1]

At any rate, neither in 1914 nor in 1939 was he a Pacifist. Less philosophical than William Temple, who would argue that force is a thing which must be used, and that the choice is therefore between using it rightly and using it wrongly, he was content to put forward simple reasoning, "Can you stand by and let a bully work his will?" or, "What would you do if a man attacked your

[1] *The Church in Time of War*, 227-9.

sister?" Sometimes he must have seemed, both to conscientious objectors and to grave publicists, too light-hearted about the thing. Meeting Dick Sheppard one day outside St. Paul's, he called out, "Hullo, old chap! Still keen about peace?" a greeting which Dick probably understood and smiled at, but the deeper part of his sensitive soul would be distressed by it. And it is certain that he believed in 1939 that George Lansbury and Dick Sheppard had made Ribbentrop think that Britain would not fight, and so had precipitated the Second War. Sometimes he incautiously expressed himself in striking phrases, which were afterwards remembered against him. There was a famous sentence about the old lion which had not, as was supposed, lost all his teeth, which went well at the time, but was afterwards criticized.

He was no pacifist, and, on the other hand, as compared with other non-pacifists, he was more honest and straightforward than some of those speakers whose balanced and qualified statements secured them, or would have secured them if anyone had remembered what they had said, a greater measure of approval afterwards. Ingram knew very well, and said in actual words, that "War is damnable." Of course he was apt to employ the usual picturesque metaphorical language, as Prime Ministers did, about "not sheathing the sword", as if it were a sort of single combat, conducted according to the accepted rules of duelling among gentlemen. Yet he was more ready than some to face the fact that the action of consenting to wage war commits the conscience of a nation and of every consenting citizen to a grim and hideous responsibility. He knew well enough that modern war means smashed faces, crushed and mangled limbs, stomachs ripped and torn with shells. He knew, none better, of the sorrow that war brings to innumerable homes and of the crippling for years afterwards of the national life. So he said that war was damnable, but he also said that, as it had been forced upon us, we must see it through.

He was always on the look-out for redeeming features. He was quick to hail any evidence—happily, not difficult to find—of chivalry among British soldiers, or to say, naïvely enough, that:

There are accepted principles of Christian Warfare; and I would have you remember that there has not been a single accusation, even

281

from the enemy, that our men have transgressed those Christian principles.[1]

And, as is said elsewhere in this book, he overestimated the volume and the permanence of the religious revival which he discerned among the fighting men. Yet always his one desire was to use this crisis, this judgment, this Day of God, as he called it, in a Christian way and for Christian ends. In this he was utterly wholehearted, and marvellously successful.

4 August 1914, found him in Camp, near Eastbourne, with the men of the London Rifle Brigade, whose Chaplain he had been since 1901. His car, which stood in the Camp and was constantly used for interviews, was always known as "Fulham Palace". Within a few days, the Brigade was sent to Bisley. He went with them, and stayed with them for two months. They were Territorials, and many of them had not yet volunteered for service overseas. There had been a sort of idea that, if war came, the duty of the Territorial Army would be to man the cliffs of Dover and repel the invader. "Put a little ginger into your sermon, Bishop," said the General before the first Sunday. He evidently did, for the whole Brigade volunteered for foreign service before nightfall, as did all the men of another Brigade which he visited, at the invitation of General Smith-Dorrien, next day. He was in fact an extremely successful recruiting-officer, before the days of conscription. And if it should seem to anyone that a Bishop of the Church of Christ should not so act, at least he put his call on high grounds. He called for sacrifice, and preached no hatred. The sort of thing that got them was, "We would all rather die, wouldn't we, than have England a German province?" This would elicit a sort of low growl of assent, and the names came in at once.

The Bishop gave that Advent a rousing call at the Guildhall. To the Archbishop and all the other Bishops the war was, day by day and hour by hour, an almost unbearable anxiety, but there were cynical and ill-informed persons who said that they were not "giving a lead". It is always a cheap and popular form of disparagement. Of Ingram it could not be said. The Bishops were all doing faith-

[1] I am not here suggesting that there were such things. The *naïveté* is to suppose that if the Germans had accused our men of such things, our Press would have been allowed to tell us of it.

fully what they had to do. Ingram did more. He broke fresh ground. He had the power of divining, and expressing, the sentiments of the ordinary Briton, and he gave to them the most Christian complexion of which they were capable. By this is meant that a Christian preacher who says "Go on with the war" is taking what must be called lower ground. But he feels driven to this by the necessity which he, with others, has already faced, of choosing the lesser of two evils, and even on the plain he can breathe the air that comes down from the mountains.

There is no doubt that in his three Guildhall Addresses, on National Freedom, National Honour and National Faith, he said something which the whole nation was waiting to hear.[1]

It had always been the Bishop's hope to visit the L.R.B., and other units, in France. The opportunity came in the Spring of 1915. The Chaplains in France, whose spokesman was Harry Blackburne, now Dean of Bristol, wanted him. The Bishops felt that one of their number ought to go, and that he was the one who could best do it. Field-Marshal Sir John French gladly invited him. What he actually wrote was:

Dear Bishop,
    Five minutes of you cheers me up. Come out for ten days.

The time chosen was Holy Week and Easter, and it was to be a Mission to the B.E.F. It has been well described by the Reverend G. Vernon Smith, now Bishop of Leicester, who accompanied him as his Chaplain, in his little book, *The Bishop of London at the Front*. He took with him a vast supply of hymn-sheets, service-papers containing a short Russian war-time Litany, and ten thousand of what the Army insisted on calling "souvenirs", containing some short prayers for private use. Many more than ten thousand could easily have been disposed of. The instinct of the men was to send them home in letters, but the Bishop, discovering this, continually exhorted them to keep the papers for their own use.

On Palm Sunday the Bishop, having celebrated Holy Communion early, preached at six services, as well as confirming in the afternoon. The remaining days of Holy Week were even fuller. Admirable arrangements had been made by those responsible, and

[1] *The Church in Time of War.*

the services, whether advertised or impromptu, were all crowded. The Bishop everywhere began at the human end, saying, that he had come to give them a greeting from home, and then went on to speak of divine things, and especially the spiritual meaning of the Week. During the last few days he constantly took as his text one or more of the Seven Words from the Cross. He had preached on these many times before, but always in more conventional sur-roundings. This was an entirely new and strange experience. Men who are to face death, and perhaps taste it, in an hour's time, are worth preaching to. He had been made by Sir John French to promise that he would not actually go up into the trenches. He often kicked at this, but he was under discipline, and he went as near to the trenches as he was allowed. At almost every service they sang, "When I Survey". The other hymns were "Rock of Ages", "There is a Green Hill" and "Jesu, Lover of my Soul".

Easter Day was a great day. He had spent Easter Eve at Ypres, where he saw the ruined Cathedral and all that remained of the famous Cloth-Hall. He noted the great Crucifix that still stood, unharmed, over the Western Door of the Cathedral. His text that evening was, "Turn ye to the stronghold, ye prisoners of hope." He reached the quarters of the L.R.B. on Saturday night, and was enthusiastically greeted by them at a concert which was being held in the hall of a convent.

On Sunday Holy Communion was at seven. There were only 250 of the regiment in the village, and of those 200 came to receive the Holy Sacrament. At eight o'clock, it appeared that there were 200 men of other units, who had walked from a distance and were waiting outside. A second Celebration was at once held for them. Other services followed during the day, and in the evening there was a great gathering at H.Q., at which Sir John French and the Chief of Staff were present.

The tour ended with visits to the large Base Hospitals at Rouen and Havre, and what were called Rest Camps. Here he confirmed many, and also had a long chat with the Archbishop of Rouen. The work at these bases was in some respects even more arduous than that of the days spent at the Front. There were no long motor-rides in which to have a little relaxation, and almost the whole of every day was spent in interviews, than which few things are more exhausting. In fact, the whole fortnight made immense demands on the spiritual and physical resources of the Missioner.

The Bishop summed up his own impression of the tour by saying to his Chaplain, "I have had the experience of my life." Sir John French wrote a Despatch to Lord Kitchener, in which, after saying that there was scarcely a unit in the command which the Bishop did not meet, and that personal fatigue and even danger were completely ignored by him, he continued:

> I am anxious to place upon record my deep sense of the good effect produced throughout the Army by this self-sacrificing devotion on the part of the Bishop of London, to whom I feel personally very deeply indebted.
>
> I have once more to remark on the devotion to duty, courage and contempt of danger which has characterized the work of the Chaplains of the Army throughout the campaign.

The Chaplains all testified with one voice that his visit had been an immense help and encouragement to them in their exacting and dangerous work.

When he returned home, the Bishop wrote, by request, a letter to the *Times*, in which he said:

> I held fifty or sixty short services all along the front of the battle-line, and at all the Bases, and visited, ward by ward, twenty-two of the hospitals in France, and have therefore had a unique opportunity of seeing that side of the British soldier's character which is often left out in people's estimate of him. We hear a great deal of his wit and humour, his grit and his splendid courage and endurance; but little is said of that simple faith which he has imbibed in some quiet home or learnt in his Sunday School, and which is to a large extent, the spring and source of his other qualities. . . . It is to this spiritual side, of course, that I went out primarily to appeal, and I chose Holy Week and Easter as the most appropriate time at which to do so. What has encouraged me so much has been the overwhelming response of the whole Army.

Mr. St. Loe Strachey, Editor of the *Spectator*, wrote to him:

April 13, 1915.

My dear Bishop of London,

Your letter is quite splendid. I will of course do what you say and submit it to the Press Bureau, but if they prevent its publication I shall

285

judge them mad. The letter could not do any harm and must in my opinion do great good. I am no mystic, but I am perfectly sure that victories in war, like victories in the moral field, are won in the brain and by a great effort of will and not in the haphazard way in which we are now going on. It is a strange paradox, but we were in a much better mood for finishing the war just after the retreat from Mons, when everyone was so stricken at heart, than we are now when everybody seems comfortable.

You did a great national service, I am sure, in going out to the front, and we were all proud of you.

In June 1915 he marched in pouring rain (the Chaplain who carried the Pastoral Staff was laid up for weeks afterwards with rheumatism) to St. Paul's with 3,000 soldiers, and addressed them from the steps of the Cathedral. His subject was "The Soul of a Nation". He began with the famous *Punch* Cartoon of the German Emperor saying to the King of the Belgians, "So you have lost everything?" and the King's reply, "Except my soul." He went on to speak of France, Russia and Italy, and then he gave "The Message of the Church to the Nation":

I come out to-day as a Bishop of the Mother Church of England to give a message to the soul of our nation. Have we got a soul? Who that knows the history of the English people can doubt it? It is a soul which gets overlaid, like the soul of other nations, with love of material comfort, with arrogance, and with worldliness; but the children would not be springing from all over the world—from Canada, Australia, New Zealand, South Africa, to the Mother's side, if the Mother had no soul; if there had been no love for freedom, no belief in honour, no care for the weak, no contempt for the merely strong, then there would have been no glad loyalty from thousands and tens of thousands who have rallied round her flag. Can we doubt for a moment that the soul of the nation which won Agincourt, which flung back the Armada, which withstood for many years the armies of Napoleon, is not as great as the soul of other nations? Rather we believe that in this equally balanced contest on the Continent it is that soul of England which is once again to face the world; no calamity can be pictured more awful than if at this supreme crisis England should fail. We must fight as one man, for we are fighting not only for the freedom of our own Country, but for the freedom of the world. As I stand in front of this great Cathedral, I cannot forget the Cathedral of Ypres, and others on the

Continent which are now in ruins. We are fighting for the right of all to live free. It is a glorious time in which we are living. You soldiers in front of me have the chance of taking part in the second Battle of Waterloo.

He ended with a stirring call to pray, to repent, to serve and to save.

This was a timely utterance and made a deep impression, not only on those to whom it was actually addressed, but on those who read it. The Lord Mayor wrote the following letter:

June 10th, 1915.

My Lord Bishop,

As Chairman of the Grand Committee of the City of London National Guard and Honorary Commandant of the Corps, I write at once to express to you the most sincere thanks of myself and my Committee for the great service you did in addressing the Regiment last night at St. Paul's. Your address to the men, my Lord Bishop, was a noble and inspiriting one and from many quarters I have heard expressions of the deepest gratitude to you for the Christian and Patriotic thoughts you brought to the minds of those in the large Congregation.

Believe me,

Yours very sincerely,

CHARLES JOHNSTON.

Lord Mayor.

A month later he sent out a Pastoral Letter to the clergy of the Diocese, in which he appealed to them to redouble their prayers, and to call upon the people of their parishes for "a great outpouring of unselfish and patriotic service". He suggested various ways in which united intercession might be organized—a great many London parishes already had war-shrines in the streets—and other methods of deepening the public morale, and ended by saying:

All this can only be done by those who live on the spot, and who have already won the confidence of the people.

In all these ways the Church must justify its claim to be the National Church at a time when the nation specially needs such help.

I am sure, dear brother, that I may trust you to rise to the level of our great opportunity, and to be yourself an example of service and sacrifice "for the people to follow".

287

He also published a Message to the People of London, of which 500,000 copies were circulated. In it he said very much as he had said to the soldiers at St. Paul's:

He also wrote a homely little letter to soldiers in Hospital:

London House,
St. James' Square, S.W.

Dear Brother and Comrade,

Here you are in a comfortable bed at last, "scaped from the winter and the storm", and what a blessed thing it is to be between clean sheets again; and to have all the loving care you will find in the hospital where you are! I know what it is myself after weeks in camp—a good *big* hot bath and clean sheets—and what must it be after the muddy trenches! But, how are you going to use your time after you have got over the feeling of the comfort and peace of it all?

You may often be lying awake at night, unable to sleep, and in any case there are the long hours of the day, and you have got to lie there until that wound has healed up, or the poison in your system has been got rid of.

I want you to look upon it as a Godgiven opportunity for coming back to God, and making God your Friend for life.

God has never ceased to love you, and knows you by name out of all the thousands in the War; has often spoken to you, but you perhaps were either not attending, or the noise of the battle or the constant chaff and jests of comrades prevented your hearing.

But now, in the stillness, you will be able to hear His Voice; He seems to say, "Be still, and *know* that I am God."

You have never been an atheist; you have never out and out disbelieved in God; but has He been the great Reality of the Universe to you?

You have come from great realities; when the shell is bursting over you, or the mine explodes, you are face to face with death, and you know it; how unreal many things sound then which you may have said lightly in days of peace about religion being only fit for women and children. As a young man wrote to me from the trenches, "nothing matters here but prayer and trust in God; we all feel it out here; War is a great purge."

It is, then by God's mercy that you were not killed by the shell or bullet that wounded you, or by the gas or trench fever. Is not this the very time:

288

1. To thank God for preserving your life, and for giving you another chance to love Him more and serve Him better.
2. To learn more about Him, as revealed in the Bible, and especially in the New Testament.

 Why not have a little Bible reading to yourself every day?
3. To *think* over what a wonderful thing it is that He came down to our little earth at Christmas, and died for us on Good Friday, and conquered death on Easter Day.
4. To learn to pray more, or to start praying again, asking Him for help and healing, and to care for the wife and children or the old people far away.
5. To resolve that if you are allowed to come back to life again that your life shall be different.

Why not resolve to be confirmed and come afterwards to the Communion—if you are not already confirmed?

I confirmed myself 200 during my short visit to the Front, and gave Communion to 350 on Easter Day behind the lines.

Anyhow, I hope you will make the Padre, as he comes round, stop and have a talk with you. He is there to help you.

You can shew him this letter and ask him if he agrees with it, and that will start the conversation.

You perhaps hardly realize how constantly we think of you all and pray for you at home, and this is just a little message from home.

Your friend and comrade,
A. F. LONDON.

The last call of those four years was his Easter Sermon in St. Paul's in 1918. It was a real Easter sermon, but it was delivered during the final crisis of the war, when the prospects in France were very formidable. He worked into it "They shall not pass". One wiseacre said to him afterwards, "If they do, shall you change your religion?" His reply at the moment is unknown, but it was certainly confident. His faith never wavered. Happily, the question did not arise, and he was able to refer to the challenge in Westminster Abbey six months later, and say, "Where are those pessimists now?"

In 1916 he was invited by Admiral Jellicoe and Admiral Beatty to visit the Grand Fleet. He went first to Rosyth, and then sailed in the *Warspite*, where Walter Carey was Chaplain, to Scapa Flow.

Within a few minutes of his boarding the *Iron Duke*, he was confirming seventy men of the Fleet. The day by day routine was,
after morning prayers in the Flag Ship, to visit four ships in the
morning and four in the afternoon. In some ships he found a
number of East Londoners, and he began by saying, "I suppose
you have *heard* of Bethnal Green, Stepney and Whitechapel," and
they all grinned with pleasure. In many ships he made use of a
favourite argument about the impossibility of a box of letters
throwing themselves into a play of Shakespeare, a consideration
which impressed officers and ratings alike.

There were Quiet Days for the Chaplains at Scapa Flow and Inver-
gordon, there was a game of golf ashore on a temporary course
with the Admiral, and there was tennis in the evenings with the
"snotties", or, as the Bishop politely called them, midshipmen, and
he was sent off from the Fleet in a ninety horse-power motor car.
Thus ended the visit to the Grand Fleet. The Bishop was enthusiastically thanked by Jellicoe for what he had done.

In 1918, just before the end of the War, he paid a visit to the
Armies in Salonika, at the request of General Milne. The journey
thither and thence to Sofia, Athens, Malta, Rome and Paris, involved much travelling by road, rail and sea, and included the
maximum number of engagements in every place. It was very
laborious. At the end of it the Bishop wrote a letter to the *Times*
paying a warm tribute to the British soldier for his courage and
endurance and the good reputation he had gained among the
Balkan peoples.

A large part of the Bishop's time during these years of war was
spent in comforting the bereaved. This was done mainly in letters
and private talks, of which there is no record, but some words
must be quoted from his Sermon at the Memorial Service for
soldiers of the London Rifle Brigade at St. Botolph's, Bishopsgate
on June 19, 1915—

> You must not think of your dear one as far away; he is close to you
> in that blessed spiritual communion. He prays for you and loves you,
> and you can pray for him and love him. He is only parted from sight
> for a little time. And he has gone to a life that a young man can enjoy.
> Do not tell me that when GOD finished making this world, with all
> its interests, and activities, and brightness and glorious service, that

His imagination became bankrupt, and that he had none left to make another world with. In that ghost-like, unattractive world which our imaginations have conjured up a young man would not be at home. But JESUS CHRIST loved young men. "JESUS, beholding him, loved him." He knows how to make young men happy. He knows your boy. He knows what he can enjoy, and the sort of life he can live, and the company in which he will be happy; and he has got it all ready for him. When that full-blooded, happy-starred spirit shoots into the spirit world, he finds there the LORD who loved him, and understands him, and Who has ready a life for him which he can enjoy. But he will not be complete without you. He will be waiting for the mother, the sister, the wife, to come over too. But he has got a life which is a man's life, for JESUS CHRIST was a man as well as GOD. And then, best of all, you will see him again. It is not for ever, the parting. You will see him again with your own eyes. Every day brings the day of meeting nearer. You will see him again, purified in character, in the sunshine of his Lord's presence, but the same person, the same son you love, with the same love for you. And when you look back from eternity, the parting will not seem so long. You will have him with you for ever. "He asked life of Thee, and Thou gavest him a long life, even for ever and ever."[1]

This chapter has been compiled partly from the Bishop's own *Fifty Years* and partly from other sources. *Fifty Years* is an ingenuous narrative, from which it would almost seem that there were no problems and everything, except, of course, the physical labour of going so far and doing so much, was easy. And, in a true sense, with Ingram, it was easy. Bishop H. L. Paget said once about some spiritual project, "Of course there are practical difficulties, but I never have believed much in practical difficulties." There is a kind of faith which does remove mountains. Ingram went straight forward, and it constantly appeared that the mountain was not so big as it had looked. He tackled men in his cheery, personal and deadly earnest Christian way, and touched something which they often had not known—but he knew—to be in them. It was of course very far indeed from being a complete victory, but it was a victory. And it was one more illustration of the truth of St. John's words, "This is the victory that overcometh the world, even our faith."

[1] *The Church in Time of War*, 298-300.

XV

RECREATION

R ECREATION was an important thing in Ingram's life, because he was convinced that without exercise he would not be equal to his work. It is also the fact that he liked playing games and thoroughly enjoyed a holiday.

On the day-off in London he usually played golf. For an occasional hour or two in an afternoon there was tennis at Fulham in the summer, or squash-racquets at the Bath Club, where his opponent was at times the Prince of Wales. In winter there was an occasional game of hockey. When nothing else was possible, there would be a sharp walk along the riverside. Only in quite exceptional circumstances was a day ever spent without some exercise. On country holidays squash was not as a rule to be had, and to the other diversions he added fishing. It would seem that golf was really his favourite recreation. "I am having," he wrote in 1917, "some capital golf, which I like more than anything." And he was no mean performer. There was a time in America when he was negotiating a particularly difficult bunker, known locally as "Hell". He got away, and the old caddie said, "Bishop, I should recommend you to take that niblick with you when you die."

He looked forward as eagerly as a schoolboy to a holiday, whether of a day or of two months. He enjoyed every moment of it. "When the ball is on the tee," he said once to one of his Suffragans, "who can remember the diocese of London?" He liked a "jolly holiday" in a country house, with a number of young people, and plenty going on, but he also liked a quiet week or week-end in a country Vicarage.

The usual plan was to spend a winter holiday, beginning the day after the Children's Party, at Bournemouth. There he stayed with his mother, while she lived. The visit always included a meeting in the Town Hall for East London. "We look upon the Bishop," said the President of the Bournemouth Rotary Club, "almost as a

Bournemouth man. He is very dearly loved in Bournemouth."
After Easter and at Whitsuntide he would spend a few days in the
home of a friend in the country. This is the account of the Reverend
H. J. Warner, who was for twenty years Vicar of Northstoke:

> For some thirty years the Bishop spent his Whitsuntide with his
> great friend, Sir John Wormald, at "Springs", a beautiful house and
> grounds on the Thames, about two miles below Wallingford, in the
> parish of Northstoke. This friendship arose, I understand, in con-
> sequence of a sermon in which the Bishop appealed to any young men
> in the congregation with time and leisure to come and help him in his
> work in the East End of London. Mr. Wormald (as he then was) put
> himself into communication with the preacher, and became greatly
> interested in the mission at Bethnal Green. Mr. Wormald helped the
> Bishop both personally and financially. The place of the Bishop's short
> holiday was kept secret from the Press, and afforded him a few days'
> rest and recreation, spent in reading books which he brought with him,
> golf at Huntercombe and tennis at "Springs". As I had two Churches
> to serve—Northstoke and Ipsden—two miles apart and no car, with
> six Services at the great Festivals, the Bishop, with characteristic
> kindness, took the 8 a.m. Holy Communion at Northstoke and assisted
> also at Mattins and Evensong. On Whit Monday each year, at the
> invitation and expense of Sir John Wormald, a party of men came
> down from Bethnal Green and Stepney, and spent a glorious day at
> "Springs," with the opportunity of meeting again their old friends,
> Sir John and the Bishop.

Here is another description of a like series of short holidays. The
Reverend M. J. Eland, Vicar of Coberly, Cheltenham, writes:

> Bishop Winnington-Ingram—108th and dearly loved Bishop of
> London was, like St. Paul, all things to all men. We had known him
> in London at the peak of his career, and we had the privilege of know-
> ing him later in another sphere as sportsman and fisherman, the simple
> lovable guest who came every summer to our Cotswold Rectory for a
> week's trout-fishing.
> As soon as the May-fly was seen on the water he would drive up to
> our door, with the ample luggage of a more spacious generation.
> There were usually fourteen pieces, which included the "Holy Bag",
> which contained his robes for Sunday, and the "Unholy Bag" of
> fishing-tackle and golf balls. He would arrive in time for a cup of tea,
> and, far more important, in time for the evening rise. He had been

accustomed to fishing the lordly waters of the Test and the Teme, but he was just as keen to throw a fly on the lake at the back of our house, or to fish the small Cotswold streams where the trout are seldom larger than a pound. Tea was spent comparing flies with the Rector, planning the campaign with the zest of a schoolboy and if he could come back with five or six trout in his bag, his day would be complete.

We would all gather round to see the fish weighed and praise his skill—it is incidentally far harder to catch these trout than the pampered inhabitants of millionaires' waters.

One day when he had hooked a large fish, his reel fell off into the water. with the result that he lost the fish. "Weren't we good Christians?" he said when he came home. "We neither of us even said 'Damn'."

As soon as he entered the house, he brought a beautiful atmosphere with him; we all behaved better, were kind, sweet-tempered, gentle, as he expected us to be, and as he was himself. Even the children noticed it. One of them, when she was only seven years old, said, "You can tell the Bishop is a very holy man," and, when questioned, replied scornfully as though we should know the answer, "Well, you can feel it, can't you?"

He called the children his Archdeacons, "Archdeacon o' London, and Archdeacon o' Middlesex", and they had their duties, fetching his books and spectacles, helping him to make his bed and lay out his clothes, reading Evensong with him before dinner. Before he left they had their wages, 10/- each, a kiss, his blessing, and they adored him as every one did who came in contact with him.

He was always known in the Parish as the "Bishop", and when word went round that he was expected at the Rectory, many little offerings for him arrived. He was extremely fond of roast duck and green peas, and a farmer's wife would walk down two miles from the hills, with a fat duck beautifully wrapped up in a white napkin "For the Bishop's Dinner". Other people would queue up for biscuits for him, since he had been heard to say that, as he didn't smoke or touch alcohol, he did think the nation might allow him two Marie biscuits with his morning tea. Another woman would bicycle four miles up a very steep hill every day for a week before he came "to give the place a thorough clean for the Bishop", a labour of love which in war-time no money could have procured. He really loved these gifts and the spirit in which they were given. "My young nephew always says that Uncle Arthur's an asset to the house," he used to say jokingly but proudly.

All through his long life he had kept a strict routine from which he never departed, even on holiday. He liked to be called at seven. "I am always so glad to wake up," he would say, "to know I've another day before me"; and he would go straight in to the cold bath which he had taken since boyhood. Then he had his morning tea, and the Marie biscuits, dressed and came downstairs to read Mattins in the sitting-room. The family were usually busy at this hour getting the breakfast and driving the children to school, so often the large black Labrador would sit in front of him and gaze up into his face all the time, and he could almost think that he joined in the Amens.

He had his breakfast at nine o'clock, and thought coffee and a poached egg *and* bacon, the nicest breakfast in the world. He ate very little, but the food that he liked he enjoyed thoroughly, as he enjoyed everything. "I love life," he used to say. "God has given us such a beautiful world, and it's all so *interesting*." After breakfast he read and answered his letters, and hardly a morning went by without his sending for his cheque-book; some poor little woman was ill and must have a holiday, or an old friend had to have a course of treatment at a Spa. Then he sat in the garden till lunch-time, reading; the Labrador asleep beside him, the hens pecking blissfully at the lawn at his feet. "I've just taken off my hat to that hen," he said, "and thanked her for laying such a nice egg for my breakfast."

He read every good book that came out, and this was one of the secrets of his perennial youth. "If you put nothing in your head, nothing will come out of it; it becomes like a river that's over-fished," he said.

After lunch he always took some form of exercise; golf, fishing or tennis. Ten years ago after his serious illness, Lord Horder told him that he must give up tennis. "Well, H'orders is Horders," he said to his chaplain. "Get them to mark out the tennis court."

At 80 he could hit hard and strong, and had a cutting serve, and it was one of his proudest memories that he had once played a match with Helen Wills-Moody. After his exercise he would come home to a hot bath, which revived him, and change into his purple cassock and buckled shoes (much admired by the children) for dinner. Either before or after dinner he liked to read Evensong with any members of the family who were free, and before he went to bed, after the news, to be read to for an hour or so, from a novel. One year it was Hardy's *Under the Greenwood Tree* and when we reached the description of the church band being replaced by an organ, he chuckled and told us that at his father's church at Stanford, when he was a boy, they had a barrel-organ for the hymns, and the old clerk used to turn it.

Every year he came to us he insisted upon taking three services on the Sunday, Holy Communion at eight, Mattins and Evensong. I think during these last years of his life he preached better than he had ever done before, and his presence was so magnificent that it brought a lump to the throat. This, I think was the secret of it: "Every time I go into the pulpit I feel a thrill to think that I am going to be allowed to preach the Gospel," he said, only last year.

Let us all praise famous men and thank God for this beautiful life.

The main holiday was in August and September. It would begin with a few days in Camp, with the London Rifle Brigade or the Church Lads' Brigade, and then he would travel up to Scotland, staying at various big houses. It was a rich man's holiday. Not that it cost him much, except railway-fares and no doubt generous tips, but there was a good deal of expenditure behind it on the big houses and maintenance of the fishing. Of course he had the services of the most accomplished ghillies, and a Midland clergyman, with whom he occasionally fished in the years of his retirement, observed that he was not handy at doing small piscatorial duties for himself. This was only because he always took those things as he found them. The best service was available. The men were eager to give it. Very well, he would receive it, and be very grateful, and he would make friends with those who gave the service. He was just as happy catching small trout in an English stream as he was when playing his salmon on the waters of the Ness or Tay.

He read a good deal on his holidays. The "book-box", often referred to, contained volumes, new and old, which had been saved up to read in holiday evenings. And he lost no opportunity of making personal contacts. Sometimes he puzzled the natives. He was talking once to an old shepherd:

"How many sheep have you?"
" 'Bout a hundred."
"I'm a sort of shepherd, too."
"How many sheep have you?"
"About four million."
"Eh! What do you do at lambing-time?"

But he always won their hearts.

The time in Scotland was not always spent in big houses. Provost

Smythe of St. Ninian's, Perth, was an old friend, and Ingram was often there. One who was at that time a child, writes:

The late Bishop of London used to visit his dear friend Provost Smythe for the fishing, and always attended the 9 a.m. Communion at St. Ninian's Cathedral, Perth, to take part in the service, and to partake of the breakfast that followed in the Chapter House. How we, as children (1924-26 I suppose) used to love him—he and the Provost were men who truly had a halo; they radiated happiness and kindness.

Here are a few holiday letters from the Bishop himself:

Inverness, N.B.
August 31, 1919.

I am really having a lovely holiday this time. I think it is the fact of the awful burden of the war being gone; one hardly realized what a nightmare it was until it was over. After the rain came, I got some big salmon, 20 lb., 18 lb., 11 lb., a nice grilse, which I sent my Mother, and I am going to have a day on the Ness to-morrow.

I am glad to find that I *can* catch them still, and play them. The old ghilly said, when I landed the huge twenty-pounder, "Eh, mon, but you played it beautifully," which I felt a greater compliment than if an Archbishop had praised my sermon.

At the same time I feel sometimes sorry for the poor creatures and want them to escape; only I suppose that God *meant* fish to be caught and eaten.

I had some glorious golf and tennis at St. Andrews. . . .

I am reading hard all the time.

August 29, 1924.

My bag, so far, has been 2 salmon, 20 sea trout and innumerable smaller trout off the boat. But I don't care much for boat-fishing; it is too easy. I move on to —— to-morrow, where I shall have more golf than fishing, and you will be glad to hear that I am thoroughly enjoying my holiday this time. God is making up to me for my sad time last winter.

September 2, 1932.

I got one salmon in the Tay, the only one caught in the week, and two in the Ness, the first caught in a fortnight, so I have been very lucky. To-day I had a game of golf, and am off to fish in the loch after tea, but I am doing a lot of reading, and am 2/3 through my book-box

Read *Charles II* by Bryant, and the *History of the A.-C. Movement*[1] by Spencer Ingram.

August 16, 1938.

I have just had a fortnight's splendid tennis, and now am settling down for a fortnight's fishing.

An amusing story is told of one of the Bishop's holidays. It sounds very legendary, but it was related in Mr. Raymond Blathwayt's *Looking Down the Years*:

Two ladies were staying in a country-house. When they came down to breakfast on the first morning they reported that they had had a wretched night and that their room must be haunted. "We were fast asleep," the elder sister said, "when we were awakened about twelve o'clock by someone rushing into the room, and suddenly all the clothes were torn off my bed." Just at that moment, to everyone's astonishment, in walked Dr. Winnington-Ingram. "My dear Bishop," said the hostess, "we had quite given you up. When *did* you arrive?"

"Oh, my dear Lady So-and-So, my train was dreadfully late. But your good butler gave me a capital supper, and then shewed me up to my old room."

"I hope everything was comfortable there."

"Well," said the Bishop, "when I came to get into bed, I found there were no bedclothes, so I just went into the next room and picked the clothes off a bed there: but I had a very good night!"

Stories develop. This cannot be taken as it stands, but there is probably some faint foundation of fact in it. Perhaps no more than the Bishop confessing at breakfast that he had been cold in the night, and someone else remarking, "Well, I was only next door, and I could have given you an extra blanket," and the Bishop rejoining, "But I could hardly have come in at twelve o'clock and picked a blanket off your bed. You would have thought the house was haunted."

Behind all the enjoyment was a serious purpose. On 26 July, 1926 the *Church Times* quoted, with comments, from the Diocesan Gazette:

[1] I am unable to identify this volume. My friend Mr. Kenneth Ingram has written books, but not with this exact title. The mention of the Christian name makes me wonder whether it is my own book *Church and People* 1789-1889, which is not a history of the Anglo-Catholic Movement, though it includes some reference to it.

"Holidays!" cries the Bishop of London, "the very word is like music to the ear of the man who has worked all the year with his nose to the grindstone." But before thinking of his own holidays, the Bishop sets an example to his diocese by thinking of other people's. He always begins his holidays by going to the camp of the Church Lads' Brigade, partly in order to encourage the fairly well-to-do, before they go for their own holidays, to send a subscription to the Council for Youth, at the Rectory, Ironmonger-lane, E.C., either for the C.L.B. or the Scouts or the Boys' Camp or the Women's Holiday Fund which the Bishop himself started for hard-working mothers.

It is the Bishop's habit to set off for his holidays with fishing rods at one end of the car, golf clubs at the other, a tennis racquet under the seat, and a huge box of books on the top. "I am sure," he writes, "people are making a great mistake about their holidays if they do not make this a time of mental refreshment and recuperation, as well as a time of physical enjoyment."

Then after a word of caution about the need of consideration, chivalry and good manners in the use of the roads, the Bishop comes to what he considers the most important purpose of a holiday: that is to get a fresh grip on spiritual realities. "The world is too much with us" during the working days, but by the ocean, with what a Greek poet calls its unnumbered smile, or beneath the great mountains, there is time to be still and know that God is God, and so far from people taking a holiday from their religion during their holidays, as some people do, it is a time to allow the great realities to get a grip on the soul, which will last into and through the coming winter".

An occasional day-off was devoted to a golf-match between the London Clergy and the Clergy of some other diocese. The Reverend A. B. Wright records that

For ten years I was Hon. Sec. of the Oxford Diocese Clergy Golf Club and we used to play London twice a year. The Bishop nearly always came, and I occasionally played against him in singles in the morning, and oftener in the foursomes, for he was about my handicap, 14. He liked to play in the top match with Prebendary Percival (their best man) so I had to play with our best man to make an even match. The Bishop always stood lunch for both sides, but not drinks. He used to tell us this in the morning. A year or two before he retired, I remember he came to me in the usual way, and I said, "I know, my Lord, *they* pay for their drinks." "Oh well," he said, "if they want a glass of port, let them have it." I think this is a notable instance of his very kind heart softening the austerity of his principles.

Side by side with this can be put a like reminiscence from a layman:

> Perhaps the following may be of interest, shewing his unbounded humour and sportsmanship. About 1931 he went to Stansted in Essex, for some dedication in the Church there, and an old friend of mine, Sydney Gold, entertained him for the week-end. About a week or so before the Bishop had taken part in a golf-match between the Clergy of the diocese of London and the Clergy of the diocese of Southwark, and during the match did a hole in one. After dinner on Saturday he and Gold were walking round the garden, and Gold remarked to the Bishop, "I saw you did a hole in one the other day." The Bishop laughed, and said it was dreadful. "I had to pay for all their lunches and goodness knows what it cost me in drinks." And he a total abstainer!

These stories prove, if proof were needed, that he never thrust his principles upon unwilling people, and even at times consented to provide for others what he neither used nor liked himself. He never sought, or seemed to need, any kind of stimulus. Nor did he ever use tobacco. The clergy are great smokers, though in recent years many of them have been driven by poverty to curtail or even abandon their smoking habits. The Bishop disliked the smell of tobacco. As far as possible he refrained from interference with the doings of other people, as the following story reveals:

> An old Oxford House friend was travelling with him in a railway-carriage and smoking. After a while he noticed the Bishop several times putting his head out of the window, and at last asked if he objected to smoke, and found that he did. The surprising thing was that he had smoked on many occasions for years in the Bishop's presence, and had of course known of innumerable young men doing so on a vast number of occasions, without ever having the slightest idea that he objected to it. I remember the intense surprise with which I learned this myself after a fairly close acquaintance with the Bishop, gained during some twenty years in London.

It was surely a remarkable example of forbearance and consideration. So, without using either of the two luxuries which have so often brought solace or stimulus to English sportsmen, he fished and played games with immense zest. The famous words of King Henry V before the walls of Harfleur could be adapted, in a less martial sense, to illustrate his keenness:

> I see you stand like greyhounds in the slips,
> Straining upon the start. The game's afoot;
> Follow your spirit; and upon this charge
> Cry, "God for Harry! England and St. George."

King Henry's game, when it was not war, was no doubt some kind of hunting. For Ingram it would be more like a game with some of those tennis-balls which the Dauphin had sent in mockery to the English king, but, when his game was afoot, he stood like a greyhound in the slips, and we only need to change "Harry" into "Arthur" to illustrate the eager and (it could be said) even devout spirit in which he always played.

XVI

THE LAST YEARS IN LONDON

In the summer of 1933 the Bishop was dangerously ill. He had only had one serious illness in his life before, and he was accustomed to say that the sole use he had for his doctor was to invite him to dine. This time he had severe congestion of the lungs, and narrowly escaped double pneumonia. One who was there at the time reports that it was touch and go. Immense sympathy sprang up everywhere. Prayers were made for his recovery in parish churches, by Free Churchmen, by Roman Catholics, and in countless homes. There is extant a sheet of paper which is evidently the rough copy in rather irregular writing of a reply to inquiries from the highest quarter:

> The Bishop of London is much touched by his Majesty's kind inquiries. He thinks he has at last got a real turn for the better.

While he was still abed, he learned that Archbishop Phelps of Capetown was to be in the neighbourhood, and said, "This is my best chance to make my confession," and the Archbishop visited him for this purpose.[1]

In the course of this illness, as in the former one, champagne was ordered and sent in by the doctors. Having been an abstainer for many years, he refused on both occasions to take it, and eventually had a "Recovery Lunch" for doctors and nurses and made them drink it. He was attended by Lord Horder and the local G.P. He is said to have been most difficult to control. He used to laugh about the doctors' restrictions, but he tried to get round them all the same. Great anxiety was felt for the strain on his heart, but one day, in the absence of the Chaplain, he persuaded the nurses to take him down to the garden. The effort of getting upstairs again strained his heart badly and prolonged the convalescence by several weeks. A few days later, having secured a carrying-chair, he inno-

---

[1] In earlier days he had resorted for this purpose to Bishop Wilkinson and Bishop King.

cently asked Lord Horder if one day next week he might sit in the
garden for a time. Lord Horder, supposing that this meant in complete isolation, agreed. The real reason was that a Boys' School was
due for a visit on the Tuesday, and he wanted to be among them.
Lord Horder was horrified when he heard about it afterwards. All
games were of course forbidden for a long time, but well before the
appointed day he was at golf, tennis and squash rackets. "This," says
the Chaplain, both in reference to that time, and in general, was
"not mere pleasure. He needed vigorous exercise to clear his head
from the interminable worries which by all and sundry were
brought to him daily."

In 1934 the Bishop reached the fiftieth anniversary of his ministerial life. His friends, above all those who had been ordained by
him, were determined to mark the occasion. It produced a great
outburst of filial affection. A large sum of money was collected.
The Secretary of the Fund was the Reverend Arthur McCheane,
the devoted Rector of St. Nicholas, Cole Abbey, who, as Minor
Canon at St. Paul's, had assisted at a great many Ordinations. There
was a very large gathering of bishops and priests in the Hall of
King's College, London, to make the presentation. The Bishop of
Willesden presided and among those on the platform were the
Archbishop of Canterbury, the Suffragan Bishops and Archdeacons,
Bishop Paget, several former Domestic Chaplains, Mr. McCheane
and the Gospeller at the Bishop's last Ordination. The total number
present was about 700.

The following telegram was read by the Chairman:

The Queen and I warmly congratulate you on the fiftieth anniversary
of your Ordination and your long life and active service rendered
during so many years to the Church in London.

GEORGE R. I.

The Chairman said:

With the exception of some on the platform, he (the Archbishop)
and I are the only people present this afternoon who were not ordained
by the Bishop of London. We represent the enormous company of
his adopted sons. Others will speak of what we all owe to this greatly
beloved Father-in-God. There are only three things that I wish to say.
First, I think it would be true to say that this is an occasion quite

unprecedented in the history of our Church, that one Bishop during the tenure of one see should have admitted into Holy Orders no fewer than 2,205 men. I like to be accurate, and I have been making a little research by the aid of a scholar into the records, and it is extremely difficult to make a complete statement. Many of the records before the Reformation have disappeared. In great Dioceses like Lincoln and Lichfield there were large numbers at Ordinations. But I do not think there is the slightest doubt that this record has never been reached by anyone, and I am told that I shall be making no mistake in making this statement. Most students would probably agree that seldom, if ever, has this record been equalled, if not surpassed. *We* here know in our hearts that there is no doubt at all that there has never been anything like it.

I have only one thing more that I must say, though others will say it after me, and that is, the remarkable fact is not to be found in regard to names or numbers, but in the depth of affection felt by this great body of men in a wonderful way for this great Father-in-God. I have seen letters which have come from all over the world, and you can understand how warmly men have written from the distant corners of the earth. We all know that the Bishop has given us a wonderful vision of a Father-in-God, who rules by love and therefore claims a loyalty which has always been gladly given.

The Archbishop of Canterbury said:

I cannot tell you how deeply moved I am myself by the thought of the fifty years of this unique and wonderful ministry. It is very fitting that it should be celebrated by this great company of those whom the Bishop has ordained. As you all can see, he has come with health and joy to his jubilee, bringing his sons with him.

I am afraid that, so far as I am concerned, I must be regarded more or less as an intruder. But my right to be here has been described by the Bishop of Willesden. There is a curious relationship between the Bishop and myself. I was his Suffragan in one sense, he is my Suffragan in another. One thing has remained constant during all these changes, and that is our friendship. It is true that of late years we have both been so occupied in our respective spheres that we have not been able to see as much of each other as I should wish. But our friendship is not one of those that needs cultivating, because its roots are so deep and strong that it flourishes whether I see him or whether I do not. As he knows, when we do meet on some occasions not as friendly and festive as this, beneath all the talk and discussion that goes on we know where we stand to one another. That is why you must not expect me to deliver an oration about the Bishop. It is always absurd to make a speech about an old friend in his presence. Yet I suppose you will wish me to say one or two words. They will be very simple and sincere. Naturally, I should be in what the newspapers call a reminiscent mood. I have known the Bishop, I expect, longer than almost any one here. That is rather a rash statement to make when I note the almost venerable appearance of some of the Bishop's sons. It is not surprising at all that he should have spiritually begotten so many sons. It is a little surprising that out of him should have spiritually come 65 dignitaries, and, what is even more surprising, that he should have begotten so many sons who outwardly seem so very much older than himself. I think I have probably known the Bishop longer than at any rate most of you here present. It is forty-six years since I first made his acquaintance. He was then just appointed Head of the Oxford House, and I remember the impression which I first received when I found myself in Oxford House, a little shy of even such quasi-ecclesiastical surroundings. I was then a student at the Temple, very ambitious of pursuing a career in politics, to which the law was to have been the introduction, but I had already made the acquaintance of East London and its settlements and all that they meant. When I came to the Oxford House as it was in the days of James Adderley and Hensley Henson, and when young Winnington-Ingram came there from Lichfield, it seemed to me that there was a different atmosphere. Instead of friendship with the poor being a matter of principle, I found it an instinct of love, and the difference made a profound impression on me. One never knows, but it may be that that impression of what the Church ought to bring to the poor was one of the reasons that led me to a complete change of my career.

Thirty-three years ago the Bishop summoned me to be his comrade and successor as Bishop of Stepney. I spent eight hard and happy years under his rule and in his fellowship. Some of you can remember, but few as I can, that wonderful springtide of the Bishop's episcopate. You will forgive me if even in his presence I say that when I look back on those radiant days he seemed to be the Bayard of the Church of England, the *chevalier sans peur et sans reproche*. He came, even more manifestly than bishops had been wont to do, preaching the Gospel of the Love of God, and whenever he went he captured the imagination and the heart of London. The reason for that conquest was not so much anything that he said but the impression he gave of his own personality.

And that has remained ever since. I am sure when you think of the days at Fulham, just before you were ordained, you will agree that it was not so much anything that the Bishop said, but the extraordinary way in which with his innate sympathy he put himself alongside of you, and you felt that you were alongside of him. The way in which that is done cannot be analysed. It is a form of spiritual genius wich is to be accepted, for which to thank God, but which cannot be explained. That sympathy has been clearly marked in his dealings with the boys at Public Schools, and even with those more complete boys at the University. They all feel in the same way that extraordinary power of human personality. I remember a boy at one of our great Public Schools to whom I said, "You were one of those hundreds of boys who went to see the Bishop the other day. What happened?" He replied, "I have not the ghost of a notion what the Bishop said, but I felt it was good to be there." So it has been all along, and that instinct of kindness and sympathy has never failed. Whenever there is any sickness or trouble in his Diocese among his priests or his people, you may be certain that the Bishop will be there. I never know how he finds time to do it, but he makes time for these things because his life of rigorous discipline enables him to do so. The flow of his lovingkindness goes on ever fresh because it has a spring of love which never fails. If I may strike a deeper note, the reason why that spring never fails is because it has itself a deeper spring, for "He that dwelleth in love dwelleth in God, and God in him." I have already said more than the Bishop will like, but I rejoice at being present with you and sharing with you memories of another kind but not less part of our lives; and I would say to the Bishop that with this offering of the love and loyalty of these your sons, will you deign to accept the unfading flower of the love of one who was once your comrade and is always your friend?

Bishop Paget said:

I can never forget the Bishop's extraordinary kindness and loyalty to those who in some capacity or other worked under him. He always reminded me of the Bethnal Green father who before his daughter's marriage was told that he would have to give her away. Looking grave, the father replied, "I could, but I won't." That was always a course that lay within the reach of the Bishop of London with regard to his Suffragans, but he never took it. The Bishop of London was simply amazing in his loyalty. I shall never forget the something more than brotherly kindness with which he met one's mistakes. But just for a moment one must get to deeper things. What must be in the minds of those who have been ordained in the Diocese of London? First, the glorious dignity of the service for those who are ordained in this Diocese, that interview with the Bishop, which I believe to many of us is just about the most critical interview in the whole of life, fraught with issues that may colour and change the whole of one's ministry. It is just in that that the Bishop has been absolutely inimitable. I remember one clever friend of mine remarking after an interview with the Bishop that he was perfectly certain that there was Someone else present in the room with them all the while. It is not so much what he says, but that the presence and the claim of Jesus Christ are made such a reality. Again, a grave old priest once said to me, "There is one thing about the Bishop of London; it is very difficult to tell him a lie. Not that any of us tell lies! But I think it is just possible to be a little bit evasive with the Archdeacon, and to muddle the truth in self-apology when one talks it over with the Rural Dean. But with the Bishop, never." To have a presence, a sincerity, a sympathy, a love, which do draw out the truth, seems to me one of the very highest things of the Bishop's episcopate. I think that perhaps in days when accuracy is less studied than it ought to be, it is an almost supreme gift in a Bishop of a great Diocese that he can be the sort of man to whom it is impossible to be wilfully untrue. We all know, too, that he has not given us the spirit of fear or of contention. He has given us the spirit of power and love and of a sound mind; and let us try to help our Bishop by living as near to all that as ever we can, being persuaded that he really has no greater joy than that he find his children walking in the truth.

The Bishop of Stepney, who was the third man to be ordained by the Bishop of London, Number one being in British Columbia and Number two being unable to attend, then made the Presentation. He said:

About a year ago I was reading Canon Barry's book, and I came across a sentence which leaped out at me as a true word, that "the real significance of a man's life is his creativeness in the lives of others." I thought about that sentence for a bit, and I pencilled in the margin as a conspicuous instance of this three letters very familiar to us, "A.F.L." And, my dear Bishop, we hail you to-day because you have been a creative force in our lives. Some of us may look back to one of your sermons heard long before we were ordained, which set our feet in the right way; or we may remember that first interview at Fulham, or recall a word of encouragement when we were rather down, when some of us deserved reproof and got undeserved forgiveness, and we realized that you believed in us quite recklessly. For every one of us there has been that gladness in all good things, that zest, by which you make the best of both worlds: that wonderful power by which in your presence we are rebuked and inspired, always infectious and always creative because we know that that joyful gladness of yours comes from a true heart. I have felt, and many have felt it too, that when you enter a room, we hear the sound of your Master's feet behind you.[1]

On the fly-leaf of the Book was written:

EMBER DAYS AT FULHAM PALACE

These whose names are recorded in this book, in number two thousand two hundred and five, went forth from this Chapel or from London House to St. Paul's Cathedral there to be ordained Deacon and Priest in the years 1900–1934 by

ARTHUR FOLEY WINNINGTON-INGRAM,
108th Bishop of London.

Some have now passed out of the sight of men; many fulfil their vocation in the far corners of the earth.

On this tenth day of July in the year of our Lord one thousand nine hundred and thirty-four, to mark with deep thanksgiving the completion of fifty years of his ministry, a great company gave to him this Roll of the names of his Sons in Christ. He is to them the Bishop of their Ordination Day, a true Father-in-God, whose love never faileth, "A man greatly beloved."

The Bishop of Stepney added:

In presenting this to you, dear Bishop, together with the cheque which I believe you are going to use for the beautifying of the Chapel at Fulham Palace, I am associated with Number 2,205. Thirty-three years separate me from my brother. These thirty-three years cover the whole of your years as Bishop of London.

The Bishop of Stepney then handed to the Bishop the Book, and the Rev. R. P. Symonds, Gospeller at the last Ordination in St. Paul's, an envelope containing the cheque. Great cheering and "For

---

[1]Many years before a priest, rather critical of the occupation of Fulham Palace by a Bishop, said, "We want our Bishop to come to us straight from Jesus Christ." This is perhaps the answer to that demand.

he's a jolly good fellow" greeted the Bishop as he rose to reply. He said:

This is the most delightful moment in my life. I have had many presentations: I was given my portrait to hang in Fulham Palace about twenty-six years ago, and you gave me a lovely motor car when I had finished twenty-five years of my episcopate, but there is a special flavour about this. In the first place, it is entirely unexpected. I know now why children hang up their stocking at Christmas. They have a sort of thrill of expectation. I have not looked yet into the "stocking", but I know it is the most lovely book, and whatever the envelope contains I am going to spend it on beautifying our chapel where we spend those happy hours before the Ordinations. The reason why this gift is so beautiful is because it comes from my sons. The Archbishop would agree with me that there is a sort of longing in one to have sons. I have some very charming nephews and nieces; I have a great nephew here with me this afternoon who is just nine years old, and he has already decided that he is going to be ordained and carry on the family tradition. I have in fact 62 nephews and nieces, but I have not got any sons. Now you are my sons. I have always tried as far as I could to make you feel that you are not all of a lump, but each separate and beloved. It is the outpouring of the sons' love back to their father that is so helpful and beautiful to me. I noticed very much what was said by Bishop Paget about the "lie". I believe the relationship of the father to his sons is the one which ought to exist between a Bishop and his clergy, and I have always told you to come to me in your difficulties. Therefore it is because this is the outpouring of the sons' love to the father that this is the most beautiful moment of my life, and all the more because some of my sons have become Fathers-in-God themselves. I am going to count the Bishop of Willesden as one of my sons and Fathers-in-God, for though he left us for a time he soon came back to the right Diocese. It is wonderful to think that I have ordained 25 Bishops—suppose I had ploughed any of them!—and to think of them as being all over the world.

I suppose you will want to know how your Father-in-God is going on. I can only say with the familiar words, "There's life in the old dog yet." Looking back upon this spring, I rejoice to think that on my Fridays I have had two rounds of golf each day, whereas old gentlemen of sixty retired at midday and rested for the remainder of the afternoon. Certainly it is a great happiness, especially after being ill last summer, to think of the extraordinary health and enjoyment of life that is given to me. But it is my zest in my work that I love to feel I have still got. It is just the same thing to me as it was fifty years ago; my delight in preaching the Good News of the Kingdom becomes more and more glorious. This year I seem to have had a revelation of the glory of the Gospel of God. It has come perhaps from reading such books as Professor Jeans' *The Mysterious Universe*, to know that it took thousands of millions of years to make the earth, and millions to make man. I ask myself, what can be the purpose of all this? We all believe that there *is* a purpose behind it. It is, surely, that God might at last have someone He could love and someone who could love Him. How could men love Him if they had never seen Him, if He had done nothing to shew His love? And so on Christmas Day, it is a wonderful thrill to proclaim what has taken two thousand millions years to prepare. "He that hath seen Me hath seen the Father." You are preaching a Gospel which is the centre and core of all creation. That ought to make us go back to our work, not only feeling the thrill of it all, but with the thought of the extreme patience of God. The wonderful patience of God seems to me to be more thrilling every day. And I revel in this work of building the Forty-Five Churches, and I hope to live to see them all consecrated.

I thank you all from the bottom of my heart for your gift. I shall put it in the chapel at Fulham, and it will be my most priceless possession. And in conclusion I wish you back "the grace of our Lord Jesus Christ, the love of God, and the fellowship of the Holy Ghost be with you all."

In November the same year (1934) the Agenda for the Church Assembly contained a motion about a compulsory retiring age for Bishops and other clergymen. The Bishop of London thought (quite erroneously, it is believed) that this was directed against him, and wrote to one of his clergy, Prebendary Merritt, asking him to speak on the motion. The Bishop himself would not be present. The Prebendary, who had been ordained by the Bishop, and, with one short exception, had spent the whole of his ministerial life in the diocese, made a speech which was reported, not in the official account of the proceedings, but in the Press. He said:

If this House were to organize a Squash Rackets contest, and if Parliament had not forbidden betting, I would put my shirt on the chance of our beloved Diocesan romping home the winner.

The motion was withdrawn, and it was decided to ask an existing Committee on Ecclesiastical Duties to consider the matter. Prebendary Merritt was of the opinion that the incident shewed that the Bishop was becoming self-conscious about his age. At the same time he was still extremely active. On 26th January 1938, he reached eighty years of age. On the day before he had taken part in the St. Paul's Day Service at the Cathedral, dealt with an unusually large correspondence, attended Meetings of the Order of the British Empire (of which he had been Prelate since 1918), the Corporation of the Church House, presided at five over a Temperance Meeting at the Memorial Hall, Farringdon Street, and attended the St. Paul's Chapter Dinner in the evening. The next morning he professed some Sisters at Kilburn at 8 a.m., at eleven he played golf at Walton Heath, and in the evening gave a birthday dinner at Fulham Palace.

At the same time it was clear that he was ageing. The impression made about 1930 on the then Headmaster of Merchant Taylors' School, where he often came to confirm, was that:

> He was getting older; there was still the heart of a boy, but his voice was failing, and he was rather too reminiscent of his own earlier days, which made him at times seem almost egotistic, an utterly false impression to those who had known him earlier. . . . We used incidentally sometimes to forget, in the strength of his popular appeals, that the Bishop was a competent scholar and wide reader.

Canon Leeson continues:

> My closing memory of him is a meeting in support of Boys' Clubs that he addressed at Winchester some three years ago. Here he was on the old pitch, and the memories of East London came back as vividly as ever, and so did the utterly undiminished boyishness and drive, though he was well over 80. He based his address on a then recent bulletin, I think of Lord Montgomery, in which came the expression that the "tanks had gone through", and you can imagine the use he made of that—left arm flung out and hand over head, as of old.
>
> I suppose he had faults as an administrator, and perhaps he became too garrulous as he grew older; but I remember hearing the late Archbishop Davidson quoted as saying that the Bishop was the greatest spiritual force in the Church of England since Wesley. From such knowledge as I have of him I believe that to be a true verdict. He was at home in

any and every society, and although the appeal was always absolutely simple and straightforward, he could adapt it to all but the most hard-boiled of his listeners. No one can think of the Bishop without immediately feeling younger; and I cannot think of any Bishop who can have meant more to his clergy as father and friend than he did to what he used to call the "Old Guard in East London", with whom he had worked for 40 years, and whose ecclesiastical peculiarities he never seemed to bother about, so long as they were doing the job.

In 1935 on 25th June the Bishop sat in St. Paul's Cathedral to receive gifts to be used for the work of establishing the Church in the new districts. In a Leaflet entitled "Thirty-four years Bishop of London" the Diocesan Office gave some startling figures about the expansion and the needs of London.

POST WAR LONDON

GROWTH

In 1901, when our Bishop was translated to the See of London, the population of Middlesex was 810,306, and of the whole Diocese 3,610,000.

In 1935, the population of Middlesex was 1,638,521 and of the whole Diocese 4,025,247.

THE BISHOP'S TASK

To be a shepherd to all these people.

This means that he must send clergy to minister in the new districts, of which 55 have been marked out as needing a Church in time.

He must see that Churches and Halls are built both for worship and to provide a centre for the social life of these districts.

With characteristic courage and faith, he has undertaken this immense task. This, for him, is the supreme task of his episcopate.

To see, before he lays down his work, these new districts established, would be the crowning joy to him.

Since 1930 he has seen:—

10 New Parishes provided with permanent Churches.

19 Other districts provided with Halls and Missioners.

10 Sites secured for further districts.

THIS YEAR.

3 More permanent Churches will be started.

6 More Halls at least and one School and Hall combined will be built.

6 More Missioners will begin their work.

£10,000 for Sites.
£50,000 for Halls.
£40,000 for additional Missioners' stipends during the next six years.

The Bishop celebrated Holy Communion in the Cathedral at 8, and sat to receive gifts from 8.30-845, 9.30-9.50, 11.45-1.30, 3.15-3.45, 5-6.30, 7.30-8.15, and conducted a Service of Offering and Thanksgiving at the end of the day. During the remaining hours of the day the Suffragan Bishops sat for him. At 1.15 the Lord Mayor attended in State to offer the City Gift, and at 3.30 the Lord Lieutenant of Middlesex. The total amount given during the day was £18,231. It included a gift sent by post from some Christian lepers whom the Bishop had met in Japan. In a note issued at the time the Bishop of Willesden explained that since the inauguration of the Forty-Five Churches Fund five years before, nine districts had become regular parishes, but other districts had developed and forty-two new districts now needed Churches. In thirty-four years sixty new churches had been built, 2,235 men had been ordained, and 546,000 confirmed.

In 1937 an interesting event occurred. For thirty years there had been published every spring a *Bishop of London's Lent Book*. It was always widely read. The Bishop invariably contributed a Preface. In 1937 he wrote the book himself, and the Archbishop of Canterbury added the Preface. The book was called *Everyman's Problems and Difficulties*. In it the Bishop described himself as an "Orthodox Modernist", after the pattern of Bishop Gore, and argued against the position of the "extreme Modernists". Its main purpose however, was not to engage in theological controversy, but to meet the needs of the ordinary, vaguely religious person, and to speak of "joy and peace in believing".

As time went on there were occasional rumours that the Bishop was going to retire. It was felt in some quarters that he ought to retire. A close friend, writing of the power of his early episcopate, says, "Some of those who loved him best half-wished that he would retire before that power waned." For some time he was himself of the contrary opinion, and indeed, except for the fact that his voice was failing and it had become difficult to hear him from the pulpit, he had undeniable, and remarkable, physical fitness on his side. In 1936 he went so far as to say at Greenford that:

Nothing short of an Act of Parliament could make him resign.

Unfortunately, this got into the Press and the Archbishop explained at the Church Assembly at the request of the Bishop that the remark had been made in a jocular way at a private meeting and must not be taken too seriously. It is probable that he would have liked to remain until 1941, and so complete forty years as Bishop of London, but he gradually realized that there were many who thought that he ought to lay the burden down.

In June 1937, he announced to the Diocesan Conference that he proposed to resign not later than 1939. He said that there were still 63 Churches to be built in Greater London, and that he hoped in two years to reduce the burden that he must leave to his successor. He added that he was not tired of the work, or failing in mental or physical vigour ("Mentally, I do not feel more of a fool than thirty-four years ago"), but that "it was only fair for an old man to make way for a younger man".

The news, when it came, was a complete surprise to the diocese. Not long before one of his senior incumbents had actually said at the dinner-table, "The Bishop's successor is not yet weaned." That was of course not literally intended, but most London Churchmen would have said that he would live for another ten years and would die Bishop of London. The news was received in the diocese and outside with very mixed feelings. Most people thought that it was right, and all were sorry to lose the Bishop of London.

Mr. C. B. Mortlock wrote in the *Daily Telegraph*:

The Bishop's decision is most touching evidence of his devotion to his beloved diocese. I doubt whether, in all his career, he had ever had to make a choice in which personal feeling and a sense of duty have been so sharply and poignantly opposed.

For a Bishop who is wedded to his diocese, as Dr. Ingram is to London, for a Father in God who is held in such affection by clergy and people alike, it must be difficult to believe that his vast family will be better cared for by a newcomer. None the less, though, as he said to me the other day, he is still "as fit as a flea", he is determined that there shall be no querulous voices murmuring, "It is high time the old man resigned."

He said later in the same article:

I do not believe there is another diocese in England in which the departure of its Bishop would be felt by men and women of every school, and by the clergy as so grievous a loss. Dr. Ingram's unbounded love for his diocese has pervaded every part of his work.

At any gathering, small or large, private or public, his presence is in sober truth an inspiration. It will not be easy to find his successor, for in any circumstances the vast charge, unlike any other in the Anglican Communion, is one that demands exceptional qualities.

and ended with what turned out to be a true forecast:

I believe that if the Bishop could choose his own successor, it would be Dr. G. F. Fisher, Bishop of Chester, who became Headmaster of Repton when he was 27, and is still a comparatively young man.

Many Ruridecanal Chapters and Conferences sent him requests to withdraw his resignation, but he was rightly adamant.

The Bishop's last Diocesan Conference was in June 1939. He said:

It is always a solemn thing to come to the end of anything, and it is a solemn thing to me to think that this is the last time I shall address the London Diocesan Conference as its President, but I am determined that it shall not be a sad thing. After all, how thankful I ought to be to have such wonderful health at my age, and to be able to take you young men on at golf and lawn tennis and squash rackets, and even hockey, and still more thankful to have maintained for so long the same mental vigour that I had as a young man.

I feel just as keen about the diocese, and building those 45 churches, as I did when the work started, and I only wish that the 91 churches, which, by the mercy of God, we have erected during my time as Bishop, could have been 100.

Then, another ground for thankfulness is the love and loyalty by which I am surrounded. One of my plain-spoken maidservants said to me the other day, "It was lucky you resigned. You wouldn't have known people cared for you, unless you had." But I am not going to be like a Vicar I heard of, who, on receiving an address and a present said, "I had no idea you liked me so much; I will withdraw my resignation."

Fortunately, the King is in Canada, and therefore I could not so do, even if I wished, but I do not wish to do so. It is quite time for a man of 81 to hand over the diocese to a younger man, and such an excellent younger man has been found.

At the end of the Conference Prebendary Wellard moved and Mr. R. C. Nesbitt seconded, the following resolution:

> That this Diocesan Conference, assembled for the last time under the presidency of the present Lord Bishop, desires to declare and to place on record its profound appreciation of his untiring and devoted labours for the Diocese of London throughout the thirty-eight years of his tenure of the See. It expresses its gratitude to Almighty God for his wide sympathies, his attractive goodness, and his loving guidance, which have made him always a true Father-in-God to all those under his care.

The Bishop of Willesden, supporting the resolution, referred to four Sermons preached in St. Paul's in 1902 on "The Afterglow of a Great Reign", and added:

> When a new day dawns in the Diocese, we shall carry with us the radiance of a great episcopate, not less glorious in the later years than in the earlier years. We shall carry with us, too, personal memories, from that influence which has been felt for fifty years at the heart of the life of London, has helped each one of us, and, directly or indirectly, a multitude which no man can number.

The Bishop's reply was in the old cheerful vein:

> We have grown together in the diocese to love and trust one another more and more every year. The party spirit that I remember thirty-eight years ago seems to have died down, and every school of thought works together for the good of the diocese and the glory of God. I wish, from the bottom of my heart, prosperity and happiness to the diocese in the future.

A friend writes:

> I shall never forget his discussing his successor with me a year and a half before his retirement. The way in which he discussed the various

names suggested was most amusing, and he was the first person to realize Bishop Fisher as the man.

He once said to another friend, "These provincial Bishops are always telling me how I ought to manage the London Diocese. I should like to see them try. Dear old ——, I wonder how *he* would handle the London clergy."

One of the most difficult last things was the last Children's Dance. One who had himself been there as a boy, and had now come with his two children, writes:

> At the end he stood on a chair and spoke to the great company, a bigger crowd than I had ever seen at Fulham before. He turned to a crowd of children just beneath him and said, "You won't forget me, will you?" Spontaneously they all shouted, "Never, never, never!" I'm afraid I had to go out into the passage-way leading to the Chapel and have a good cry on my own.
>
> What a miracle this is! Here was a man who kept the child-heart to the age of 80. The light was undiminished, the joy increasing as the years went on, the love of souls ceaselessly expressed..

The end came with a vast meeting at the Albert Hall of twelve thousand of the clergy and the laity, who came, as *The Church Times* puts it, "to say good-bye *en masse* to the radiant, devoted personality whom it has been their good fortune to have for their Father-in-God for thirty-eight years."

The Archbishop of Canterbury presided, and with him on the platform were other diocesan and suffragan bishops, the Dean and Canons of St. Paul's, the Archdeacons, Eric Hamilton and E. A. Dunn to represent the London clergy, Lord Sankey, Mr. George Lansbury, Dame Beatrix Hudson Lyall. The Archbishop spoke once more of "that springtide of his episcopate. . . . Well, now it is the autumn, but the man is the same."

> His Grace went on to enumerate some of the Bishop's characteristic qualities, speaking first of the courage with which he had waged, for thirty-eight years, a warfare against every form of evil in this great city; wielding his sword in this cause with the more effectiveness because there was no man living who was less of a killjoy. He spoke of the loving kindness of his heart, his unquestioning faith and invincible hope. There had been within him a spring of spontaneous, un-

ceasing loving kindness which had gone out to all sorts and kinds of people, clergy and laity alike, in this vast city. "It must have meant much to you, my friends, that all these years there has been at the heart of the diocese this heart of a father and brother open to you all, and I know that this evening it is the great heart of London that goes out to him in ever-flowing affection." The Archbishop illustrated the youthfulness of the Bishop by a charming little story. He recalled that he had once invited Dr. Winnington-Ingram, when he was still the young Bishop of London, to his Highland home, and instructed the driver of the coach to be attentive to his distinguished passenger. The coach arrived, but no Bishop; and on asking the driver where he was, the reply came, "There was nae Bishop; there was only a lad wi' a bicycle." The Bishop of London had always been, so to speak, "a lad wi' a bicycle", setting forth day by day to meet its duties and difficulties, with the same sort of eager expectancy of a boy riding out on his bicycle. And still he was to be "the lad wi' a bicycle", revolving round the whole world, with greater freedom because he would no longer have the heavy burden of the diocese of London on his back.

There could be no sort of sadness in this farewell. In the case of most old men it was natural to pray that God's peace might be within them and around them. But he found it difficult to associate the word "peace" with this happy and undefeated warrior. He would rather pray for him that, in the years that remain, as in the years that were past, he would find his unfailing strength in the joy of the Lord.

Dame Beatrix said that she felt very diffident at following such accomplished speakers, but she scored the success of the evening when she described the Bishop as:

the Peter Pan of the episcopal bench and as the youngest man in the Hall to-night.

Equally successful was her Catechism:

"Have you ever seen our Bishop come into a meeting without a smile?" she asked.

"No!" came the reply from thousands of lips.

"Have you ever seen our Bishop look bored?"

"No!"

"Haven't you always felt happier after you have been in a room or a hall with him?"

"Yes," they cried.

She turned to the Bishop, "You have made thousands of people better," she said, "and shewn to everyone the attraction of real goodness."

The Address was as follows:

To
ARTHUR FOLEY WINNINGTON-INGRAM
Bishop of London

We who offer you to-night our gratitude for your long ministry—a ministry whose influence has extended to the ends of the world—know that we are only a few of the multitude who have you in thankful remembrance. A great company has passed out of the sight of men, fortified by your courage, cheered by your constant confidence in God, upheld by the message of the everlasting gospel you have preached.

Untiring as a Father in God to all the people of this City and Diocese; ceaselessly given to hospitality in the ancient home in Fulham which you have made an open house; the Friend of Everyman; drawing together in Christ, East and West here and in the wider world; constantly handing the torches of truth and Christian service to each new generation; you have fought the good fight and kept the Faith. From Oxford House to the Rectory of Bethnal Green: from Amen Court to Fulham Palace, for fifty years you have been our dauntless and most Christian leader—a man greatly beloved. Though still young in heart and mind you generously pass the work you love to younger hands. You go forth now from the diocese, but never from the heart of London: alone, but for ever in the company of friends.

Lord Plender then handed to the Bishop a book containing the names of those who had contributed to the farewell offering, which amounted to £5,056.

The Bishop rose to reply, but the applause was so loud and long that it was some minutes before he could make himself heard. He said:

"I am a very ordinary man! And if what has been said to-night encourages any other ordinary man to try and do his job, that is the best it can do." He owned that he was an ordinary man, with a grave defect—a dislike of saying "No." "I am much too kind-hearted to be a good Bishop. A Bishop should be made of sterner stuff. But in spite of all my infirmities, I think I have proved, to my own satisfaction and, I hope, to yours, that love never fails. We are very proud in this diocese of never having prosecutions." He had been accused in a news-paper of being a chameleon. In answer to that he would say that he was not ashamed to be seen one day in a cope and mitre, surrounded with incense, and the next day almost in his shirtsleeves. They were all preaching the same Gospel, each in his own way. He had come from church to church four times a week for thirty-eight years, visiting the parishes of London. He knew the clergy and their wives, and had blessed their babies in bed many a time. That was how they came to know and love and trust one another so well.

It was a total misreading of the situation to say that the Church was divided into hostile groups. He had tried to make the Church in London one happy family of God. He had tried, too, with the aid of the different denominations at work in the diocese, to give a clean and happy London to the children and young people. Here he paused to read a message from General Evangeline Booth, expressing the great esteem in which he was held by the Salvation Army.

Then, because it has always been the Bishop's way to speak of religion as naturally as other men pass the time of day, he dwelt on his attempts to teach his people the power of prayer. To him, prayer is manifestly "the secret of happiness", which is the title of his new book containing his last message to his people.

Finally, he thanked them for their splendid gift, and told how he intends to spend it. All unbeknown to him, his Secretary, Miss Catton, fearful that his own generosity would beggar the Bishop, had been putting by several hundreds a year, and this accumulated to sufficient to live on. He therefore proposed to spend part of the farewell offering on three missionary tours, to the West Indies, to Africa and to India. Then if he came back from all these, he would spend the remainder on a lovely, shiny car, in order that he could get about the country and refresh himself in readiness for another tour. He felt it right to do this, because he had tried to make London the most missionary-hearted diocese in the world, and in this way he would be carrying on the same work.

The meeting ended when Cosmo Gordon, by divine providence Lord Archbishop of the Province, laid his hands in blessing on the bowed head of Arthur Foley, by divine permission Lord Bishop of London.

There had never been anything like that Meeting, and it may well be that there will never be anything like it again. Emerson said, "All mankind loves a lover." He meant no doubt that other people observe with satisfaction a happy betrothal or a marriage in which love manifestly continues, but the words could also mean that when a man for many years has flung out his own love broadcast, it will come back to him a thousandfold. The Bishop's pastoral affection was bread cast upon the water of the Thames.

The Bishop himself, writing in 1941 in *The Secrets of Fortitude* about the Albert Hall Meeting, said:

> The verse which follows, "Love never faileth," is associated in my mind with one of the most touching days of my life. There were about twelve thousand people in the Albert Hall to say farewell to me before I left London, and I was fairly overwhelmed and surprised by the love and affection displayed towards me on that occasion. The love seemed coming up in great waves from that huge audience, and there were many outside who never got in. It was a trying occasion. I had to listen for an hour to many far too kind speeches, but I had to say something in reply, and what I did say was that I was a very ordinary man (as, indeed, I am), but this wonderful ovation proved that, even with an ordinary man, "Love never faileth." I certainly had loved those people for fifty years. I blessed their children in bed, I buried the priests when they died, and visited for the last forty years four or five parishes every week. I had done it as a matter of course and as part of my duty; but it was no doubt the return of love for love which produced that wonderful gathering and has given me a happy memory for life. I remember giving in my speech an illustration of a priest, whom I had had to depose from his living for an improper letter, but whom I never gave up taking care of for the rest of his life. When he died in my arms, he said, and I shall never forget it, "Do realize, Bishop, that nothing but Love does any good to a man like me." His children are my devoted friends still. But enough about myself.

After that came the sad business of packing up, reading again and destroying old letters,[1] and preparing to evacuate Fulham Palace. The intention to go overseas again had to be laid aside. He was of course disappointed, but the Archbishop of York commented to a friend on the utter incapacity of disappointment to interfere with his happiness. The remainder of the Bishop's days were spent in two

[1]See p. 85.

W

places. During the summer he lived with his niece and her husband (Colonel and Mrs. C. B. Grice-Hutchinson) at the Boynes, Upton-on-Severn, and during the winter months (October to April) at the Crag Head Hotel, Bournemouth, not far from where his sister, Miss Winnington-Ingram, lived, and just opposite to St. Peter's Vicarage, where the Reverend Hedley Burrows, now Dean of Hereford, was Vicar. The story of those years is the Epilogue of this book.

XVII

SUMMARY

WHAT manner of man was this? The reader has probably come to a conclusion already, but the question must here be asked, and, so far as is possible, answered.

Such a question is sometimes very difficult to answer, because some men disclose very little of what is in them. Ingram himself had a story of a London merchant, of whom a fairly close business-friend did not know until the day of his death that he had been Warden of a City Church for many years. Ingram was not like that. He disclosed a great deal. His little weaknesses were apparent on the surface, as they are in the life of a child. He was, in fact, that rare and happy thing, a child-like character. In Canada in 1910 he was presented by a group of children with a large bouquet, inscribed "For the Children's Friend". The flowers remained in his hand until the company presently reached the grave of an eighteenth-century missionary, which was the object of the pilgrimage. The quick-witted wife of one of the clergy present whispered in his ear, "Why don't you put the flowers on the grave?" This he immediately did, saying that here was someone more worthy to be called the Friend of the Children of Canada. In this way he eased himself of an embarrassment, and did a graceful thing, but in fact few men have been more of a children's friend. And he achieved this, as he achieved all his triumphs, by being exactly like all children, only better. It was also his secret with adults. It has been said that our Lord may quite properly be thought of as "Myself, only perfect". Something like that, only of course within the human and therefore the imperfect, fallible sphere, might be said of Ingram. Multitudes of those who met him, and looked into his eyes, felt, "He understands me. He makes me feel that I want to be a better man. I should like to be a man like that. I ought to be a man like that." He would throw himself into their circumstances, and it made them want to grow into his character.

It seems to his biographer, after the reading of many letters, press-cuttings and reminiscences, and the Bishop's own intensely self-revealing books, that, while his constant purpose in life was "to spread happiness", his outstanding characteristics were faith, simplicity, and a concentrated power of living in the present and caring for the person who was there. That these qualities may be a little dashed by concomitant defects is in theory undeniable. It is of course not certain that faith will be easily deceived, or that the simple character will lack wisdom, or that concentration on the here and now will cause that to be forgotten which should have been remembered. But it does sometimes happen, and it did occasionally happen with Bishop Arthur Foley.

(1) Of his clear, unfaltering religious faith enough has been said elsewhere. With it he had a great belief in man. Not for him the profound pessimism of Karl Barth, who declares that, when God saves a man, it is as if a swimmer had rescued in deep water a man who could not swim a stroke. Ingram rejected that theology, and looked upon his fellow-man, however unpromising, as having much more than the bare "capacity for salvation", which is all that Barth allows. His practice followed his theology. He believed in almost everybody because he loved everybody. Above all, he was for the under-dog. In Bethnal Green he had believed in the essential soundness of the East-Londoner. As Bishop of London, he more than once came back from the Church Assembly, and said that he had made a point of supporting a speaker from the back-benches, because he did not think that he was having a fair deal. Macaulay used to say that in his young days, whenever he heard an opinion expressed, every possible answer and objection to it rushed into his mind. Of Ingram almost the exact opposite might be said. His zeal for orthodoxy came largely from this. He loved to think that he had the whole mind of Christendom behind him. He was not a Dissenter because, he said, "I don't dissent." He was anxious to agree, and he was above all anxious to defend the faith of the plain man. He did not live to read Bishop Barnes' *The Rise of Christianity*, but he would have been inexpressibly shocked by it. In fact, he once permitted himself to speak with some indignation, not, of course, about Dr. Barnes as a man (they were colleagues and friends), but about the propriety of making him a Bishop. And his distress

at the book would have been in the interests of *la foi du charbonnier*. Like St. Athanasius, he knew that there were controversies in which the doctrine of Redemption was at stake, and so he contended earnestly for the Faith.

Apart from this, he knew and liked an enormous number of people, many of them quite ordinary. He had a very remarkable knowledge of many hundreds of clergymen in the diocese of London, and of some outside. He was in that way a true Father in God. And he had an astonishingly large circle of lay friends, whom he loved to entertain. His abundant hospitality was almost entirely of the kind prescribed in the Gospel—

When thou makest a dinner or a supper, call the poor, the maimed, the lame, the blind.

He did not entertain the "big people of the diocese", a practice for which there are reasons quite other than the expecting of invitations in return. His guests were as a rule quite ordinary people, but behind what often looked like mere sociableness there was almost always a specific reason. They were people who needed some kind of help. Again and again he would return from a visit in East London and say that some priest's wife was looking very tired, and that he had invited her and the children to spend a few days at Fulham. And there were many others who had been invited because they were sick at heart or had lost faith. The Bishop would sometimes say jokingly, with perhaps twenty people in the house, "This is a lost dogs' home." A chaplain testifies that "when the time came to leave, tears were not far away in numberless quite unlikely instances".

That is why the London clergy never felt the "drop-down-dead-ativeness" which Sydney Smith said was characteristic of the clergy in the presence of their Bishop. And they were hardly conscious of the inequality between his stipend and theirs. They knew that he lived simply and that his resources were, as far as possible, at their disposal. Actually, his hospitality and his generous gifts came out of the profits of his books. His official stipend was spent in maintaining his official residence.

He was always on the look-out to do a kind act. He would not only take opportunities; he would make them. Once at a Royal

Academy Dinner, he saw a clerical figure alone, looking a little out of it, and he went over to be friendly. The stranger turned out to be the Roman Catholic Archbishop Downey, of Liverpool. When the Bishop left, as his custom was on those occasions, rather early, after a quick walk round the room, the Archbishop hurried to him, and said, "I wish to thank you for your kindness. Now I know that you are not only a great prelate, but a great gentleman."

He was occasionally taken in. He enjoyed being popular ("We all like to be liked", he said) and he was not impervious to flattery, though there was in him an intense, fundamental humility which was a spiritual antiseptic. His large charity and unfailing optimism caused him at time to be over-easy with offenders, and to embarrass his brother-bishops by a quick, and, as they sometimes thought, not quite consistent readiness to re-instate an erring priest. Men who had been suspended elsewhere were sometimes very quickly given work in the diocese of London. His kind heart misled him, and occasionally there were scandals. He himself always felt sure at the time that he was right. He saw the man personally, whereas other bishops sometimes only acted through a lawyer. He claimed that he always knew if a man was lying. Once at least he said to a man, "Go into the Chapel for half an hour, and then come back and talk to me," and there is actual evidence that it was found difficult to lie to him. He gave careful attention to each case, and he believed in "discerning the spirits", constructively, as a doctor would, and he rejoiced, with the angels of God, over one sinner that repented.

The cause of the error, if there was one, was that he sometimes mistook a present state of feeling penitent for a permanent change of life. He was temperamentally a "non-hanging judge". It used to be said of Devon Assizes that the Juries too often returned a verdict of "Not guilty". The Bishop's easiness was much more meritorious than that. There is evidence that other bishops were disturbed at "what seemed to be the light-hearted way with which the Bishop dealt with moral problems", but there was no *laissez-faire* about it, no careless toleration of things intolerable. Nor was there inability to understand. Bishop Westcott, pattern of scholarly and devout life, was unable to understand how men could really be guilty of some sins. Ingram knew a great deal about men, and the sins of

326

which men were capable. But he had an immense belief in forgiveness, and in ministering it, he sometimes took too much for granted. Sin he detested. With all his bonhomie, he was himself a man of Puritan, ascetic life. Sin was to him a nasty, hateful thing. His easiness can perhaps be illustrated if it is possible to imagine the Second Epistle to the Corinthians as it might have been written by Barnabas or Timothy. It would not have been so good in the long run for the Corinthians. And it might have made things rather difficult in other Churches for Peter and John. Archbishop Whately is said to have expressed satisfaction on his death-bed that he had never given a penny to a beggar in the street. He may have been right in his economic practice, but not in his self-praise. Most of us are glad that we are not like that. Ingram was not at all like that. His trust was from time to time misplaced, but as Chesterton says in his book on Dickens, "With torches and trumpets, like a guest, the greenhorn is taken in by life. And the sceptic is cast out by it".

(2) Ingram's simplicity was that of a child. He enjoyed winning a game, and he did not like losing. He was not easily provoked; he had a sweetness of temper which cast out that little demon. There was no jealousy in him, and he was marvellously free from pride. He had a little occasional vanity in small matters. He must have known that he could do a great many things much better than most of the other bishops, but there is no sign of anything which suggests that he ever thought of that, or envied those who could do other things better than he. Yet he liked to think that he had done things, and could do things. He passed a letter once to a London priest who was in his study, and said, "What book shall I recommend him?" The priest, on the spur of the moment, mentioned one of Gore's books. The Bishop said, a little huffily, "Oh, I thought perhaps you might have suggested one of my books." And the man said to himself, "Bang goes my chance of promotion in the diocese of London." The priest was probably quite mistaken in his conclusion, and it is unquestionable both that the huff was only for a moment, and that Ingram had no jealousy of Gore, whom he admired intensely as man, scholar and theologian, from whom he was content to learn much. Nevertheless, the story shews a wish to be appreciated.

Another story tells of a perhaps not even momentary irritation. The late Prebendary Bernays, Rector of Finchley, told it at a St. Paul's Day Chapter Dinner. As the junior Prebendary, he had to propose the health of the Bishop. He spoke of "the only time I have ever seen the Bishop ruffled":

> We were playing golf, and the Bishop was addressing his ball. Just then an old sheep on the other side of the hedge uttered a loud "Baa!" The Bishop looked up, "Bernays, I wish you wouldn't cough just when I am making my stroke."

The operative words of a rather top-lofty review of his "Fifty Years Work in London" in the *New English Weekly* (25 July, 1940) are "unquenchable adolescence". At the same time the reviewer is driven to admire:

> Despite its title, the principal impression that this book conveys is one of unquenchable adolescence. Hardly a single fundamental issue is even glanced at in these pages. No wonder that in the closing chapters of a book revealing so much credulity and complacency the author is forced to say, "I feel I have really failed to convey what my fifty years has really been." He has failed, for when all is said, there *was* something to convey, which is suggested even here, as in the Chapter "A Bishop of London's Day". For beneath all the complacency, beneath all the superficiality, beneath even the "charm", there was something true and real—an enormous and unflagging zeal for work, a wonderful fidelity to a gigantic task, a warm and discriminating sympathy for persons in every office and every class. Nothing that could bring happiness or consolation was ever too much trouble; no parish was too unimportant to be remembered; no soul too obscure for the simple message to be given to it. The fatuities which this book records will soon be forgotten, while there will long remain a memory of fifty years of energy and love.

It is certain that this simplicity was an immense spiritual asset. From the early days when he was "Mr. Ingram" at Bethnal Green to the time when he was "the old Bishop", his simple, sincere, uncomplicated character forged countless links with other lives which the hesitations and qualifications of an academic psychology could never have won. His own psychological insight, like that of St. Francis, was natural, not studied. He was human, and it is possible that sometimes he was unable completely to banish from his mind the unworthy thought, "Now what sort of impression am I making on this chap," but in the main his thought was always of God and the welfare of the chap. He talked often, in later years too much, about himself and what he had done, but there was in that something of the Pauline naturalness. That was the thing he had to give. He threw himself, his vitality, his experience and his example quite simply into the common stock. He never actually said, with St. Paul, "Be ye imitators of me," and he would have shrunk from such a form of words. But like St. Paul, he would do anything, he would strip off the coat of an Englishman's reserve and stand in his shirt-sleeves, though they would be very white and would have the familiar starched cuffs, that he might by all means save some.[1]

Like King David, he danced before the Lord with all his might. And if he had had a wife, and she had been offended, like Michal, he would have smiled at her, and said, "Never mind, old girl, it's for the glory of God." A close friend of his writes:

> His egotism was always about trivialities. "Occasionally, he let me into what he had done for someone whose life had been transformed, but very rarely, and then under his breath. . . . No one knew less how to describe his own power and influence than he did himself. At times I used to think that he had no conception of what he was effecting. But at other times he was so shrewd and understanding."

(3) His power of concentration was remarkable. Few things are generally found more tiring than to have a succession of interviews for some hours or all day, with the consequent necessity of applying the mind to a number of quite different sets of needs and circumstances. The Bishop was often weary at the end of a long series, but his sympathy was always fresh. He was absorbed in each man's case, and he diagnosed very swiftly. Love gave him this capacity. The Holy Spirit does illuminate the mind. The seven Gifts of Confirmation are, to an extent which sometimes surprises, in-

---

[1] A generation ago the Rev. Frank Swainson was the vigorous and effective Vicar of a North London parish. He sometimes visited the public houses in order to invite customers to come to his men's services. One of the men offered as an excuse that he was poorly dressed. "Would you preach to us in your shirt-sleeves?" "I will next Sunday, if you and your mates will come." And he did. The incident was reported to some busy-body to the Bishop, who sent for Swainson and gave him a mild wigging. "What would you have done, my lord, in my place?" "Oh, I should have done just the same."

tellectual. The reason is that if, or in so far as, the adviser can get rid of pride and self-pleasing, and have in him that supernatural love which is the gift of God, the gift somehow produces the solution of the puzzle.

That this concentration on the man in his study or the thing in hand sometimes betrayed him is certain. There were times when he would promise or half-promise an appointment to some man, and then later give it to another. There were times when he would be induced by pressure from the diocesan staff to make, rather reluctantly, some appointment. It would be in course of time a great success. He would then completely forget his former reluctance, and would say, *optima fide*, "Of course I knew that old so-and-so was the man for that job. So I put him in, and look what he has done." And those who knew the facts would smile and say, "Well, the old Bishop, he's like that. He can't help it. It's only because he so wants the parish to go well."

More serious harm, arising from the same moment-to-moment benevolence, were the verbal permissions to Vicars to do something which was officially forbidden, and the acceptance for Ordination of men who were not really qualified. Other Bishops, loving him dearly, as they all did, for himself, were sometimes embarrassed by the fruits of his perpetual kindness of heart.

His power of understanding documents or some ecclesiastical or political situation was much like that of any other intelligent man. He could study a programme or schedule and make himself master of its contents. His view of it would be simple, perhaps even conventional, though always there was the magic touch of his own chivalry and charity. He had not the large judicial mind, with its capacity to hold together a great number of considerations and to sum up, which belonged to Lang, or Temple, or to his own successor in the diocese of London. He could not possibly have made the masterly speech, covering a large range of very intricate ground, which Bishop Fisher delivered in the Church Assembly in introducing the Reorganisation Areas Measure in 1943. But confront him with a person, and he would bend on the needs of that person at that time the whole resources of what was, for such purposes, a singularly powerful mind.

The Bishop of North Queensland wrote in the Australia Church Quarterly for June, 1946:

He would unravel the knots in complicated characters, and astonish people by shewing them that he understood them far better than they did themselves. It is a power that is notably found in confessors of long experience, and he had gone far to perfect it. He reminded me in his discerning sympathy and rapid intuitions—sometimes verging on the miraculous—of the Curé d'Ars; and in his wisdom of men like Father Puller, or St. Vincent de Paul. Yes, he knew human souls, and he had the gift of counsel to a wonderful degree. It was because he loved them all so generously.

And his judgments were not always favourable. They were sometimes shrewdly critical. He wrote in 1907:

Dear ——,
   Old —— is just what you described him, a blether-headed old bore. There is no good talking to him. I don't suppose he will do any harm. I am glad that —— is getting on all right. I always thought that he was a good Cavalry Officer spoilt. These two criticisms must go no further than you.

All sorts of people, Ordination candidates, priests who had come for encouragement or to be put on the carpet, or appointed to a benefice, undergraduates, schoolboys or schoolgirls, men and women old and young, who knew, or perhaps till then had not known, that they were in need of Christian counsel. All these had for long, among their most treasured memories, some ten or fifteen minutes in the study at Fulham. Of course he failed occasionally. A hard-boiled layman would come out and say, "I didn't want to have a pi-jaw." But perhaps that was not altogether a failure. And again and again the interviews were indubitable victories.

He had a good memory for faces, and very often, when the same person appeared again after an interval, the situation would come back into his mind, and he would begin again where they had left off. Sometimes of course he had forgotten the face. The Suffragan-bishops and the Archdeacons remember the quick undertone in a crowded room. "Who am I talking to?" And sometimes he was reduced to playing for time, or some other device, until he could remember.

It was sometimes said in the later days of his episcopate that he was surrounded by a group of flatterers, who encouraged him to go on too long in his tenure of the see. There may be something in this —in any case he certainly did go on too long. At the same time it is always difficult, when an old man says to you, "Do you consider that I ought to resign?" to say "Yes." And it was always possible to say to him with perfect truth, "But you are still physically fit." But the real answer to the implied criticisms of the Bishop and his entourage is the fact that those who were nearest to him loved and admired him most. Their evidence is quite unanimous. And it comes out of continuous and intimate experience. His friends were "those of his own household".

This is, in all that matters most, a great tribute. But it may have an incidental drawback.

A shrewd observer notes that there was a tendency in him to like dependants, a habit which reduces criticism and hinders that stretching of the mind that comes from meeting people who are not affinities. The same writer, however, goes on to say that "his kindness never faltered", and that he was "simply wonderful" with his nephews or near relations. No "nepotism", but "genuine affectionate duty meticulously fulfilled".

And he was the same everywhere. Some people are better at home than they are outside, and some *vice versa*. What Ingram was in his own home, he was everywhere. One of his Chaplains writes:

No experience could have been more remarkable than, when having the great privilege of acting as Chaplain to the Bishop, to see the genuine affection and personal enthusiasm with which he was greeted everywhere. Regard and respect, of course there was always. Never did I see or hear of anyone attempting to take liberties with him. Enthusiasm is not too strong a word, it is the only adequate word, and should always be coupled with affection. Typical instances come to mind. Wherever he moved, month after month, year in year out he seemed to create the same atmosphere. His expressed purpose was "to spread happiness". Certainly smiles and delight seemed to await him wherever he went. Not only the parish priests when he visited their Church but the Church-wardens, choir-men and boys, vergers, police on point duty, railway and shipping servants, all alike seemed genuinely moved. It was no one class or kind of person, believer or unbeliever, but all alike. In the House of Lords, on those rare occasions when he spoke on some moral question, the Lord Chancellor would normally in the last years rise from the Wool-sack and accompany him to the door as he left, thanking him for having come. At public functions in the City all stiffness and boredom vanished from faces as he appeared, there always seemed to be genuine eagerness to greet him. On the occasion of the opening of a great new building in the City (The Association of Insurance Companies) by the King and Queen about 1933-4, the windows of all the buildings around were filled with city workers watching and cheering the "great" as they departed. As the Bishop emerged to enter his car he was greeted with a tremendous outburst of cheering. He was greatly surprised and touched.

To another Chaplain, considering whether he should undertake the duty, Archdeacon Holmes said:

> You will often find it very, very difficult, but you must remember all the time that the Bishop's greatest desire is to love everyone and to be loved by everyone.

Bishop Maud, whom Ingram called "Jack Kensington", said on his deathbed, when his chief visited him, "It must be terrible to be loved as you are loved."

One of the most life-like pictures of him appeared in March, 1901, in the *St. James's Gazette*. It was written by, or founded upon recollections of, an old Oxford House man:

> Arthur Foley Winnington-Ingram is one who compels love, for the reason that his own heart is full of it. From the moment that the kindly grey eyes rest upon one, and the ready smile begins to play around the corners of the humorous mouth, one feels that he is a man to whom all may be told, and all trusted, and that his sympathy and help are assured. That is a true instinct. No man of wider sympathies ever yet existed. You may see him walk down the Bethnal Green Road, his arm linked in that of the rowdiest larrikin; you may see him clap an apparently irreclaimable ruffian on the shoulder with a genial "Hullo, old boy!" it is because his eyes, lightened with the love within, can discern the faint spark of better things. But there is no easy-going toleration of wrong. In the presence of meanness or deceit the mouth sets, the jaw tightens, and forked lightning plays round the head of the delinquent. No man can be sterner; but no man melts more readily at the first sign of repentance. No man is without the pale of Ingram's love,

provided that he be sincere, for sincerity, open and transparent, is the keynote of his own character.

It might also be said of the Bishop that he works twenty-four hours in the day the whole year round. He is far too sane a man not to take his due proportion of sleep and recreation, but each is taken with one sole end in view—how best he may renew his powers for his Master's service. So he plays as earnestly as he works. He plays every game but cricket, and plays it a little better than most other people. When he goes on his holiday he leaves instructions that no letters are to be forwarded, and climbs mountains with as much enthusiasm as, by faith, he removes them in East London.

In that word "enthusiasm" is contained the main secret of his power. Of the inner spiritual life it befits not to speak, and none may know; but the evidence is in all his acts, glorifying every particle of the work to which he sets his hand, and driving him on at a white-hot glow of zeal. The promise of Joshua rings ever in his ears; discouragement is not possible to him, for the strength which is not his sustains him. Hear him in the pulpit; the elocution is faulty; the thought is not profound; the language is often common-place and the words ill put together. Yet few men can so move a congregation, or are listened to with such rapt attention. It is the spirit which profiteth—the profound conviction, the joy in his service, the certainty of victory. In this power he conquers alike the drawing-rooms of the West End, the college halls of Oxford and Cambridge, and the tenement dwellings of the most abandoned slums.

That he will succeed as Bishop I have the profoundest conviction. Difficulties he will have, of course, and some of his own making, for that very quality of enthusiasm sometimes leads him into ill-considered action, but he will succeed because he is human and manly, broad-minded, tolerant, and sympathetic, gifted with imagination and the saving grace of humour. He will succeed because scattered through London to-day there is a band of devoted clergy trained in his school who look on him as the best friend they ever had, and will follow him and obey him. He will succeed because, where another would be painfully seeking a way round, he, in his enthusiastic fashion, will smash right through the obstacle, and be unaware that it ever existed. He will succeed by the power of a life which knows no selfish aim, but is consecrated to the service of God and man.

An old friend said to his wife at the time of Ingram's appointment to London, "Oh, no, it will be quite simple for him. He will make them all love him, and then do as he likes with them." The wife, reporting this, added in a letter to the Bishop, "There's a good deal of truth in his hopeful view of overcoming difficulties. Indeed, I will pray more and more for you. It is my only way, and the best, of returning some of your unfailing love and goodness to me and mine."

Tubby Clayton, never a member of his household, but of his diocese, and a shrewd and experienced judge of men, has written this considered estimate:

DR. WINNINGTON-INGRAM

In my last year at St. Paul's School, I achieved the one ambition which was within my reach, and by devious means became the junior Editor of the *Pauline*. The retirement of our old Highmaster, F. W. Walker, in my last term enabled me to summon the pen of G.K.C. to write of him. Gilbert began with a " *Tremendous Trifle*", so simple and sincere that I repeat it after forty years. "Schoolboys forget everything they are taught, but never can forget the man who teaches them." Apart from their father and the family lawyer, the schoolmaster is the first grown-up whom they have ample opportunity of studying. They may dislike him or approve of him; but he is utterly indelible. Their minds are focussed on an estimate which is not transient. It endures for life; and when the middle-aged at Old School Dinners hear that the mighty Possos is now pensioned, they can still imitate his tone of voice or recapture a classroom crisis, which for ten minutes dwarfed the siege of Mafeking.

If we remember all our schoolmasters, it is not strange that I should be possessed of vivid recollections of *the* Bishop; for he was integral to all my early years.

As it were yesterday, I can recall the first of many visits paid by my Mother to the new regime at Fulham Palace, when a bold translation brought the Bishop of Stepney to the Chair of Erkenwald. I can see my Mother setting forth, laden with problems. She was then Head of the largest Branch of the Girls' Friendly Society in London and on the Council of the Mothers' Union. Earlier visits paid to the previous Diocesan had not returned her very much relieved. But she now came back, glowing and rejoicing. My Mother was not easily impressed. Her life in Queensland gave her qualities rare in Churchwomen of indoor upbringing. She had a work-a-day respect for scholars, but, most of all, her energetic spirit sought for a Bishop who could understand. Winnington-Ingram did this to perfection. He promised her his prayers. He gave his Blessing. He recognized in her those qualities which made her not only a resourceful Mother, but a distinctive personality who had no compare in our neighbourhood. And to the end he always dealt with me principally as her son. That was my claim on him, twenty years after she had passed to rest. Having said this, I must explain that my instructions are not to indulge in an appreciation of his outstanding gifts and saintly virtues. My orders are to play the devil's advocate, and to put down what incidents I may which tend to illustrate his limitations.[1] I must obey; since otherwise the picture drawn in this whole Biography may suffer a lack of balance.

What were his defects? He had the defects of his qualities. One of these qualities was innocence. As you shall hear, he was not destitute of elements which indicate diplomacy; but these came later. They were no part of him. He used them rarely, mainly money-raising, an art then most untoward in a Bishop. He would go down to Brighton for the benefit of his East London Fund, year after year. He would praise Brighton overflowingly as "London by the Sea", which carried with it the same great heart of charity towards the poverty of Bethnal Green. Having extracted what he could from Brighton, he would transfer his flag and his Appeal to Eastbourne, where the Duke of Devonshire's tenants and leaseholders in affluent stagnation (which they mistook for life) were next informed that even the poor people of Brighton—reporters please omit!—had given a sum of £25,000. Now (he would continue) I come to Eastbourne! Eastbourne is the Queen of Sunshine in Sussex. Her parks, promenades, hotels and splendid shops are patronized by the élite of Europe. I expect, indeed the whole Fund confidently leans upon the princely tone of your response. Eastbourne then doubled Brighton's contribution.

On one occasion, for a special urgency, he went back once again to his first friends at Brighton. Reporters were not present at this meeting, but the tradition is that it began with a thumb jerked backwards over the shoulder and the words: "When I left you, I just looked in at Eastbourne, upon the way to see my dear old Mother. Those nobs or snobs at Eastbourne—they dunno nofing of Befnal Green; but they planked down twice the first round of Brighton by the Sea. I knew that Brighton wouldn't be content to play second fiddle to that stuck-up place. So I've come back, to give you all a chance of putting Eastbourne in its proper place."

[1] This is an interpretation of the words used in a humble request for some discriminating recollections.

Yes, there was guile, inclining to deceit, but it became him as a touch of humour. His transfer of hard cash to East End needs was unexampled. Money was given straight from the heart, for it was to compassion and to Church loyalty that he addressed his overwhelming flow of East End stories, repeated in the terse vernacular which he espoused. He was a coster-king; and his best pearls were pearls of Cockney wit and intonation. He introduced to the platforms of West End Meetings and Drawing-rooms the loving, daily study of three million, who had no equivalent ambassador; unless we so account Albert Chevalier, who by a single song (based on a phrase with which a cabman preferred wife and home to a drink offered by his famous fare) told the West End that the East End regarded the marriage bond as one which did not snap. Chevalier, in his lesser inspirations, parodied and even travestied the uncouth gaiety of the coster folk; but Winnington-Ingram carried Cockney speech to a fine art. He held up a true mirror of Bethnal Green—not as it is to-day, but as he came to it from Marlborough and Keble.

Neither of these academies of learning were of a kind to injure innocence. Sophistication may be premature in London day-schools, where boys live at home and watch the breadwinner dive for his City train and come back tired and careworn from the office. Winnington-Ingram had no economic or antiquarian tastes. The "One Square Mile" was a mere Home of Mammon to be blamed, and to be plucked. Long dinners, wines, cigars, rumours of markets, continental openings —all these were very foreign to his nature. The City Churches were anathema; and had he had his way, he would have sold nineteen of them at prices now absurd. Churches should never hold a watching brief. They should be full and near poor people's homes, or they should be dissolved into hard cash. That was his thesis, logical enough; but too staccato for the City Fathers. Many devoted Churchmen in the City, who loved the sportsman and the saint in him, deplored his inability to view with a constructive eye the open and effective door to a rapprochement between Church and Business which the reformed use of the City Churches could hope to compass, had they been encouraged.

Armitage Robinson, perhaps the most erudite Dean possessed by Westminster Abbey since the Reformation, took an immense delight in Winnington. He spoke of him, not always privately, as a "Bus Bishop", an amusing contrast with the historian who had reigned at Fulham. He felt that, in the Diocese of London, a Bishop who was loved in the East End was a most valuable experiment. Necessities of

learning and research could—for a space—be left in more leisured
hands; and Cosmo Gordon Lang, his successor in Stepney, brought
to the East abilities only comparable with Cabinet rank. But we can
go too far in poking fun at Arthur Foley's lack of scholarship. He carried
on his reading steadfastly, and seized upon the pith of every book. He
was a teacher with a following now unexampled in the Church
of England. The rumour of his presence at a meeting was quite
enough to fill the largest hall; and in the West End and in Court
Society he shone as an inspiring Missioner. Gore and Scott Holland
in that golden age could not bring in the rich and poor together with
half the certainty won by his name. Friends knew what he would say,
almost by heart. But repetition did not stale his magic. Dick Sheppard,
in the years between the Wars, commanded West End London in a
manner which no successor of to-day inherits. But Arthur Foley, at
his happiest zenith, was equally beloved in East and West.

Once more, his innocence could bring a downfall sufficient to dis-
count a lesser man. On one occasion, when the new Club game called
Bridge was all the fashion in the card-rooms, and the inexpert paid for
their bad luck, a meeting patronized by Royalty was held at a great
house in the Green Park. The Court came in a body. Lords and Commons elbowed each other in the pillared entrance. Clubland was there,
ready to kiss the rod, which this Godgiven Father of his people would
break that afternoon across their backs. The Bishop came and put all
at their ease, as only he could do with such a throng. He talked with
passionate simplicity. He praised them to their face. He thanked God
for them. Then he grew stern—a rare mood in his nature. His audience
were tense. The blow was coming. He would ban Bridge from every
Christian household, and they would have to choose between the
Church and "sans à tout". A shudder ran through them. For once, he
chose the way of compromise. Gambling was a great curse—it is
to-day! No, he would not forbid them to stake money upon the new
card game; but he adjured the leaders of Society in London, to whom
the world looked for a moral lead, not to make stakes which led to
instances of ruin and despair and suicide. As Bishop, he would beg
them to go forth, back to their Clubs, back to their drawing-rooms
with firm obedience to his grave concession. Henceforward, let them
play for shilling points!

The meeting broke up in a festive mood. Their Bishop had indeed
sprung a surprise. Clubland was then playing a 2/6 a hundred points.
Gamblers alone would then have dreamt of playing at five shillings
for a hundred. The Bishop had left the Club rate far behind!

It proves the merit of our odd conventions that all those present tacitly concurred in a conspiracy of understanding. The Bishop was not chaffed for his mistake, nor made aware of it by witty laymen. Indeed, I always heard that certain clergymen, priding themselves on being bridge-players, were the first to demonstrate to him the blunder he had made. The laymen present generously judged that he was caught and bowled on a poor wicket, with no discredit to his character They felt they knew precisely what he meant. They recognized that he had strained his conscience to give them leave to play, even for pennies. They would not take advantage of his slip, which went to prove his honesty of purpose. His reputation actually was heightened. "The quality of mercy is not strained." Even the gentry of that period could, now and then, be generous in their judgments towards a saint who was a thorough sportsman.

The magic influence exercised by Winnington-Ingram, and the unwisdom of some of his prophecies came almost to a head in the dark autumn of 1914 and in the following spring. As senior Chaplain to the London Rifle Brigade—commonly called the Bishop of London's Own—he knew almost each Officer and Rifleman. His voluntary services at Deepcut were treasured as profound and all-convincing by almost every member of the Regiment. Crisford and Vernon Smith took them to France as Chaplains to the First and Second Battalions. The First Battalion—what was left of them—made their Christmas Communion in Talbot House in 1915, when five hundred and forty-two Communicated out of seven hundred. With the sole exception of the 16th Battalion K.R.R. (Church Lads' Brigade) no regimental unit, of the half a million officers and men who patronised Talbot House, came to Communion as a corporate whole. This was, to a degree past estimate, the Bishop's influence upon his Regiment.

It was a pity that he came to France, or rather that he talked of his experience in an unguarded manner, on his return. His optimism led to disappointments, which were not very easily forgotten. He saw a great revival of religion as likely to begin with troops in Flanders. Visitors often made the same mistake. It is not one which augments reputations.

In 1920-21, Toc H, reborn in London, found itself set up in an old-fashioned house in Stucco Gardens. Here we discovered that we were invading certain amenities, which were confined by legal covenant to private residents. We begged the Bishop to become our champion, and we held a meeting, open to our neighbours. Several who came and heard his explanation were wholly won; but one old legalist got up and left the meeting in high dudgeon. We were alarmed. The Bishop, like a sportsman, stood in the gap and saved our reputation with his own. Then two years later, he inducted me into the living of All Hallows', henceforth to be the Guild Church of Toc H. Here he came seldom, for he was far too busy; but once he held a Mission on Tower Hill. He was now failing, but his energies outlasted the alertness of his mind. In such a man, it is a crude misnomer to say that the source of energy was solely physical. No doubt his lifelong abstinence from alcohol and from tobacco served him in good stead. Regular habits, weekly exercise, came to his aid, when friends felt bound to hint that the Diocese needed a younger hand upon its helm. But in his heart, the flame of Orders burnt as ardently at eighty as at forty. He was increasingly misunderstood. The Church of England, in his final years, was no longer amply equipped with scholarship and learning. Catholic clergy were, indeed, more numerous, but they now tended to regard his outlook as that of a by-gone age. He was no other than a veteran boulder, viewed from a bridge, a disused stepping-stone. He had outlived his friends and his disciples. Stepney and Bethnal Green had been transformed and new ambitions (which excluded Charity) were now the panacea for all their troubles. He was no longer their interpreter.

But he had been raised up at the right time, and from the moulding of his hands there came to the East End the voice of joy and health. The cinema to-day has ruled right out those entertainments of a homely nature which only men of my age can recall. Down East and on the Surrey side, cheap theatres provided plays where virtue was triumphant in the Final Act. A frequent hero was in those distant days a muscular Curate, who, to the cat-calls of the sixpenny gallery, removed his black coat and soliloquising, "If I am a parson, I am also a man," laid out the villain in the gas-chamber, with the trap-door conducting to the Thames. This flood of reinforcement for the Church in the East End was Winnington's achievement, inherited by Lang, who with all his abilities could not have introduced them to the spot. *Noblesse oblige* is now a ghostly motto, but it was real in Arthur Foley's hands. Shrewdness he lacked. Administrative gifts were painfully apart from his make-up. I like to think of him in the same terms as Dr. John Brown uses in describing the sheer simplicity of Dr. Chalmers:

"His emotions were as lively as a child's, and he *ran* to discharge them . . . he was quite singular for his simplicity; and taking this view of it, there was much that was plain and natural in his manner of thinking and acting, which otherwise was obscure and liable to be misunderstood."

Bishop Curzon, who, as Secretary of the London Diocesan Church Fund, and an incumbent in the diocese, and afterwards as Bishop of Stepney, worked with him for many years and knew him as well as anybody, considering the appropriateness of the epithet "great", summed up his recollections in the words "creative in the lives of others". And this was not only from the pulpit, though his work as a preaching evangelist is not wholly unworthy to be compared with that of John Wesley. His creativeness was manifested even more clearly in arresting decay and building up sound fabrics by individual pastoral care. To have ordained more than two thousand priests is to have performed a remarkable service to the Church. To have communicated, as he unquestionably did, some of his own enthusiastic faith and love to all those men means that the Church of God in all parts of the world has been notably strengthened. To have attracted, as he did in his prime, enormous congregations wherever he preached, was a proof that the Bishop was a power in London. The fact that large numbers of them thought of him ever after as a friend, and that a good many had actual talks with him, or received from the pulpit answers to their questions, made a great difference to their lives.

He was always thinking of the people of London. Of others, too, as he had strength, but of London above all. He often used to say, "As I drive through the streets of London, I think of the boys and girls who are putting up a fight against temptation." Sometimes he would feel about Londoners with the Apostle, "My little children, of whom I am again in travail, until Christ be formed in you" (Galatians iv. 19), and sometimes more hopefully, "For this cause, brethren, we were comforted over you through your faith; for now we live, if ye stand fast in the Lord" (1 Thessalonians iii. 7, 8). In general his conviction is fairly expressed by two sentences with which St. Paul ends two paragraphs of the stormiest of his Epistles, "I rejoice that in everything I am of good courage concerning you," and "Thanks be to God for his unspeakable gift". (2 Corinthians vii, 16, ix. 15).

There are other passages in literature, which come crowding into the mind as he is remembered. One is that in which Francis Thompson speaks of childhood:

Know you what it is to be a child? It is to be something very different from the man of to-day. It is to have a spirit yet streaming from the waters of baptism; it is to believe in love, to believe in loveliness, to believe in belief; it is to be so little that the elves can reach to whisper in your ear; it is to turn pumpkins into coaches, and mice into horses, lowness into loftiness, and nothing into everything, for each child has its own fairy godmother in its own soul; it is to live in a nutshell and to count yourself the king of infinite space: it is

> To see the world in a grain of sand,
> And a heaven in a wild flower,
> Hold infinity in the palm of your hand,
> And eternity in an hour.

Another is from Bede's account of St. Cuthbert. It needs a little translation to carry it from the outward circumstances of a seventh-century monk to those of a twentieth-century Bishop, but its relevance springs from the fact that the best kind of Christian goodness is the same in every age. Bede says that:

This man Cuthbert had such a grace and skill in utterance, such a zeal in persuading, such an angel's face and countenance, that none that was present durst presume to hide the secrets of his heart from him; but did all openly declare in confession the things that they had done.[1]

He goes on to say that Cuthbert visited remote places in the craggy hills, "which other men were afraid to come at, or else, being learned, loathed to visit because of the unseemly dwelling and uplandish rudeness of the inhabitants." To all such places Cuthbert went with joy.

Our Bishop would go anywhere and do anything to help a soul in need. He approved himself as a minister of God "by pureness, by kindness, by the Holy Ghost, by love unfeigned, by the armour of righteousness on the right hand and on the left".

[1]Stapleton's Translation.

EPILOGUE

A T Bournemouth the Bishop lived in the Crag Head Hotel, just opposite St. Peter's Vicarage, where his old friend Hedley Burrows, now Dean of Hereford, lived. This is how the Dean describes it:

From 1939 to 1943, from October to April we had the priceless happiness of having him as a near neighbour. During Holy Week he used to come and stay under our roof. I had had three years at Bournemouth while he was still Bishop of London and I shall never forget the joy of having him as preacher at St. Peter's in 1937. At last the man who had influenced my life so much was functioning in a Church of which I had charge. He could not be heard very well, but it made no difference. The Church was filled to capacity if it was known that he was preaching. He preached some remarkable sermons at St. Peter's during the years of his retirement. He came regularly to the 8 o'clock service. We took him down with us in the car every Sunday, and on Saint's Days. He always preached on Christmas morning, and often at other times. Some of the sermons stay in the mind. A sermon on Ahab, in preparation for Lent ("There is an Ahab in every heart")[1] or a remarkable sermon on Quinquagesima Sunday, when he shewed that he knew instinctively what was passing through the mind of youth about love—or the challenge in war time to see the necessity and righteousness of resistance to the advancing tyranny and lust for power which Nazism represented—these forthright utterances shewed that he possessed to the end the direct power of the prophet (I had seen him in the 1914-1918 war and he had visited my hospital at Rouen in 1915, and I remember well the direct moral force that he brought to bear on our men in war time).

He celebrated at 8 a.m. on the first Christmas of his retirement, 1939. There was a very large number of communicants, and it completely exhausted him. When he turned to give the Blessing, he collapsed and fell. I thought he had gone. My server and I carried him to the sacristy, set him in a chair, and life began to revive. I got a doctor, and together we took him back to his hotel. I asked the doctor

[1]See *The Secrets of Fortitude.*

343

to see that he went to bed, and I told him that I should preach in his place at 11.15. If you please, he turned up at 11.15, and greeted the Churchwardens with the words "See how the Church revives." He insisted on preaching in a crowded Church. The doctor watched him from one side and I from the other. It was a perfect Christmas Sermon, well delivered, lasting ten minutes. Then at the end he gave the Blessing, which, as he said, he failed to give at 8 a.m. I never let him celebrate at 8 o'clock on Festivals again. On that particular Christmas Day, he had his Christmas dinner at the hotel, went out to tea with his sister, went on to a Christmas party at the Royal Exeter Hotel, and played eighteen holes of golf the next day.

His life was a benediction in Bournemouth, and a vital influence in the hotel where he stayed. He couldn't grasp rationing for some time: "I'm a great believer in austerity at this time, but, when it comes to finishing your butter by Wednesday, what are you to do?" Some of the ladies in the hotel helped him out!

The owner and the staff all came under his influence, and it was priceless to see leisured old dames being invited up to his room to say Evensong with him after dinner. Some of them had never contemplated such a thing in their lives, but it all seemed quite natural under his direction. The outgoing of the virtue of spiritual power remained with him to the end. His blessing in bedroom or drawing-room was a benediction from on high. The Bishop was a great help to the clergy of the other parishes too, preaching in turn for all of them, and his presence in Bournemouth meant that the annual Sunday meeting for East London in connection with the Bournemouth Churches was sustained.

It was a moving thing to see that his influence on my children was the same as that on my brother and sister and myself. We all miss his presence and his love; we thank God for the glorious witness to the Presence and the love of Christ which he brought to mankind.

Any clergyman who has ever stayed in an hotel will know that it is not the easiest thing in the world to evangelize the people in the hotel. It is perhaps less difficult if the evangelist is a bishop and lives there for months at a time. But most men wait until they are approached. To Bishop Winnington-Ingram it was quite easy to take the initiative. It was natural. It was inevitable. He could not do otherwise. He formed the habit of asking residents in turn to dine at his table. Newcomers, especially if they were honeymoon couples, were greeted and invited to coffee and a chat. A lady writes:

My husband and I met the late Bishop of London, Dr. Winnington-Ingram, in 1944, at his hotel at Bournemouth just after we had been married. The moment he came into the dining-room he seemed to notice us, and came up to us at once, then asked our name and invited us to dine with him the next night. He then wanted to know all he could about us, where we came from, and what we had been doing, and finally invited us to have coffee up in his room after dinner. Before saying "good-night" he asked us if we would like him to give us Holy Communion in his room on Sunday morning at 8 a.m. He took the service beautifully and we loved it. We shall never forget his charming personality, for he seemed to radiate charity and happiness, wherever he went. That Sunday we heard him preach a beautiful sermon for the Bible Society, quite *extempore*, and without a single note—his memory was wonderful, and his voice so pleasing and distinct. On leaving we asked him for his photograph, which he sent in due time.

Whether or not such contacts brought people to Holy Communion, or led them towards Confirmation or whatever was their next step in the life of religion, they did not remain unaware of the Master, Whose he was and Whom he served. One who saw him from time to time in the hotel said it was reminiscent of "The Passing of the Third Floor Back". Or we might say that it was as if an angel of God had said to him, as to St. Paul on board the ship of Alexandria sailing for Italy, "God hath granted thee all them that sail with thee." He knew all the hotel staff, and called them by their Christian names.

Here is his own description of his life at Bournemouth. It came in the course of an interview given him to the *Bournemouth Times*:

"Whom the gods love die young." You know the old saying, and it is perfectly true. And that does not mean that we die young in years. It means that however old you may be in the space of time, you are still young in heart and mind. Your head is above the mists. It is not bowed. . . . I have enjoyed every minute of my life. . . . I mean to live my life right out to the end.

He kept his eighty-sixth birthday (1944) at the hotel. He had about two hundred letters and telegrams of good wishes, all of which he answered during the next day or two. About forty guests came to tea, at which there was a cake, with eight large candles and six small ones. The year before, when conditions were a little easier, there had actually been eighty-five candles. About his eighty-seventh (and last) birthday in 1945 he wrote:

> I had a lovely birthday, and fifty to tea, and a large cake, which the whole hotel helped to eat.

He preached somewhere every Sunday and took a keen interest in all the Church activities of the town. The Vicar of a new parish (St. Mark's, Talbot Village) writes:

> He took the utmost interest in our effort, just as though it had been in his own Diocese in earlier years. He told me of his great interest in Church extension work, and of the Churches he had built in and around London. He told me that the happiest days of his episcopate were those on which he went to consecrate these Churches. He remembered the happiness of the people in the parishes who after years of effort had been able to build their Church. Though we are a little Church on the very outskirts of Bournemouth he was intensely interested in our plans. On his way from golf on the Saturday he took the trouble to drive through our housing area and to study the need.
>
> In Church on the Sunday he charmed everybody with his simplicity and geniality; though physically frail and apparently rather weary, once in the pulpit, his voice clear and strong, he spoke with remarkable ease and wisdom, giving a message of great encouragement and wise advice.

Nor did he lose his old concern for the Services. He preached to soldiers as often as he could, and once he went to a tiny Church to confirm six Service candidates. An officer writes:

> To give you some idea how small the church is, the length of the ordinary church pew is the width of the church.
>
> The R.A.F. Padre soon got the place in order and imagine how pleased I was when I received a photograph of the Altar and Altar Window and an invitation to attend the first Confirmation Service to be held in the Church when three W.A.A.F.s and three R.A.F. men were to be confirmed by our friend, Bishop Winnington-Ingram.

The Officers and men of the R.A.F. Station, Hurn, I am certain will always remember the kindly advice given by the Bishop on that day and remember his wonderful spirit of duty before self that he shewed, then as always, in going over to conduct that first Confirmation Service at their own little church.

During his years of retirement he did not a little writing. He published:

The Secrets of Happiness (1939),
Fifty Years Work in London (1940),
A Second Day of God (1940),
The Secrets of Victory (1941).

Of the *Fifty Years* Artifex wrote in the *Manchester Guardian*:

The whole book from cover to cover is a characteristic mixture of interesting side-lights on things of almost world-wide importance and of streamlets of small beer so small that one wonders anyone should have felt it worth while to record them. And all is, so to speak, fused into a unity by the personality of the writer. The man's personality has triumphed over everything. Few men can have influenced more of their fellow-creatures throughout the English-speaking world, and, if in recent years his influence waned, it was because the world changed while he remained unchangeable. It would not be true to say that he created his age or any part of it. Rather he succeeded because he was in perfect harmony with it. The mixture of optimism, belief in the goodness of human beings, and refusal to look much below the surface or beyond the passing moment was perfectly in harmony with the thought of the time up to the outbreak of the last war, during which his influence was greatest.

The *Spectator* writes:

With a naïveté which has always been one of his outstanding characteristics, the lately retired Bishop of London paints his own features with a fidelity surpassing all the efforts of the great artists whose self-portraits hang in the Uffizi Gallery. Dr. Winnington-Ingram takes his readers through the half-century of his life and work in London as one turning the pages of a vast album of snapshots in every one of which he is himself the central figure. Here he is as he was known to thousands during his long episcopate, always happy, always enjoying to the full what were to him, at all events, "the sweets of office", moving from Bethnal Green, *via* St. Paul's to Fulham Palace, consorting with royalties, statesmen, merchant princes, the leaders of Big Business in America, and with "all (other) sorts and conditions of men" (not to say women) with the smile of a happy schoolboy, and, be it said in all sincerity, the unbreakable serenity of a saint.

Those fifty years were pregnant with change in every department of life. All through them, as we know only too dreadfully, the world was moving towards the climax which is now upon us, but from first to last the Bishop of London remained the one inveterate optimist, temperamentally incapable of seeing any other interpretation of the facts than the rosiest one possible. The reader will not find in them any profundity of analysis of the movements, ecclesiastical and political, religious and social, which were at work in the world outside Fulham Palace during the years 1899 to 1939, not even thumbnail sketches of the multitude of personalities with whom the Bishop came in contact, but only the record of how he enjoyed meeting them and all the rest of "the dog's life" of a Bishop of London. In plain words, if you seek in these pages for guidance as to why the world and the Church are where they are to-day you will not find it, but if you are curious as to the spiritual and psychological secrets which made Dr. Winnington-Ingram one of the most discussed, acclaimed and criticized figures in the world for fifty years, you will read this book (which, incidentally, bears many a trace of the haste with which it was written) with interest—and some smiles.

In the *Sunday Times* the Dean of St. Paul's wrote:

There is no word in it which is not inspired by charity, even when criticism or even resentment might have been excused; there is no thought which is not cheerful and hopeful. No one could claim that Dr. Winnington-Ingram is a great religious thinker, and perhaps there might be a question as to whether he was a great administrator, but few would deny that he was a great Christian, and it was by reason of his fervent Christian faith and his human sympathy that he was a great bishop.

He played golf three afternoons a week, twice at Queen's Park Links and once at Ferndown. He travelled from time to time, avoiding London, for the sake, as he said, of his successor, except to preach once a year at St. Paul's Cathedral. Before leaving London he would pay a visit to King's Cottage, on Kew Green, and have a long talk with Archbishop Lord Lang.

The last public engagement that he fulfilled was a meeting of the Keble College Council.

He was all the time preparing for his own death. He said in *Secrets of Fortitude* (1941):

> I think my friends would say that I am the least morbid of mankind, but I should be a fool if I did not realize that there is a day coming when "heavy footsteps" will be carrying something down some house or other, and that will be my body, and that there will be a grave in some cemetery, which will be different from all other graves, inasmuch as it will be my grave, and the world will go on just the same when I am dead. There will be the same cries in the streets, and the milkman will come on his round, and someone will say, "He is gone, you know," and very soon the best of us will be *almost entirely forgotten*.

He had quoted to many mourners, "He asked life of Thee, and Thou gavest him a long life: even for ever and ever," and, "Let thy loving Spirit lead me forth into the land of righteousness," and soon he must go himself, to verify, as all must do, those of a great faith and those of a lesser faith, the truth of his convictions.

It may be supposed that this preparation for death came more naturally in the other half of each year. In the country God seems nearer. The time from April to October was spent at the Boynes, Upton-on-Severn, in his native county of Worcester. He lived there with his niece and her husband, Lieut.-Colonel Grice-Hutchinson, who counted it a privilege to give him during the summer a happy country home. There for the first time for any long period he tasted the delights of the country. He sat in the garden, and read, and wrote letters in an increasingly illegible hand. He was surrounded by all his personal possessions and he loved to shew them to visitors. From his bedroom window he could see the Malvern Hills, where "on a May morning" Piers Ploughman had seen his vision. Piers said some hard things about the bishops of his day. He saw in his vision Reason admonishing prelates and priests:

> That ye preach to the people,
> Prove it on yourselves,
> And do it in deed;
> It shall draw you to God:
> If ye live as ye learn us,
> We shall love you the better.

but Piers, translated to 1940, once he had got over his surprise at the appearance of a modern prelate and the terminology of this one, would have hailed Bishop Arthur Foley as a true shepherd of Christ's sheep.

Here is a letter from Upton:

June 4, 1940.

I have settled down here very happily, and I am writing this in a lovely garden, about as big as Fulham, with a beautiful view of the Malvern Hills. I am not allowed to play tennis yet (I tried but it hurt too much), but I can play golf, which is a great thing, and now I am "digging for victory" every day, besides preaching to the troops and Boys' Schools every Sunday. I quite believe that the miraculous salvation of the B.E.F. was the answer to the Day of Prayer. "Heaviness may endure for a night, but joy cometh in the morning."

Mrs. Grice-Hutchinson, in simple, moving words, tells the story of this period.

He came to live with us at the beginning of the war, and stayed with us from April to October every year.

Sayings. His favourite ones were:

"Look straight into the Light, and leave the shadows behind."

"Take one day at a time, and trust God to see you through."

"One worry drives another out."

"God's in His Heaven; all's right with the world" (Browning).

His sensitiveness. He was very sensitive to the opinion of others, both in private and public life. He had such a universal love for all that he was not happy unless this was reciprocated. He got on best with demonstrative people, although he took endless trouble to know those who were more reserved.

His love of beauty. He loved the beauties of nature, such as lovely views, brightly-coloured flowers. He appreciated flowers in his room, and always noticed them. In spite of this, he knew little about gardens or botany, although much enjoying the finished product. He was anxious to garden during the war, and proudly dug up a row of lettuces as being noxious weeds. After this we tactfully guided his war-work into other channels. He often referred to the lettuces afterwards and we had a good laugh over his "digging for victory", as he was wont to describe his efforts.

His humbleness. He was outstandingly humble in some respects. For instance, he would attend our little country Church service and listen to the new curate, sometimes a deacon, nervously preaching his first sermons, and say after, "You must not be timid of me, old boy; I am just here to receive a crumb of comfort, like the rest of the congregation." Then afterwards, in the vestry, he would try to help him if he could by making such remarks as "An excellent sermon, old boy, but what a good point you might have made about so and so. You want to make your points strong and concise, and not be too long, end up at the right moment." The curates grew to love him, and often said what a help he was to them. He would also lend them books. He always gave the Blessing, standing at the chancel steps.

His interest in the country parish in which he lived. He liked to talk over parish worries with the Rector and his wife, of both of whom he was very fond. He was anxious to back up the campaign started by the Bishop of the Diocese, which called for more co-operation between the clergy and laity. He attended a P.C.C. Meeting and gave a little address on the subject, and suggested ways of helping on the cause. He always contributed to the Rummage Sale got up for the little Chapel-of-ease in the hamlet where he lived. He stayed in the country from April to October, and then he went to his Bournemouth hotel to be near his sister.

Food. Just at the beginning it was hard for him to understand the regulations of food-rationing, having come straight from the land of plenty at Fulham to a district invaded by evacuees. This made the food-question doubly hard just at that time. However, kind friends and relations helped out with his rations and made life easier for him.

Personal appearance. He was very particular about this and always shaved twice a day. He also had three baths a day, a cold one at 7 a.m. Bathing was as quick as washing, he always said. He always looked nice, and had a beautiful clear complexion and twinkling grey eyes.

It is well known that his games were tennis, golf and, up to a few years ago, squash racquets at the Bath Club. Later, he took to golf-croquet. He was easily put off his game. On our tennis court the shadows made by the sun shining through the trees worried him, and he would be quite upset if he played badly until he had had his evening bath and his Evensong, and then his wonderful tranquillity would return.

Health. He often looked tired as he grew older, but he had a wonderful power of recuperation and would change quickly from a state of exhaustion to one of exhilaration. He observed very regular habits, but I am afraid he did not always obey doctors' orders.

Adaptability. When he first came to live with us, he did not realize the difficulties of procuring domestic labour in war-time. He did not like doing small things for himself, such as stamp-sticking, telephoning, etc., but his adaptability was great and he soon saw that he could save someone's valuable time by attending to these matters for himself, and when his sister came to stay she noticed how much more independent he had become.

Last Years. As he grew older, he gradually relinquished his tennis owing to his "tennis elbow" and failing sight, and took more to golf and golf-croquet. My husband gave up much time to brightening his last years by playing this game with him. There was a time when my uncle had formerly despised croquet of any sort, but he became a great G.C. enthusiast and was much disappointed if the weather or any other reason prevented him from playing. The evening he was first taken ill he had been playing golf as usual on the Malvern Links. He came into my room about 3 a.m., and said he felt very ill. I managed to get him back to bed and gave him brandy, as I knew he was suffering from his heart, and sent for the doctor. He was given a sleeping-draught and next day rallied surprisingly. The third night he had a similar attack, and the doctor came again. He lived for a week after this, some days seeming better than others, but remaining in bed of course. He was not allowed visitors, and only few relations were able to come. He spent the time up to the last in reading religious books and dictating his letters to my brother, and also in writing part of a foreword for a book which he was not able to finish.

On the last night he was alive I was getting him ready, helping him in his room, and he talked a great deal to me about my mother, who was his eldest sister. He had been devoted to her, but she had died some years ago. He also talked about his affection for his youngest sister Mary, and he mentioned all his brothers. He then said quite suddenly, "But we are all full of iniquity," and he repeated these words. It seemed almost as if he were making his Confession, although few were so well prepared to die. Next morning was Sunday, and at about 8.15 a.m. I went to his room to see what he would like for breakfast, and found him with his head very low and looking much exhausted. I asked him if I should arrange his pillows, but he said he would wait as he was tired, but he gave orders about his breakfast. I rushed down to prepare this quickly when a former maid looked in to inquire after the Bishop. The breakfast was ready then, and she offered to take it for me. She came back quickly, much distressed, to say that he had died. I went up and found it all too true. But such a beautiful end! He had been reading his Mattins, and his spectacles were still in his hand, and it was Sunday. Thus ended a life of service.

And there we might well leave the old warrior, tired and ready to be taken:

> Father, in Thy gracious keeping
> Leave we now Thy servant sleeping.

And yet, another picture rises to the mind, the last Children's Party at Fulham, with the Bishop standing on a chair and saying to all the boys and girls, "You won't forget me?" And hundreds of young voices shouted, "Never, never, never!" And the father of two children, who had himself as a schoolboy been a guest at the first party, went out into the corridor to hide his tears. "Never" is a long time. Yet some of those who in 1938 were ten years old will live to the end of the century. They will carry with them all their lives the remembrance of a Happy Warrior, who was their friend.

The private funeral was at Upton Church, where some members of the family were present. They then went to Cheltenham for the Cremation, and the urn was kept in Upton Church until 7 June. The hymns were "The radiant morn hath passed away" and "The strife is o'er". The public funeral was at St. Paul's Cathedral on 7 June.

INDEX